PROGRESSIVES, PLURALISTS, AND THE PROBLEMS OF THE STATE

Progressives, Pluralists, and the Problems of the State

Ideologies of Reform in the United States and Britain, 1909–1926

Marc Stears

OXFORD
UNIVERSITY PRESS

OXFORD
UNIVERSITY PRESS

Great Clarendon Street, Oxford OX2 6DP

Oxford University Press is a department of the University of Oxford.
It furthers the University's objective of excellence in research, scholarship,
and education by publishing worldwide in

Oxford New York

Auckland Bangkok Buenos Aires Cape Town Chennai
Dar es Salaam Delhi Hong Kong Istanbul Karachi Kolkata
Kuala Lumpur Madrid Melbourne Mexico City Mumbai Nairobi
São Paulo Shanghai Singapore Taipei Tokyo Toronto
with an associated company in Berlin

Oxford is a registered trade mark of Oxford University Press
in the UK and in certain other countries

Published in the United States
by Oxford University Press Inc., New York

British Library Cataloguing in Publication Data

Stears, Marc.
Progressives, pluralists, and the problems of the state: ideologies of reform in the
United States and Britain, 1909--1926/Marc Stears.
p. cm.
Includes bibliographical references.
1. United States—Politics and government—1901–1953. 2. United States—Intellectual
life—20th century. 3. Progressivism (United States politics)—History—20th century.
4. Radicals—United States—History—20th century. 5. Pluralism (Social sciences)—
United States—History—20th century. 6. Great Britain—Politics and government—
1901–1936. 7. Great Britain—Intellectual life—20th century. 8. Socialism—Great
Britain—History—20th century. 9. Radicals—Great Britain—History—20th century.
10. Pluralism (Social sciences)—Great Britain—History—20th century. I. Title.
E743.S757 2002   320.5—dc21   2001058829

ISBN 0–19–829676–2

1 3 5 7 9 10 8 6 4 2

Typeset in Stone Sans and Stone Serif by
Cambrian Typesetters, Frimley, Surrey
Printed in Great Britain
on acid-free paper by
T.J. International Ltd,
Padstow, Cornwall

To Jane Stears, Derek Stears, and Liz Irwin

ACKNOWLEDGEMENTS

This book was begun at Nuffield College, Oxford and finished only two hours away in Emmanuel College, Cambridge, but in between I travelled to many places and incurred many debts. As with all historical investigations, most of the actual business of researching and writing for this book was conducted in a wide range of libraries and I have had enormous pleasure working in them all: the Bodleian, Balliol College, Nuffield College, Rhodes House, and Ruskin College Libraries of Oxford University, the Emmanuel College and University Libraries of Cambridge, the Butler Library of Columbia University, and the University Libraries of Bristol, Harvard, Rutgers, and Yale. Special mention must go to three collections: the Social Welfare History Archive at the University of Minnesota, the Labor-Management Center at Cornell University, and the Workers' Educational Association archive, Temple House, London. The exceptional kindness, professionalism, and enthusiasm of the staff at these institutions were inspirational. These archivists and librarians must have assisted in the production of hundreds of scholarly works and I am conscious that this acknowledgment is an inadequate form of thanks for their contribution to this one.

From the very outset, this project was dependent on the financial support of a number of institutions. By far the greater parts of that funding came from the Warden and Fellows of Nuffield College who generously elected me to a Prize Research Fellowship on the basis of the proposal and provided seemingly limitless funds towards research expenses thereafter. Very generous additional resources also came from the British Academy and Oxford University's Andrew Mellon Fund. I am grateful too to David Johnston at Columbia University, for arranging visiting scholar status for me for the summer of 1998, and to Stuart White, then at the Department of Political Science at MIT, for welcoming me to Cambridge, Mass. in the spring of 1999, and offering continual insights into the work. Without these visits, I would have been unable to conduct archival research in the United States and the book could never have been written. The Department of Historical Studies in the University of Bristol created the most pleasant scholarly environment in which to finish the writing of this book. I cannot think of a nicer group of people among whom to work; and I miss their company enormously.

The ideas that generated the arguments in this book also owe much to others and I have been immensely fortunate in my guides. Brian Harrison and Nigel Bowles expertly took me through my initial studies in politics and both also directed me back to Oxford when I lost my way. On that return, Michael

Freeden introduced me to the study of ideologies, provided an unrivalled education in conducting historically sensitive research in political theory, and was constantly supportive even at the most trying of times. David Miller also offered important guidance and demonstrated a continued commitment to the project even when it left the terrain of analytical political theory and entered a more antiquarian genre. Any credit for the idea of an Anglo-American comparison must go, however, to Dominic Byatt at Oxford University Press, who shared his exceptional understanding of political theory throughout the book's development. Dominic had to wait too long for the final manuscript as I struggled to cope with a series of professional and personal upheavals. I am sorry for that and I am enormously grateful for his patience and support. I thank Amanda Watkins, too, for her efficient answers to tedious questions, and for helping me come up with the title.

Many others individuals have bestowed acts of kindness. An enormous number of exceptional scholars commented on the ideas in the book, among them Robert Bickers, Nigel Bowles, John Burrow, Edward Carmines, Tak Wing Chan, Jayant Chavda, Ali Cheema, John Darwin, Michael Freeden, Brian Harrison, Sudhir Hazareesingh, Mathew Humphrey, Shin Kambe, Desmond King, Anna Gambles, Lawrence Goldman, Cecile Laborde, Man To Leung, Eugenia Low, Rodney Lowe, Meira Levinson, Paul Martin, Robert Mason, James Meadowcroft, David Miller, Gautam Mody, Karma Nabulsi, Richard O'Leary, Kirsty Reid, David Runciman, Byron Shafer, Richard Sheldon, Laura Slatkin, Antonia Taddei, Federico Varese, Stuart White, Laurence Whitehead, and Ray Yep. Lively audiences at seminars in Atlanta, Belfast, Bristol, London, Nottingham, Philadelphia, Oxford, Washington DC, and York also provided trenchant criticisms of individual arguments, as did each and every member of the Nuffield College Political Theory Workshop from 1992 to 1999. With so many helpful interlocutors, all of the errors that remain in this book can be due only to my inability to follow the expert lead that they have provided.

Others also listened to me enthuse and complain far too much and kept me going as a result; they include Jocelyn Alexander, Ewen Bowie, Sudhir Hazareesingh, Catherine O'Rawe, Adam Sandell, Brendan Smith, Tabitha Tuckett, Mary Whitby, Ian Wei, and Hughie Wong. Ray Yep taught me how to survive in the intimidating and utilitarian atmosphere of Nuffield College and also showed that it was worthwhile sacrificing things for the sake of completing a work of scholarship, however inevitably flawed that work would be. I should also very much like to thank three families—Eileen Gillooly, Dan, Kate, Ben, and Jake Polin; Amy, Cordelia, and Clare Johnson; Regina, Carole, and Laura Slatkin—for demonstrating in their everyday lives the generosity, hospitality, and sense of common purpose which the thinkers in this book strove to create in society at large. These acknowledgments could not conclude without a special mention of Karma Nabulsi, who is the embodiment of these lessons. Her scholarship alone was inspirational, her total commitment to constructing a better world, locally, nationally, and internationally, more valuable still. The fact that she could combine these remarkable gifts with a commitment to the value of the ideas and the people discussed in this book and a belief in my ability to tell their story is all but impossible to comprehend.

I have left three people to last. They are my parents, Derek Stears and Jane Stears, and Liz Irwin. These were the only people with me and with this project from beginning to end. The value of their continual support is both immeasurable and indescribable. I hope a dedication says enough.

Marc Stears
Emmanuel College, Cambridge
August, 2001

CONTENTS

ABBREVIATIONS

AALL	American Association for Labor Legislation
AFL	American Federation of Labor
COS	Charity Organisation Society
DORA	Defence of the Realm Act
ILP	Independent Labour Party
IWW	International Workers of the World
LSE	London School of Economics
NCLC	National Council for Labour Colleges
NGL	National Guilds League
TUC	Trades Union Congress
WEA	Workers' Educational Association
WEB	Workers' Education Bureau of America

INTRODUCTION

The three decades that surrounded the First World War were among the most dramatic years in the modern political development of Britain and the United States. These were years within which the terms of politics changed for ever, years which witnessed the dawn of a new era of bitter political struggle and momentous social change. In this time, the widespread beliefs of the late nineteenth century rapidly began to lose adherents. It was no longer certain that partisan allegiance was essentially a matter of region and religion, that individual enterprise was the only reliable means to economic growth, or that the size and the scope of state power should always be limited. Instead, political argument was increasingly structured around a new series of cleavages. The problems of mass urban centres, the economic power of large industrial corporations, and the fierce discontent of an increasingly organized working class shaped the new order of the day.[1]

As the terms of political debate shifted in both countries, a whole series of interest groups and issue-oriented pressure groups sprang up, each demanding reform. In addition to serving the demands of their constituents, these movements presented a myriad of opportunities for politically engaged intellectuals clamouring for influence. A new generation of academic enthusiasts thus abandoned the confines of the universities, determined to blend the insights of innovative philosophies and the findings of empirical social science into concrete proposals for reform. The cacophony of voices that emerged yielded little immediate agreement. Proposals ranged in scale from minor changes to the distribution of poor relief to the total reconstruction of the social order. The ideals upon which these were based and the mechanisms designed to achieve them were also fiercely contested. But whatever the disputes, all the activists shared one central object of faith: modern nation states were witnessing a widespread attack on a whole range of 'social notions' that had rightly been 'conceived as fundamental' only a decade or so before.[2] It required 'no profound insight' in such a context to note that Britain and the United States were on the threshold of grave and far-reaching change.[3]

---

[1] For recent introductions, see S. J. Diner, *A Very Different Age: Americans of the Progressive Era* (New York: Hill and Wang, 1998) and J. Harris, *Private Lives, Public Spirit: A Social History of Britain, 1870–1914* (Oxford: Oxford University Press, 1993). For a comparison, see D. Rodgers, *Atlantic Crossings: Social Politics in a Progressive Age* (London: Belknap Press, 1998).

[2] H. Laski, 'The Temper of the Present Time', *New Republic*, 18 February 1920, 335–8.

[3] H. Laski, 'A Labor Programme', *New Republic*, 9 March 1918, 179.

That the early twentieth century offered its activists a moment of potentially epochal change is well known to most students of British and American
politics. It is much less frequently acknowledged, however, that the political
thinkers swept up in the excitement refused to restrict their attention to their
country of origin.[4] Just as the problems of trade union militancy, of urban
poverty, and of the concentration of economic power all appeared to recognize no national boundaries, so there seemed no reason why the search for
solutions should be confined within the limits of individual states. The international similarities implicit in the new political era fundamentally altered
the aspirations of reformers. In such an age, the *Manchester Guardian* dramatically declared, 'space has been eliminated' and 'frontiers no longer exist'.[5]
After generations of expecting that the course of political development would
be sharply different in the New World than in the Old, activists and intellectuals now began to believe that the 'problems' facing Great Britain and the
United States were 'essentially the same'.[6] In the twentieth century, the
Guardian argued, 'the problems of Great Britain interest every American of
good-will who labors for a readjustment in the United States'.[7] American
reformers themselves confirmed the judgement, contending that 'they and
their British counterparts were facing a similar enemy and fighting much the
same kind of fight for comparable ends'.[8] Altogether, those of 'advanced
thought' in Britain and the United States were 'uniting for an ideal'.[9]

There was, of course, a substantial degree of over-optimism in these expectations. Despite the shared challenges that modern industrialism posed,
Britain and the United States maintained sharply distinct political systems,
social structures, and public cultures throughout the twentieth century,
which guaranteed that their national responses would also remain unique.
But even if the belief in political convergence eventually turned out to be
mistaken, it nonetheless shaped the activity of a generation of reformers.
During the first three decades of the twentieth century, formal and informal
commissions of inquiry continually criss-crossed the Atlantic seeking expert
witnesses to every conceivable political, social, and economic change.
Scholarly exchanges brought professors from the United States to Oxford,
Cambridge, and the London School of Economics, and sent lecturers from
these institutions back to Harvard, Yale, and the New School for Social
Research in New York. Political journals and political weeklies mushroomed,
targeted often at an international audience and drawing increasingly on an
international set of contributors. If a new political and social order was to be

---

[4] See Rodgers, *Atlantic Crossings*, esp. 1–6.
[5] Advertisement, 'World Liberalism', *New Republic*, 3 September 1915, 157.
[6] Editors, 'Towards Industrial Democracy', *New Republic*, 1 September 1917, 123.
[7] Advertisement, 'World Liberalism', 157.
[8] M. Stokes, 'American Progressives and the European Left', *Journal of American Studies*, 17
(1983), 28.   [9] Advertisement, 'World Liberalism', 157.

built, all those engaged agreed, it was to be transatlantic in its orientation and inspiration.

Amongst this plethora of discussions between British and American thinkers, one ongoing discussion stood out as particularly intellectually intense and politically controversial. This was the debate between the British socialist pluralists, led by Harold Laski, G. D. H. Cole, and R. H. Tawney, and the American nationalist progressives, directed by Herbert Croly, Walter Lippmann, and Walter Weyl. These movements fiercely disagreed on the single most important question facing reformers of the day: the size, scope, and legitimate role of the central state. Indeed, these groups appeared to occupy positions of polar opposition on the issue. Laski, Cole, and Tawney rejected every aspect of the bureaucratic and centralizing socialism then dominating the British left. They demanded that reformers should *resist* an over-reliance on the central state and look instead to the work of smaller, localized, and democratized associations as the agents and units of meaningful reform. In contrast, Croly, Lippmann, and Weyl formulated a vision known as the 'new nationalism', which maintained that significant intervention by the central state should be *introduced* into American politics. These theorists self-consciously broke from what they took to be the dominant American political tradition of anti-statist, Jeffersonian, liberalism and insisted instead on increased order, structure, and centralized discipline in the American politics of reform.

Yet despite this startling discrepancy, each of these two movements openly valued the contribution of the other. Indeed, as the First World War drew to its conclusion, each movement grew to believe that a common dialogue was the means to provide the answers to 'the inspiring challenges of the new world'.[10] For the British pluralists, this was a discussion that proved that radicals could 'look to America for a help that would not fail';[11] while to the Americans, these British theorists demonstrated how intellectuals could lead workers into 'taking strides towards co-operative socialism'.[12] This optimism was not misplaced. For all of their disagreements, these movements eventually constructed programmes of reform which shared many essential features in common. Both groups called for the extension of democratic mechanisms into private and public industries, rejecting the established polarities of the private market or state nationalized control that pervaded most discussions. They also outlined measures for the radical expansion of educational opportunities for working adults, arguing that the construction of a truly democratic polity was dependent on an informed and involved electorate. Both also proposed an extensive system of social welfare that sought to balance

---

[10] Editors, 'American Labor Politics', *New Republic*, 29 June 1918, 250.

[11] H. Laski, 'Birthday Greetings', *Nation (NY)*, 26 August 1925, 33.

[12] A. Gleason, *Inside the British Isles* (New York: Century Co., 1917), 19.

compulsory and voluntary means of contribution and provision. As contemporaries observed, these detailed political programmes appeared remarkably similar. When the programmes' individual units are analysed closely themselves, the resemblance becomes more marked still. Yet all of this was achieved while their rhetorical disagreements on the role of the central state remained fierce. Somehow, when it came to identifying individual programmes of real reform, two movements that seemed dramatically opposed actually spawned agreement.

This book offers the first detailed analysis of this transatlantic debate. It examines the evolution of both movements' distinctive ideological systems in order to provide a resolution of the startling paradox their exchange presents. The book rejects the dominant scholarly interpretation of the socialist pluralists and nationalist progressives as simplistic advocates of starkly polarized anti-statist or statist opinion.[13] Instead, it argues that both of these groups offered ideological programmes of great subtlety and sophistication. Neither movement was dedicated to any knee-jerk rejection or confirmation of the central state. Rather, the book argues, both were committed to experimenting with a series of new political mechanisms in the search for an institutional settlement which would allow them to realize a series of more fundamental ideals. In pursuing this analysis, the book examines the forces that shaped each movement's ideological evolution. It explores the arguments which the movements themselves considered most important and investigates the contrasting political challenges which they faced. As it does so, it continually focuses on the transatlantic dimension to their work, tracing the impact of their international exchange of views and identifying the role played by the peculiarities of their political environments. Taken together, these aspects enable a re-evaluation of the intellectual credibility of both of these movements and a reassessment of their legacy. By re-establishing the centrality of international exchange in this story, the book also offers a unique perspective on the broader evolution of modern ideological politics in Britain and the United States.

Building Movements, Beginning a Debate

The world in which Herbert Croly, Harold Laski, and their colleagues worked was characterized by an almost unique combination of intellectual innovation,

---

[13] For examples of such interpretations, see A. Eisenberg, *Reconstructing Political Pluralism* (Albany: State University of New York Press, 1995); R. J. Lustig, *Corporate Liberalism: the Origins of Modern American Political Theory* (Berkeley: University of California Press, 1982); J. A. Nuechterlein, 'The Dream of Scientific Liberalism: The New Republic and American Progressive Thought, 1914–1920', *Review of Politics*, 42 (1980), 167–90; D. Nicholls, *The Pluralist State: The Political Ideas of J. N. Figgis and his Contemporaries* (London: St Martin's Press, 1994); B. Zylstra, *From Pluralism to Collectivism: The Development of Harold Laski's Political Thought* (Assen: Van Gorcum, 1968).

dynamic social change, powerful opportunities for reform, and an increasingly transatlantic focus to political debate. In later years, reformers would look wistfully back on an unprecedented set of shared opportunities, some taken, others not, all now passed. In retrospect, the first few decades of the twentieth century would appear as 'glad years of faith and hope', when a new generation developed a series of ideas that they hoped would 'spread . . . swiftly over this weary world and capture it and make it young'.[14] It was not surprising, therefore, that the theorists at the centre of this book commenced their working lives in the belief that they could achieve a great deal. What was more surprising was the astonishing degree of scholarly and political attention that they actually enjoyed. The early twentieth century was well provided for with radical political movements, stretching from mugwumps and populists through to liberal progressives and state socialists. The six leading theorists under examination here always chose to stay somewhat distanced from mainstream developments, continuing to stand opposed to many of the contentions of the dominant movements. Yet, despite this distance from the mainstream, they exerted a truly remarkable hold on the attention of thinkers and politicians in the early twentieth century. Amongst the intelligentsia they were often described as the 'outstanding figures' of their age, and their influence spread far wider.[15] They provided the motivation for many activists, legitimized a whole range of new policy proposals, reordered people's thinking, provoked discussion on themes previously taken for granted, and indicated alternative courses of political action. As the *Economic Journal* put it, although these movements never achieved all their goals, the ideas they espoused nonetheless became the 'living political issues' of the day.[16]

This success sometimes came from rather inauspicious beginnings. The leader of the American nationalist progressives, Herbert Croly, struggled through Harvard in the 1880s and 1890s. Leaving and returning to the college several times despite the continual support of a highly intellectual and financially secure family, Croly eventually suffered from a series of nervous illnesses.[17] Having completed his less than successful formal education, he eked out a living as an architectural journalist in New Hampshire. His enduring hope for a place in the annals of progressive reform, though, maintained his enthusiasm for political thought, and such hope proved not to be misplaced. When his first book eventually emerged as *The Promise of American Life* in 1909, it was almost instantly revered as a classic. Although sales were

---

[14] E. Poole, 'Exploration', in M. Weyl (ed.), *Walter Weyl: An Appreciation* (Philadelphia: Privately Published, 1922), 52.

[15] Anon., 'Book Supplement', *The Highway*, February 1919, 10.

[16] As even sceptics recognized. See H. Philips, 'The Control of Industry', *Economic Journal*, 33 (1923), 396.

[17] See D. Levy, *Herbert Croly of the New Republic: The Life and Thought of an American Progressive* (Princeton: Princeton University Press, 1985), esp. 44–67.

relatively poor, critics declared *The Promise* to be the most able synthesis of reformist suggestions yet produced and noted that it offered a significant reorientation of progressive ideals. In *The Promise*, Croly imposed a distinctly national and state-centred emphasis on reformist politics, outlining a programme which called for the active involvement of the federal government, and not just for State legislatures or voluntary organizations, in the task of building a new political order. This aspect of *The Promise* above all others brought Croly immense prestige. Former Republican President Theodore Roosevelt himself turned to Croly for advice, suggesting that the ideas in *The Promise* could provide the platform for a new political campaign and even a new political party.[18] Even if Roosevelt's attention was more cosmetic than intellectual, mixing in such circles brought Croly to the notice of a range of wealthy benefactors. Together with one of them, Willard Straight, Croly talked of the need to build an extended intellectual and political movement around *The Promise*'s ideas. The result was the founding of the leading weekly journal of opinion, *The New Republic*. Explicitly 'modeled on the English *Nation* and *New Statesman*'—political weeklies that frequently set the agenda for British radicals—the *New Republic* was soon required reading for the American left.[19] By 1918 it was widely believed to make 'history week by week'.[20]

In developing the essential idea of the *New Republic* and in editing the journal, Croly drew on the assistance of Walter Lippmann and Walter Weyl, two thinkers who would quickly became the other leading theorists of 'nationalist progressivism'. His choice of colleagues was both inspired and courageous. Lippmann and Weyl were far more at home in the formal world of academia than Croly ever had been; and they were also less enamoured with the existing progressive movement, believing that it lacked any real sense of purpose or direction. Indeed, some years before joining the *New Republic*, Lippmann and Weyl had both flirted with the idea of working with the radicals of the American Socialist Party rather than with the more mainstream reformers of the American progressive movement. When Walter Weyl left the Wharton School of the University of Pennsylvania with a Ph.D. in economics, he set out immediately to work with John Mitchell's United Mine Workers of America as a political adviser. Walter Lippmann accepted a similar position as political adviser to George Lunn, the first Socialist mayor of Schenectady, on graduating from Harvard.[21] As with Croly, though, the publication of their first major theoretical works located them at the very heart of the emerging nationalist progressive

[18] See M. R. DiNunzio, *Theodore Roosevelt: An American Mind* (New York: Penguin Books, 1995), esp. 16–18.

[19] H. Croly, 'Memorandum on the New Republic' (1914) in Yale University Library, The W. Lippmann Papers, I/22/875.

[20] H. Laski cited in R. Steel, *Walter Lippmann and the American Century* (London: Bodley Head, 1980), 155.

[21] See C. Forcey, *The Crossroads of Liberalism: Croly, Weyl, Lippmann, and the Progressive Era, 1900–1925* (New York: Oxford University Press, 1967), esp. 66–7.

movement. In 1912, Walter Weyl published *The New Democracy*, a clear scholarly advance on the foundations Croly had laid in *The Promise*, and probably the fullest and most sophisticated account of the nationalist progressive agenda. But if Weyl's book contained the academic substance, Walter Lippmann's *A Preface to Politics* in 1913 and *Drift and Mastery* in 1914 caught the public imagination. Lippmann seized attention with the staggering wit and subtlety of his prose and with his unerring eye for anecdote. Nor was it only the 'sheen of quip, quote, and paradox' that was so effective.[22] His astonishing youth enhanced his status still further; Lippmann was only 24 years old when his first work was published. Combining on the *New Republic*'s staff, Croly, Lippmann, and Weyl brought their diverse talents and their disparate advantages together. There they forged a movement in political theory the work of which was not only read by every progressive intellectual and activist of note but which sought to transform American understandings of the possibilities of politics for ever.

In Britain, the movement that became known as 'socialist pluralism' was characterized by a similar diversity of talents and personalities. This movement began with the work of a precocious young talent, G. D. H. Cole. His *World of Labour* was published in 1913 to astonishing critical acclaim and instantly endeared Cole to the very highest echelons of the British labour movement. The message of *The World of Labour* was uncompromising. The tendency of the British left to look to central governmental agencies to play the leading role in the politics of reform was essentially misplaced. The mechanisms of the central state and the agents who ran them simply could not be trusted. British reformers had to look elsewhere for support and they had to design a programme of reform that would not be dependent on an overbearing state. It was a widely popular call in the first decade of the twentieth century. Cole, indeed, was one of an exceptionally broad alliance of thinkers advancing it regularly in the London-based weekly newspaper, *The New Age*. On publication of *The World of Labour*, Cole rapidly became the most prominent figure of the *New Age* set, publishing an extensive article almost every week. Despite the prestige the paper allowed him, however, Cole was never entirely satisfied with a publication that presented attacks on the state from anarchists, laissez-faire liberals, disgruntled churchmen, medieval revivalists, and arch-conservatives. Such breadth had its limitations even for someone ideologically committed to diversity. In the search for greater ideological unity he led a break away in 1915, forming his own political organization, the National Guilds League (NGL), producing his own series of journals—*The Guildsman*, *Guild Socialist*, and *New Standards*—and even drawing up his own constitution for an ideal society in the so-called 'Storrington Document'.[23]

---

[22] Forcey, *Crossroads of Liberalism*, 117.
[23] For an introduction, see A. Wright, *G. D. H. Cole and Socialist Democracy* (Oxford: Oxford University Press, 1979).

The foundation of the NGL marked the beginning of a more intellectually serious and politically coherent ideological movement, but it was still far from fully formed. Beyond their strong distaste for the centralizing tendencies of traditional British socialism, even the self-described 'guild socialists' who followed Cole into the National Guilds League often shared relatively little in common. Members of the NGL themselves recognized that the League had 'as many positions as it has adherents'.[24] During the First World War, however, a more focused movement emerged from among these members. At its heart was one occasional contributor to the guild socialist journals with whom Cole could agree more often than disagree, R. H. Tawney. Like Walter Weyl on the other side of the Atlantic, Tawney was more skilled as an academic economist than as a political propagandist and his contribution to debate tended to be more rarefied than Cole's. His major work of the period, *The Acquisitive Society* (1921), nonetheless presented a powerful statement of the emerging position. There, Tawney outlined a clear vision where decision-making power was to be removed from both capitalists and from the central authority of the state and redistributed towards manual workers themselves. Tawney also provided a thorough theoretical defence of the ideals which underlay such a suggestion. This single work itself was enough to guarantee Tawney's place at the heart of the new reformist drive towards the devolution of power and authority then capturing the British left.

Vital as Cole and Tawney's work was, however, it was Harold J. Laski who finally provided the political focus and intellectual credibility necessary to establish a distinctive ideological movement. Three books published within four years guaranteed his authority. Laski's *Studies in the Problems of Sovereignty* (1917), *Authority in the Modern State* (1919) and *The Foundations of Sovereignty* (1921) expounded the most academically sophisticated and the most groundbreakingly radical attack on the British state, an attack that quickly came to be known as 'pluralist'. Although, Laski's relationship with the organizations that Cole had constructed was rather distant—Laski refused to join the National Guilds League, worrying that too many of Cole's colleagues were 'little more than third-rate'[25]—his intellectual similarities with Cole and Tawney were obvious to everyone. He openly admitted finding himself in 'admiring agreement' with Cole's central arguments.[26] Tawney too came in for praise, being described as one of 'the most brilliant of our younger thinkers'.[27] Detailed disagreements between the three would continue, as will

---

[24] R. H. Tawney, 'What I Think of National Guilds', in Nuffield College, The Bedford Papers, 10/33/1. For a detailed account of disputes within *The New Age* and the National Guilds League, see M. Stears, 'Guild Socialism and Ideological Diversity on the British Left, 1914–1926', *Journal of Political Ideologies*, 3 (1998), 289–305.

[25] H. Laski, 'The Meaning of National Guilds', *Political Science Quarterly*, 34 (1919), 668.

[26] H. Laski, *Authority in the Modern State* (New Haven: Yale University Press, 1919), 83, and 'Meaning of National Guilds', 668.

[27] H. Laski, 'Mr Wallas as Social Analyst', *Nation*, 9 April 1921, 60.

be revealed in the pages that follow, but the combination of these three thinkers' work collectively offered a distinctive and radical position in British political thought. Through their academic contributions and political campaigning, Cole, Tawney, and Laski crafted a distinctive alternative to dominant trends in the British reform tradition, carefully outlining both a concrete policy programme and a complex theoretical system to defend it. By the end of the war, an identifiable British 'socialist pluralist' movement had been born.[28]

Although the individual success of each of these movements was easily explicable, the intellectual and political relationship between them was complex and confusing. Indeed, given the plethora of available options, a whole host of alternative transatlantic ideological relationships suggested themselves. The British socialist pluralists could have been expected to strike up a rapport with the theorists of the American Socialist Party or with thinkers like Louis Brandeis who advanced a decentralizing vision eventually embraced by Woodrow Wilson's 'New Freedom' Democrats.[29] The nationalist progressives likewise would seem more likely to have found the state-centred theorists of the British Fabian Society and the Independent Labour Party more natural allies than the socialist pluralists. And yet, although some discussions did emerge from these other links and many lessons were learnt, the most startling intellectual relationship of the war years and after was that between the socialist pluralists and nationalist progressives.

The relationship between these groups was sometimes direct, at other times conducted at a considerable distance. Harold Laski established the most important personal connections between the two movements. Laski wrote his first three extensive books in the United States, where he both taught and studied at Harvard. Laski became especially popular at the informal court of the progressives' idol, Supreme Court Justice Oliver Wendell Holmes. It was Laski's privileged place within that group that enabled him to meet the leading American theorists, activists, and politicians of the day. An extended correspondence with Holmes, which lasted long after Laski's return to England, maintained the connection, and was quickly joined by continual and often highly intellectual exchanges with other members of the nationalist progressive circle. Laski's friends and confidants included the progressive jurists Learned Hand and Felix Frankfurter, and all of the *New Republic* set of

[28] For more details, see Stears, 'Guild Socialism'. Laski, Cole, and Tawney were often identified as a 'group' or 'movement' by contemporaries. See Anon., 'Liberty and the Law', *Nation*, 18 August 1919, 594–5; Anon., 'The Pluralist State', *Manchester Guardian*, 12 February 1922; Anon., 'The Foundations of Sovereignty', *New Statesman*, 25 March 1922, 708–10; W. Lippmann, 'Authority in the Modern State', *New Republic*, 31 May 1919, 148–9.

[29] For instructive alternatives, compare L. D. Brandeis, *The Curse of Bigness: Miscellaneous Papers of Louis D. Brandeis* (Port Washington, NY: Kennikat Press, 1965) and J. Hughan, 'Changing Conceptions of the State', *Socialist Review*, 7 (1920), 165–8 with Laski, *Authority* and G. D. H. Cole, *Self-Government in Industry* (London: G. Bell and Sons, 1917).

Herbert Croly, Walter Weyl, and, especially, Walter Lippmann. The other leading theorists of both movements also occasionally worked together, teaching
in the university lecture rooms of the London School of Economics and the
New School for Social Research in New York and debating in the conference
halls of the American Academy of Political Science. When distance kept them
apart, they exchanged views in the pages of their academic monographs and
contributions to scholarly journals. They also pursued their endeavours at a
less elite level. They employed the review, comments, and correspondence
columns of politically involved weeklies and newspapers, especially the *New
Republic*, to critique each others' work and to respond to those criticisms.
They also involved themselves directly in advising trade unions and worked
most closely together by collectively designing educational agendas for the
Workers' Educational Association in Britain and Workers' Education Bureau in
the United States.

Despite the importance of this direct collaboration, though, this was not a
connection born simply out of personal friendship or the ties of collegiality.
On the contrary, relations between and within the groups were often very
strained. Lippmann was close to Laski, but he had little personal contact with
Tawney, and he never warmed to Cole.[30] Many in the American nationalist
progressive movement, indeed, took against Cole's 'temperamental disposition' even as they admired 'his most brilliant [intellectual] qualities'.[31] The
antagonism was probably mutual. Although Cole left no direct indications of
dislike, he was frequently to be found publicly exhibiting disdain for the
personal manners of Americans in general and American reformers in particular.[32] Such distaste of things American among the British was also more
generally noted. One *New Republic* correspondent suggested that there was 'a
certain faint condescension' in the attitude shown to American nationalist
progressives by their British contemporaries. 'It is not intentionally insulting
or hostile', this commentator conceded, but it did display a distinctive if
'subconscious' sense of 'superiority'.[33] Nor were these personal disagreements
confined to matters of cultural difference. Even within the national movements themselves there was often palpable tension. Laski enjoyed company,
especially the company of the rich and famous; Cole, on the other hand, was
dismissive of the trappings of political power and preferred to settle in the
aristocratic academic environment offered by early twentieth century Oxford.
The result, their biographers tell us, was that the even when the two were
working on closely related projects, they 'actively disliked each other' and

---

[30] See Steel, *Walter Lippmann*, 70.

[31] J. P. Frey to A. Gleason, 29 July 1921, Social-Welfare History Archive, University of Minnesota,
Survey Associates Records, 77/576.

[32] See G. D. H. Cole, *The World of Labour: A Discussion of the Present and the Future of Trade
Unionism* (London: G. Bell, 1913, 2nd edn 1917), 165.

[33] A. Gleason to P. Kellogg, 8 July 1919, Survey Associates Records, 77/576.

were inclined to avoid 'continuous personal contact'.[34] Within the American movement too there were clear personal strains. Herbert Croly was painfully shy, often unable to communicate with even the most affable of his colleagues. Meetings at the *New Republic*'s offices were often characterized by his 'settling like a stone crab in the middle of lively company'.[35] Lippmann, on the other hand, was gregarious to a fault, although he was prone to a form of self-aggrandizement that did not sit well with many of his high-minded progressive allies.[36] Partly as a result, Walter Weyl, like R. H. Tawney, maintained a somewhat aloof distance from all the goings-on, preferring the pastoral peace of Woodstock in upstate New York to the political and intellectual hothouse of the *New Republic* offices in downtown Manhattan.[37]

All of these tensions implied that these movements' intellectual exchange was not a straightforward matter of swapping opinions and information. Rather, it was a vigorous debate between theorists not immediately well disposed towards each other. It is unsurprising, in such a light, that the prolonged argument between these two movements never resulted in complete consensus; the British socialist pluralists always remained essentially wary of central government intervention, the American nationalist progressives were ever eager to extend the role of America's federal authorities. It is essential, nonetheless, to recognise that both movements developed intellectually and evolved politically precisely as a result of their discussions. Through their period of debate, their own arguments continually grew in subtlety as new avenues of philosophical and political enquiry were opened up by the intervention of their interlocutors. More important still, the ongoing dialogue between the movements directly shaped their joint recommendations for concrete political reform. They may never have resolved either the intellectual or the personal tensions between them but eventually the socialist pluralists and nationalist progressives advanced a series of proposals that shared many essential features in common.

Shaping an Approach

The absence of any previous attempt to conduct a detailed comparative study of this compelling debate between socialist pluralists and nationalist progressives is difficult to explain. It springs neither from an absence of historical awareness nor from any lack of interest in the subject matter itself. Few periods

---

[34] I. Kramnick and B. Sheerman, *Harold Laski: A Life on the Left* (London: Hamish Hamilton, 1993), 250, and M. Cole, *The Life of G. D. H. Cole* (London: St Martin's Press, 1971), 163.
[35] See Levy, *Herbert Croly*, p. xiii.   [36] See Weyl (ed), *Walter Weyl*, 91.
[37] See Weyl (ed), *Walter Weyl*, esp. 55–74.

in twentieth century history have been accorded as much scholarly attention as the progressive era in the United States and the Edwardian and inter-war years in the United Kingdom. And as the period itself has been the subject of close and careful analysis, so the lives of the leading theorists in this book have also been the subject of detailed biographical scrutiny.[38] A whole series of works has recently revitalized the study of their lives and work and has sparked many compelling and wide-ranging academic controversies. The best of these studies of individual figures have also made significant efforts to set the theorists into the context of the movements to which they belonged.[39]

All of these previous scholars have, however, restricted themselves to single-country studies: the nationalist progressives have been analysed in relation to developments in American politics, the socialist pluralists in the context of events in Britain. In earlier generations, this reserve was the straightforward consequence of a broader scholarly trend. At least into the 1970s, the academic orthodoxy asserted that the development of American ideological identity was singular, continuous, and 'exceptional' and that there was little to be gained from exploring its evolving links with the traditions of other nations.[40] The only major work to trace international ideological exchange between British and American reformers in this period was Rose Martin's truly bizarre *Fabian Freeway* (1967), a McCarthyite study motivated by a desire to illustrate that the American left was controlled by British socialists who were themselves in hock to Moscow.[41] More recently, however, this reluctance to analyse the history of these two countries together has evaporated. Ground-breaking works like James Kloppenberg's *Uncertain Victory* (1996) and Daniel Rodgers' *Atlantic Crossings* (1998) have confirmed beyond doubt that that the essential foundations of American social and political thought from the 1880s right up to the New Deal were rooted in a dialogue conducted across the Atlantic ocean. As a result, the 'story of the impact of the British labour movement on American reform', and vice versa, has begun to be told.[42]

---

[38] For fine examples, see Kramnick and Sheerman, *Harold Laski*, Levy, *Herbert Croly*, Steel, *Walter Lippmann*.

[39] For other studies see J. Jordan, *Machine-Age Ideology: Social Engineering and American Liberalism, 1911–1939* (Chapel Hill: University of North Carolina Press, 1994), Lustig, *Corporate Liberalism*, and J. Thompson, *Reformers and War: American Progressive Publicists and the First World War* (Cambridge: Cambridge University Press, 1987).

[40] For an excellent overview of this argument, see B. E. Shafer (ed.), *Is America Different? A New Look at American Exceptionalism* (Oxford: Oxford University Press, 1989). There have, of course, always been notable exceptions to this view. See, especially, A. Mann, 'British Social Thought and American Reformers of the Progressive Era', *Mississippi Valley Historical Review*, 42 (1956), 672–92 and K. O. Morgan, 'The Future at Work', in R. Thompson (ed.), *Contrast and Connection: Bicentennial Essays in Anglo-American History* (London: Bell, 1976), 245–71.

[41] R. L. Martin, *Fabian Freeway: High Road to Socialism in the USA, 1884–1960* (Chicago: Heritage Foundation, 1966).

[42] J. T. Kloppenberg, *Uncertain Victory: Social Democracy and Progressivism in European and American Thought, 1870–1920* (New York: Oxford University Press, 1986) and Rodgers, *Atlantic Crossings*. For earlier demands, see A. F. Davis, 'Welfare, Reform and World War One', *American Quarterly*, 19 (1967), 533.

That this general trend has still not resulted in a close study of this particular relationship is due, in part at least, to the considerable difficulties that a study of the collective efforts of these movements presents. This cannot, after all, be a study of a straightforward direct and unmediated personal relationship between two groups of theorists. The tensions between the individuals involved meant that their correspondence was often indirect and occasionally extremely strained. It must, instead, be a careful analysis of the evolution of two contrasting sets of *ideas*. Unfortunately, though, neither can this study straightforwardly rely on the established practices of historians of political thought. These thinkers saw themselves as political activists as much as intellectuals or philosophers; and this implied that Croly, Laski, and their colleagues operated in two distinctive sorts of arena simultaneously. They worked in the academic settings of international journals and academic book markets *and* in the more public realm of the distinctive political environments of Britain and the United States. As a result, many of their texts were intended for two very different audiences: first, for an international community of scholars, both British and American, who possessed a set of shared assumptions and enjoyed a series of shared experiences; and second, for nationally specific wider British and American publics, who, for all the hope of political convergence, still possessed conflicting agendas, assumptions, and prejudices. Any study of this exchange has, therefore, to examine the manifold ways in which theorists located in different political environments, facing different challenges, and fighting for different goals, managed both to get a clear message across at home and to engage in fruitful philosophical and practical exchange abroad.

This book overcomes the difficulties of analysing such a broadly based endeavour by offering a synthesis of available methodological approaches. It borrows tools from a broad collection of intellectual disciplines, ranging from social history through the history of ideas to modern analytical political philosophy. Most importantly, it seeks to combine the insights of two particular sub-disciplines: the historical study of 'ideologies', as recently described by Michael Freeden, and the historical and institutional study of comparative political development, as expertly practised by Ann Orloff, Theda Skocpol, and Stephen Skowronek.[43] If employed individually each of these approaches would offer important insights in and of themselves; but by seeking effectively to reconcile these two dimensions—the philosophical and the practical, the ideological and the institutional—it is possible to understand how the groups sought to combine their contrasting roles as international philosophers and domestic reformers.

---

[43] See T. Skocpol and A. Orloff, 'Why Not Equal Protection? Explaining the Politics of Public Social Spending in Britain, 1900–1911, and the United States, 1880–1920', *American Sociological Review*, 44 (1984), 726–50 and S. Skowronek, *Building a New American State: The Expansion of National Administrative Capacities, 1877–1920* (Cambridge: Cambridge University Press, 1982).

Recent methodological work in the study of ideologies provides an essential guide as to commencing this form of enquiry.[44] Analysis must begin with an identification of the core ideals that structured the primary arguments of each the group. It is crucial to recognize the central ideals for which both movements worked, to appreciate the nature of the essential commitments which gave structure to their overall ideological programme. The ideologies the two movements constructed were not 'irrational, arational, or imperfectly reflective' schemes of thought; rather they were built up around carefully thought-through conceptual arguments.[45] It is necessary, therefore, to read the texts these thinkers produced closely, carefully, and logically, to examine the complex ways in which their arguments unfolded, to see how their conceptual definitions related to one another: to employ, in short, the strategies of analytical political theory. It is also essential, however, to recognize that no set of political thinkers can have totally free rein. These theorists could not have constructed their ideologies out of logic alone, for to persuade their audience of the rectitude of their conceptual arguments they had to work within a language comprehensible to their target audiences. In order to understand this process, it is necessary to develop a rich picture of the broad 'idea environment' within which these thinkers were operating. It is crucial to trace their intellectual predecessors, understand their cultural and intellectual inheritance, analyse the 'consumption' as well as the 'production' of their arguments.

Fundamental as all of this is, it is only part of the story. For in addition to their efforts at subtle conceptual argumentation the socialist pluralists and nationalist progressives also made continual efforts to translate their theoretical arguments into tangible, concrete proposals for reform.[46] But when they entered the world of concrete politics they were confronted with a further series of problems and constraints, all of which were qualitatively different from those that presented themselves in the world of academia. Consequently a different method of analysis is required. In order to understand these concrete problems it is necessary to take the traditional elements of explanation in political science—including political events, social structures, formal and informal governing institutions—extremely seriously. Most of all, it is essential to note that as these movements sought to institute programmes of reform they came up against the opposition of groups committed to maintaining the advantages of entrenched patterns of political

---

[44] The approach is masterfully spelt out in M. Freeden, *Ideologies and Political Theory: A Conceptual Approach* (Oxford: Oxford University Press, 1996). See also J. Tully and Q. Skinner (eds), *Meaning and Context: Quentin Skinner and His Critics* (Cambridge: Polity Press, 1988), esp. 13–16 and 119–32.

[45] Freeden, *Ideologies*, 551.

[46] This process was, of course, closely linked with the first: as their philosophy constantly informed their politics, so their politics shaped their philosophy. For a critique of the distinction itself, see M. Freeden, 'Practising Ideologies and Ideological Practices', *Political Studies*, 48 (2000), 302–22.

behaviour, patterns that were largely generated by ideals, interests, and expectations themselves shaped by pre-existing political institutions. Both socialist pluralists and nationalist progressives were continually forced, therefore, to adapt themselves to the demands of their specific political environments. To understand the movements, it is vital to understand the peculiarities of these political environments themselves.

That the two approaches need to be intertwined in this case should be clear to see. The necessity begins with recognition of the enormous, even over-arching, ambition of both of these movements. Politics always involves discussions about the role, shape, and scope of governing institutions as it is a practice that inevitably 'involves struggles over the authority to establish, enforce, and change the rules governing social action'.[47] Yet the groups under investigation demanded far more extensive restructuring of the centre of power than most of their contemporaries. One movement, the British social-ist pluralists, possessed ideological commitments that sought to delegitimize the authority of the central government. The other, the American nationalist progressives, possessed principles that led them to attempt radically to enhance the effective authority of those selfsame institutions. And, further-more, both movements attempted this within political and scholarly commu-nities that were often sceptical and occasionally deeply hostile. The means both movements employed to overcome such hostility were both 'philo-sophical' and more directly 'political'; and each of these efforts requires distinctive methods of analysis. It is the groups' own dual purpose, therefore, that itself determines the necessity of this dual approach.

The advantages of a synthesis of methodologies do not stop here though. For it also enables us to reveal the very reason why these two contrasting groups found it so worthwhile to collaborate. It helps us explain, that is, why it was possible for these movements to agree on concrete proposals even while they disagreed so violently on fundamental matters of conceptual principle. It does so by enabling us to trace the consequences of the groups' efforts to implement the recommendations of their very different ideological systems within two equally different political systems and political traditions. By employing the dual approach described above, this book shows that it was actually this combination of differences that paradoxically generated almost exactly the same political outcome. To be more precise, this study demonstrates that by forging a concrete reform programme from an anti-statist perspective in a state-centred society, as the British did, or from statist ideals in a radically decentralized polity, as the Americans tried, the groups were sometimes led to advocate exactly the *same* proposal. Their similarity, their shared resolution to the concrete problems of the state, it will be seen, was actually a result of their difference.

[47] P. Pierson, 'Increasing Returns, Path Dependence, and the Study of Politics', *American Political Science Review*, 94 (2000), 259.

The Structure of the Book

The structure of this book is directly shaped by this multi-layered approach. The book is presented in three parts, each of which aims to fit a central piece of the puzzle in place. Part I traces the contours of each movement's fundamental ideals. It begins by noting that, for all their disagreements, these movements grounded their philosophical arguments in a discussion of the same set of intellectual predecessors, including the idealists, positivists, Fabians, pragmatists, and social psychologists. By examining the intellectual response of each group to these earlier movements, Part I then demonstrates that neither the socialist pluralists nor the nationalist progressives believed that the size and scope of state power per se was the central theoretical question of the age. Rather, in both cases, the movements' theoretical work began with an effort persuasively to redefine two fundamental political concepts: those of 'liberty' and 'community'. Both movements believed that these values lay at the heart of modern social problems and that a better understanding of them would provide the essential guide to political reconstruction. Socialist pluralists and nationalist progressives thus built their entire ideological programme upon a subtle and analytically precise reworking of these key political terms. They also used these two conceptual arguments to help define other concepts, including 'equality', 'democracy', and even 'state' itself. Where the movements differed, however, was in the particular definitions they gave to each term. The nationalist progressives offered a radically socialized account of human nature and thus sought to combine the demands of liberty and community. They then transformed these commitments into a normative agenda capable of motivating significant state intervention in the lives of American citizens. The arguments of the socialist pluralists, on the other hand, were characterized not by any communitarian assumptions but by a philosophical individualism of exactly the type the nationalist progressives had sought to spurn. They then utilized this individualism in developing a conception of liberty that demanded a radical diminution of state activity.

Having presented this new account of the underlying motivations of each movement, the book turns in Part II to a detailed investigation of each group's response to the key conceptual contentions of the other. It illustrates how an explicit and implicit dialogue was conducted against the background of the dramatic developments of the First World War. It shows also that the political difficulties each movement faced in the immediate aftermath of the conflict led them to consider adapting their programme in a wide range of ways suggested by their opposite numbers. It illustrates the nationalist progressives' flirtation with pluralism and the socialist pluralists' attempts to reconsider the importance of social harmony. It also argues, however, that both of the movements ultimately remained loyal to their original philosophical contentions, and explains why.

Part III of the book continues this analysis of the exchange of ideas, beginning with a recognition that the conceptions outlined in the first two parts were not designed for a purely academic audience but were intended to motivate and legitimize detailed public policy suggestions. It seeks to analyse more explicitly the differing approach of these two groups to political practice and emphasizes, in particular, that it was the conceptual positions highlighted earlier in the book rather than some antecedent pro- or anti-statism that provided the foundations for policy preferences. This point is developed in detail in two chapters that examine central arenas of political debate in which both groups were actively engaged: the provision of education to working people and the emergence of a welfare state. Within both arenas it is shown that although the essential ideological commitments of the two movements remained opposed, the differing political circumstances the groups found themselves faced with led to the development of startlingly similar positions.

This structure is, as shall be seen, primarily thematic and explanatory in purpose; it aims to enable us better to understand the underlying ideological assumptions of each group and to appreciate their consequences. As a secondary aim, however, it also maintains an important sense of chronology. Institutions and ideals both evolve over time in reaction to changing events, and although this book does not intend to trace each precise stage of these developments, it does nonetheless take us from the theorists' own education in the late nineteenth century through the groups' initial debates during the First World War to the more desolate years of the mid-1920s and the movements' eventual decline. As it does so, it also draws heavily on a collection of diverse sources. As these thinkers operated in a wide range of forums—from universities, through international academic conferences, to newspapers and national politics—any real attempt to understand their activities requires access to an equally wide range of material. A study of single classic texts—even of magisterial works like Croly's *The Promise of American Life* or Laski's *Grammar of Politics*—simply will not suffice. It is necessary to look to editorials in the *New Republic* and columns in the *New Statesman*, to speeches in political meetings and contributions to official committee reports, and to personal correspondence as well.

What follows, then, is dependent on an acceptance of diversity: in methodological approaches, in themes, and in sources. But not *everything* can be here, of course. As Croly, Laski, and their colleagues often seem to have worked in almost every available forum, so too they appear to have written on almost every major issue. In addition to their contributions to the debates discussed here—debates on democracy, industrial organization, welfare, and education—they also made informed observations on race and immigration, on foreign policy, on the justifiability of the war or of war itself. If coverage of these themes is rather limited in this work, it should not be taken as a dismissal of the movements' consideration of them. It is, rather, a recognition that these themes were not central to the ongoing debate between these groups and thus do not lie at the heart of this particular study.

Conclusion

Whatever the absences, this book's purposes remain extensive and ambitious. By its conclusion, it hopes to have enabled renewed comprehension of the development of two ideological movements, both of which are continually revisited by historians of both the political and the ideological development of Britain and the United States. The ideas these movements discussed were of central importance to the politics of reform in both countries. As they sought to resolve the tensions between their apparently anti- and pro-statist perspectives, these movements engaged in a whole series of more fundamental debates. Each group had to choose between the sanctity of individual choice and the need for a coherent social order, between the protection of privacy and the possibilities of democratic governance, and between the devolution of power and the effective organization of authority. Even where they failed to attain the goals they set themselves, the answers they provided to these difficult theoretical questions informed the debates of generations of reformers that followed them. A better understanding of each of these movements thus contributes to a better understanding of the extensive reform traditions of Britain and the United States.

As these theorists' work helped to structure the aspirations of the generations that succeeded them, so their ideas also continue to have purchase today. Indeed, both movements' theoretical arguments have enjoyed something of a renaissance of late. In the 1990s, communitarian political philosophers, led by Michael Sandel, have cast their attention back to the work of Croly, Lippmann, and Weyl in their search for inspiration and for a distinctive political agenda. The American nationalist progressives' work, Sandel and his colleagues claim, offers a programme of reform premised on the value of social solidarity lacking from contemporary American discourse, but still potentially politically viable today. The British socialist pluralists, on the other hand, find their champions in the form of those political theorists dubbed 'associationalists' and led by Paul Hirst. As they seek to construct practical alternatives to the nation state, these associationalists turn to the pluralists of old for both practical direction and philosophical inspiration.[48]

---

[48] See, for example, M. Sandel, *Democracy's Discontent: America in Search of a Public Philosophy* (Cambridge Mass.: Belknap Press, 1996), 201–26 and P. Hirst, *Associative Democracy: New Forms of Social and Economic Governance* (Cambridge: Polity Press, 1994).

Without a detailed and accurate analysis of these two movements' endeavours, however, both contemporary normative theorists and political historians are prone to misinterpretation. As this book will show, theorists now frequently invoke texts to defend arguments that they would actually be better employed to refute, just as historians continue to overlook or misunderstand the detailed policy positions which the groups outlined more frequently than they appreciate them. Greater sensitivity to the ways in which these movements' arguments evolved will provide the necessary corrective.

This particular investigation makes one further contribution to the study of political theory. By conducting a comparative examination which concentrates closely on the ways in which very different political environments shaped these movements' arguments and their outcomes, the opportunities and the pitfalls of their international debate should become clear. Such a revelation takes the lessons of this exchange beyond the specific and the narrow, for it brings with it a better sense of the *generic* possibilities of international ideological exchange. When armed with an understanding of the forces that shaped this remarkable ideological relationship, that is, we should come closer to appreciating the forces that shape the opportunities of all those who attempt to exchange ideas for reform across national boundaries. This book, therefore, should also be seen as a study that sets out to examine the structure of international exchanges of political ideas. If this comparative analysis can help us to better understand this, then even those scholars who continue to resist the attractions of socialist pluralism and nationalist progressivism should agree that their debate continues to assert its relevance well into another new century.

I
BEGINNINGS

1

Conceptual Foundations

Introduction

'The crying need of our days is the need for freedom', insisted G. D. H. Cole as the First World War drew to its conclusion.[1] It was a call that was widely echoed on both sides of the Atlantic in the first three decades of the twentieth century. As radical political theorists faced new practical political challenges and developed ever more subtle theoretical and practical programmes in response, they began to argue that the 'supreme evil of modern industrial society' was not 'poverty', the original target of the left, but 'the absence of liberty'.[2] But it was not liberty alone for which reformers strove. For together with the desire to liberate the citizen from the confines of the new city, and the worker from the enslavement of the large corporation, progressive thinkers shared a commitment to developing a new coherent and stable social order. Reacting to the apparently continual growth of social conflict, and especially the conflict of the classes, reformers in Britain and the United States insisted on the need to construct a social order built on communal harmony and social solidarity, and not on individual competition or sectional conflict. The ideal society of the future, almost all reformers agreed, would 'bring out a larger and better measure of human fulfillment' only by enabling everyone to realize the essence of genuine freedom and communal commitment.[3]

As widespread as these aspirations were, they did not mark the end of ideological debate. Rather, they marked a new beginning. For the British and American theorists at the centre of this book were sharply divided on the questions of what the absences of 'freedom' and 'community' actually entailed and how they should be rectified. The very understanding of these concepts, an account of their conceptual components, normative prescriptive recommendations, and a 'continuous wrangle' concerning the nature of the relationship between them provided the chief battleground of their overall

---

[1] G. D. H. Cole, *Self-Government in Industry* (London: G. Bell and Sons, 1917), 114. 'Freedom' and 'liberty' are used synonymously, as they were by the theorists themselves.

[2] R. H. Tawney, *The Commonplace Book* (Cambridge: Cambridge University Press, 1972), 34.

[3] Editors, 'The Nationalism of the British Labour Party', *New Republic*, 7 August 1918, 65.

ideological dispute.[4] As R. H. Tawney succinctly summarized, the central, fierce disagreement of the age was a debate as to 'what exactly' it was that 'freedom mean[s]' and how it was to be reconciled with the desire for 'social unity'.[5] The debate was found everywhere in intellectual circles from the late 1880s and well into the 1920s. Even a whole range of novelists, from H. G. Wells and Edward Bellamy on the left to G. K. Chesterton on the right, structured their fictional tales around the puzzling divide between 'order' and 'anarchy', 'society' and 'individual'.[6]

The intellectual arguments surrounding these concepts were from the very start deeply political. They did not suffer from the form of philosophical abstraction that has blighted so much late twentieth century political thought. 'The idea of liberty', as Harold Laski thus recognized, 'has its own special history' because 'each age has problems peculiar to itself and the meaning of liberty is the answer it makes to those problems.'[7] That said, however, there was nothing *crudely* political about the debates over freedom or community, in either genesis or development. The late nineteenth and very early-twentieth centuries witnessed a vigorous and far-ranging conflict between subtle theoretical movements advocating different conceptual approaches to these two key concepts. A whole range of philosophical and political movements proffered their own views and enjoined theorists in both Britain and the United States to take their side. Some viewed liberty and community as essentially connected, others thought them agonisingly opposed. Some contended that genuine freedom and social harmony required an expansion of material equality, others celebrated existing inequalities. Some saw liberty and the gradual growth of the central state machinery as antithetical, still others built the state into their very conceptual definitions. Even when there was agreement on the conceptual essentials, differences grounded in the groups' contrasting educational, social, and cultural traditions obscured and complicated the picture still further. More concretely empirical judgements also continually informed the theoretical arguments. Views as to what was possible—politically, socially, and economically—sometimes reinforced, and other times undercut, the conceptual imaginations of competing movements.

An understanding of all of these arguments is essential for any attempt to understand the debates between the socialist pluralists and the nationalist progressives. Both movements' ideological programmes were shaped by the

---

[4] G. D. H. Cole, *Labour in the Commonwealth: A Book for a Younger Generation* (London: Headley Bros, 1918), 193.

[5] R. H. Tawney, 'Lecture to Stroud WEA', British Library of Political Science, London, The R. H. Tawney Papers, 19/6.

[6] For examples, see H. G. Wells, *The New Machiavelli* (London: John Lane, 1911), E. Bellamy, *Looking Backward* (Toronto: G. N. Morang, 1897), and G. K. Chesterton, *The Man Who Was Thursday* (Bristol: Arrowsmith, 1908).

[7] H. Laski, 'Freedom', *New Republic*, 21 December 1918, 228.

conceptual arguments that they inherited from their immediate predecessors and which they then reworked as their own. In seeking to understand the ideological systems the movements constructed, it is vital to begin with the positions that they learnt as students themselves. These earlier contentions not only set the agenda that socialist pluralists and nationalist progressives would address, but provided the essential intellectual language without which their transatlantic dialogue would have been entirely impossible. In seeking to appreciate the subtleties of these debates of the late nineteenth and early-twentieth centuries, it is important consciously to avoid the use of any of the superficially straightforward dichotomies that have dogged many previous scholarly analyses. In particular, it is necessary to reject the argument that the late nineteenth and early-twentieth century debates about freedom that our theorists inherited are best categorized as a contest between 'positive' and 'negative' accounts.[8] This positive-negative divide signally fails to provide the means necessary for a thorough theoretical comprehension, let alone an attempt at normative evaluation, of the complex debates of the age, because it is both analytically simplistic and historically anachronistic. It neither directs the latter-day interpreter to a rich and complex set of central issues that perennially constitute debates on freedom nor centres on the issues with which the groups themselves were concerned. This is not to claim that the terms 'positive' and 'negative' were entirely unknown to early-twentieth century theorists. Yet it is to argue that this heritage has led all too many latter-day interpreters astray, especially in the aftermath of Isaiah Berlin's seminal—but for our purposes largely unhelpful—contribution to the debate. For although contemporaries may have been prone to use the terms 'positive' and 'negative' as tags to eliminate the necessity of continued detailed discussion, this was largely because they assumed that their audience already possessed a deeper understanding of the rich and complex debates that lay behind them. Today, such an assumption is no longer acceptable and the beguiling simplicity of the tags obscures the actual interchange of conceptual and practical positions. An understanding that is both more nuanced and more carefully contextualized is thus demanded if the conceptualizations of liberty and community that provided the ideological foundations for British socialist pluralism, for American nationalist progressivism, and for the debate in which they were engaged is to be understood. It is in pursuit of such an understanding that this chapter begins.

---

[8] Many previous analyses rely heavily on these categories, see W. H. Greenleaf, 'Laski and British Socialism', *History of Political Thought*, 2 (1981), esp. 584; D. Nicholls, *The Pluralist State: The Political Ideas of J. N. Figgis and his Contemporaries* (London: St Martin's Press, 1994), 26; E. Eisenach, *The Lost Promise of Progressivism* (Lawrence: Kansas University Press, 1994), 189; E. Stettner, *Shaping Modern Liberalism: Herbert Croly and Progressive Thought* (Lawrence: Kansas University Press, 1994), 50–1.

The Foundations of a New Conception: Idealism

Surveying the academic scene on both sides of the Atlantic in 1882, the Harvard philosopher William James noted that 'we are just now witnessing a singular phenomenon in British and American philosophy'. 'Hegelism,' he continued, 'has found among us so zealous and able a set of propagandists that to-day it must be reckoned one of the most powerful influences in the higher walks of thought.'[9] While 'idealism' was a safer title than 'Hegelism', as the primacy of the debt to Hegel himself was an issue of some debate, James's observation was apposite at the close of the nineteenth century, and it would be equally so three decades later.[10] For although idealism's hold on the academic imagination never went unchallenged, the movement was strikingly resilient. By the time of the United States' entry into the First World War, the *New Republic* could report that 'the idealistic tradition still is and perhaps will long continue to be the prevailing basis of philosophic instruction' in America. For the British, Harold Laski would argue at the same time that any new movement in philosophy was a response to the 'idealistic canon of T. H. Green and [Bernard] Bosanquet'.[11] And nowhere was idealism's attraction more keenly felt than in the Harvard which educated Herbert Croly and Walter Lippmann, or in the Oxford which set Harold Laski, R. H. Tawney, and G. D. H. Cole upon their careers. Whatever other steps these thinkers had already taken, and would in the future take, the formal philosophical education of the major British pluralists and American progressives began with idealism. It was knowledge of idealism that would provide the intellectual playing field for their aggressive ideological disputes. It offered a shared language and a shared set of interests. In order to understand late nineteenth and early-twentieth century debates about freedom, it is necessary to start where it all began.

The academic origins of the British idealist movement itself lay in the 1870s in the work of the Oxford philosopher Thomas Hill Green, and the movement continued into the early 1920s led by F. H. Bradley and Bernard Bosanquet.[12] In

---

[9] W. James, 'On Some Hegelisms', first published 1882, republished in W. James (ed.), *The Will to Believe and Other Essays* (New York: Longmans, Green and Co., 1909), 263.

[10] On the controversy of nomenclature, see S. den Otter, *British Idealism and Social Explanation: A Study in Late Victorian Thought* (Oxford: Oxford University Press, 1996), 10–50. For the longevity of idealism in philosophical circles see M. Cohen, 'On American Philosophy: The Idealistic Tradition and Josiah Royce', *New Republic*, 3 September 1919, 148–50 and T. V. Smith, *The American Philosophy of Equality* (Chicago: Chicago University Press, 1927), 207–9.

[11] H. Laski to O. W. Holmes, letter dated 23 May 1918, M. de Wolfe Howe (ed.) *The Holmes–Laski Letters: The Correspondence of Mr Justice Holmes and Harold J. Laski* (Cambridge, MA: Harvard University Press, 1953), 156.

[12] The literature on British idealism is voluminous. Especially good introductions are: P. Nicholson, *The Political Philosophy of the British Idealists: Selected Studies* (Cambridge: Cambridge University Press, 1990); den Otter, *British Idealism*; M. Richter, *The Politics of Conscience: T. H. Green and his Age* (London: Wiedenfield and Nicholson, 1964); A. Vincent and R. Plant, *Philosophy, Politics and Citizenship: The Life and Thought of the British Idealists* (Oxford: Basil Blackwell, 1984).

the United States, it was Henry Brockmeyer, a self-imposed exile from Heidelberg University, and his protégé William Torrey Harris who initially brought Hegelian and quasi-Hegelian ideals into mainstream philosophical circles, again in the 1870s. In the United States, though, it really fell to Josiah Royce to confirm the ascendancy of the idealist approach with a sparkling Harvard career lasting from the early 1880s until his death in 1916.[13]

The relationship between the British and American idealists displayed many of the features that characterized the later transatlantic connection between the pluralists and progressives. Initially united through their joint interest in the same set of intellectual predecessors—especially early-nineteenth century developments in German philosophy and the re-readings of Plato and Aristotle that these developments provoked—their relationship was cemented still further by a set of shared academic institutions. Most prominent among these was the *International Journal of Ethics*, founded in 1890 by Royce and his American colleagues. *Ethics*, as it was later to become, was explicitly designed to bring idealist thinkers from Britain, America, and further afield together into an identifiable intellectual community.[14]

Differences did, of course, emerge between the British and American idealist camps. Josiah Royce fiercely resisted being labelled a disciple of the British. Even though most observers suggested that the American idealists took their lead from idealism 'as developed by British writers like Green, Bradley and Bosanquet', Royce insisted that American idealism had developed alongside, rather than in debt to, its British equivalent; and although its central contentions were shared, many of the particularities of their arguments were sharply distinct.[15] Even within the national groups arguments demonstrated variation in academic substance and political orientation.[16] Yet, regardless of the disagreements, the patterns of interconnection between British and American idealists generated a series of complex shared understandings ranging from underlying metaphysical theory to a set of precise normative arguments. Moreover, the idealists and their critics agreed that at the very centre of those commitments lay a reconsideration of the concept of liberty.

In their own mind, there was no doubting the audacity of the idealists' conceptual innovation. All the idealists consistently contended that the dominant strand of British and American political philosophy in the nineteenth

[13] The American idealists are rather less well served than their British counterparts but good introductions include J. Clendenning, *The Life and Thought of Josiah Royce* (Nashville: Vanderbilt University Press, 1999); P. Fuss, *The Moral Philosophy of Josiah Royce* (Cambridge, MA: Harvard University Press, 1965); J. E. Smith, *America's Philosophical Vision* (Chicago: Chicago University Press, 1992).

[14] See J. H. Muirhead, *The Platonic Tradition in Anglo-Saxon Philosophy: Studies in the History of Idealism in England and America* (London: George Allen and Unwin, 1931).

[15] Cohen, 'On American Philosophy', 149 and J. Royce to F. Thilly, letter dated 6 May 1898, J. Clendenning (ed.), *The Letters of Josiah Royce* (Chicago: Chicago University Press, 1970), 346.

[16] See J. Morrow, 'Liberalism and British Idealist Political Philosophy: A Reassessment', *History of Political Thought*, 5 (1984), 91–108.

century was a form of liberalism, whose leading proponents stretched from Thomas Hobbes to John Stuart Mill in Britain and from Thomas Jefferson to Ralph Waldo Emerson in the United States. Prefiguring the arguments of Louis Hartz by almost a century, the idealists argued that this tradition saw human fulfilment almost entirely in terms of the attainment of liberty, and understood liberty as essentially a celebration of individual difference and particularity. A world which valued human development, on this view, was a world in which diverse individuals were able to pursue their own goals and ambitions independent of the pressures of others. It required the guarantee of a protected sphere of life within which the non-interference of state, society, and other individuals could be assured. What was demanded, on this account, was a 'paucity of restraint' on individual behaviour.[17]

While the actual conceptual position of the idealists' predecessors was, of course, much subtler than this account was capable of admitting, the idealists' historical caricature allowed them all the more easily to map out new conceptual terrain.[18] The idealists did not reject the importance of freedom or liberty to human flourishing. Rather, they attempted radically to reconstruct the concept itself. Adapting the contentions of a quasi-Hegelian metaphysical philosophy to the realm of political philosophy, they constructed a conception of human freedom directly opposed to the individualist contentions of their—constructed—predecessors. It was this new conception that would eventually be used to recommend and legitimize a series of new practical political measures. It is crucial to recognise that the idealists' view was not simple. Rather than seeking to replace one monolithic conceptual approach with another, the idealists consciously attempted to replace one complex conceptual construct with another 'cluster concept', composed of five component parts. Only when each aspect was combined one with another could the extent of the idealists' conceptual innovation become evident. So vital would each of these components turn out to be that each requires to be spelled out in some detail.

Five components of a conception of liberty

The first component of the idealists' conception was that freedom itself should be understood as a 'perfectionist' concept. Idealists, that is, insisted that freedom was not straightforwardly concerned with protecting or enabling an individual's pursuit of his own desires. Instead, idealists argued

---

[17] For details of this tradition, see A. Vincent, 'Classical Liberalism and its Crisis of Identity', *History of Political Thought*, 11 (1990), esp. 156–61.

[18] For America, see B. A. Shain, *The Myth of American Individualism: The Protestant Origins of American Political Thought* (Princeton: Princeton University Press, 1994). For Britain, see P. Berkowitz, *Virtue and the Making of Modern Liberalism* (Princeton: Princeton University Press, 1999). Inventing or manipulating the past is, of course, one of the stocks in trade of any ideologist. See M. Freeden, *Ideologies and Political Theory: A Conceptual Approach* (Oxford: Oxford University Press, 1996), esp. 239.

that liberty was concerned with the pursuit of the more essential qualities of human life. As freedom was one of the most sought-after of moral and political goals, it could not be concerned with protecting the average individual 'in his ordinary moods, when he sees, or thinks he sees, nothing in life but his own private interest and amusement'.[19] Rather, freedom had to refer to individuals seeking to be something *better*. To idealists, freedom involved individuals pursuing the total 'fulfilment of one's possibilities', seeking to 'become the best they have it in them to be'.[20] Liberty entailed the search for perfection rather than the pursuit of each individual caprice or whim.

Following from this, the second component of the idealist conception argued that freedom involved the absence of *all* obstacles to the pursuit of individuals' worthy goals. Freedom was not thus confined to the absence of 'external' obstacles, such as the deliberate coercion of others or the accidental obstruction of circumstance. 'Internal' psychological states, emotional weaknesses, or moral dispositions also counted as constraints on freedom.[21] Bernard Bosanquet explained that on such a view what individuals had to be 'freed from' was not only 'the constraint of those whom we commonly regard as others, but the constraint of what we commonly regard as part of ourselves'.[22] In order to be described as free, individuals had to be able to prevent themselves from pursuing 'unworthy' goals and to direct their attention instead to ends which were more significant. Free individuals were thus those who had developed significant control of their own urges or desires, lest those desires themselves constitute obstacles to the pursuit of more worthy goals.[23] For the idealists, as F. H. Bradley made clear, the 'slave of his lusts is not a free man'.[24]

Absent from these first two components was the means of distinguishing 'whims' from 'worthy goals'. Idealists had, then, to provide an account of the process by which it was possible to distinguish the pursuit of desire from the pursuit of perfection. What was required, therefore, was a precise description of the goals that the free man had to seek to acquire, and an account of the psychological disposition, moral strengths, and emotional states that individuals' had to possess to be able to detect and pursue those 'perfect' goals. The third component of the idealist conception of freedom provided the

[19] B. Bosanquet, *The Philosophical Theory of the State* (London: Macmillan, 1899), 125.

[20] T. H. Green, *Lectures on the Principles of Political Obligation* (Reprinted: Cambridge: Cambridge University Press, 1986), 9, 17–18. Bosanquet, *Philosophical*, 127.

[21] On debates between earlier theorists on the 'externality' of 'obstacles', see Vincent, 'Classical Liberalism', 156–7.

[22] Bosanquet, *Philosophical*, 138.

[23] It was sometimes thought to follow from this that the only adequate test of whether an individual was free was to assess whether these worthy goals had actually been *attained*. As Bradley phrased it, 'the man is free who *realises* his true self'. For the idealists, then, liberty was occasionally understood to be an 'exercise' rather than an 'opportunity' concept. See F. H. Bradley, *Ethical Studies* (Oxford: Oxford University Press, 1927), 57.

[24] Bradley, *Ethical*, 56.

beginnings of just such a definition. It insisted that the substance of all individuals' real and valuable ends could be deduced from the importance of
human 'interrelatedness'. A worthy goal was one that somehow recognized the
essential connection of each individual to every other and to an over-arching
social whole. In defending this view, the idealists argued that any individualist account of human nature that did not situate the human within a definite
social context was 'but a mere fancy' or a 'delusion of theory'.[25] In its place,
the idealists constructed a thoroughly social view of humanity. As F. H. Bradley
described the individual, 'if we suppose the world of communal relations in
which he was born and bred, never to have been, then we suppose the very
essence of him not to be; if we take that away, we take him away'.[26]

From this perspective, the idealists thus insisted that since humans were
inevitably and unambiguously communal creatures, the attainment of
human perfection, freedom itself, must also be recognized as essentially
social. This then translated into a close connection between the pursuit of
freedom and the necessity of pursuing a common good. Human perfection
lay in the collective pursuit of goods which individuals could enjoy together.
This did not entail that all individuals' goods must be exactly the same;
perfection was not thought to be identical for each and every one of us. But
it did require that each human's perfection must involve mutual support and
connection. As Josiah Royce outlined, 'the law of freedom that we seek is
determined by the fact that there are many of us living together, and that, if
we are rational beings, we are deeply concerned for one another, to organize
our wills into some sort of universality, to live in spiritual union, to give our
common life the most complete wholeness possible'.[27] In a society where
individuals had achieved perfection there would be no conflict, as the perfection of each individual would involve and assist that of all other members.
The third idealist component of freedom thus demanded 'that one realize, as
far as may be possible, the inner life of one's fellow men'.[28]

These first three elements of the idealist re-conceptualization of liberty—
freedom as the pursuit of perfection, as the absence of external *and* internal
obstacles to that perfection, and as the definition of that perfection in terms
of essential human communality—led in turn to the fourth and fifth elements.
These last two elements were more clearly political in character than the first
three. The fourth component concerned the role of external authority in the
pursuit of freedom. Before the advent of idealism, the idealists themselves
argued, freedom had been thought to consist in allowing individuals to pursue

[25] Bradley, *Ethical*, 174. Idealists, of course, credited earlier British and American liberalism with
just such an individualist view; but see note 18 above.

[26] Bradley, *Ethical*, 166.

[27] J. Royce, cited in C. M. Bakewell, 'Royce as an Interpreter of American Ideals', *International
Journal of Ethics*, 27 (1916), 309.

[28] Royce in Bakewell, 'Interpreter', 31. See too B. Bosanquet, 'The Function of the State in
Promoting the Unity of Mankind', *Proceedings of the Aristotelian Society*, 17 (1917), 38.

their own goals independent of the constraint of others. As such, early-nine-teenth century theorists had emphasized the importance of a sphere of individual non-interference. Indeed, free individuals were often pictured simply as those who enjoyed privacy and protection from the activities of others. Theories of liberty of this earlier variety were especially interested in removing the pressures of state and society, seeing them as posing the greatest threat to the individual's ability to 'pursue his own good in his own way'.[29] For the idealists, however, such a recommendation relied upon a fundamental distortion of the essential human condition. 'According to these ideas', Bosanquet raged, 'the self is something less in society than, if it could so exist, it would be out of society.'[30] Rejecting this approach, the idealists offered an entirely opposite claim. The fourth idealist component argued that rather than requiring *protection* from the interference of society, individual liberty demanded proactive *assistance* from that society. Far from providing hindrances or constraints, the activity of an external authority could positively help the individual's search for liberty.

This assistance itself could, of course, take several forms. Most mildly, idealists argued that an external authority could help an individual's search for freedom by providing the environment that was required to inculcate in him both the desire and the ability to pursue a communal form of perfection. The early British and American idealists, with T. H. Green and William Harris to the fore, thus advocated an expansion of education provision. The discipline of the classroom and the comradeship of the schoolyard, it was argued, would enable future citizens to learn emotional and psychological control and appreciate the merits of cooperation, enabling them thus to identify and to pursue their social perfections.[31] More strongly, these early idealists also occasionally asserted that certain 'anti-social' activities could effectively be prohibited, without such a prohibition threatening the individual's liberty. As freedom involved the pursuit of perfection, and given that perfection was social rather than distinctly individual, the prohibition of anti-social desires did not involve an infringement of liberty, not even of the liberty of the individual being constrained. As the British social commentator C. Delisle Burns summarized in true Rousseauian style, for the idealists 'the anti-social ability to do as I like is not freedom at all, not even my freedom'.[32] As the years progressed, some of the later idealists took this fourth conceptual argument still further. Bernard Bosanquet suggested in his magisterial *Philosophical*

[29] See J. S. Mill, 'On Liberty', reprinted in M. Warnock (ed.), *Utilitarianism, On Liberty, and Essay on Bentham* (London: Fontana, 1979).

[30] Bosanquet, *Philosophical*, 124.

[31] See W. T. Harris, *Psychologic Foundations of Education: An Attempt to Show the Genius of the Higher Faculties of the Mind* (New York: Macmillan, 1898); Green, *Political Obligation*, 162; N. G. McCluskey, *Public Schools and Moral Education: The Influence of Horace Mann, William Torrey Harris, and John Dewey* (New York: Macmillan, 1958), 99–176.

[32] C. D. Burns, *The Philosophy of Labour* (London: George Allen and Unwin, 1925), 28.

Theory of the State that if a positive control of the behaviour of an individual forcibly directed him towards certain activities that led to him to follow more socially useful activities than he otherwise would have pursued, then, paradoxically, he was more free when externally coerced than when not. The idealist conceptual scheme made it possible to describe an individual as 'free', Bosanquet insisted, even 'at the very moment' when 'law and order is constraining [his] particular private will in a way which [he] resent[s].'[33]

The final component of the idealist conception of freedom identified the organization to be responsible for deciding the nature and extent of the assistance, restrictions, and prohibitions recommended above. All the idealists were certain that there had to be some such body because, as Royce argued, the 'comprehensive harmony of the conflicting wills of men' could be achieved only through 'the organization of the larger life of mankind'.[34] All idealists also agreed that the body 'which is to be in sole or supreme command of force for the common good' must be representative of 'a genuine community sharing a common sentiment and animated by a common tradition'; an authority to be charged with shaping social harmony must be contiguous with the boundaries of a community in which such harmony is attainable.[35] It was here, though, as they sought to locate this community that the British and American strands of idealism appear to have diverged, with each national group turning to a different level of community to provide its focus.

In Britain, most of the leading idealists asserted that 'such communities are not now to be found except in the nation-state'.[36] Turning against the celebration of regionalism and localism characteristic of much of earlier British political thought, these theorists argued that individuals in the late nineteenth century were primarily socialized in nations. The social harmony within which each individual's perfection could be found was thus nationally based.[37] Drawing on this claim, the idealists concluded that the authority to be charged with assisting the pursuit of perfection had to be the one organization that was synonymous with the boundaries of the nation; this was, of course, the state. For British idealists, as H. S. Shelton summarized, the pursuit of a national communality led to the 'desire to extend, so far as possible, state activities and state control'.[38] For the American idealists, on the other hand, the community required was distinctly not the nation, and the central organization was thus

[33] Bosanquet, *Philosophical*, 127. See too H. C. Brown, 'Human Nature and the State', *International Journal of Ethics*, 26 (1915), 177–92. The *Philosophical Theory of the State* was published in 1899 and quickly became a centrepiece of the idealist canon.

[34] Royce in Bakewell, 'Interpreter', 312.

[35] Bosanquet, 'Function', 29.

[36] Bosanquet, 'Function', 48.

[37] For earlier celebrations of locality in British political thought, see J. Burrow, *Whigs and Liberals: Continuity and Change in English Political Thought* (Oxford: Oxford University Press, 1988).

[38] H. S. Shelton, 'The Hegelian Concept of the State', *International Journal of Ethics*, 24 (1913), 25.

not the state. Individuals in America, Royce argued, were not socialized in nations because the American nation itself was too 'vast' to provide any social focus. The very scope of the country entailed that it was without any essentially shared culture, or sets of values, or traditions. Rather, American culture was characterized by extensive social diversity and its geographical space allowed too much social isolation. Moreover, the government of so large a nation 'seems [more] like a great nature force', an entity that is large, imposing, and existent external to each individual himself, 'than like his own loyal self, writ large.' American citizens could not hope to recognize the means for providing the necessary 'social unity' in their central government. The alternative focus lay in the American localities. For Royce and his followers, American communities were found in small towns, counties, or even the several States, all of which Royce went on to call the 'provinces'. It was within these provinces that human character was forged, and it was within these that 'the social mind is naturally aware of itself as at home with its own'.[39] American idealism thus became a celebration of the *local*. American idealists demanded a 'sort of provincialism' which makes people 'want to idealize, to adorn, to ennoble, to educate, their own province; to hold sacred its traditions'.[40]

This apparently stark divergence between Americans and British idealists, however, was far more notable in pure academic theory than in recommendations for political practice. For when it came to drawing concrete conclusions from conceptual speculation, the British idealists did not celebrate 'big government' and the expansion of centralized state authority any more than the Americans did. Indeed, insofar as they were politically involved at all, the vast majority of British idealists were extremely cautious as to the merits of interventionist programmes of reform. The primary theoretical reason for this apparently paradoxical conservatism rested in the British idealists' understanding of the 'state' itself. The early idealists who followed T. H. Green in Britain saw the 'state' itself as something far broader than the organs of central government, understanding the concept to refer instead to all of a single society's institutions and associations unified in some mystical form of harmonic relationship. Often, indeed, when the idealists used the term 'state' they simply meant 'society'. As Bernard Bosanquet argued, to 'identify the State either with the governmental machine, or with what is ordered by a plebiscite over a certain area' is a serious error. For British idealists the state involved 'all parts of the community', with localities and voluntary organizations all 'being expressly intended'.[41] Despite all the conceptual innovation, there was, thus, no demand for nation-wide homogeneity or for the dominance of one central institution over others.

[39] J. Royce, *The Philosophy of Loyalty* (New York: Macmillan, 1908), 239. See too Smith, *America's Philosophical Vision*, 147–52.

[40] Royce, *Loyalty*, 245–6. For a detailed account, see Smith, *America's Philosophical Vision*, 147–52.

[41] B. Bosanquet, 'A Note on Mr Cole's Paper', *Proceedings of the Aristotelian Society*, 15 (1915), 162.

Idealist politics

Idealist politics emphasized the role of the local, the voluntary, and the social. In place of the efforts of the central government, idealists rather aimed to shape the ethos of the voluntary social work characteristic of London's Toynbee Hall and Chicago's Hull House.[42] Indeed, their most significant success was in the Charity Organisation Society (COS), which became the one Anglo-American organization to adopt idealism as its house philosophy. By emphasizing the importance the idealists attached to 'internal' moral, psychological, or emotional, obstacles to freedom, the COS used the conception to argue against the use of centrally provided welfare benefits and to legitimize instead a series of prescriptive educative measures designed to improve individuals' 'moral character'. These measures themselves were intended to enhance a capacity for self-reliance as the best example of civic responsibility. They thus further fed a suspicion of direct government aid and activity.[43] In the politics of the late nineteenth century, therefore, British and American idealists were generally found arguing for one of two political programmes. They either urged the maintenance of prevailing notions of laissez faire or, at most, demanded that reformers strike an harmonic balance between emerging patterns of industrial conglomeration, whether public or private, and the old-style capitalism of small businesses and entrepreneurs.[44] As the twentieth century began, idealists in both Britain and America largely continued in the same vein. In Britain, Bernard Bosanquet complained bitterly at the expansion of government power overseen by the radical Liberal administration that took office in 1906. In the United States, Josiah Royce argued at the same time that any 'further centralization of power in the national government . . . can only increase the estrangement of our national spirit from its own life'.[45]

    All of this entailed that there was no significant disagreement between British and American idealists when it came to political prescription. It also meant, though, that there was something paradoxical about their five-part

---

[42] See J. Harris, 'Political Thought and the Welfare State, 1870–1940', *Past and Present*, 135 (1992), 116–41.

[43] For Charity Organisation Society work in Britain, see H. Bosanquet, *Rich and Poor* (London: Macmillan, 1896); B. Bosanquet, *Essays and Addresses* (London: Swan Sonnenschein and Co., 1899); A. Vincent, 'The Poor Law Reports of 1909 and the Social Theory of the Charity Organisation Society', *Victorian Studies*, 27 (1984), 343–63. For America, see F. D. Watson, *The Charity Organization Movement in the United States: A Study in American Philanthropy* (New York: Macmillan, 1922); R. A. Mohl, 'The Abolition of Public Outdoor Relief', in W. I. Trattner (ed.), *Social Welfare or Social Control?: Some Historical Reflections on Regulating the Poor* (Knoxville: University of Tennessee Press, 1983), 35–50.

[44] As the essays collected in D. Boucher (ed.), *The British Idealists* (Cambridge: Cambridge University Press, 1997) bear witness. See the editor's introduction, pp. xxi–xxii. There were exceptions to this general rule, however, of whom D. G. Ritchie was the most notable. See D. G. Ritchie, *Studies in Political and Social Ethics* (London: Swan Sonnenschein and Co., 1902), 43–65.

[45] Royce, *Loyalty*, 248.

reconceptualization of liberty. For the idealists, liberty was to be understood as the pursuit of perfection independent of internal as well as external obstacles, where perfection was social rather than individual in orientation, where it often required assistance rather than abstinence from external authority, but where the nature of that authority and the scope of its activity were often both vague and limited. It was, therefore, a radical theoretical agenda but a moderate practical one. In comparison with the Millian liberalism from which they fled, the idealists certainly offered conceptual innovation, but they did not intend that it should be followed by substantial political change.

The Alternative: Evolution, Fabianism, and Freedom

All five central components of the idealists' conception of liberty, and especially their dedication to a communal view of human nature, were initially advanced through the haze of a quasi-Hegelian metaphysical philosophy. They were ideas propagated through the peculiar logic of the 'Absolute' and of the 'Whole' characteristic of that brand of thought. Idealists thus argued that their conception of liberty was grounded in the conviction that a full account of life must involve an acceptance of a thoroughgoing holism. They argued for the essential interrelationship of 'every phenomenon to every other in the universe', an interrelationship captured in a universal reason, a 'reason' which rested at the centre of all possible human understanding. Such a view was intended to rid philosophy of the dualism between the 'natural' and the 'ideal'. At root everything was connected in a spiritual union. The 'real' involved the relationship of both nature and ideas, of both facts and values. As a result, idealists also argued that an understanding of the 'whole' could not be captured through empirical observation alone. The essential 'togetherness' of life had, instead, to be inferred from a belief in the universality of the 'Absolute spirit'. Furthermore, as these metaphysical speculations were frequently coupled with a restatement of the essentially Christian bases of Western philosophy, acceptance of the importance of the Absolute was often born from religious conviction and faith.[46]

Such a defence for the new view of freedom was neither academically satisfactory nor particularly attractive among the wider public. For although these rather obtuse defences became popular in the philosophy and theology faculties of leading British and American universities, and were more attractive still to those who studied in the overwhelmingly Hegelian atmosphere of turn-of-the-century Germany, they could never be widely asserted beyond the

---

[46] See F. H. Bradley, *Essays on Truth and Reality* (Oxford: Oxford University Press, 1914), 1–18, and, for an overview, den Otter, *British Idealism*, esp. 76–80.

confines of these select branches of academia. Indeed, few beyond the walls of the academy could probably even comprehend the underlying logic of the approach. To begin with, therefore, the attractions of the idealist conception of freedom were obscured by the unattractive underlying philosophical justification.[47] And yet, despite these initial limitations, as the nineteenth century closed the central five contentions of the idealist conception of liberty began to find a far larger group of disciples in both Britain and America. By the beginning of the twentieth century the idealist conception of freedom comprised one of the central topics of discussion of political theory. The change was initiated not by any fundamental reconsideration by the idealists themselves but rather because their conception of freedom began to find a series of new theoretical and empirical underpinnings. These new patterns of support would not only encourage the wider dissemination of the idealist contentions but would also allow a shift in practical interpretation and, eventually, in political usage. Moreover, these arguments were not confined to philosophy but were to be found in a broad range of other, often initially quite distinct, intellectual traditions. The first came from contemporary natural science, and especially evolutionary Darwinism.

Society as organism

If idealism dominated philosophical speculation in Britain and America in the late nineteenth century, the discoveries of evolutionary biology dominated almost every other branch of academic inquiry. Seized by excitement at the possibilities of offering 'scientific' explanations for social phenomena, students of society in particular turned to the new techniques and discoveries. As Mike Hawkins has impressively shown, by the 1870s, 'social and psychological development, class, race and gender, religion and morality, war and peace, crime and destitution' were all in the process of being explained with reference to the evolutionary model that biology, and especially Darwinian biology, was providing.[48]

Central to these developments was the organic analogy. It was increasingly argued in the late nineteenth century that society could be best understood if it was treated as an organism, enjoying a status 'above and beyond' the aggregate identities of its parts. Constructed out of a variety of differing but intricately connected parts, society had a 'common . . . life, character and purpose', which could not be resolved into, but was nonetheless dependent upon, 'the life, character and purpose' of its individual components. Groups within society could thus be seen as various and vital 'organs' of the single

---

[47] For a detailed account of idealism's initial difficulties, see M. Freeden, *The New Liberalism: An Ideology of Social Reform* (Oxford: Oxford University Press, 1978), 16–18 and *Ideologies*, 180–3.

[48] M. Hawkins, *Social Darwinism in European and American Thought* (Cambridge: Cambridge University Press, 1997), 61.

societal 'organism'. Individuals were understood likewise, seen as the indispensable 'cells' out of which both 'organs' and the whole were constructed. As an animal with a clear identity of its own is constructed out of cells, hearts, lungs, and kidneys, so a distinct society emerges from a collection of individuals and associations.[49]

Such organicism could have augured well for idealism, insisting as it did on the interconnectedness of the parts to the whole in a way seemingly reminiscent of the idealist insistence on essential holism. As it first impacted on political theory, though, the biological analogy actually did remarkably little to benefit idealist conceptual speculations. The methods of the two movements were clearly distinct: the essentially empirical underpinnings of natural science kept it distant from idealism's faith-bound metaphysics.[50] More importantly, those who employed the organic analogy also reached normative conclusions that appeared to contradict several idealist essentials. At the outset, there appeared little reason for conflict. All of the social and political theorists who were first touched by the desire to base their philosophy on an analogy with Darwinian biology were convinced that, as an organism, society must be in a continual process of evolution. That in itself caused idealists few problems, for although they were often socially rather conservative the idealists were not entirely opposed to change. The emphasis Darwin and his successors placed on *competition* as the essential driving force of that evolutionary progress, however, swiftly entailed that a central aspect of biological thought stood in direct conflict with idealism.[51] At the centre of Darwinian evolutionary explanation was the belief that an unavoidable, relentless 'struggle for existence' was the root of all progress. As such, when sociologists and political theorists, led by Herbert Spencer in Britain and William Graham Sumner in the United States, first began to import Darwinian observations into their discipline it was no surprise that they gave priority to the maintenance of vigorous competition. Their recommendations directly contrasted with the emphasis on the fundamentally communal, harmonic and cooperative nature of human fulfilment characteristic of idealism. As the British idealist D. G. Ritchie put it, '[f]raternity ... seems clearly impossible when ceaseless struggle and ruthless elimination of the unfit are the very means of progress'.[52]

---

[49] J. A. Hobson, *The Crisis of Liberalism: New Issues of Democracy* (London: P. S. King and Son, 1909), 73.

[50] For an instructive discussion of the underlying differences between these 'scientific' and 'philosophical' brands of organicism, see J. Meadowcroft, *Conceptualizing the State: Innovation and Dispute in British Political Thought, 1880–1914* (Oxford: Oxford University Press, 1995), 59–68.

[51] For recognition of this conflict, and attempted resolutions, see H. Jones, 'The Social Organism' (1883) and B. Bosanquet, 'Socialism and Natural Selection' (1895), reprinted in Boucher, *British Idealists*, 3–29 and 50–67.

[52] D. G. Ritchie, 'Ethical Democracy: Evolution and Democracy' (1900), in Boucher, *British Idealists*, 70.

The acceptance of the inevitability and desirability of competition infused every aspect of Spencer and Sumner's political vocabulary; and their understanding of liberty was no exception. For Spencer and Sumner, freedom was to be understood in distinctly individual and competitive terms. Liberty was a 'status created for the individual' that included a guarantee that each man should be allowed 'the use of his own powers exclusively for his own welfare'. Translated from potentially convoluted philosophical language 'into blunt English', Sumner concluded, the conceptual definition of freedom would read 'mind your own business'.[53]

A new organicism

These arguments persisted in related forms right throughout both the nineteenth and twentieth centuries. Yet they did not exhaust the contribution that evolutionary science had to make to political thought. From the 1880s, new developments in evolutionary theory enabled organic theories to move away from this position of diametric opposition to idealism towards a stance of mutual comprehension and eventual acceptance. The original Darwinians argued that evolution was dependent upon struggle: progress was reliant on the potentially brutal 'survival of the fittest' and competition was thus the dominant tendency in all forms of natural life. As the nineteenth century aged, though, a later generation of Darwinians began to argue that the obsession with struggle as the *means* of evolution had obscured the quite different *direction* that such evolution was taking: a direction of which Darwin himself had professed ignorance but which more 'recent empirical researches' were supposed to have discovered.[54] These new biologists, led by August Weismann, were convinced that if one investigated carefully it became apparent that although evolution did indeed progress through natural selection, through 'the survival of the fittest', its results actually consisted in a trend towards ever more sophisticated models of *social interaction* and *communal cooperation*. The individuals or groups that survived through the evolutionary process were, on this account, those whose lives had become 'integrative'; those who survived were those who had learnt to 'work more in co-operation and less in competition with each other'.[55]

Claiming to be 'profoundly impressed' by the 'triumphs in Natural Science' of the post-Darwinian era, a whole new generation of political theorists began towards the end of the nineteenth century to employ the organic

---

[53] Sumner cited in Hawkins, *Social Darwinism*, 112.

[54] See S. Webb, *Towards Social Democracy: A Study of Social Evolution during the Last Three-Quarters of a Century* (London: Fabian Society, 1909), 10–13.

[55] From the excellent summary of these trends, J. A. Thompson, 'Progress in Evolution', *New Statesman*, 3 July 1920, 360–1. See too R. Balmforth, 'The Influence of Darwinian Theory on Ethics', *International Journal of Ethics*, 21 (1911), 448–65; Bosanquet, 'Socialism and Natural Selection', 56; Webb, *Towards*, 9–13; Hobson, *Crisis*, 71.

analogy in a way that allowed them to come to very different conclusions to their immediate Darwinian predecessors.[56] In the United States, these ideas were seized on in particular by the positivists led by Herbert Croly's father, David. The notion of an inevitable and scientifically detectable socializing trend in evolution chimed well with the essentials of their Comtean philosophy. Edward Bellamy's fabulously popular positivistic utopian novel *Looking Backward* that predicted the emergence of a society of communal harmony and order was based almost entirely on the union of Comte and Darwin.[57] Impressive as these developments were, and extensive as their support was, the new evolutionary ideas found an even more significant political following in Britain. That following began in the academic circles around the radical wing of the Liberal Party, and included the leading 'New Liberal' theorists John A. Hobson and Leonard T. Hobhouse. It reached its apex, though, with those theorists who comprised the nascent Fabian Society and the intellectual wing of the Independent Labour Party. It was through these organizations that such influential figures as the social investigators Sidney and Beatrice Webb, the novelist H. G. Wells, and the political philosopher and later Labour Prime Minister, J. Ramsay MacDonald, all turned to the discoveries of the new evolutionary science.[58] They used it both to resuscitate and then to transform the idealists' approach to freedom.

Social evolution

For all of these thinkers, the chief lesson of the new developments in evolutionary science was the assurance that a greater 'state of affairs ahead of us, less marked by failure, less chaotic, better organised.'[59] In society's current relatively primitive state, disharmony characterized the relationship between vital component parts of the societal body. As Ramsay MacDonald phrased it,

---

[56] As described in R. H. Tawney, *The Webbs in Perspective* (London: George Allen and Unwin, 1953), 11. The debate over whether these scientific discoveries provided the motivation for or merely a *post hoc* legitimization of the new conceptual and practical programmes is difficult to resolve. The two views are expertly presented in Freeden, *New Liberalism*, 90–115 and S. Collini, *Liberalism and Sociology: L. T. Hobhouse and Political Argument in England, 1870–1914* (Cambridge: Cambridge University Press, 1979), 147–209 respectively.

[57] 'Comte in America meant Darwin', as R. J. Lustig argues in his *Corporate Liberalism: The Origins of Modern American Political Theory 1890–1920* (Berkeley: University of California Press, 1982), 231. For positivism and Bellamy, see G. J. Harp, *Positivist Republic: Auguste Comte and the Reconstruction of American Liberalism, 1865–1920* (University Park, Pennsylvania: Pennsylvania State University Press, 1995), 97–104.

[58] Contemporaries, and especially American commentators, often included all these thinkers under the umbrella term 'Fabian'. Although there is some inaccuracy in this use of the term—the Independent Labour Party was just as important an organization as the Fabian Society in this regard—such generic usage will largely be followed here in order to maintain consistency with the original texts. The complex pattern of actual interconnections between Fabians, members of the ILP, and radical 'New Liberals' is presented in M. Freeden (ed.), *Minutes of the Rainbow Circle* (London: Royal Historical Society, 1989). See too Meadowcroft, *Conceptualizing the State*, esp. 59–68 and 168–204.

[59] J. R. MacDonald, *Socialism and Society* (London: Independent Labour Party, 1907), 9.

while mixing the metaphor, 'the chief characteristic of existing society is the incoherence of its functions. It is a machine out of gear'.[60] All was not despondency, though. For the evolutionary development of society was heading towards a greater coordination of the various component parts of the societal organism. As the Webbs evocatively summarized, 'where our forefathers saw a jostling crowd of individuals . . . each fighting for his own hand', these new developments forecast the emergence of a 'highly organised, far reaching, patiently pursued communal enterprise'.[61]

As an evolutionary step, this development was considered to be inevitable. Indeed, at the turn of the twentieth century, many theorists claimed to have detected this shift already at work in their society and particularly in the economy. In the struggle for industrial success, they argued, capitalists had recognized the futility of certain forms of disharmony, and had thus unconsciously initiated a progression towards the essential evolutionary goal of an increasingly coordinated society. The development of capitalistic combinations and the formation of monopolistic cartels, these thinkers frequently claimed, illustrated the inexorable drift to cooperation.[62] A further advantage of the new evolutionary understanding, however, entailed that reliance on such an ad hoc evolutionary progress had been rendered unnecessary; it was, these theorists held, now possible to 'transcend the process of struggle' and to achieve evolutionary goals another way.[63] The new recognition of the direction of evolution entailed that 'instead of [continuing to be] unconscious factors' in social evolution, human actors and their associations could 'become deliberate agents to aid the developments coming to our notice'. Whereas initial Darwinian ambivalence as to the direction of evolutionary change had led theorists of the Spencer and Sumner school to conclude the intervention was at best misguided and at worst counter-productive, the opposite was now the case. 'Human selection', Webb concluded the argument, 'accordingly becomes the main form of natural selection . . . Man becomes the midwife of the great womb of Time, and necessarily undertakes the responsibility for the new economic relations which he brings into existence.'[64]

The advantages of this conscious interference over its unconscious counterpart were manifold. American Positivists and British Fabians were convinced that not only would the evolutionary process reach its apex more swiftly when controlled, but also that 'evolutionary shocks'—unfortunate

---

[60] MacDonald, *Socialism and Society*, 9.

[61] S. and B. Webb, 'The Principles of the Labour Party' (London: The Labour Party, 1918), 4.

[62] See J. R. MacDonald, *Socialism: Critical and Constructive* (London: Cassell and Company, 1921), 143–8. See too Webb, *Towards*, 31–3.

[63] See Hobson, *Crisis*, 132.

[64] S. Webb, 'The Difficulties of Individualism', first published 1891, reprinted in S. Webb (ed.), *Socialism and Individualism* (London: Fifield, 1909), 7.

events along the path of evolutionary adjustment—could be avoided.[65] More fundamentally, these thinkers maintained that a consciously directed evolution could be a fairer, more just, evolution. There was no reason to suppose that an undirected evolution should proceed in accordance with conscious human moral principles: biology, after all, 'has no standard of value'.[66] If, however, reliable agents and associations, possessing moral integrity, could be charged with directing the evolutionary process they could ensure that the process would give substantial weight to *ethical* considerations. For example, a directed evolution could ensure that all parts of society would benefit from coordinated integration. The demands of efficacy and equity would harmonize only in the process of directed evolution. As J. A. Hobson phrased it, 'it is doubtless [in] the real interest of the organism as a whole to distribute blood in accordance with the needs of the individual . . . cells'.[67] The healthier each of the parts was, the healthier the whole would be.

From evolution to freedom

All of this had important consequences for the understanding of liberty. The new organic view, with its joint emphasis on the interconnectedness of all in society and the notion of a coordinated pursuit of a communal progress, allowed essential elements of the idealist view of freedom to reappear. The perfectionist claim was the first to return. In 1897, Sidney and Beatrice Webb declared on behalf of Fabian thinkers that 'we ourselves understand by the words "liberty" or "freedom" . . . the utmost development of faculty in the individual human being'.[68] MacDonald concurred, with 'real liberty' for him being the 'liberty of a man to fulfil his true being'.[69] Second, it also entailed that individuals would have to learn to control themselves, to overcome their internal weaknesses, to temper their own demands, to privilege the common good above their own short-term desires. In order to ensure evolutionary progress, the 'community' would have to 'enter at every point into the life of the individual', and in order for that to be possible it would be vital to teach individuals how to 'broaden [their] sympathies . . . into the wide sympathy of community'.[70] To be genuinely free, Sidney Webb thus wrote in 1889, each individual would have to 'abandon self-conceit . . . and bend his jealous mind . . . to subjection to the higher end'.[71] Third, the new organic vision clearly designated individual perfection as communal in essence: the new organicism

---

[65] See Webb, *Towards*, 8–10.
[66] L. T. Hobhouse, *Democracy and Reaction* (London: T. F. Unwin, 1909), 137.
[67] Hobson, *Crisis*, 81.
[68] S. Webb and B. Webb, *Industrial Democracy* (London: Longmans, Green and Co., 1901), 847.
[69] J. R. MacDonald, *Socialism and Government* (London: Independent Labour Party, 1909), 154.
[70] J. R. MacDonald, *Democracy and Character* (London: Independent Labour Party, 1905), 10.
[71] S. Webb, 'Historic', in G. B. Shaw (ed.), *Fabian Essays in Socialism* (London: George Allen and Unwin, 1st edn 1889, Jubilee edn 1948), 54.

demanded that only 'the individual in society can attain to a state of complete development'.[72] Indeed, as evolutionary progress depended on the development of an ever closer communal union, then the only way to true liberty was to be found by ensuring that each and every individual rendered 'faithful service' to the community.[73]

When it came to the more prescriptively political fourth and fifth components of the idealist conception—the idea that an external agency could assist in the liberation of the individual and the identification of the authority to be charged with such a duty—this straightforward acceptance was transformed by the Fabians into more sophisticated adaptation. Their faith in the identification of the science of society entailed that these thinkers were even more willing to insist that external authorities could be of use to individuals in finding their freedom than the idealists who had preceded them. As an ordered evolution was to be overseen and directed, so the 'liberty' to pursue social perfection could not be understood as the 'negative demand to be let alone'; there was no longer any antithesis between 'liberty and coercion'. Well-advised external agencies, those that knew where evolution was going and how to get there, would assist individuals in the development of their social perfection rather than hinder them, even if those individuals may not initially recognize it themselves.

The amended conception of social evolution also enabled Fabians and their colleagues to lay down clear guidelines for the choice of external agencies that were to be charged with the task of enabling individuals to pursue their social perfection. Any institution that was to be able to direct the whole course of societal evolution would have to satisfy at least three criteria. First, and most straightforwardly, such an agency would have to be powerful enough successfully to direct, when necessary, every one of society's functioning organs. It must have a 'force strong enough to be thrown against' any obstructive individual or sectional interest, to be able to override any temporary, short-sighted opposition. Second, the agency would have to be well informed. It would have to be aware of the overall 'science of society', the needs and demands of all the constituent parts, and possess solutions to the many important technical questions that would arise. Third, it would have to be impartial. The agents involved would need to possess a high level of moral integrity, which would make them capable of ensuring that each part of the societal body was maintained in health.[74]

The Fabians and their allies were convinced that only one institution met these demanding conditions: the central government of the nation state. As MacDonald spelt the conditions out, employing his own unique brand of

---

[72] MacDonald, *Socialism*, 3.   [73] MacDonald, *Socialism and Society*, 195.
[74] Webb, *Towards*, 38–9.

organic imagery, the search for evolutionary progress demanded that '[s]ome organ must enable other organs and the mass of Society to communicate its impressions to a receiving centre, must carry from that centre impulses leading to action, must originate on its own initiative organic movements calculated to bring some benefit or pleasure to the organism'.[75] This series of conditions, he continued, happily coincided with 'the Socialist view of the political organ on its legislative and administrative sides'. It was central government, and only central government, MacDonald concluded, that 'carries up experience, carries it to a centre which decides corresponding movements, and then carries back to the parts affected the impulse of action'.[76] The state in this sense, at least when properly reformed and staffed, was the only agency capable of guaranteeing that the inevitable socializing evolution was conducted effectively and fairly. It was the agency that should be charged 'systematically to think out the function that each person has to perform and the relation in which each must stand to others and to the whole', and in so doing it would guarantee both social progress and individual development: the combination of which made for the expansion of real freedom.[77] 'When critics suggest that individual liberty and a thick statute book are inconsistent', the Fabians and their colleagues thus argued, we 'confess we do not follow the argument'. For '[t]here is no opposition between these things' as long as one accepts 'that the law of individual well being is a law of social personality'.[78] With all of these arguments in place, Sidney Webb could insist that a policy of 'growing collectivism', whereby individuals' lives are positively directed by a central authority operated 'more and more [by] . . . persons elaborately trained and set apart for the task', would be 'the mother of freedom'.[79]

The faith that progress would come through an ever-increasing communal endeavour that the new form of Darwinism provided for allowed both for the re-emergence of all of the idealists' conceptual essentials and the use of those essentials to argue for a far more radical position. These political differences were important, and the methodological dispute between 'science' and 'philosophy' remained severe; but in an important sense they made the similarities of the conceptual position with that of idealism all the more startling. Even for the most diehard of philosophical and political rivals, 'significant features' of their conceptual system were rendered 'completely consistent'.[80]

---

[75] MacDonald, *Socialism and Society*, 14–15. [76] Ibid.
[77] S. and B. Webb, *A Constitution for the Socialist Commonwealth of Great Britain* (London: Longmans, Green and Co., 1920), 202.
[78] MacDonald, *Socialism and Society*, 134–5.
[79] Webb, 'Difficulties', 27, and 'The Necessary Basis of Society', *Fabian Tract* 165 (London: Fabian Society, 1906), 6.
[80] The same was true of idealism and American positivism, on which see D. Levy, *Herbert Croly of the New Republic: The Life and Thought of an American Progressive* (Princeton: Princeton University Press, 1985), 31 and Harp, *Positivist Republic*, 190.

It was a recognition from which the Fabians and their colleagues did not flinch. As Sidney Webb himself admitted, as the twentieth century began, the Fabians and their colleagues advocated an approach to freedom indisputably shaped by 'the teaching of Thomas H[ill] Green', even if, when placed within a new ideational context, this 'idealist doctrine' was now offered not as a defence of the status quo but 'as a justification for socialism'.[81]

Challengers: Psychology and Pragmatism

The British Fabians and their Positivist colleagues in the United States were not the only movements to employ the new developments in evolutionary thought to reconsider the idealist conception of freedom in its theoretical and practical aspects. Drawing further on these conclusions in the 1890s and very early 1900s, other philosophers and social theorists began to employ their own evolutionary analysis to challenge the arguments that had been developed by Fabians and their idealist predecessors. At the forefront of these investigations was the emergence of the discipline of social psychology, which, as shall be shown below, challenged fundamental features of Fabianism. Also to emerge was the philosophy of pragmatism, which was closely related to speculations in psychology. The pragmatists provided a new opposition both to the new organicism associated with Fabianism and, initially at least, to the bases of the idealist conception itself.

Initial opposition: social psychology

There were important British contributors to the development of social psychology—the most notable of whom was Graham Wallas of the London School of Economics—but the discipline was generally an American invention. At its head was Charles Horton Cooley of the University of Michigan, who laid out a manifesto for the discipline in his masterful *Human Nature and the Social Order*, published in 1902. Cooley and his colleagues, including the economist turned psychological investigator Simon Nelson Patten of the Wharton School in Philadelphia, rejected the deterministic and mechanistic aspects of the approach to evolution that Positivists and Fabians had suggested. Although sound in essentials, Cooley and colleagues argued, the Fabian-style theory overstated the malleability of each individual in the evolutionary process. By treating individuals as units in a larger system that can be directed towards improvement by an impartial central state, the

---

[81] Webb, 'Difficulties of Individualism', 154. And G. D. H. Cole, 'Conflicting Social Obligations', *Proceedings of the Aristotelian Society*, 15 (1915), 148.

Fabians were overemphasizing their flexibility. The social psychologists understood the initial determinant of an individual's behaviour as inherited psychological characteristics, none of which could be easily eroded. Humans were not as plastic as Fabians and other reformers seemed to suggest. Each man is born with energies and 'tendencies', Cooley contended in 1902,[82] and any theory of social change would have to take those forces into account.

This insistence on the pre-existence of set human 'tendencies' did not, however, entail that social change was impossible. Rather, the social psychologists argued that humans do adapt, but they do so only slowly, and only when an individual continually mixes with others within a particular society. Through the processes of social interaction, Cooley and Patten argued, each individual comes to have a 'character and a career' in addition to the psychological blueprint that he passively inherits from his parents. 'If an English couple settles in this country,' Cooley explained, 'the children will contract from our climate and society peculiarities of appearance and behaviour that will mark them as Americans.' Furthermore, Cooley concluded, it is quite 'uncertain whether they can in any degree be transmitted by heredity'. When these sorts of human characteristic and attributes are passed from generation to the next—thus giving the impression of biological heredity—they are in fact largely communicated through the formal and the informal social processes of teaching and learning.[83] All of this implied, therefore, that intentionally led social change as desired by the Fabians was theoretically possible as inherited psychological tendencies could be redirected in the right environment, but that such change would both be slow to come about and could result only from the immersing of individuals in a different social environment. It distinctly could not be achieved simply by the dictate of the state. 'The possibility of a progressive evolution', Simon Patten explained, primarily depends not upon 'the conditions of the objective world' coming under the right direction but rather upon 'the development of new mental qualities' in each and every individual in a society.[84]

Initial opposition: pragmatism

If the psychologists began to pick away at the apparent certainties of Fabianism, the American philosophical movement of pragmatism initiated an

[82] C. H. Cooley, *Human Nature and the Social Order* (New York: C. Scribner's Sons, 1902), 423.

[83] C. H. Cooley, 'The Process of Social Change', *Political Science Quarterly*, 12 (1897), 65. Other excellent first hand examples of this argument can be found in G. Wallas, *Human Nature and Politics* (London: Constable and Company, 1910); F. Carrel, *An Analysis of Human Motive* (London: Simpkin, 1905); W. McDougall, *Psychology* (London: Macmillan, 1912), 183–9, and D. G. Ritchie, *Darwinism and Politics* (London: S. Sonnenschein and Co., 1901). For more details of the sources of this development in Britain and America, see respectively R. Soffer, *Ethics and Society in England: The Revolution in the Social Sciences, 1870–1914* (Berkeley: University of California Press, 1978) and Hawkins, *Social Darwinism*, 159–66.

[84] S. N. Patten, *The Theory of Social Forces* (Philadelphia: American Academy of Political and Social Science, 1896), 7.

even more aggressive campaign against idealism itself. Led by Harvard's William James, and specifically designed as a refutation of idealist metaphysics, pragmatism was the most serious challenge to idealism's dominance of the American philosophical world. It also posed a challenge, initially at least, to the Darwinian underpinnings of Fabian thought. The pragmatists' most celebrated contention was that 'truths' of all sorts were to be derived neither from Hegelian metaphysical speculation nor from Darwinian evolutionary theory building, but from the processes of action, experience, and experiment. No theory or argument possessed any status above a mere 'probability', to be tested against the continual unfolding nature of events, and accepted only insofar as they succeeded in providing explanations that met the demands of the time. All the apparent certainties of metaphysics, religion, and evolutionary science were equally susceptible to such a test.

For William James such an approach represented the death knell for every aspect of idealism, including, most importantly, the idealist conception of freedom in all its guises. The dedication to experimentation inherent in pragmatism, James argued, implied that 'our sense of freedom supposes that some things at least are decided here and now'. '[T]he passing moment', he continued, 'may contain some novelty, be an original starting-point of events, and not merely a push from elsewhere.' Such a view tore the heart out of the idealists' communal assumption and replaced it with an individualism more reminiscent of traditional liberalism: 'some parts of our world, [pragmatism] admits cannot exist out of their wholes; but others, it says, can.' When this was accepted, James concluded, the idealists would have to abandon the entirety of their conceptual vision. Their 'ridiculous' theory of freedom as the 'freedom to do right' simply could not be maintained, James insisted, when the essential contingency of life and understanding was conceded. It would have to be accepted, he concluded, that all freedom could actually be was simply the ability 'to do as *I* think right'.[85]

Conceptual compromise: pragmatism, psychology, and the idealist conception

Stark as James's rejection was, many of the other early pragmatists, including most notably John Dewey, did not join James in his renunciation of the idealist view of freedom. Almost as if to illustrate just how resilient the idealist conception was in the late nineteenth century, Dewey lent warm support to the move away from philosophic individualism and towards a heavily socialized approach to human nature, characteristic of both idealism and evolutionary Fabianism. Dewey explained this startling conviction in 1888 by arguing that

---

[85] W. James, *Some Problems in Philosophy* (London: Longmans, Green and Co., 1911), 139–40 and *Will to Believe*, 271. For a persuasive interpretation, see J. A. C. Pemberton, 'James and the Early Laski: The Ambiguous Legacy of Pragmatism', *History of Political Thought*, 19 (1998), 264–97.

'[e]ven from the pragmatic standpoint, the theory that men are not isolated social atoms, but are men only when in intrinsic relations to men, has wholly superseded the theory of men as an aggregate, as a heap of grains of sand needing some factious mortar to put them into semblance of order'. Further, when it came time to turn to specifically political philosophy, Dewey argued that the idealists and the Fabians had indeed been right in thinking that such a socialized view of humanity had important consequences for conceptual understandings. As Dewey continued, one of most the significant results of the acceptance of such a theory was the alteration to understandings of the concept of liberty. The organic assumption entailed that 'freedom is not mere self-assertion, nor unregulated desire'—the first two of the idealist components—and that 'liberty is not' to be found in the maintenance of 'isolation' but rather that the essence of liberty demanded 'the realization of personality through the formation of a higher and more complete unity amongst men'.[86] Here within pragmatism itself, perhaps the least likely of philosophical settings, the essential elements of the idealist conception had emerged once again.

This pattern of conceptual convergence also appeared in the work of many of the social psychologists. Again, although there were clear methodological differences between the psychologists and their idealist or Fabian rivals, their inherently social view of human development allowed many of the essential components of the idealist conception of freedom to be warmly endorsed. The agreement started, of course, with the acceptance that freedom must be essentially communal rather than distinctly individual: 'if the word [freedom] is to have any definite meaning it must . . . be separated from the idea of a fundamental opposition between society and the individual', Cooley contended. He then moved to endorse all of the other key conceptual components too. For these social psychologists, just as for the idealists, liberty was a perfectionist concept, requiring the 'opportunity for right development'. It demanded, further, the absence of internal as well as external constraints: being led to do 'wrong' by one's own desires was to be rendered essentially 'unfree'. Furthermore, it also required the sensible use of external authority. 'So far as discipline is concerned', Charles Cooley insisted with a vigour reminiscent of Bosanquet, Royce, and Webb, 'freedom means not its absence but the use of higher and more rational forms . . . It is freedom to be disciplined in as rational a manner as you are fit for'.[87]

As with the earlier Fabian response to the idealist conception, though, disagreement followed agreement when conceptual discussion was transformed

---

[86] J. Dewey, 'The Ethics of Democracy', 1888, reprinted in *John Dewey: The Early Works* (Carbondale: Southern Illinois University Press, 1988), 231, 244–5, 248. See too J. Dewey and J. H. Tufts, *Ethics* (New York: Macmillan, 1908). On pragmatism and social ethics more generally, see R. Bourne, 'American Uses for German Ideals', *New Republic*, 4 September 1915, 117–19 and A. Ryan, *John Dewey and the High Tide of American Liberalism* (New York: W. W. Norton, 1995), 84–106.

[87] Cooley, *Human Nature and the Social Order*, 422–6.

into political suggestion. The institutional recommendations that flowed from these conceptual commitments—the fifth component that followed the first four—were clearly distinct from those of either the idealists or the Fabians. Within the pragmatist vision of Dewey, understanding freedom as the pursuit of a communal perfection leant legitimacy to a decidedly *democratic* vision. 'Disguise it as we may', Dewey argued of the idealist conception, 'this theory can have but one result, that of the sovereignty of the citizen'. Although, he continued, '[t]here are various theories which have served to keep this in the background . . . it is the logical outcome of the organic theory of society'.[88] The social psychologists reached an identical conclusion. If the lessons of the psychological enquiry were heeded, Patten insisted, 'human society must tend towards a mobile democracy'. Individuals, Charles Cooley likewise argued, should be 'satisfied with no other' system.[89] More dramatically still, for all three thinkers democracy had to stretch far further than its current representative stage. Democratic institutions should be introduced almost everywhere—in politics, in industry, even in the schoolroom—and everyone should be involved in an almost day-to-day process of democratic deliberation and decision-making.

Both psychologists and pragmatists advocated participatory democracy because they believed that it was the only institutional system that combined three essential elements. First, it was experimental, enabling and encouraging individuals and communities continually to respond to changes in their environment. For Dewey democratic society was 'a restless society . . . an innovative society', where necessary changes demanded by experience would not be hindered by the weight of custom or the inertia of bureaucrats.[90] Second, democracy succeeded because it encouraged communication. Democratic systems with an emphasis on continual dialogue would allow individuals to develop bonds of communal loyalty with one other. Through discussion, these psychologists and pragmatists claimed, people would come to see the value of each others' points of view, would learn the value of working through problems one with another, and would come to empathize with the position of their fellow participants. Real 'sociability' and a genuinely common mind-set, Cooley contended, would surely emerge if 'the people' were to come continuously 'to exchange views'.[91] Third, and perhaps most importantly, participatory democracy was demanded because it was the only system that recognized the necessity of social change coming from *within* the individual, from a change in personal convictions, rather than from outside direction. As Dewey summarized this, the distinction between pragmatism and other movements did not lie in the

---

[88] Dewey, 'Ethics of Democracy', 235.
[89] Patten, *Social Forces*, 130; C. H. Cooley, *Social Organization* (New York: C. Scribner's Sons, 1909), 309.   [90] Ryan, *John Dewey*, 134–5.
[91] Cooley, *Social Organization*, 85.

conceptual understanding: pragmatism as well as idealism and Fabianism allows that 'the full significance of personality can be learned by the individual only as it is already presented to him in objective form in society; it admits that the chief stimuli and encouragements to the realization of personality come from society'.[92] The difference came because pragmatism 'holds, none the less, to the fact that personality cannot be procured for any one, however degraded and feeble, by any one else, however wise and strong'.[93] A participatory system was the way to square the circle. By being involved continuously in collective decision-making, individuals would learn to temper their demands, to desire to seek compromise rather than conflict, to pursue the goods of the overall community rather than their own selfish priorities. Democratic involvement, in short, would produce communal discipline without the need for disciplinarians.

Conclusion

Both methodologically and ideologically all of these groups—the idealists, Fabians, and social psychologists and pragmatists—continued to disagree. The bases of their approach remained distinct and, as political movements rather than as philosophical schools, they each demanded different forms of institutional change. The idealists celebrated the loyalties of traditional localities in the American case, and the work of a whole range of voluntary organizations in the British. The Fabians and Positivists, though, argued that social progress would best come from the purposeful direction of an informed elite: 'we believe in a government of the people, and for the people, but not by the people', as David Croly declared.[94] Finally, the pragmatists and psychologists urged the development of an ever more participatory democracy, so distanced from the Fabian ideal of rigid instruction from the centre that its citizens 'would not understand what a state is if the word were used in its present sense'.[95] These political divisions had other dimensions too. To take an important example: whereas idealists saw tradition and continuity as providing the essential cement of social life and thus tended to celebrate continuity and custom as a result, Fabians and pragmatists demanded, or at least expected, continual experimentation, innovation, and change.

As the next two chapters will show, the following generation of theorists would continue to revel in these debates and put many of their competing contentions to work. But the conceptual similarities that rested beneath the

---

[92] Dewey, 'Ethics', 244.   [93] Ibid.
[94] D. Croly cited in Harp, *Positivist Republic*, 46.   [95] Patten, *Social Forces*, 98.

surface of these arguments were, nonetheless, of still more fundamental import. As the nineteenth century ended, even the idealists' most fierce philosophical opponents were able to embrace at least some of the basic precepts of the conception of freedom that the idealists had first offered in the 1870s. Seen the other way, as the twentieth century began the idealist conception of liberty was effectively freed from the confines of idealist metaphysics and could be put to a large variety of uses by those who radically differed on questions of philosophy or methodology. It was in this way that the textbook writers of the new century could argue that their predecessors had left an admirably clear legacy. 'Political theory during the nineteenth century', Columbia University's W. A. Dunning wrote of trends in Anglo-American thought, 'was largely devoted to the task of adjusting the conceptions of authority and liberty'. And in the end, Dunning concluded, a solution had been found: 'society, as an entity comprehending the whole range of human relationships, was declared to be the holder and distributor of authority over all.'[96] For many at the turn of the century, this 'convergence of results'—the fact that those who came from very 'different sides' of philosophical and ideological disputes could nonetheless share certain conceptual understandings—was 'one of the most hopeful signs' for political philosophy in the new century.[97] In John Jordan's elegant phrase, all these varying movements had grown into 'mutually energizing intellectual traditions'.[98]

Despite the remaining differences, then, some sort of consensus of conceptual usage was beginning to emerge: a consensus that spread across competing political and philosophical movements, and, as this was a distinctly transatlantic phenomenon, across international boundaries as well. A conceptual agenda had been set and all the new movements in political theory that would emerge in early twentieth century Britain and America could not but respond to this shared set of ideals and understandings. In another way, however, the outlook was far less clear-cut. For the different groups who inherited these ideas would not respond to them in the same way. Indeed, as the twentieth century unfolded, the central claims of the idealist conception of freedom were destined to become some of the most fiercely contested items of both theoretical and political debate. The history of American nationalist progressives and British socialist pluralists is, as will be seen, essentially a combination of this tension between shared sources and divergent responses. It was the idealists' conceptual agenda that brought the American nationalist progressives and British socialist pluralists together. It allowed them to speak the same conceptual language and to

---

[96] W. A. Dunning, *A History of Political Theories*, iii (New York: Macmillan, 1920), 422.

[97] D. G. Ritchie, *The Principles of State Interference* (London: Swan Sonnenschein and Co., 1891), 168.

[98] J. M. Jordan, *Machine-Age Ideology: Social Engineering and American Liberalism, 1911–1939* (Chapel Hill: University of North Carolina Press, 1994), 69.

understand each other's theoretical terms. But as these thinkers developed their own responses to that agenda it would also break them intellectually apart. It was the response to the idealist agenda that provided the philosophical essence of their ideological dispute. The next two chapters trace the contours of that response.

2

Building the New Nationalism

Introduction

At the outset of the twentieth century, a series of philosophical, sociological, and psychological movements stretching from idealism to Darwinism, and from Fabianism to pragmatism, were radically reshaping the way in which educated and informed Britons and Americans thought about the nature of their society, of each individual's place within it, and thus of the meaning of freedom. Herbert Croly and Walter Lippmann both came directly across all of these major traditions during their formal education at Harvard. There the idealists Josiah Royce and George Palmer expounded their Hegelian vision with great charisma; H. G. Wells and Graham Wallas brought news of Fabianism and its critics from Britain; and William James tried his best to redress the balance by promulgating his highly sceptical version of the pragmatist creed. The third of the nationalist progressives, Walter Weyl, escaped the direct influence of these great philosophical figures by training as an economist, first in Halle and Berlin, Germany, and then at the Wharton School of Political Economy in Philadelphia. Despite the difference in formal education, however, he was also exposed to the new ideals of social philosophy, as he came under the influence of that most remarkable of polymaths Simon Nelson Patten at the Wharton School. Patten combined insights from Hegelianism, Darwinism, and pragmatism, and the form of social psychology he eventually produced offered a powerfully concentrated distillation of the developments of the previous two decades.[1] With Patten as a teacher, one did not need the individual attention of each of the groups in turn to grasp a sense of the direction of the whole.

In their reflections on this remarkable inheritance, recent commentators on the work of Croly, Lippmann, and Weyl have tended to divide into two groups. The first group has attempted to evaluate which of these many, often conflicting, philosophical traditions engaged which of this new generation of theorists most. Unpacking their respective allegiances is thought to provide

---

[1] See S. N. Patten, *The New Basis of Civilization* (New York: Macmillan, 1907) and M. Weyl (ed.), *Walter Weyl: An Appreciation* (Philadelphia: privately published, 1922).

the key to understanding each of the theorists. But while there has been agreement on the project, the many biographers of each of the major figures have often starkly disagreed. Herbert Croly's lineage is traced by some through Roycean idealism, while others detect the centrality of Jamesian pragmatism, and still others identify his creed with the Positivism of his father, David.[2] The disagreement is equally intense over Lippmann's origins: while some accounts accredit his philosophical outlook to the direct influence of the Fabians' visits to Harvard, and especially to Wallas and H. G. Wells, others place extensive emphasis on the pragmatists James and Dewey.[3]

The second scholarly tradition leaves these debates aside and argues that while efforts at tracing intellectual ancestry are undeniably intriguing they are also just as certainly inevitably flawed. On this view, the young Croly, Lippmann, and Weyl are understood as being irrevocably divided in their philosophical allegiance. As Walter Lippmann's biographer Ronald Steel has argued, Lippmann's work was an 'intellectual *pot pourri*, stuffed with nearly everything' he had learned 'at College and after'.[4] From this perspective Croly, Lippmann, and Weyl should be seen as both parasitic and potentially incoherent: reliant on a collection of social and philosophical theories that had been 'more fully articulated' by others.[5] Eldon Eisenach has particularly disparaged the contribution of Herbert Croly in this way. To Eisenach, Croly's work was 'derivative both in content and [in] methods of analysis'; and when Croly's *Promise of American Life* appeared in 1909 it was not 'seen as anything exceptional or new' in progressive circles.[6]

Of these two views, there is probably more of value in the second than in the first.[7] Croly, Lippmann, and Weyl did not resolve the ongoing metaphysical and epistemological disputes between the different groups of predecessors, nor did they loyally and consistently follow the lead of any one group. Rather, their mentors pulled them in different directions simultaneously.

---

[2] E. Stettner, *Shaping Modern Liberalism: Herbert Croly and Progressive Thought* (Lawrence: Kansas University Press, 1994) makes the case for Royce; whereas for David Levy, Croly's ideas 'came from several places, but the heart of them Croly took from his father, who, in turn, had borrowed them from the French philosopher Auguste Comte'; *Herbert Croly of the New Republic: The Life and Thought of an American Progressive* (Princeton: Princeton University Press, 1985), p. xv. The dispute is investigated in depth in David Levy's admirably good-natured review of Stettner's book, *American Historical Review*, 99 (1994), 1407–8. An earlier but still deservedly influential account is C. Forcey, *The Crossroads of Liberalism: Croly, Weyl, Lippmann, and the Progressive Era, 1900–1925* (New York: Oxford University Press, 1967).

[3] See B. Lloyd, *Left Out: Pragmatism, Exceptionalism and the Poverty of American Marxism, 1890–1922* (Baltimore: Johns Hopkins University Press, 1997), esp. 223, and J. Hoopes, *Community Denied: The Wrong Turn of Pragmatic Liberalism* (Ithaca: Cornell University Press, 1998), esp. 100–3.

[4] R. Steel, *Walter Lippmann and the American Century* (London: Bodley Head, 1980), 47.

[5] E. Eisenach, *The Lost Promise of Progressivism* (Lawrence: Kansas University Press, 1994), 40.

[6] Eisenach, *Lost Promise*, 39–40.

[7] Although both groups are an advance on the work of earlier commentators, many of whom suggested that Croly, Lippmann, and Weyl were 'intellectual maverick[s] unrestrained by any prior commitments'. See, for example, H. N. Dam, *The Intellectual Odyssey of Walter Lippmann: A Study in his Protean Thought 1910–1960* (New York: Gordon Press, 1973), 17.

Croly himself described their underlying philosophical thought as displaying an 'incoherent eclecticism'.[8] Their major works were often vague, confusing, and conflicting on the questions of method and philosophical allegiance. Where this second group of scholars go awry, however, is in drawing conclusions from these observations. None of Croly, Lippmann, or Weyl even *tried* to contribute to the underlying methodological debates that engaged idealists and Darwinists, Positivists, and pragmatists. These thinkers were *ideologists*, not philosophers or sociologists, and, as such, their interest did not lie in the imponderable contentions of pure academic analysis. Rather, they sought to adapt the conceptual understandings upon which these competing traditions were coming to agree to the business of *politics*. This is where their major contribution lay and in this respect there was little that was either incoherent or unoriginal.

They made such a contribution in two stages. First, by examining aspects of the patterns of conceptual change in more detail they sought more explicitly to draw out the particularly *political* implications of the developing philosophical movements. Armed with a richer appreciation of the potential implications of the new conceptions, their second task could then begin. This involved the construction of an array of concrete recommendations, derived in part from the combination of these conceptual understandings. The new conceptual approaches—what Croly called the new '*terms* of human liberation'—thus helped establish an account of institutional reform—what he dubbed the '*conditions* of individual emancipation'.[9] In these two ways, Croly, Lippmann, and Weyl strove to outline 'a revised scale of national values' and then to base a new 'project of future national development' upon them.[10]

Seen in this way, far from being merely parasitic on the results of others, these thinkers were actually both innovative and radical.[11] Their *innovation* lay in the fact that, in the United States at least, remarkably few of the late nineteenth century thinkers had sought to draw out the political implications of the understandings thrown up by new strands of thought in any detail. There was little of concrete practicality in the speculations of Josiah Royce, George Palmer, or even of William James. The work of Croly, Lippmann, and Weyl was an 'expedition into territory hitherto not very well occupied', just as Croly himself described.[12] The *radicalism* derived from the fact that those few American theorists of the earlier generation who had sought to expound a political view from the conceptual speculations—including Charles Horton Cooley and Weyl's own mentor Simon Nelson Patten—had tended, when

[8] H. Croly, 'Autobiographical Fragment', in *The Felix Frankfurter Papers* (Frederick, MD: University Publications of America, 1986), Reel 136, 14.

[9] H. Croly, *The Promise of American Life* (New York: Macmillan, 1909), 409 (emphasis added).

[10] Croly, 'Autobiographical', 21. For more on this duality, see *Promise*, 150.

[11] As contemporary reviews of their works clearly recognized. See H. J. Ford, 'The Promise of American Life', *American Political Science Review*, 4 (1910), 614–16.

[12] H. Croly to L. Hand, letter dated March 1909, Harvard Law Library, Harvard University, The L. Hand Papers, 102/17.

push came to shove, to fall back on the political certainties of old. The reformed system of government these thinkers offered, although further democratized, would not differ too dramatically from American institutions as they already existed.[13]

In the United States, at least, politicians were even more culpable than academics in this regard. While by the beginning of the twentieth century a large number of progressive activists up and down the country were willing to admit the necessity of change, Croly, Lippmann, and Weyl found their reform proposals far too timid.[14] Rather than being comfortable settling into the existing ranks of progressive and reformers, these new thinkers searched for an equivalent in the United States of the Fabian Society in Britain. But they could not find one. Walter Lippmann thus complained that in the United States even those who 'know there is a new world' to be formed, preferred to 'dream of an older' one.[15] Although many reformers thus accepted it was 'nonsense' simply 'to talk of liberty as a happy-go-lucky break-ing of chains', he continued, they still behaved as if that was *exactly* what the word implied.[16] While Lippmann's tone betrayed his characteristic self-satis-faction, the young theorist was certainly right to suggest that his predecessors had not developed as impressive a political vision as his own generation would fashion.

If the origins and originality of Croly, Lippmann, and Weyl's conceptual understandings are often disputed, the nature of their political programme is the subject of an even more intense debate. Some scholars characterise their form of progressivism as a demanding, elitist authoritarianism, requiring social homogeneity unconcerned with individual difference and redolent of the most unattractive aspects of British Fabianism. Others, though, brand their programme as excessively timid, shirking from their major challenges of the times and looking almost like a throwback to the Jeffersonian liberalism of an earlier era.[17] This chapter provides a new interpretation through an analysis of Croly, Lippmann, and Weyl's use of the conceptual debate on liberty. It proceeds in two sections that mirror the theorists' own structure. First, the chapter examines the theorists'

[13] See the excellent D. E. Price, 'Community and Control: Critical Democratic Theory in the Progressive Period', *American Political Science Review*, 68 (1974), 1663–78.

[14] For a classic account that still stands out in an enormous literature, see R. Wiebe, *The Search for Order, 1877–1920* (New York: Hill and Wang, 1967).

[15] W. Lippmann, *Drift and Mastery: An Attempt to Diagnose the Current Unrest* (New York: M. Kennerley, 1914), 133.

[16] Lippmann, *Drift*, 197. As Byron Dexter once put it: 'To the reforming politicians who read *The Promise of American Life*, the theoretical definition of the place of the individual in this more central-ized (or nationalized) state did not then greatly matter. The relationship of the individual American to his government seemed just what it always had been, as stated in the Declaration of Independence: of course man came first, his rights preordained and unquestioned.' See B. Dexter, 'Herbert Croly and the Promise of American Life', *Political Science Quarterly*, 70 (1955), 212.

[17] See Lloyd, *Left Out*, 223, and Hoopes, *Community Denied*, 101–3.

immediate response to the conceptual agenda of their predecessors, as outlined in the previous chapter. Through this examination Croly, Lippmann, and Weyl are shown first to have adopted and then significantly radicalized the conceptual understandings their idealist, Darwinist, and pragmatist predecessors in the United States had outlined. These nationalist progressives reached a conceptual position that had as much in common with that of the British Fabians as with their American predecessors. Then, second, the chapter analyses the distinctly political uses to which this conceptual approach was put, exploring the ways in which conceptual agenda and political programme were closely related together. It analyses a series of potentially disparate reforms the nationalist progressives suggested, stretching from a repudiation of the American system of judicial review, through an ambiguous relationship to the celebrated democratic reforms of the progressive era, to a firm rejection of several central elements of the separation of powers. The conceptual understanding provided demonstrates how all of these suggestions were connected by the underlying conceptual arguments that motivated them. Through this analysis, a new interpretation is presented of the theoretical structure and the practical scope of the ideological movement that was known as the 'new nationalism'. That study begins with thinkers' response to debates surrounding the new conceptions of human flourishing and of the deep connection between liberty and community.

Conceptual Understandings

The conception endorsed

At the very heart of the idealists' late nineteenth century reconceptualization of human flourishing was the contention that the their central concern lay not in enabling the pursuit of desire but rather in the development of something qualitatively *better*. Whatever else divided them, almost all of the major nineteenth century movements—idealists, Fabians, pragmatists, social psychologists—had all been dedicated to the pursuit of human *improvement*. People should not be left as they are; rather, they should be transformed. Croly, Lippmann, and Weyl all shared that ideal. An insistence on human 'improvability' was a constant refrain of all these new progressive theorists.[18] Progressive reform, Croly, Lippmann and Weyl insisted, was essentially concerned with the 'creation of a higher type of

---

[18] See W. Weyl, *The New Democracy: An Essay on Certain Political and Economic Tendencies in the United States* (New York: Macmillan, 1912) 129.

individual'.[19] Fulfilling individuals' preferences was not the question, improving their character was. Real human liberation required an effort to redirect pre-existing human passions from unworthy ends to worthy ones. Within the early work of Herbert Croly and Walter Weyl this argument was taken, as in idealism itself, to its fullest extent, as a dedication to 'human perfectibility'.[20] Liberty itself, Walter Weyl could thus conclude, does not entail the pursuit of desire. Rather, it means 'the right to do the things which one *should* have the right to do'.[21] For Lippmann the ideal was slightly weaker, if none the less deeply felt: liberty for him was 'a searching challenge'. In order to be truly free, each individual must ensure that his goals are 'disciplined by a knowledge of what is possible, and ordered by the conscious purpose' of his life.[22] 'The outlook of the free man', Lippmann continued, directed his attention to the underlying 'needs of our natures and the possibilities of the world'.[23] Perfection itself might be elusive, but it should be pursued nonetheless.

This argument entailed advocacy of the second component of the idealist conception of liberty. Croly, Lippmann, and Weyl all argued that, in addition to removing 'external' obstacles from individuals' lives, each individual's liberation also required the absence of 'internal' constraints. An extended capacity for emotional, moral, and psychological control was an essential prerequisite for personal freedom. Individuals interested in freeing themselves must learn not to 'follow impulse wherever it leads'.[24] 'The glutton and the rake can satisfy only their gluttonous and rakish impulses', Walter Lippmann insisted, 'and that isn't enough'.[25] The list of potential 'internal' obstacles to be overcome was also extremely broad. 'Every victorious selfish impulse, every perverse and cowardly thought, every petty action, every irresponsibility and infirmity of will', Croly insisted with almost Hegelian zeal, could potentially be an impediment to personal freedom. Such psychological weaknesses impoverished not just the lives of *other* people, those let down by the negative behavioural patterns they implied, but limited the lives of those who *possessed* them as well.[26]

---

[19] Croly, *Promise*, 284. See too 413.   [20] Croly, *Promise*, 400 and 454.

[21] Weyl, *New Democracy*, 353 (emphasis added). Compare with James's definition of the idealist conception: W. James, 'On Some Hegelisms', in W. James (ed.), *The Will to Believe and Other Essays* (New York: Longmans, Green and Co., 1909), 271.   [22] Lippmann, *Drift*, 197 and 272.

[23] Lippmann, *Drift*, 277.

[24] This stands in contrast to the interpretation in Stettner, *Shaping Modern Liberalism*, esp. 52–5.

[25] Lippmann, *Drift*, 272.

[26] H. Croly, *Progressive Democracy* (New York: Macmillan, 1914), 427. An example illustrates the point. In analyzing the effects of capitalism on the liberties of the citizen, Herbert Croly noted that the lack of material resources suffered by the poor presented them with genuine difficulties that should be correctly understood themselves as obstacles to their freedom; but he went on to argue that the most important 'vice' of the capitalist system is not 'the bondage imposed upon its victims'. '[M]uch more insidious', he contended, is 'the bondage imposed upon the conquerors and their camp followers.' It was, for Croly, the 'moral' damage that the competitive system perpetrated—the

This endorsement of freedom as improvement and as the condemnation of both 'external' and 'internal' obstacles was followed by an endorsement of the third component of the idealist-inspired conception. The distinction between human improvement and human deterioration was to be derived from an account of the essential communality of man. Although their reasoning was vague, Croly, Lippmann, and Weyl all followed their predecessors who had advanced the inescapably social reading of human nature, insisting that human personalities were essentially forged through social interaction. Any system of thought that took the 'individual simply in the sense of a man who inhabits a certain body and possesses a certain continuity of organic sensations' as the central unit of analysis was grounded in 'illusion'.[27] In order fully to understand any individual, they argued, it is essential to realize that 'his acquisitions, his capacities, his wills . . . are all the creation of his time and his people'.[28] The move from this view of social 'fact' to the expression of necessary human 'value' followed effortlessly. If humans are shaped by positions in communities then the 'enhancement of human life', freedom itself, must also be inextricably linked with the enhancement of social life. Individual self-development had to be integrally connected with the 'realization of a common purpose'.[29] As a result, a new theory of freedom must ensure that individual and communal lives are understood together: it must 'emphasize social rather than private ends' since only 'socially valuable' goals and capacities led the way to human improvement.[30]

This emphasis on the inextricably social aspects of humanity did not, though, crowd out all discussion of the importance of individual difference. Real individuals are not 'cast in moulds', Lippmann argued, and there 'is nothing' in the communalistic view of human nature 'which need make it inevitably hostile to the variety of life'.[31] Indeed, to stress their own acceptance of human diversity, Croly, Lippmann, and Weyl often described the pursuit of freedom as the development of real 'individuality'. People freed from internal and external constraints and able to pursue perfection enjoy the opportunity to become genuine *individuals*. Such a description has confused many commentators. It has led otherwise astute observers such as Edward Stettner and Charles Forcey to follow Louis Hartz in concluding that, when push came to shove, Croly, Lippmann, and Weyl were not willing to move far

misleading picture it inculcated of the nature of worthy ends and of righteous characteristics—which mattered most. Individuals could not pursue perfection in an unreformed capitalist system because living within the psychological environment that capitalism fosters they would not learn the right values, they would not learn to distinguish worthy goals from unworthy ones. Croly, *Promise*, 410. Compare with the counter claim in Stettner, *Shaping Modern Liberalism*, 52–3.

[27] Croly, *Progressive*, 198.
[28] Editors, 'Bill of Rights Again', *New Republic*, 17 April 1915, 273.
[29] Croly, *Progressive*, 120. See too Levy, *Herbert Croly*, 116.
[30] Weyl, *New Democracy*, 162 and 329.
[31] W. Lippmann, *A Preface to Politics* (New York: M. Kennerley, 1913), 201, and *Drift*, 295.

beyond the individualist philosophical commitments of a much earlier political philosophy. This commitment to 'individuality', Hartz and colleagues argue, illustrates that these progressives eagerly abandoned the 'European' communal 'Hegelian notion' with which they began and moved back towards an 'individualism' more in tune with the liberal heritage of America's past.[32]

This interpretation is, though, seriously misguided. For Croly, Lippmann, and Weyl's use of the term 'individuality' was not straightforward, and it certainly was not intended to signify a rejection of the idealist hypothesis and a return to earlier forms of liberalism. Rather, in *The Promise of American Life* and other major works, the conception of 'individuality' itself was the subject of significant reconsideration. Herbert Croly outlined a fundamental 'antithesis' between the 'old' and the 'new' understandings of 'individuality'. For Croly, the *old* view, the one he associated with earlier, Millian, liberalism, accepted individuals' goals as it found them and rendered individuals themselves necessarily the best guides to their own improvement. On these terms, the pursuit of 'individuality' was to consist in the pursuit of desires felt by and justified to only the individual who possessed them. But there was no sympathy for this conception in Croly's work. To understand 'individuality' in this way, he explicitly argued, was to see the notion 'deprived of all serious moral and intellectual meaning'.[33] Such an interpretation transformed 'individuality' into nothing more than a celebration of jealous, egotistical 'particularity' because it overlooked the essence of communality. In place of this 'old' view, Croly offered a new approach to the concept. This view was of an individuality 'which is selective', where some goals were judged necessarily better than others. Furthermore, it was an approach that took the 'fact' of human communality seriously, as the process of selection was to be made precisely on communal grounds.[34] This new view placed individuals firmly within their social context and argued that individual growth was an inescapably social affair. It exalted 'social obligations above mere competitive egoisms', it ensured that 'socially valuable individualities' were the ones that were enhanced.[35] Far from being in conflict, 'individuality' and 'communality' were inextricably related.

Croly's decision to describe freedom as the striving for 'individuality' was, though, not without substantial conceptual purpose. It was not simply a ruse to mislead his more liberally minded readers. Rather, it was intended to demonstrate that a dedication to communality did not necessitate complete abandonment of all interest in individual peculiarities. Croly argued that although individual perfection was essentially communal, each 'genuine individual possess[es] some special quality which distinguishes him from other

---

[32] L. Hartz, *The Liberal Tradition in America: An Interpretation of American Political Thought since the Revolution* (New York: Harcourt Brace, 1955), 233. See Levy, *Herbert Croly*, 54; Forcey, *Crossroads*, 39; Stettner, *Modern Liberalism*, 54.   [33] Croly, *Promise*, 413.   [34] Ibid.
[35] Weyl, *New Democracy*, 329 and 319.

people'.[36] No progressive wished all individuals to exhibit the same personalities, develop the same skills, or pursue the same goals. The communal assumption suggested nonetheless that a full account of human flourishing was inescapably tied to the emergence of a harmonious relationship between those goods pursued by individuals in a given society. Bringing these two potentially contradictory ideas together was the notion, so familiar to idealism, of 'unity in difference'.[37] From *The Promise of American Life* to the outbreak of the First World War, Croly, Lippmann, and Weyl argued, just as Josiah Royce had a generation before, that although individuals were bound to differ from one another in important ways, personal improvement would come only through the pursuit of goods that involve and assist the goods of all other members. Differing goals must connect together seamlessly so as to produce a new and undisturbed harmony. The condition of 'genuine individuality', Croly astutely summarized, saw individuals 'divided from one another by special purposes' but 'reunited' when 'these individual purposes [are] excellently and successfully achieved'.[38]

This definition of freedom and individuality as requiring the pursuit of communal perfection led to the fourth component of the idealist-inspired conception; to, that is, the understanding of the role of external authority distinctly different from that described in earlier brands of liberalism. Understanding freedom as the pursuit of a communal perfection, independent of internal as well as external obstacles, demanded 'an effort to develop, train, and nurture men's impulses'.[39] It further suggested that such training could often be provided only from the outside. This theme was ever present in the early Croly, Lippmann, and Weyl. Croly argued that external authorities could 'contribute positively to the liberation of the individual' primarily by shaping the environment in which individuals found themselves. External agents could help individuals perfect themselves by aiming to 'substitute attractive virtues for attractive vices'.[40] Most importantly, authorities could assist an individual by 'diminishing his temptations, improving his opportunities, and by enveloping him in an invigorating rather than an enervating moral and intellectual atmosphere'.[41]

Lippmann added to these thoughts with concerns derived from the social psychology and pragmatism of Charles Horton Cooley, the young John Dewey, and Simon Nelson Patten. Although outside agencies could shape options, choices, and environments, he thus argued, they must always hold back from their inclinations to guide individuals in any particular direction by means of direct coercion. The attempts of external authorities to aid

---

[36] Croly, *Promise*, 410.
[37] Compare Croly, *Promise*, 409 with J. Royce, *The World and the Individual*, ii (New York: Macmillan, 1901), 274. See too T. V. Smith, *The American Philosophy of Equality* (Chicago: Chicago University Press, 1927), 222–4.
[38] Croly, *Promise*, 411.   [39] Lippmann, *Preface*, 80.
[40] Lippmann, *Preface*, 46.   [41] Croly, *Promise*, 409.

individuals' liberation had always to stop with offers of assistance. As Lippmann insisted, '[t]he use of the club can never be applauded' for its 'use is a confession of ignorance'. 'Instead of tabooing our impulses, we must redirect them', he continued, instead 'of trying to crush badness we must turn the power behind it to good account'.[42] Croly and Weyl, though, were not so half-hearted. They were willing to evoke the need forcefully to coerce individuals for the sake of their own development, just as those idealists who followed Bernard Bosanquet had suggested.[43] Indeed, at times Croly seems to have positively revelled in the explicitly directive elements of this part of the conceptual approach. Seeing the search for individual improvement as a form of 'schooling', he suggested, entails that it may 'frequently demand severe coercive measures', for 'what schooling does not?'[44] '[C]onstructive regulation' of individuals' lives for their own good, Croly and Weyl recognized, may occasionally imply 'the imposition of certain . . . limitations upon *traditional* individual freedom'; but such limitations were of little consequence to either ideologist, equipped as they were with a 'new conception' of the roots and the goals of 'both of individual and of national development'.[45]

The conception radicalized

Croly, Lippmann, and Weyl all thus endorsed the first four component parts of the conception of liberty that had been first expounded by idealism, despite the confusions sometimes caused by their language. But this is far from all there is to say. Still remaining from this perspective was the question of the *locus* of the community in which individuals were to find their perfection and, thus, the nature of the authority to be charged with providing the conditions for individual improvement. As the previous chapter outlined, it was these questions that had previously divided idealists, Fabians, social psychologists, and pragmatists. It was here too that Croly, Lippmann, and Weyl were at their most distinctive and at their most assertive.

Most American theorists of the late nineteenth century had sought to develop social harmony in patterns of social connection grounded in rural locality, social homogeneity, and predictable economic relations. For both American idealists like Josiah Royce, and social psychologists such as Cooley and Patten, although their reasons were different, 'the home, the church, the club' were the places where individuals should forge communal attachments. They celebrated the local, the provincial, and the face-to-face.[46] For the nationalist progressives, though, those solutions were bound to times and

---

[42] Lippmann, *Drift*, 46 and *Preface*, 49–50.
[43] See Weyl, *New Democracy*, 353 and Ch. 1.   [44] Croly, *Promise*, 283.
[45] Croly, *Promise*, 421 (emphasis added).
[46] S. N. Patten, *The Theory of Social Forces* (Philadelphia: American Academy of Political and Social Science, 1896), 89.

conditions that had passed. 'We live' now, Walter Lippmann instructed the more nostalgic of his predecessors, 'in great cities without knowing our neighbours ... our associations are stretched over large territories, cemented by very little direct contact'.[47] In such an era, the immediate community structures of the small town or the village hall could no longer be relied upon to provide the necessary opportunities for communal interaction. The search for a set of communal attachments in the new industrial age necessitated instead a turn to the *nation*. This was the contention that distinguished Croly, Lippmann, and Weyl from their American predecessors. It was the idea that forged the 'new nationalism'.

The dedication to the nation began as a judgement as to the scale of social and economic change in the United States since the founding of the republic. At the root of this transformation was industry. The United States began the nineteenth century with an overwhelmingly rural economy, consisting largely of small businesses and independent entrepreneurs working within an ever expanding economic base symbolized by the frontier. It entered the twentieth century utterly transformed. By 1900, over 80 per cent of the work-force was employed by large-scale corporations, with over 60 per cent of it engaged in industrial labour.[48] Croly, Lippmann, and Weyl believed that such industrial expansion entailed that the concrete realities of American life were now inevitably national in scope. Innovations in transport and communications enabled further development. As railroads spanned the entire continent, they facilitated new means of communication and trade that brought the country increasingly close together.[49] In this new industrial era, the United States was no longer a collection 'of villagers', Lippmann argued. Economic and social change had 'made the nation a neighborhood'.[50]

Such a set of observations had radical implications for these thinkers' description of community. Croly, Lippmann, and Weyl were not the first to notice these trends, nor were they the first to draw political conclusions from them. They were, however, the first important group of active American political theorists to celebrate them and to integrate them fully into their conceptual scheme. In common with the British Fabians, Croly, Lippmann, and Weyl believed that this nationalizing trend was both inevitable and desirable. It brought with it vastly increased resources that would provide individuals with greatly enhanced opportunities for self-development. As the objective, empirically ascertainable realities of American life had become increasingly

[47] Lippmann, *Drift*, 153–4.

[48] See R. F. Bensel, *The Political Economy of American Industrialization, 1877–1900* (Cambridge: Cambridge University Press, 2000).

[49] See Croly, *Promise*, 110–14.

[50] Lippmann, *Drift*, 121, and W. A. White, *The Old Order Changeth: A View of American Democracy* (New York: Macmillan, 1910), 250.

national, Croly argued, 'political, economic and social organization' must be increasingly 'coordinated with [people's] actual needs'.[51]

Unlike some of the Fabians, though, Croly, Lippmann, and Weyl believed that the primary requisite of such a successful nationalizing trend was a prioritization of national *loyalties* in the lives of everyday people. Again deriving lessons from social psychology, Croly, Lippmann, and Weyl all argued that effective coordination of national activities could not be achieved without the immediate conversion of the mass of the people to the national cause.[52] 'The dynamics for a splendid civilization are all about us', but before it could be realized Americans would have to 'learn to co-operate on a large scale'.[53] Croly emphasized the point most vividly in *The Promise of American Life*. 'Americans' had to be made 'more sensitive to a national idea and more conscious of their national responsibilities'.[54] '[L]oyalty', he wrote, was the necessary 'subjective aspect' of 'inevitable mutual association'. It was 'the recognition that as a worldly body [citizens] must all live or die and conquer or fail together'.[55] '[Y]ou cannot institute a better industrial order by decree', Walter Lippmann complementarily declared. 'It is of necessity an educational process, a work of invention, of cooperative training.'[56]

As Croly, Lippmann, and Weyl all believed that an enhancement of the bonds of national loyalty was instrumentally valuable, so they also contended that it would bring *intrinsic* benefits; the subjective sense of national belonging was an integral part of human development itself. As Herbert Croly insisted, the development of a sense of loyalty 'to the national interest the improvement and the intensification' of subjective feelings of national unity is the means by which to bring about a higher form of 'human relation'. In the new industrial world, national loyalty, and national loyalty alone, would allow the 'conviction and feeling of human brother-hood' to enter 'into the possession of the human spirit'.[57] It was 'an essen-tially formative and enlightening' transformation' the aim of which was the attainment of a 'better quality of human nature effected by a higher type of human association'.[58]

Vitally important as they were, unfortunately these attachments could not be developed easily. For Americans, the nationalist progressives argued, did not realize the essential interconnectedness of their lives. 'The construc-tive public spirit' of America, these theorists held, is at best 'fragmentary,

---

[51] Croly, *Promise*, 273.

[52] See Croly, *Progressive*, 282. Contrast with R. M. Smith, *Civic Ideals: Conflicting Visions of Citizenship in U.S. History* (New Haven: Yale University Press, 1997), 414–15.

[53] Lippmann, *Preface*, 317, and *Drift*, 145.   [54] Croly, *Promise*, 169.

[55] Croly, *Promise*, 284.

[56] Lippmann, *Drift*, 169. This was an argument inherited from G. Wallas, *Human Nature and Politics* (London: Constable and Co., 1910)

[57] Croly, *Progressive*, 211, and *Promise*, 453.   [58] Croly, *Promise*, 273 and 166.

temporary, of sporadic interest'.[59] This problem was held to be, at root, the result of a deeply ingrained cultural trait. Writing only three years prior to the publication of Croly's *Promise*, H. G. Wells diagnosed the malady: the 'typical American', he argued, 'has no "sense of the state"'. 'I mean', Wells continued, 'that he has no perception that his business activities, his private employments, are constituents in a large collective process; that they affect other people and the world forever, and cannot, as he imagines, begin and end with him'. 'The American', the British Fabian concluded, had yet to achieve 'the conception of a whole to which all individual acts and happenings are subordinate and contributory'.[60] Unflattering as this critique was, Croly, Lippmann, and Weyl all adopted the argument as their own. They changed it only in so far as they sought material explanations for the cultural actuality. Weyl saw the emergence of this culture of extreme individualism on the remarkable geographical expanse that faced the first settlers: 'The open continent intoxicated the American', he argued. 'It gave him an enlarged view of self. It dwarfed the common spirit. It made the American mind a little sovereignty of its own, acknowledging no allegiances and but few obligations.' Whatever the cause, though, the effect was the same: 'It created an individualism, self-confident, short-sighted, lawless, doomed in the end to defeat itself.'[61]

In addition to this long-standing cultural peculiarity, Croly, Lippmann, and Weyl also emphasized the role of two more nascent problems in perpetuating the United States' lack of a spirit of national solidarity. Americans were no longer solely driven by a culture of individualism. They *were* able and willing to craft communal loyalties. Unfortunately, though, these were loyalties not to the nation but to new, divisive, sectional interests.[62] The first of these new sectional divisions was largely distinct to the United States: allegiance to ethnic group. Throughout the late nineteenth and early twentieth centuries, immigrants flocked to the United States from an increasingly disparate series of countries of origin. As they did so, arguments over the perpetuation of a 'hyphenated' citizenry found a central place in American public debate; they fed demands for immigration requirements and eugenic testing of incoming groups.[63] Of the nationalist progressives, it was Walter Weyl, himself the son of German Jewish immigrants, who expressed the most concern as to the

---

[59] P. Kellogg, Untitled MS in Social Welfare History Archive, University of Minnesota, The P. Kellogg Papers, 3/28/12.

[60] H. G. Wells, *The Future in America: A Search After Realities* (New York: Harpers and Bros, 1906), 153–4. For Croly's support see *Promise*, 4, and Lippmann, *Preface*.

[61] Weyl, *New Democracy*, 36. See too H. Croly, 'State Political Reorganization', *Proceedings of the American Political Science Association*, 8 (1911), 127.　　　[62] See Weyl, *New Democracy*, 235–8.

[63] For thorough descriptions of these arguments and trends, see G. Gerstle, 'Liberty, Coercion and the Making of Americans', *Journal of American History*, 84 (1997), 524–58, and D. King, *Making Americans: Immigration, Race, and the Origins of the Diverse Democracy* (London: Harvard University Press, 2000), 85–126.

consequences of the new immigration. He argued that the 'babel of traditions' that it brought to America's shores would 'hamper and delay the formation of a national consciousness'. His *New Democracy* fiercely contended that the danger 'of too near a contact' with those fleeing 'European poverty can hardly be overestimated'. Only if the immigrants were 'especially selected for their adjustability to American conditions', Weyl concluded, could the United States 'advance in the task of improving the economic, political, and psychological development of the masses as to render inevitable the progressive attainment of the social goal'.[64]

Croly and Lippmann were far more circumspect as to the validity of these underlying assumptions. Lippmann especially argued clearly that neither the number nor the quality of immigrants provided any difficulty. It was rather the economic destitution and the social isolation that awaited them in the United States. If each immigrant is condemned to arrive in the 'slums of New Haven, assaulted by din and glare, hedged in by ugliness and cynical push', Lippmann asked, is it surprising if he 'becomes brutal, greedy, vulgar' or if he appears to fail 'to measure up to the requirements of citizenship'?[65] Nonetheless, even though he was sceptical as to the motives of those who demanded immigration restriction, the value Lippmann invested in the nation still demanded the erosion of the cultural differences brought to the United States by ethnically diverse immigrant groups. Developing the bonds of national loyalty involved eroding the bonds of ethnic and cultural difference. The 'singular strength' of America in the past, they would all happily remind their readers, was that it was 'the world's melting pot'. Its major difficulty now was that 'the melting is not over'.[66]

While the question of such extensive immigration was largely peculiar to the United States, the second of the new sectional divisions lay less in American distinctiveness than in the country's apparent convergence with the older industrial world. It lay in the increasing importance of social class. As one progressive commentator put it, with industrialization came not only the nationalization of everyday life but also the emergence of continual 'warring across the boundary line between labor and capital'.[67] Whereas well into the nineteenth century it had been plausible to argue that the United States potentially possessed enough natural resources for everyone, such optimism dissipated as the frontier closed and as ownership of capital became more and more concentrated in the hands of a few large corporations. Wealth began to be 'distributed in so unequal a manner', Croly contended, that the old solution for poverty, a simple increase in economic activity, could no longer be expected to 'help unify and consolidate the American people'.[68]

[64] Weyl, *New Democracy*, 347.   [65] Lippmann, *Drift*, 211.
[66] W. Weyl, *Tired Radicals and Other Papers* (New York: B. W. Huebsch, 1921), 222, and Weyl, *New Democracy*, 239–40. See too Smith, *Civic Ideals*, 413–19.   [67] Kellogg, Untitled, 12.
[68] Croly, *Progressive*, 97.

Indeed, a straightforward increase in economic activity was now more likely to drive them further apart. Vicious 'antagonisms between class and class' were beginning to dominate industrial life. There was a fivefold expansion of American union membership during the first decade and a half of the twentieth century alone and with the increase in size came an increase in militancy.[69] All the major industries of the new economy—coal mining, iron and steel production, railroad transport—were almost continually racked with discord and that discord was often violent. Indeed, the strength and discontent of organized labour was, it seemed, daily 'forced upon the attention of the public at large'.[70] 'The sword of class consciousness is being whetted', Walter Weyl concluded, 'and its sharp edge will cut through the body social, sundering us into two mutually antagonistic groups.'[71] The necessary bonds of nationhood were 'in danger of being torn to pieces by irreconcilable class enmities'.[72] It was thus fundamental to any effort to inculcate the national ideal to fight 'a desperate battle' against 'accepting class war as the order of our life'.[73]

Faced with these apparently intractable problems of ingrained cultural individualism and expanding sectional infighting along ethnic and class lines, Croly, Lippmann, and Weyl searched for a new solution. It lay, they argued, in the growth of strong, organized, national activity. Given the changes in American social and economic life, and the goal of national unity to which they aspired, a genuinely all-encompassing organization was essential both to identify actual needs and to inculcate the new sense of national identity. A 'basis of association narrower than the whole complex' of new 'human powers and interests will not serve', as Croly said.[74] To begin with, it seemed as if such an organization might arise naturally from the processes of industrial development. It was as such that these nationalist progressives welcomed the emergence of large-scale capitalistic monopolies and trusts. These rapidly expanding industrial corporations provided a pattern of interconnections that seemed to be a step in the right direction.

---

[69] See G. Marks, *Unions in Politics: Britain, Germany, and the United States in the Nineteenth and Early Twentieth Centuries* (Princeton: Princeton University Press, 1989), esp. 83–5, and J. A. McCartin, *Labor's Great War: The Struggle for Industrial Democracy and the Origins of Modern American Labor Relations* (Chapel Hill: University of North Carolina Press, 1997).

[70] A. Gleason, *What the Workers Want: A Study of British Labour* (London: George Allen and Unwin, 1920), 5, and C. Beard, 'Introduction', in S. Zimmand (ed.), *Modern Social Movements* (New York: Bureau for Industrial Research, 1921), 2. For overviews, see D. Brody, *Workers in Industrial America: Essays on the Twentieth Century Struggle* (New York: Oxford University Press, 1993).

[71] Weyl, *Tired Radicals*, 24–5. Again these arguments were strikingly familiar to Fabianism. See A. M. MacBriar, *Fabian Socialism and English Politics, 1884–1918* (Cambridge: Cambridge University Press, 1962) and J. T. Kloppenberg, *Uncertain Victory: Social Democracy and Progressivism in European and American Thought* (New York: Oxford University Press, 1986), 349–58.

[72] Croly, *Progressive*, 98.

[73] H. Croly, 'A School for Social Research', *New Republic*, 8 June 1918, 168, and W. Lippmann, 'Unrest', *New Republic*, 12 November 1919, 316.

[74] Croly, *Promise*, 283. See too Lippmann, *Drift*, 160.

Their organizational centralization and sheer size ensured that they were more stable and more socially coherent than a series of small capitalist enterprises. Monopoly and nationwide concentration of industrial organization were to be prioritized as a replacement for 'the wasteful, the planless scramble of little profiteers'.[75] The trusts brought 'plan where there has been clash, and purpose into the jungles of disordered growth.'[76]

This welcome famously distanced Croly, Lippmann, and Weyl from most of their reforming contemporaries. As is well recorded, most progressives at this time were committed to a programme of 'trust-busting'. Led intellectually by thinkers such as Louis Brandeis and politically by Woodrow Wilson, these progressives argued that the growth of large-scale, potentially monopolistic industry was an integral part of the problem rather than the solution.[77] Croly, Lippmann, and Weyl, though, could not have disagreed more vigorously. 'If the anti-trust people really grasped the full meaning of what they said, and if they really had the power or the courage to do what they propose', Lippmann thus argued, 'they would be engaged in one of the most destructive agitations that America has known.' In attacking trusts, they 'would be breaking up the beginning of a collective organization, thwarting the possibility of cooperation'. That trust-busters sought to do all this in the name of liberty was all the more shocking. For only 'silly anarchists', those equipped with outdated political conceptions, or those who misunderstood the importance of the new ideals could 'talk as if such organisation were a loss of freedom'.[78]

The welcome these new nationalists gave to the trusts should not, though, be overstated. In the long run, the inequalities of both wealth and power that industrial reorganization produced ensured that these straightforward private monopolies would not do even for Croly, Lippmann, and Weyl.[79] 'The rich men and the big corporations have become too wealthy', Croly thus warned, so that 'while their work has been constructive from an economic and industrial standpoint, it has made for . . . social disintegration.'[80] 'We don't imagine

---

[75] W. Lippmann, 'Our Stupid Anti-Trust Laws', *New York Call*, 6 July 1914, 6.

[76] Lippmann, *Drift*, 137. Exactly the same welcome was found among British Fabians. See N. Thompson, *Political Economy and the Labour Party: The Economics of Democratic Socialism* (London: University College London Press, 1996), esp. 62–3.

[77] This distinction is extensively debated. For standard guides to the practical and theoretical arguments, see respectively A. Link, *Woodrow Wilson and the Progressive Era, 1910–1917* (New York: Harper and Row, 1954) and M. Sandel, *Democracy's Discontent: America in Search of a Public Philosophy* (London: Belknap Press, 1996), 211–21. A recent attempt to cast doubt on the effectiveness of such a divide is M. Sklar, *The Corporate Reconstruction of American Capitalism, 1880–1916* (Cambridge: Cambridge University Press, 1988). Additional progressive forces, of course, were gathered around the more populist message of Robert M. La Follette. For discussion of the relationship between the nationalist progressives and La Follette, see D. Horowitz, *Beyond Left and Right: Insurgency and the Establishment* (Chicago: University of Illinois Press, 1997), 1–18 and D. P. Thelen, *Robert M. La Follette and the Insurgent Spirit* (Madison: University of Wisconsin Press, 1976).

[78] Lippmann, *Drift*, 124 and 69. For support of corporations see, amongst many examples, Lippmann, 'Anti-Trust Laws', 6; Weyl, *New Democracy*, 85–94.

[79] On equality, see Chapter 7; on industry, see Chapter 7.   [80] Croly, *Promise*, 117.

that the trusts are going to drift naturally into the service of human life', Lippmann wrote.[81] The trusts would have to be carefully monitored, regulated, and eventually, even, overtaken by other forms of industrial organization. Furthermore, the only agency capable of taking on such a task was the central state, in the guise of a reformed federal government.

The dedication to 'nationhood' was thus translated into an express desire for an expansion of activity from the organized state. '[W]ithout a vivid sense of the possibilities of the state we abandon the supreme instrument of civilization', Lippmann argued, and his new nationalist colleagues did not dispute it.[82] These progressives further delineated the idea of 'state' action itself far more specifically than many of their predecessors had.[83] State activity was no longer to be understood as a vague harmonization of a wide collection of social organizations. The new hostility to sectional interests implied that it simply could not be so understood; instead, when these progressives demanded state intervention, it was clearly the mechanisms of government that they required to be put to use. In so far as nationalist progressivism required 'the substitution of a frank social policy for the individualism of the past', it demanded in turn, 'the use of efficient governmental instruments'.[84] It was the governmental organization of the modern nation state, Croly continued, that 'constitutes the best machinery as yet developed for raising the level of human association'. A well-structured government could also help achieve the necessary transformation of citizens' subjective sensations. A properly reformed central administration would thus be one that 'really teaches men how they must feel, what they must think, and what they must do, in order that they may live together amicably and profitably.'[85]

There were clear echoes of the British Fabians here: they too had welcomed industrial conglomeration as the first signs of an evolutionary trend towards ever greater cooperation, to be overseen and eventually superseded by state activity.[86] Indeed, so similar were these developments in Britain and the United States that one contemporary commentator suggested that nationalist progressivism was becoming 'the American equivalent of Fabianism'.[87] Nor was this entirely hidden by Croly, Lippmann, and Weyl themselves. Although there was little immediate to gain from identifying with a 'foreign' ideological phenomenon, and many political reasons to avoid it, the 'socialist' tag did not unduly worry any of the nationalist progressives, at least in the early years. A series of personal links with the British Fabians initially inured them from any such worry. As early as the 1890s, efforts had been made to found a

[81] Lippmann, Drift, 145.   [82] Lippmann, Preface, 266.
[83] See Eisenach, Lost Promise, 131–6.
[84] Croly, Progressive, 15. See too Lippmann, Drift, 69–71.   [85] Croly, Promise, 284.
[86] See Chapter 1 and S. Webb, Towards Social Democracy: A Study in Social Evolution During the Past Three Quarters of a Century (London: Fabian Society, 1909), 31–3.
[87] E. A. B., 'American Notes', New Age, 7 January 1915, 249.

journal called *The American Fabian*, and although it did not last members of the Fabian Society were still welcome visitors in American reformist circles during the last decade of the nineteenth century.[88] The more charismatic and less doctrinaire Fabians made a regular series of journeys to the United States during the first few decades of the twentieth century and many of the nationalist progressives came directly across them. Indeed, Professor Graham Wallas's term teaching at Harvard introduced his variant of Fabian socialism directly to younger scholars; and Wallas's impact was outstanding.[89] 'Wallas is the teacher', Walter Lippmann later recalled, and 'we are all of us his pupils.'[90] And Lippmann was clearly an impressive charge. On leaving Harvard, Wallas dedicated his next and possibly most successful work, *The Great Society*, to him.[91]

More important than these personal connections, though, was the fact that the nationalist progressives' major theoretical works often openly accepted that a pattern of conceptual similarity existed between their brand of progressivism and moderate forms of socialism. 'The proposed definition' of freedom and its consequences, Croly recognized, 'is socialistic, if it is socialistic to consider democracy inseparable from a candid, patient, and courageous attempt to advance the social problem towards a satisfactory solution. It is also socialistic in case socialism cannot be divorced from the use, wherever necessary, of the political organization in all its forms.'[92] In such a tone, Croly was happy to argue that even careful regulation of industrial life was only 'a make-shift'. Government regulation was 'inevitable during the transitional period' but to be up-graded 'when the state becomes competent to assume its proper function'.[93]

The details of that 'proper function' is for the next section of this chapter to investigate. For now, it is essential only to note what this meant for these progressives' conceptual foundations. Armed with such an understanding,

[88] See A. Mann, 'British Social Thought and American Reformers of the Progressive Era', *Mississipi Valley Historical Review*, 42 (1956), 687–8.

[89] See Lippmann, *Drift*, 36.

[90] W. Lippmann to L. Hand, letter dated 12 May 1922 in Hand Papers, 106/15.

[91] See M. Stokes, 'American Progressives and the European Left', *Journal of American Studies*, 17 (1983), 5–28; D. Rodgers, *Atlantic Crossings: Social Politics in a Progressive Age* (Cambridge, MA: Belknap Press, 1998), 65–6; M. Horn, *The Intercollegiate Socialist Society, 1905–1921: Origins of the Modern American Student Movement* (Boulder: Westview Press, 1979).

[92] Croly, *Promise*, 209.

[93] H. Croly to L. Hand, letter dated 20 December 1911, Hand Papers, 102/19. As he himself admitted, Croly's attitude to socialism owed much to the work of F. W. Taussig, Henry Lee Professor of Economics at Harvard, who had argued: 'The discussion of socialism is by no means barren. It centers attention on the fundamental problems of society, on the basis of existing institutions, on the sources from which coming growths must proceed . . . But it affects in so serious degree *present* endeavours and aspirations. As to these, there is a noteworthy accord of opinion [between socialists and reformers]. The course which society should take for the next generation or two is not obscure, and all men, socialists as well as social agnostics, can joint in efforts to turn it to the direction admitted by almost all to be that of progress.' F. W. Taussig, *Principles of Economics*, ii (New York: Macmillan, 1911), 501.

these progressives saw a future characterized by a remarkable combination of developments. America was to witness an increase 'in the number of legal inhibitions *and* in the sum total of the liberties of the citizen'.[94] Conceptual ideas inherited from the movements of the nineteenth century were now arranged and put to use in a way that would have shocked even the most reform-minded of their predecessors in the mainstream of American reform. The nation state would build the 'better American individual'. The conception of freedom as pursuit of communal improvement developed in a previous era was now the foundation stone for an ideology that would call on the United States to turn 'to the law, to the government, to the state'.[95]

Institutional Reconstruction

There were many remarkable similarities between the conceptual accounts offered by the nationalist progressives and the British Fabians, similarities that came, in part, from an extended period of joint academic activity. There were also, however, important differences. If these two groups were *intellectually* engaged in a joint enterprise, *politically* the Fabians held a distinct advantage. For whereas the Fabians crafted their theory of a single community to be directed by a centralized state in a nation that already possessed a fairly unified and increasingly centralized set of governmental institutions, in the United States was that there simply was no such state available.[96] As Croly himself recognized, 'the British have organized a political system which is probably more sensitively and completely responsive to a nationalized public opinion than is the political system of the American democracy'.[97] Indeed, Croly should have gone even further. For if anything was ill suited to the conceptual understandings these nationalist progressives developed, it was the United States' structure of governance: the institutional system of American government accorded directly with the old conceptual view of liberty. 'To the early Americans', Walter Weyl wrote, the essential political values were 'negative' in character—'an absence of kings, of nobles, of political oppression, of taxation without representation'—and as such they crafted an American institutional order marked by a remarkable lack of centralized power.[98] American government was distinctly not a system designed constantly to intervene in individuals' lives; indeed, key factors of

---

[94] Weyl, *New Democracy*, 354 (emphasis added).

[95] Croly, *Promise*, 428, and Weyl, *New Democracy*, 50.

[96] For an exceptional overview of American institutions at this time, see S. Skowronek, *Building a New American State: The Expansion of National Administrative Capacities, 1877–1920* (Cambridge: Cambridge University Press, 1982).   [97] Croly, *Promise*, 232.

[98] Weyl, *New Democracy*, 20.

its institutional design were created just to ensure that it did not. The separation of powers in the central institutions ensured that temporary electoral majorities would find it difficult to legislate either quickly or effectively: '[e]xecutives, legislatures, and courts were all granted abundant power to prevent others from doing things, and very little to do anything themselves', as Croly put it.[99] Further, a unique system of federalism guaranteed power to localities to halt the march of any nationalizing legislative initiatives. 'In dividing the government against itself rulers, whether representing a majority or a minority, could not and were not supposed to accomplish much', Croly complained.[100] It was, Walter Lippmann pithily insisted, a 'political system' suitable for 'a totally different civilization'.[101]

Given this lack of fit between nationalist progressive conceptual ideals and the realities of the state in which they found themselves, it was no surprise that their overwhelming political ambition was the need to overcome the 'inadequacy of American institutions in their traditional form'.[102] It was here, then, that these progressives became associated with reform intended to increase the authority of the state. Croly, Lippmann, and Weyl wished to craft a set of governing institutions informed by their new conceptual understandings. Such a task was, though, far more easily conceived that acted upon. The relatively rigid nature of the codified American Constitution made American institutions especially impervious to change; and the respect in which the Constitution was widely held exacerbated that difficulty. Through their 'embodiment in specific constitutional documents', Croly complained, the conceptual ideas of the eighteenth century and their institutional counterparts had derived an 'appearance of definiteness and finality'.[103] This rigidity was further ensured by the component of America's institutional structure that marked the most significant difference with Britain: the notion that courts, and especially the United States Supreme Court, had the right judicially to review acts passed by State and federal legislatures and to render them invalid if they were believed to stand in breach of the Constitution. It was in regard to this that conceptual argumentation first was transformed into recommendation for institutional reform, where intellectual debate became political battle. As one astute commentator put it in 1911, the first 'fight' of the 'new nationalism' was a fight against the 'powers of the judiciary as they exist today'.[104]

---

[99] Croly, 'State Political Reorganization', 128.

[100] Croly, *Progressive*, 40. For a more even-handed analysis of contemporary events, see T. R. Powell, 'Separation of Powers: Administrative Exercise of Legislative and Judicial Power', *Political Science Quarterly*, 27 (1912), 215–38.   [101] Lippmann, *Drift*, 159.

[102] Ford, 'The Promise of American Life', 614.

[103] Croly, *Progressive Democracy*, 29. See too 36–7.

[104] L. B. Boudin, 'Government by Judiciary', *Political Science Quarterly*, 26 (1911), 238.

Liberty and the courts

As every student of American politics should know, in 1905 in the celebrated case of *Lochner v. New York* the United States Supreme Court struck down a New York State law setting maximum working hours for employees in bakeries. Three years later, in *Adair v. United States*, the Court rejected an act of Congress making it a criminal offence for a carrier engaged in interstate commercial activity to dismiss an employee solely on the grounds that he was a member of a trade union.[105] These cases, and dozens more like them, caused outrage amongst the progressive reformers who had sponsored and supported the legislation. It appeared to many that the economics of laissez faire were finding their champion in the Supreme Court. Such decisions demonstrated that the doctrine of judicial supremacy was little more than 'a balm to the timid heart of reaction'.[106]

These decisions were the catalyst for Croly, Lippmann, and Weyl's involvement in the politics of the judiciary, as they joined a whole host of reformers in rejecting the Court's decisions. The nationalist progressive dismissal of judicial review was, though, more than a partial response to an institutional system temporarily failing to generate the desired results. It was also more than an attack on the Court's focus on economic as opposed to other forms of regulation. For even when progressive economic regulation was accepted by the judiciary, as when the Supreme Court upheld hour limitations for women in *Muller v. Oregon* in 1908 and for railwaymen in *Baltimore and Ohio Railroad v. Interstate Commerce Commission* in 1911, the process itself was still rejected. Such positive judgements and the opinions that accompanied them were dismissed as 'vague, conflicting, turgid, abstract'.[107]

Beyond its practical instantiation, Croly, Lippmann, and Weyl dismissed the very *idea* that constitutionally protected rights, as interpreted by the courts, should be granted supremacy over broader collective decision-making. The real importance of the *Lochner* and *Adair* judgements for the nationalist progressives was that the ways in which they were decided illustrated the case against judicial review particularly well. The basis of both judgements was a reading of the fourteenth and fifth amendments, amendments that prohibit State and federal authorities respectively from depriving any individual of 'life, liberty, or property, without due process of law'. In *Lochner* and *Adair*, the

[105] For details, see C. G. Haines, *The American Doctrine of Judicial Supremacy* (Berkeley: University of California Press, 1932), 440.

[106] Editors, 'Bill of Rights Again', 273. See too R. Meeker, 'The Promise of American Life', *Political Science Quarterly*, 25 (1910), 693.

[107] Editors, 'Bill of Rights Again', 273. For Court details, see E. Brandeis, *History of Labor in the United States Vol. III: Labor Legislation* (New York: Macmillan, 1966), 660–701. From 1880 to the First World War indeed, the Court upheld more regulatory statutes than it struck down, and the trend towards judicial restraint increased as the years passed. See H. Hovenkamp, *Enterprise and American Law, 1836–1937* (Cambridge, MA: Harvard University Press, 1991), 199.

Court explicitly read these as guarantees providing a series of rights ensuring 'the liberty of the individual' against the unwarranted intervention of governing authorities. In *Lochner*, the Court reasoned that hour-restrictions posed a 'meddlesome' interference 'with the rights of the individual' to reach whatever contractual arrangement he sought fit. In *Adair*, it argued that binding an employer to recognize trade unions was an unacceptable 'invasion of . . . personal liberty'.[108] Common to both judgements was a particular conceptual approach. As the New York State judge and respected legal scholar Learned Hand summarized, as far as the Court was concerned liberty 'has come to mean the right to pursue one's individual purposes as one likes'.[109]

For Croly, Lippmann, and Weyl, such an interpretation was based on the very notion of liberty that they and their immediate predecessors had been striving to replace. It was a view that placed the individual above society, an argument that posited 'the existence of certain individual rights as incontestable, indefeasible and inalienable', and which was, therefore, dependent on an erroneous 'analysis of the origin and meaning of society'.[110] For these progressives, of course, 'outside of society' the individual 'has never existed and could not exist'. As such, it was simply self-contradictory to talk of an individual possessing any inalienable rights 'against the community that made him and supports him'.[111] Individual liberty consisted in growing *with* the community, in becoming a more harmonious unit within the whole, not in distancing oneself from it. With reference to the cases at hand, if it was in the general interest to regulate the hours of bakery workers, then it was also, at least in the long run, in the bakery workers' interest as well. Similarly, if trade unions added to social stability, then employers were simply short-sighted if they tried to hinder their growth.[112] As Walter Lippmann put it, it was simply the 'the bad sociology of judges' that caused them to believe otherwise.[113]

The argument over the role of the courts did not end here. For even some thinkers who accepted the new socialized definition of freedom, and who therefore rejected the Court's reading of the fourteenth and fifth amendments, offered an alternative general justification for the institution of judicial review. These thinkers argued that the Constitution as interpreted by the Justices should be granted supremacy because it rather than legislation passed through representative assemblies represented the authentic voice of the people. Derived from Alexander Hamilton's 71st and 78th numbers of the *Federalist Papers*, this argument suggested that assemblies and legislatures were easily corrupted by the dominance of special interests, whereas the Constitution itself was crafted by the people themselves and designated by

---

[108] Lochner v. New York, 198 U.S. 45 (1905); Adair vs. United States, 208 U.S. 161 (1908).

[109] L. Hand, 'Due Process of Law and the Eight Hour Day', *Harvard Law Review* 21 (1908), 495.

[110] Croly, *Progressive*, 35.   [111] Editors, 'Bill of Rights Again', 273.

[112] See Weyl, *New Democracy*, 164.   [113] Lippmann, *Drift*, 158.

them as their fundamental law.[114] By striking down statutes passed by legislators in violation of the Constitution, the Court was merely protecting the
ultimate democratic rights of the broader citizenry against the possible intru-
sion of temporarily empowered legislators.[115]

Unsurprisingly, the nationalist progressives had little time for this suggestion either. They reminded their readers that the Constitution was not
produced by the American people as a whole but was drafted by 'a convention, the members of which were never expressly elected'. Further, it was 'rati-
fied, not directly by the electorate' but by a series of additional State-based
conventions. Following the work of a new generation of critical constitutional historians led by Charles Beard and J. Allen Smith, Croly, Lippmann,
and Weyl argued that if the Constitution represented the views of anyone it
was only of a 'small minority' of economically privileged American citizens.[116] This argument against the democratic status of judicial review was
also conjoined with another: one that was derived and adapted from the
experimental pragmatism of John Dewey. This second argument emphasized
that one of the central strengths of a democratic political system as opposed
to a non-democratic one was its capacity actively to respond to change. The
supremacy of the Constitution hindered rather than assisted such flexibility,
the nationalist progressives charged. The process of amendment was too
cumbersome and ineffective—only three decisions of the Supreme Court had
been overturned by constitutional amendment in the whole history of the
republic, Croly reminded his readers[117]—and judges, who could more easily
initiate change through interpretation, tended to be distanced from popular
sentiment. Roscoe Pound, the Dean of Harvard Law School, thus argued that
as between Court decision making and the activities of elected legislatures,
the latter had to be preferred as 'the more truly democratic form of law-
making'. '[W]e see in legislation', Pound concluded, 'the more direct and
accurate expression of the general will.'[118] Croly ensured the point did not go
unheeded in his progressive circles. Constitutional judicial review merely
ensured that the 'human will in its collective aspect was made subservient to
the mechanism of a legal system'.[119] As Walter Weyl still more evocatively put
it, although 'no King was set to rule over America' in 1787, the priority
implicitly granted to courts over more democratic mechanisms 'was more

[114] See Croly, *Progressive*, 276–7.

[115] See L. Hand, 'The Bill of Rights', Hand Papers, 136/1, pp. 8–12.

[116] Croly, *Progressive*, 43. See too Weyl, *New Democracy*, 15–16, and Meeker, 'Promise', esp. 693.

[117] The eleventh amendment reversed the decision in Chisholm v Georgia 2 Dall. 419 (1793),
Dred Scott V. Sandford 19 Howard, 393 (1857) was set aside by the thirteenth amendment, and
Pollock v Farmers Loan Trust Co 157 U.S. 429 and 158 U.S. 601 (1895) by the sixteenth amendment.
More decisions were, of course, reversed through the Court's own changes of perspective or through
legislation.

[118] R. Pound, 'Common Law and Legislation', *Harvard Law Review*, 21 (1908), 406.

[119] Croly, *Progressive*, 39.

subtly subversive of the popular interest than might have been a dozen Georges'.[120]

Even beyond the direct political reasons for resisting judicial review, there were further indirect cultural effects of the institution that added to its discredit. By leading people to look to the courts for the resolutions of conflicts rather than to the processes of collective decision-making, Croly, Lippmann, and Weyl all argued, the institution fostered an American culture that valued intransigent individual choice and sectional interest over the pursuit of a common good. The Court's talk of individual rights taking priority over collective decisions provoked 'mutual suspicion and disloyalty' and was 'confusing, distracting, and at worst disintegrating'.[121] At worst, such an institution would 'prevent us from imposing a social ideal, and compel us to leave a social anarchy'.[122] But even if judicial review did not result in such dramatic division, it would still stifle the emergence of a widespread national engagement in politics. '[S]ubordinating the community's power of action to specific rules derived from past political experience', Croly insisted, 'not only enfeebled the power of collective action, and forced the democracy to create an unofficial method of accomplishing its necessary purposes, but it also enfeebled its thought.'[123] If populations knew that their ideas and their commitments could be overturned by judicial decree, why would they make the intellectual effort required to shape new proposals for the new American age? Croly provided the simple negative answer. The population would not engage 'candidly, sincerely and vigorously' in political thought 'because its thinking, like its action, was circumscribed by the supposed authority of a system of rules'. Only 'the emancipation of its power of collective action will bring . . . the emancipation of its power of thought.'[124]

For all of these reasons, Croly, Lippmann, Weyl and their colleagues strove to guarantee that the early twentieth century was to be the 'twilight of natural rights' in theory and in practice, and such a dedication entailed a commitment to far-reaching institutional reform.[125] At the very least, these theorists thought, Supreme Court Justices themselves should come explicitly to acknowledge a far greater role for public opinion when they settled on their judgements. It 'is to be hoped that as the years roll on', Walter Weyl opined, that 'the nine Supreme Court judges, making and remaking a Constitution for a hundred million people, will more and more feel the impact, the psychological attraction, of all these millions.'[126] Such sentiment was crystallized in the widespread progressive enthusiasm for one Supreme Court Justice: Oliver Wendell Holmes. Although Holmes's

---

[120] Weyl, *New Democracy*, 14. Croly employed the same metaphor, *Progressive*, 131.
[121] Croly, *Promise*, 184–5.   [122] Editors, 'Bill of Rights Again', 273.
[123] Croly, *Progressive*, 329.   [124] Croly, *Progressive*, 329.
[125] R. L. Duffus, 'The Twilight of Natural Rights', *New Republic*, 2 March 1918, 139–40.
[126] Weyl, *New Democracy*, 317.

decisions and personal politics were not always favourable to nationalist progressives—he thought their suggested 'swing toward government activity' regrettable as it 'expects too much, and will lead to things worse done'[127]—he nonetheless advanced a jurisprudence that explicitly argued that judges should be responsive to democratic change. Indeed, referring himself to the very conceptual debate at the heart of the argument, Holmes insisted that 'the word liberty . . . is perverted when it is held to prevent the natural outcome of a dominant opinion'.[128] Croly, Lippmann, and Weyl were desperate to attract more Justices with such views to the bench. When Woodrow Wilson nominated the radical lawyer Louis Brandeis to the Supreme Court in 1916, the *New Republic* waged a fierce campaign on his behalf. It did so even though Brandeis, like Holmes, was no immediate friend to the new nationalism: he had backed Wilson while the new nationalists preferred Roosevelt, and favoured the decentralization of authority over its centralization. Nonetheless, the *New Republic* considered that he was alert to the need to interpret constitutional law in a way that reflected the changing demands of the people, and that was at the centre of the debate.[129]

This advocacy of democratically sensitive judges was, though, only the lower limit of progressive ambitions. The eventual goal was the effective abolition of judicial review itself, at least in the form it currently took. As Croly aggressively insisted, a properly reformed state would effectively pursue a single common good from which every individual would benefit, and when such a time came 'the government should no longer be subjected to the Law'. This was not to argue that the United States should do without a codified constitution at all but rather that such a constitution should be limited in scope only to those procedural regulations required for proper democratic governance.[130] As Croly explained, '[w]hile its own necessities will compel democracy to attach the utmost importance to the preservation of legal forms and methods, it cannot allow its respect for legal methods to outweigh its fidelity to its own needs and purposes.' The conclusion was relentlessly pursued: 'Orderly procedure must not only remain orderly, but it must also remain or become procedural.'[131]

---

[127] He nonetheless believed that these essentially personal economic opinions were irrelevant to judgements as to the constitutionality of government intervention in the economy. O. W. Holmes to H. Laski, letter dated 12 September 1916, M. de Wolfe Howe (ed.), *The Holmes-Laski Letters: The Correspondence of Mr Justice Holmes and Harold J Laski, 1916–1935* (Cambridge MA: Harvard University Press, 1953), 19. Excellent discussions of Holmes' jurisprudence in this period are S. J. Konefsky, *The Legacy of Holmes and Brandeis: A Study in the Influence of Ideas* (New York: Macmillan, 1956), esp. 139–62, and G. E. White, *Justice Oliver Wendell Holmes: Law and the Inner Self* (New York: Oxford University Press, 1993), esp. 298–353.   [128] Holmes, 198 U.S. 45.

[129] See A. T. Mason, *Brandeis: A Free Man's Life* (New York: Viking, 1946), 465–508.

[130] This, of course, left large questions unanswered. For a broader analysis of these themes, see S. Holmes, *Passions and Constraint: On the Theory of Liberal Democracy* (Chicago: Chicago University Press, 1995), 134–77.   [131] Croly, *Progressive*, 122 and 227.

These ideas may now appear largely redundant in our age, when theorists prioritize the 'right over the good' and where many radical activists in both the United States and Britain welcome ever-expanding judicial oversight over legislative behaviour.[132] In the first decade and a half of the twentieth century, however, such progressive aspirations seemed far more timely. At the outbreak of the First World War, Felix Frankfurter, Learned Hand, and Roscoe Pound led a large number of radical but well-respected legal scholars into becoming heavily critical of the Supreme Court's willingness to intervene on behalf of individual right at the expense of collective decisions. Partly in response to this academic trend, levels of court activism rapidly began to decline.[133] Stretching beyond legal circles, the vague ideal of limiting judicial power also made it right into the core of the political agenda of the broader progressive movement. Theodore Roosevelt's Progressive Party platform in the 1912 presidential election contained a plank demanding that controversial judicial decisions be referable back to the public in referendum. And, although the theorist declined the compliment, Roosevelt attributed the idea to Croly himself.[134]

More important than any of these trends, significant reform to limit the powers of the courts was actually realized in several of the States, where constitutional amendment was generally much easier than at federal level. By 1917, direct legislation from the electorate in the form of referendum or initiative had already been established in twelve States, often justified as a measure that could overcome the power of State courts to stall popular legislative proposals.[135] As they looked on at these reforms, the nationalist progressives thought they saw 'the system of [judicial] prohibitions imposed upon state legislation' being 'swept away'.[136] Founded as it was on what appeared to be a huge ground-swell of popular opinion, moreover, this trend looked unstoppable. The people, Herbert Croly continued, were beginning 'to move in a body', and as they did the constitutional 'superstructure' was about to 'crumble to the ground'. The principle institutional hindrance to the new ideal of freedom as the pursuit of collective improvement was about to disappear. '[E]xcept for the ruins' of an old constitutional order, Croly concluded,

---

[132] For this change in popular attitudes to the role of the courts, see J. J. Dinan, *Keeping the People's Liberties: Legislators, Citizens, and Judges as Guardians of Rights* (Lawrence: Kansas University Press, 1998), 151–66. For the philosophical tendencies that these attitudes exemplify, see M. Freeden, *Ideologies and Political Theory: A Conceptual Approach* (Oxford: Oxford University Press, 1996), 226–75.

[133] For contemporary accounts of the arguments and their impact, see T. R. Powell, 'The Logic and Rhetoric of Constitutional Law', *Journal of Philosophy*, 15 (1918), 645–58, and F. Frankfurter, 'The Constitutional Opinions of Justice Holmes', *Harvard Law Review*, 29 (1916), 683–99.

[134] See M. R. DiNunzio (ed.), *An American Mind: Selected Writings of Theodore Roosevelt* (New York: Penguin, 1997), 157, and Croly to Hand, Hand Papers, 102/19.

[135] For a good account of these institutional devices and the arguments used to defend and promote them, see Dinan, *People's Liberties*, 61–79.

[136] Croly, 'State Political Reorganization', 126.

'there promises to be nothing left to hinder the unrestrained movement of the popular will.'[137]

The puzzle of progressive democracy

These attacks on judicial review apparently revealed a strong emphasis on democratic decision-making within nationalist progressive thought. And indeed, recourse to arguments about democracy was frequent in these thinkers' works. As claims to democratic status enabled Croly, Lippmann, and Weyl to deride the institution of judicial review, so such a priority also enabled these progressives to shrug off the doubts that some more liberally minded critics had harboured about the conceptual scheme that they had adopted. Understanding liberty as the pursuit of communal perfection, free from internal as well as external obstacles, could, Croly admitted, be seen to urge an 'amount of self-subordination which would be intolerable and tyrannical'. What made all the difference was the characterization of America as 'a self-governing community'.[138] In democratic America, individuals were not in need of protection, either from the courts or from anywhere else. Each individual can safely trust his 'interest to the national interest', Croly concluded, 'because American national cohesion is dependent, not upon certain forms of historical association, but upon fidelity to a democratic principle.'[139]

This combination of a rejection of the priority of rights and an emphasis on the importance of democracy entailed that worries about untrammelled majoritarianism did not strike Croly, Lippmann, or Weyl too deeply. The processes of democratic deliberation and decision-making would enable the discovery of a common purpose that would allow individuals to find perfection together, which would let them live a life of freedom in the common good. Croly, Lippmann, and Weyl had little concern that it may be hard for individuals or groups to pursue ways of life that were unpopular in a society governed solely by democratic decision-making. '[S]o far as individual Americans are not capable of making their good things look good to a sufficient number of their fellow countrymen', Croly insisted, those 'good things' will 'deserve any neglect which they may suffer.'[140] Worrying about the illiberal implications of such a charge was purely a function of the residual 'early nineteenth century' approach to liberty with its 'principles of an essential opposition between the state and the individual'.[141]

Despite all these assertions, however, the democratic credentials of Croly, Lippmann, and Weyl were, in fact, far from clear-cut. In addition to these professions of democratic faith, their work displayed a considerable concern

---

[137] Croly, 'State Political Reorganization', 126.
[138] Croly, *Progressive*, 405.
[139] Croly, *Promise*, 267.   [140] Croly, *Promise*, 444.
[141] Croly, *Promise*, 414.

as to the apparent intellectual and ethical failings of the mass of the population. Moreover, from those failings they cast doubt on both the efficacy and moral desirability of unfettered democracy. '[I]f the younger critics are to meet the issues of their generation they must give their attention, not so much to the evils of authority, as to the weaknesses of democracy', Lippmann argued.[142] Walter Weyl expressed similar concerns. Borrowing from contemporary trends in social psychology, he insisted that if American democracy was left as it was, it would be 'the crowd', that collection of unthinking people which 'is intellectually at the level of its lowest members' that would 'most completely gain ascendancy'.[143] Croly too reached the same conclusions. Before democracy was actually desirable, he contended, '[p]ublic opinion requires to be aroused, elicited, informed, developed, concentrated and brought to an understanding of its own dominant purposes'.[144]

The institutional consequence of this series of doubts appears to have been a willingness to grant significant political power to a carefully selected elite. In another remarkable echo of the British Fabians, Croly, Lippmann, and Weyl all urged that a series of experts, in both a moral and a practical sense, should be charged with directing governance. In spite of their explicit democratic commitment elsewhere, these thinkers spoke easily of the need to seek 'exceptional individuals' and to charge them with certain fundamental roles in a progressive society. 'Men endowed with high moral gifts and capable of exceptional moral achievements', Croly insisted, have 'their special part to play'. Not until the constitutional reorganization which they directed 'has been accomplished' and the ordinary 'individual released, disciplined, and purified' as a result, would a truly democratic regime be either possible or desirable.[145] Even then, it was not clear how far democratic mechanisms were expected to stretch. Even intelligent citizens such as himself, Lippmann immodestly reminded his readers, 'cannot question everything radically at every moment . . . We all of us have to follow the lead of specialists'.[146]

All of these issues have caused much concern amongst recent commentators. James Hoopes sees Walter Lippmann's political faith lying 'less in democratic systems of government than in the elite who ran government'.[147] Even such astute critics as Rogers Smith have suggested that 'to modern ears some of Croly's views suggest fascism as much as democracy'.[148] Nor are these just the views of hindsight. Many contemporary critics also seized on these arguments and combined them with a suspicion that Croly, Lippmann, and Weyl believed that the necessary ethical and practical expertise required was manifested not

---

[142] Lippmann, *Drift*, p. xx.
[143] W. Weyl, 'The Sovereign Crowd', *New Republic*, 9 October 1915, 266.
[144] Croly, *Progressive*, 304.   [145] Croly, *Promise*, 452–3. For Lippmann, see *Preface*, 95–116.
[146] Lippmann, *Drift*, 261.   [147] Hoopes, *Community Denied*, 103.
[148] Smith, *Civic Ideals*, 415. See too R. J. Lustig, *Corporate Liberalism: The Origins of Modern American Political Theory, 1890–1920* (Berkeley: University of California Press, 1982), 198–221.

just in the heroic figure of Theodore Roosevelt, whom they all constantly cited, but also in people exactly like themselves. Furthermore, whereas some latterday critics have suggested that this trend moderated over time, the progressives' contemporaries seem not to have noticed any such development. Croly's second major theoretical work *Progressive Democracy* is often cited as an exception to this authoritarian trend: a more radical work that tried to allay fears as to the theorist's democratic credentials. On that book's publication in 1914, though, the moderate socialist critic William English Walling derided it as much as any earlier work for its 'frank reliance upon the privileged or ruling classes to bring about social progress'.[149]

Although these reservations are clearly not unwarranted, they overlook one essential element of the argument. At the same time as Croly and colleagues were expressing doubts as to the ability of the public to meet their democratic obligations and emphasizing the need for expert guidance, they were also continually emphasizing the need to construct more, not less, democratic structures. Croly was absolutely insistent on this point, almost as much in his early work as in *Progressive Democracy*. '[T]he "watch word" of progressives has become "trust in the people"', he asserted, continuing 'that such a trust constitutes manifestly the only possible foundation on which a democracy can erect an enduring superstructure of political institutions.' For as much as they believed in elite direction, Croly, Lippmann, and Weyl hoped that democratic involvement itself would provide the necessary education. By encouraging individuals to think through problems and by forcing them to be responsible for their own decisions, it would be possible to transform the 'crowd' into a knowledgeable and reliable 'public', Weyl wrote.[150] Similarly, while Lippmann argued that 'men will do almost anything but govern themselves', that they constantly search 'for some benevolent guardian', he also declared that none of the possible 'substitutes for self-government is really satisfactory'. '[Y]ou can't expect civic virtue', he concluded, from those who are formally or effectively 'disfranchised'.[151] Here among the Fabian-style demands for centralized elite direction were dedications to expanding democratic mechanisms and involvement at every possible opportunity, dedications more at home in pragmatist philosophy.

From these apparently contradictory positions, the solution for democratic troubles had to involve striking a balance between expert guidance and democratic involvement. That required new roles for expertise and leadership but it also demanded an expansion, rather than a retraction, of democracy. 'If democracy is to endure', Herbert Croly conclusively argued in *Progressive Democracy*, 'its own essential good-will is the function which must

---

[149] W. E. Walling, 'Progressive Democracy', *American Economic Review*, 5 (1915), 380. See too D. A. Hollinger, 'Science and Anarchy: Walter Lippmann's *Drift and Mastery*', *American Quarterly*, 29 (1977), esp. 470–2.   [150] Weyl, 'Sovereign Crowd', 267.
[151] Lippmann, *Drift*, 189, 190, 93. See too Weyl, *New Democracy*, 190.

be fortified; and its good-will can be fortified, not by the abdication but by the exercise of its own proper activity.'[152] A 'political system which offers the opportunity of participation to them places them on their best behaviour. It challenges them to be good.'[153] Democratic mechanisms were even to be extended into industry. While the nationalist progressives' proposals in this regard were of course much weaker than the syndicalist suggestions then being vigorously advanced by the International Workers of the World, Croly, Lippmann, and Weyl were interested in significantly more than simply strengthening trade unionists' input in decision-making.[154]

Despite the strength and frequency of such assertions, though, there remained one genuine ambiguity in these progressives' emphasis on democracy. Croly, Lippmann, and Weyl were not uniformly supportive of the *methods* that progressive activists had employed to expand democratic involvement: the recall, the referendum, and the initiative, all devices by which the people themselves could bypass the legislature and initiate and pass legislation themselves.[155] These suggestions found a wide range of progressive supporters; indeed, it was the centrepiece of much local progressive reform. But among the new nationalists they were far from warmly welcomed. While Weyl grudgingly accepted the necessity of most of the suggestions, Lippmann remained largely ambiguously silent, and Croly expressed fierce dislike of the emerging institutions of 'direct democracy'.[156] All of these were, he argued, largely a 'barren and mischievous addition to the stock of democratic institutions'.[157]

---

[152] Croly, *Progressive*, 152. See too 163–83.

[153] Croly, *Progressive*, 424. The shocking exception to this advocacy of expanded democratic participation concerned the denial of the suffrage to African-Americans in the South. Here Croly abandoned the logic of the educative effect of democratic participation, arguing instead that communal loyalty was a precondition for, not a result of, democratic involvement: 'A substantially universal suffrage merely places the ultimate political responsibility in the hands of those for whose benefit governments are created; and its denial can be justified only on the ground that the whole community is incapable of exercising such responsibility. Such cases unquestionably exist. They exist wherever the individuals constituting a community, as at present in the South, are more divided by social or class ambitions than they are united by a tradition of common action and mutual loyalty.' Weyl was more awake to the demands of consistency, yet he was eventually still as essentially contradictory, contending that '[i]t is perhaps possible to evade this issue of Negro suffrage if we can satisfy ourselves that the vote is not immediately essential to Negro civilization; if we can honestly believe that the denial to the Negro of the vote is advantageous, not only to us, but to him.' Lippmann evoked a similar argument, although his group of outcasts was larger, and their common factor was class rather than race: 'You can't build a modern nation out of Georgia crackers, poverty-stricken negroes, the homeless and the helpless of the great cities. They make a governing class essential.' See Croly, *Promise*, 199; Weyl, *New Democracy*, 343; and Lippmann, *Drift*, 255. For broader discussions on race and nationalist progressivism, see G. Gerstle, 'Theodore Roosevelt and the Divided Character of American Nationalism', *Journal of American History*, 86 (1999), esp. 1304–7, and Smith, *Civic Ideals*, 410–69.

[154] See, for example, Lippmann, *Drift*, 81, and Croly, *Progressive*, 384–5. Chapter 4 returns to this theme.

[155] See J. Allswang, *The Initiative and Referendum in California, 1898–1988* (Stanford: Stanford University Press, 2000) and T. E. Cronin, *Direct Democracy: The Politics of Initiative, Recall and Referendum* (Cambridge, MA: Harvard University Press, 1989).

[156] For Weyl's support of these ideas, see *New Democracy*, 306–8. Even he, though, worried that the 'results may not always be good': 307.   [157] Croly, *Progressive*, 270.

The primary problem with such suggestions lay with the encouragement they gave to sectionalism. Croly laid out his opposition to these reforms in detail at a meeting of the American Political Science Association in 1911. By enabling popular associations to mobilize support for their particular ends, influence was provided for 'groups of individuals, who occupy no intimate or responsible relation to the state administration or to the whole body of state public opinion'. Such people were not interested in seeking the common good; instead they 'merely want to push their own ideas or advance their own interests'.[158] Staunch as these objections were, Croly was all the more insistent in private. Writing to Learned Hand in the same year, Croly dismissed the 'insurgents' who recommended such changes as 'deceitful' for 'disguising a class and local agitation with the mask of a wholly public-spirited reform movement'. 'They do not want to drive special interests out of politics', he continued, 'they want to replace one group of special interests for another group . . . They are only faction, and some of them at least will eventually become a faction of an anti-national, unprogressive democracy.'[159] The view that 'all direct popular government' in whatever form it took must lead to the 'disinterested and public spirited' pursuit of communal perfection was thus dismissed as 'preposterous'.[160]

The resolution of this apparent paradox—the welcome of enhanced democratic involvement and an apparent dislike of the mechanisms by which it was to be achieved—lay in a theoretical argument that owed much to an earlier American ideology, that of radical republicanism. Republicans had often drawn a distinction between the 'will of all' and the 'general will', whereby 'the latter considers only the common interest, while the former takes private interest into account, and is no more than a sum of particular wills'.[161] On this account, democratic decision-making is legitimate not because it allows the simple aggregation of preferences but rather because it enables the identification and pursuit of a single common good. Such an argument was to be found throughout these nationalist progressives' work. Democracy was important to all of the progressives—it is wrong to suggest otherwise—but it was always essentially of instrumental value.[162] American citizens 'are not [necessarily] Sovereign in reason and morals even when united into a majority', Croly thus insisted; they 'become Sovereign only in so far as they succeed in reaching and expressing a collective purpose.'[163] An institutional settlement would be favoured, therefore, so long as it enabled the creation of an identifiable 'public interest which was more than a collection of private and local interests'.[164]

---

158 Croly, 'State Political Reorganization', 129–30.
159 Croly to Hand, letter dated 24 February 1911, Hand Papers, 102/18.
160 Croly, 'State Political Reorganization', 135.
161 See G. D. H. Cole (ed.), *J. J. Rousseau: The Social Contract* (London: Everyman, 1993), 203.
162 Croly, *Progressive*, 270.   163 Croly, *Promise*, 280.
164 Croly, 'State Political Reorganization', 131.

Democratic deliberation and action could allow an identifiable common purpose to be discerned and pursued, and a subjective sense of national loyalty to be fostered, but only if the institutions created the right incentives and encouraged the correct motivations. The construction of a widely dispersed spirit of social unity—the subjective sense of nationhood—together with the detection of an objective common purpose, the themes which were themselves the fundamental elements of human liberation, were all more important than any particular mechanisms; they were more important even than any commitment to democracy per se.[165] 'Democracy does not mean merely government by the people, or majority rule, or universal suffrage', Herbert Croly insisted. 'All of these political forms or devices are a part of its necessary organization but the chief advantage such methods of organization have is their tendency to promote some salutary and formative purpose.'[166] 'The end of democracy', Walter Weyl all the more transparently put it, 'is thus a social goal.' It was 'the improvement, physical, intellectual, and moral of the millions' who make up the nation that was at stake.[167]

A coordinated state

From these speculations on democracy, the task remaining to the nationalist progressives in seeking to develop a set of institutions compatible with their new understanding of freedom was clear. They had to design a set of governing institutions that could combine a system of democratic participation which would be truly educative in its effect with a system of efficient and expert administration capable of identifying and pursuing an actual common good.[168] It was here, rather than in any significant ideological change of heart, that Croly's *Progressive Democracy* marked a fuller development of progressive ideas. In this work, Croly pieced together earlier speculations into a carefully spelt-out thorough institutional vision.

At the core of that vision was the desire to channel power at both the State and the federal levels into the executive.[169] In Croly's new ideal set of governing institutions, at the State level governors were to be nominated by petition, elected by a system of preferential voting that would require the successful candidate to attain the approval of an actual majority of the electorate, and subject to recall. These governors were then to be allowed to initiate legislation and given control of appropriations, subject only to the formal approval of the legislative branch. At the federal level, the president was to be elected in the same way and charged with the same authority. The executive would oversee all developments in legislation, initiating many himself. Such

---

[165] See Lippmann, *Drift*, 81–2, and *Preface*, 8–9. [166] Croly, *Promise*, 207.
[167] Weyl, *New Democracy*, 319.
[168] For a particularly clear view of this goal, see Croly, *Progressive*, 283.
[169] See Croly, 'State Political Reorganization', 134, and Croly, *Progressive*, 290.

a strong central leader was then to be supported by an effective administration. The executive branch required a permanent bureaucracy staffed by 'expert administrative officials, which shall not be removed with every alteration in the executive, but which shall be placed and continued in office in order to devise means for carrying out the official policy of the state, no matter what that policy may be.'[170] These were to be scientific experts, whose skills would be recognized partly by their results and partly by their role in guaranteeing the continuing education of the people at large.[171] Working together with a powerful executive, they would be checked only by the oversight of other governmental branches.

Even that caveat, however, was weaker than it seemed, for within the nationalist progressive blueprint there was also to be an effective end to the separation of powers. This doctrine had been a new nationalist bugbear from the start. Separation merely hindered the necessary activity of government. 'Every statesman is hampered by conflicts of jurisdiction, by divided responsibility, by the fact that when he tries to use the government for some public purpose, the government is a clumsy instrument', Walter Lippmann contended.[172] 'If in a government there is a lack of proper coordination among the parts; if certain parts are weak which should be strong, and certain parts are strong which might be weak . . . then no true efficiency can be maintained', Walter Weyl similarly outlined.[173] The erosion of judicial review mentioned above would lessen the difficulty but they were to be complimented by efforts to reduce tension between the executive and the legislature. In *Progressive Democracy* Croly suggested that the entire legislature and the executive should be elected on the same day so as to reduce the possibility of divided government.[174]

This system would, of course, require extremely able executive leadership. Recent political developments, though, led the nationalist progressives to presume such inspiring direction would not be hard to find.[175] It was former Republican President Theodore Roosevelt who 'bestrode the wave' of these 'high aspirations and hopes'.[176] If Roosevelt and his admirers could just succeed and transform both State and federal government, the only remaining worry among these thinkers would be the balance between the two. Federalism was subjected to just as rigorous an examination as the other central aspects of the American institutional settlement; and the suggested reform was equally far-ranging. The 'national advance of the American democracy', Croly argued, demands 'an increasing amount of centralized action and responsibility'.[177] 'We are increasingly perceiving that many of our

---

[170] Croly, *Progressive*, 356.

[171] See Croly, *Progressive*, 375–8.

[172] Lippmann, *Drift*, 160.

[173] Weyl, *New Democracy*, 314.

[174] Croly, *Progressive*, 293.

[175] Croly, *Progressive*, 297.

[176] M. Schutze, 'As I Knew Him in Woodstock', in Weyl (ed.), *Walter Weyl*, 66.

[177] Croly, *Promise*, 273 and 274. For Lippmann, see *Drift*, 95 and Weyl, *New Democracy*, 314.

problems are national problems and cannot be solved by any governmental unity less than the nation', Weyl argued.[178] The prevailing 'delimitation of powers between the federal and the State governments' was thus held to be woefully inadequate.[179] Despite their justified insistence that their programme for the 'nationalizing of American political, economic, and social life' meant 'something more than' and 'something very different' from straightforward 'Federal centralization', all the nationalist progressives were insistent—indeed, as Croly said, they insisted 'in the same breath'—that an enhanced federal executive was the centrepiece of nationalist reform.

There were manifold advantages to such a scheme, all of which were intricately connected to the aim of relating the educative and the directive aspects of these theorists' notion of democracy as outlined above. To begin with, this was a system in which at each election *everything* was at stake and *everyone* had a chance significantly to shape the direction of the polity. The significance of the stakes would, it was thus argued, encourage people to take democratic governance seriously; it would draw out their enthusiasm and their commitment. As Croly put it, the 'educational value' of democratic participation 'is slight under a system of government organized chiefly to safeguard individual rights . . . But its educational value may be considerable under a system of government organized to accomplish positive social purposes.'[180] It would also encourage and enable widespread practical experimentation, enabling America to search through the possible options and discover some very real common goods. As Croly again summarized, American administrations 'would tend to be a government in which the ideas and the preferences of a great majority of the people would at some time or another be put to the test'.[181]

Beyond the seriousness of elections, the nationalist progressives' policy of favouring executives over legislatures was also thought to assist the development of communal unity. It would help avoid the factionalism inherent in the American legislature: the 'organization of congress makes it a bad agent of . . . an essential national function', Croly told Learned Hand, as the direct accountability of congressmen to their constituents meant that '[l]ocal interests are too powerfully entrenched'.[182] Making the election of the President the centrepiece of democratic life would provide politicians with clear incentives to seek broad support, and thus to phrase their appeal in terms of communality rather than in terms of sectionalism. Here leadership took on almost Hobbesian importance. It was indeed because Theodore Roosevelt seemed able to stretch over the heads of special interests and appealed to the American people en masse that he became such a hero to

[178] Weyl, *New Democracy*, 314.   [179] Ibid.
[180] H. Croly, 'The Obligation of the Vote', *New Republic*, 9 October 1915, 10.
[181] Croly, *Progressive*, 323.   [182] Croly to Hand, letter dated 1911, Hand Papers, 102/19.

the new nationalists. Here was a statesman capable of being the 'translator of agitations', they argued, someone who could 'guide and purify the social demands he finds at work' and forge a new social order.[183] To many progressive commentators it appeared as if a leader of Roosevelt's quality was capable drawing a vast social coalition together, especially if he was guaranteed effective use of central government institutions.[184] This was the only way, it was charged, 'to focus the scattered . . . energy of our vast nation and to direct it into practical reforms.'[185] Here was a means to 'represent the action and passion of the times' to 'make social reform a political issue of national dimensions' and to 'inaugurate an educational campaign . . . advocating its measures to the remotest parts of the country'.[186] If the federal government could just be reformed to ensure that both legislative and executive branches could be controlled by the same party, or even just by the same collection of interests, then real progress could be made. For then, a president of Roosevelt's ability would be surely able to fulfil his 'duty . . . to propose desirable measures of state policy' and would be more likely to possess the 'authority . . . sufficient to carry out its measures'.[187] Once the common good was decided upon, there would be little to stop its attainment.

The nationalist progressives offered a complex pattern of institutional reform, each element of which was related as a single component of a central transformation. Within the American political system as they found it, 'active government was divided, weakened, confined and deprived of integrity and effective responsibility, in order that a preestablished and authoritative Law might be exalted, confirmed and placed beyond the reach of danger'.[188] The American system as they wished to leave it, though, would offer the possibility of 'a government of the whole people' capable of ensuring that 'the obstacles to social unity' would be 'gradually eradicated'. Through such institutional reform, an 'effective desire for a genuinely social consummation' would come into being.[189] In this group of suggestions, therefore, the new nationalists' conceptual understandings, and especially the desire to enable individuals to pursue a national communal perfection, found their institutional counterpart. Humans would be 'raised to a higher level by an improvement in institutions and laws'.[190]As war approached, bringing with it a series of remarkable institutional reforms, the test of the desirability of these changes was actually far nearer than even the most optimistic of the nationalist progressives anticipated.

---

[183] Lippmann, *Preface*, 97.

[184] On Republican appeal to the working class, see Bensel, *Political Economy*, 462–66.

[185] J. Addams, 'The Progressive's Dilemma', Kellogg Papers, 35/331.

[186] Addams, 'The Progressive's Dilemma'.   [187] Croly, *Progressive*, 296.

[188] Croly, *Progressive*, 41.   [189] Croly, *Progressive*, 323.   [190] Croly, *Promise*, 399.

Conclusion

From the publication of *The Promise of American Life* in 1909 to the outbreak of the First World War, the nationalist progressives Herbert Croly, Walter Lippmann, and Walter Weyl developed a new ideological programme. On the basis of a set of conceptual understandings adapted from idealism, Fabianism, and pragmatism they set out to justify a collection of sweeping reforms to the American system of governance. Had such reforms been initiated, the American people would have been charged with electing a 'government in the English sense of the word', where a powerful executive would lead a legislature in implementing a far-reaching programme of political reform.

Although clearly related to their conceptual agenda, there were two ironies hidden in the advocacy of such patterns of institutional reform. Herbert Croly himself argued that nationalist progressivism was 'manufactured out of American material and in order to meet an American need'.[191] Yet this movement of reform that had begun by demanding change to meet new *American* conditions, that had promised to fulfil the promise of *American* life, ended up advocating a system remarkably similar to that already in existence in Great Britain. Second, in the country which already possessed such a system, namely Britain, these institutions and the conceptual case which was used to defend them were about to be engulfed in great criticism. Just as Herbert Croly was instructing American citizens that the 'pretence of divided sovereignty is at the root of [more] trouble than is usually supposed', in Britain the notion of a singular undivided governing authority was beginning to lose its appeal to reformers.[192] With one half of the ideological debate between nationalist progressives and socialist pluralists in place, it is to the criticism that forged the second half that it is necessary now to turn.

[191] Croly, 'Autobiographical Fragment', 21.
[192] Croly to Hand, letter dated 17 June 1912, Hand Papers, 102/19.

3

Socialist Pluralism

Introduction

As the nationalist progressives were outlining their vision for the United States in the first 15 years of the twentieth century, so the Fabian Society was continuing to expound a remarkably similar political philosophy in Britain. On the foundations of conceptual understandings derived and adapted from the idealists, both nationalist progressives and Fabians demanded far greater state intervention in the lives of individual citizens, arguing that only then could the social harmony necessary for genuine personal growth be attained. In Britain as in the United States, it appeared that the leading radical political theorists of their day had come to broadly the same conclusions. 'We have established the basic fact of social cohesion', one commentator put it, 'and we have been attempting, simultaneously, the discovery of some political hypotheses which may help us to the interpretation of its meaning'. The result was that 'today, the state enjoys its beatification. We turn to it almost blindly in sure faith that its way spells salvation.'[1]

This blind faith in the mechanisms of the state was, however, not to last. For almost at the very moment that Croly, Lippmann, and Weyl were founding *The New Republic* in 1914, the literary critic A. R. Orage was redesigning a cultural weekly newspaper in Britain into a journal specifically intended to question the state-centred assumptions of the idealist, Fabian, and nationalist progressive left.[2] This was *The New Age,* and through its pages an eclectic group of young theorists offered a stinging critique of the dominant philosophical and political position. This was a group possessed of a series of startlingly varied political views and partisan allegiances but loosely held together nevertheless by a suspicion that the influence of the central state was just as likely to be malign as benign. They sought, as such, to build an alternative set of conceptual understandings that would be capable of generating political responses to the problems of the age that were independent of an

---

[1] H. Laski, 'Can the State Survive?', *New Republic*, 21 April 1917, 14.
[2] See W. Martin, *The New Age under Orage: Chapters in English Cultural History* (Manchester: Manchester University Press, 1967).

expansion of state power.[3] And they all looked hopefully, instead, to the activity of smaller, voluntary organizations, ranging from churches to leisure societies, from cooperatives to trade unionism. If only these groups could be released from the burdens currently placed upon them, these thinkers argued, then perhaps between them they could provide the solution to the ills of modern society.[4]

Previous scholars who have studied *The New Age* and its authors have tended to suggest that these discussions led to the emergence of a single identifiable ideological movement; a movement that has come to be known as 'English political pluralism'.[5] It is, however, a significant mistake to approach the topic in this way. For whatever similarities did obtain between these individual thinkers, these debates did not lead to the emergence of *one* pluralist movement in Britain but *two*. Each of these presented a series of different conceptual arguments and employed these arguments to legitimize a different package of concrete policies. Seen in this way, the two groups that emerge are an initial pluralist movement, led by the Anglican theologian John Neville Figgis, and a successor group led by G. D. H. Cole and Harold Laski, joined later by R. H. Tawney. The first group may have originally inspired the second but fundamental theoretical and practical differences soon divided them. Moreover, it was the second group who provided the greatest intellectual and political challenge to the British Fabians and whose prestige would eventually cross the Atlantic as well to pose the most serious threat to the American nationalist progressives.

This chapter introduces the development of this second movement, a movement known here as 'socialist pluralism'. It does so in three sections. First, it presents an overview of the emergence of the initial pluralist movement in Britain, illustrating the ways in which it simultaneously rejected the practical political manifestations of the idealist conceptual scheme while failing to challenge its central philosophical assumptions. Second, it examines the far more thoroughgoing challenge that Cole and Laski propounded during the war years, analysing in particular the ways in which these theorists strove to develop a conception of liberty to rival that of the idealists, Fabians, and nationalist progressives. This new conceptual approach returned in many ways to an earlier form of liberal individualism, and left these pluralists closer to John Stuart Mill than to Thomas Hill Green. Finally, the chapter outlines the radical set of institutional ideals that Cole and Laski

---

[3] See M. Stears, 'Guild Socialism and Ideological Diversity on the British Left, 1914–1926', *Journal of Political Ideologies*, 3 (1998), 289–305.

[4] For such a view, see J. Stapleton (ed.), *Group Rights: Perspectives since 1900* (Bristol: Thoemmes Press, 1995).

[5] For recent studies, see C. Laborde, *Pluralist Thought and the State in Britain and France, 1900–1925* (Houndmills: Macmillan, 2000); D. Nicholls, *The Pluralist State: The Political Ideas of J. N. Figgis and his Contemporaries* (London: St Martin's Press, 1994); D. Runciman, *Pluralism and the Personality of the State* (Cambridge: Cambridge University Press, 1997).

built upon the foundations of their new conceptual commitments; plans not
just for the decentralization of political power but for the radical democratization of almost all of society's major institutions and organizations. Taken
together, these three parts will provide a full and novel guide to a series of
conceptual and institutional arguments which were soon destined to become
the centrepiece of a major transatlantic debate. This analysis must begin,
however, with a series of environmental characteristics which were distinctively British.

The Foundations of Pluralism

Although British Fabians and American nationalist progressives shared a
state-centred political agenda, the actual growth of state-centred politics was
far more dramatic in early twentieth century Britain than in the United
States. In the United States, nationalist progressives were faced with an
ingrained culture of individualism, a diverse social base, and a set of governing institutions characterized more by separation of powers than by unity of
purpose. In Britain, though, cultural norms and the framework of politics
seemed far more conducive to advocating expanded governmental activity.
The culture of individualism in Britain was undercut by an emerging structure
of working-class norms that lent value more to collective effort and general
sociability than to the pursuit of individual advancement. There had also
been relatively little significant immigration to break up the social homogeneity apparently required for a stable social order.[6] British reformers fared
even better in terms of governing institutions. British radicals did not have to
face a Supreme Court capable of hindering the implementation of legislation,
and if there was not exactly 'presidential' governance of the sort Croly desired
in the United States there was at least extensive executive dominance of the
legislature.[7] Nor were these advantages solely of theoretic interest; they
increasingly shaped the actualities of British politics. By 1914, reform of the
kind advocated by nationalist progressives in the United States was well
advanced in the United Kingdom. The election of a reforming Liberal government in 1906 brought dramatic increases in state authority: this government
increased taxation, introduced old-age pensions, instituted a national health
and unemployment insurance programme, and established governmental
commissions into minimum wages. It also initiated significant institutional

[6] See R. McKibbin, *Classes and Cultures: England, 1918–1951* (Oxford: Oxford University Press,
1998), 179–205.
[7] For an overview of these differences, see B. E. Shafer and M. D. Stears, 'From Social Welfare to
Cultural Values: The Puzzle of Postwar Change in Britain and the United States', *Journal of Policy
History*, 10 (1999), 331–66.

change too: a prolonged struggle ended the unelected House of Lords' ability to veto legislation after it had attempted to block the Liberals' redistributory 'People's Budget' of 1909.[8]

Attention was focused still further on the genuine growth of state authority by a range of judicial decisions. Two cases that enhanced the role of centralized governmental authorities in fixing the limits of the activity of non-state social groups particularly seized the public imagination. First, in 1903, the House of Lords, in its guise as Britain's highest court of appeal, declared that the Free Church of Scotland had no right to merge with the United Presbyterians even though such a merger had overwhelming support amongst the members of both churches. The Lords decided that such a merger was *ultra vires*, ruling that the doctrinal differences between the two religious organizations as specified in the Free Church's original charter prohibited any union between it and the Presbyterians in perpetuity. When theological chaos threatened to break out in response, an Act of Parliament invested responsibility for the Church and its possessions in a Parliamentary Commission, resolving the immediate crisis but further emphasizing the supremacy of the organized state. The second case was perhaps more important. In 1908, W. V. Osborne, a branch secretary from the Railway Servants Union, sued the trade union for demanding that he pay a contribution to the Labour Party as part of his dues. Osborne's lawyers charged that the Trade Union Act of 1871 limited unions to involvement in specifically industrial activity and that contributions to political parties went far beyond that purview. The Court of Appeal and the House of Lords agreed and the judges explicitly argued that it was the duty of the central state to fix the terms of voluntary associations' activity.[9]

Both of these judgements met with fierce resistance from across the political spectrum, a resistance which soon provided the catalyst for a thoroughgoing rejection of state-centred political reform and for an increasing demand that groups and associations should be left to run their own affairs. By 1913, indeed, it was easy to argue that 'everywhere' in the country 'faced . . . the uprising of the group'.[10] Responding to the Free Church case, religious leaders demanded that churches should be run by clergy and churchgoers and not by the central state. After the Osborne judgement, trade unionists and sympathetic industrial commentators similarly began to argue for a liberation of trade unions from governmental regulation. Many union leaders even threatened to adopt a form of radical syndicalism, demanding that industries should be run by their own workers and operate independent of the direction

---

[8] See M. Freeden, *The New Liberalism: An Ideology of Social Reform* (Oxford: Oxford University Press, 1978).

[9] For a clear summary of the Osborne case, see H. Pelling, *A History of British Trade Unionism* (Basingstoke: Macmillan, 1992), 128–31.

[10] G. D. H. Cole, *The World of Labour* (London: G. Bell, 1913, 2nd edn 1917), 19.

either of employers or of the central state. It was through such arguments that the first 'guild socialist' movement was born, soon taking institutional form in the National Guilds League (NGL), backed by a series of major trade unionists led by Frank Hodges and Robert Smilie of the Miners' Federation, and supported by a wide range of *New Age* contributors.[11] 'The state has attempted to make its authority commensurate . . . with the social life as a whole', the call went, but 'from a whole variety of associations, churches, trade unions, private fellowships of men, denial of the claim has been sharply made.'[12]

Looking on at these mounting protests, it quickly appeared to those engaged in academic analysis that the philosophical foundations of state-centred politics were being challenged by developments in the practical political world. For if the movement towards state power had been legitimized by idealist-style contentions, as that power itself was rebuffed so those contentions themselves could have been thrown into doubt. Although the 'theory of State Sovereignty' has 'won an almost universal triumph in abstract political theory', as G. D. H. Cole thus argued, 'it now seems likely that, under pressure from religious and industrial theorists, it will suffer . . . a defeat no less decisive.'[13] To many, then, it seemed that the essence of the idealist conception was under threat. Those leading the first academic pluralist response to idealism and its followers, however, actually offered very little in the way of fundamental disagreement with the essential components of the idealist conceptual scheme. Indeed, John Neville Figgis, the leading pluralist of the twentieth century's first 15 years, used a series of major works, stretching from *The Gospel and Human Needs* (1909), through the widely celebrated *Churches in the Modern State* (1914), to *The Will to Freedom* (1917), to offer warm support to most of the central elements of the idealist conception. The idea of freedom as concerned with the pursuit of perfection rather than with fleeting desire was reiterated, as for Figgis an individual's 'truest freedom' was not concerned with 'mere personal caprice' but 'with realisi[ng] himself'.[14] This dedication also brought with it the idealists' second contention that individuals need to be able to control their desires and to channel their energy towards worthy goals, to 'alter not only what you do but what you *want* to do', as Figgis elegantly put it.[15] The third idealist essential was also continually emphasized as the early pluralists' view of human nature followed precisely that outlined by the idealists. For Figgis just as for Green,

[11] See Stears, 'Guild Socialism', 289–305.

[12] H. Laski, 'The Responsible State', *New Republic*, 14 September 1918, 203.

[13] G. D. H. Cole, 'Conflicting Social Obligations', *Proceedings of the Aristotelian Society*, 15 (1915), 141.

[14] J. N. Figgis, *The Gospel and Human Needs* (London: Longmans, Green and Co., 1909), 138. See too J. N. Figgis, *The Will to Freedom* (London: C. Scribner's Sons, 1917), 289, and A. Ulam, *Philosophical Foundations of English Socialism* (Cambridge, MA: Harvard University Press, 1951), 83.

[15] J. N. Figgis, *Churches in the Modern State* (London: Longmans, Green and Co., 1914), 89 (emphasis added).

Bosanquet, Webb, and Croly, each human personality is an irreducibly social creation.[16] 'The notion of isolated individuality', Figgis insisted, 'is the shadow of a dream.'[17] Individuals were shaped and continually reshaped by the processes of socialization, their personalities constantly changed by their fellowship. For the early pluralists, then, as much as for the idealists, an individual's ideal values and goals, his perfection, and thus his liberty took an essentially communal form. Figgis was also more than willing to endorse the idealists' fourth contention that the restriction of some activities of an individual could paradoxically lead to an increase in the level of that very individual's freedom. 'Authority is . . . the expression of the social nature of man', Figgis insisted, and thence of 'the true character of personality'. Each individual needs 'the discipline . . . of group-authority' in order to 'guard against his own caprice' and ensure that he actually pursues perfection.[18]

Figgis did have one central disagreement with the dominant philosophical approach, however. He fiercely contended that the British idealists and their followers had made one fundamental sociological mistake. That mistake regarded the idealist, Fabian, and nationalist progressive assumptions about the *locus* of the relevant fellowship, the nature of the community through membership of which individuals would reach communal perfection. Whereas the British idealists and the Fabians who had followed them emphasized the centrality of the modern nation state to achieve this, the Figgisian pluralists firmly rejected such a view. Indeed, Figgis took exactly the opposite view to the American nationalist progressives as to the impact of the dominant social and economic trends of the early twentieth century. Whereas Croly, Lippmann, and Weyl saw a move towards ever wider and broader interaction between individuals in a national context, Figgis stressed that the vast increase in the size and diversity of twentieth century nations entailed that 'in the modern world . . . no such assertion is possible'.[19] While it may have been possible for the much-admired small city-state of the ancient world to be the locus of socialization, the 'mother of all her citizens', that certainly could not be the case today. For Figgis, humans in the twentieth century were socialized not in a community conterminous with the boundaries of the nation state but rather within small, tight-knit, local groups. Individuals were thus to find perfection in a family or locality, a 'parish or county, union or regiment'.[20] As the British idealist philosopher A. D. Lindsay noted, these pluralists 'do not and cannot deny man's social nature.' Rather, '[w]hat they are concerned to deny is that the social nature finds expression in one single organisation called the state.'[21]

It was on these lines that the first pluralist theorists connected a concern

---

[16] Figgis, *Churches*, 88.   [17] Ibid.   [18] Figgis, *Freedom*, 299.
[19] Figgis, *Churches*, 72.   [20] Figgis, *Churches*, 48.
[21] A. D. Lindsay, 'The State in Recent Political Theory', *Philosophical Quarterly*, 1 (1914), 131.

with liberty and human development with the need to resist the encroaching central state and to insist on a doctrine of group autonomy or 'associational independence'. In so far as the central state was not conterminous with the community in which socialization occurred, it could not legitimately claim to be the appropriate authority to charge with the detection and development of individuals' communal perfection. Associations had to be left to run themselves. Furthermore, if it was to be for associations to detect and promote the 'perfection' of their own members, they could legitimately ask of those members a great deal. Entry requirements could be made as strict as the group demanded, and, occasionally at least, it appeared that the possibility of exit for disaffected individuals could be severely restricted.[22] This did not involve the pluralists, as the political philosopher Ernest Barker appears to have believed, in an inevitable prioritizing of 'group liberty' over a concern for individual freedom.[23] Rather, it meant that individual liberty demanded group liberty, for if individual members were to reach their communal perfection, only their group itself would legitimately be able to decide what rules and regulations should govern its own internal affairs, what goals ought to be pursued, and how they ought to be developed. It was as such that the first pluralists urged the disintegration of the powers and responsibilities of the central state and its replacement with a nexus of many small, decentralized, independent associations, each of which would govern its own affairs. Only then could associations assist their own members' attainment of their particular communal, interdependent, perfection.

A new generation of pluralists: Cole and Laski

In addition to gaining a significant notoriety of its own, this theoretical justification for the programme of associational independence captivated a generation of young British political theorists. Both G. D. H. Cole and Harold Laski became keen disciples of this early brand of pluralism as they began their academic careers in Oxford.[24] Having been thoroughly introduced to the central claims of idealism and its critics as an undergraduate, Cole quickly used the leisure of a research fellowship at Magdalen College to develop theoretical arguments of great sophistication in the Figgisian tradition. 'Freedom is not the absence of restraint', Cole insisted in 1914 for the *New Age*, but 'it assumes a higher form': 'A man is not free when he allows himself to remain at the mercy of every idle whim; he is free when he governs his life according to a dominant purpose.'[25] Soon after, in his first serious philosophical paper,

---

[22] See, for example, Figgis, *Churches*, 45.

[23] See E. Barker, 'The Discredited State', *Political Quarterly*, 5 (1915), 106.

[24] For a telling example of this youthful conversion see H. Laski, 'The Apotheosis of the State', *New Republic*, 22 July 1916, 303.

[25] G. D. H. Cole, 'Freedom in the Guild', *New Age*, 5 November 1914, 7–8. At the Aristotelian Society he declared that idealist 'principles were almost always far more true than their ways of

Cole made a ferocious attack on state-centric theories conducted along lines almost indistinguishable from those suggested by Figgis.[26] The problem with arguments that concentrated on the nation state as the locus of their social-izing community was that they treated non-state 'associative acts as rather of the individual than of the social type'.[27] The core elements of the idealist understanding—freedom as a communal perfection independent of internal and external obstacles—were clearly present in the young Cole's work. Idealism only went astray in so far as it was 'infected with a bias' for seeing the national community, conterminous with the boundaries of the nation state, as the locus of socialization.[28]

Harold Laski, too, publicly and privately demonstrated allegiance to the Figgis school in his earliest academic works. Rejecting the 'ancient but tena-cious individualism' which was the centrepiece of earlier British liberal theory as 'the coronation of anarchy', Laski welcomed Figgis's work as one of the greatest sources of his political inspiration.[29] The young Laski came to plural-ism through legal scholarship rather than through the concerns for trade union autonomy that motivated Cole, but his dedication was nonetheless equally deep. The great 'churchman' was 'among those who have perceived the real significance' of recent judicial decisions such as 'the Osborne case' as illustrating the threat to associational independence, the young Laski insisted.[30] His early works accordingly demonstrated the same balancing act between an idealist interpretation of the nature of freedom and a political call for a radical decentralization that Figgis had continuously made in the previ-ous decade.[31] Indeed, he went on throughout his career to recommend Figgis to his students in the Workers' Educational Association.[32]

Despite this early support, as the years progressed, both Cole and Laski drifted away from their mentor's approach.[33] It was the outbreak of the First

---

applying them'. He also agreed that the task of political and social speculation was not to protect the individual against the claims of society but rather to identify the nature of the individual's 'ulti-mate obligations'. See 'Conflicting Social Obligations', 151.

[26] Cole, 'Conflicting Social Obligations', 148. For explicit acknowledgement of Cole's debt to Figgis, see G. D. H. Cole, *Labour in the Commonwealth: A Book for a Younger Generation* (London: Headley Bros, 1918), 209.

[27] Cole, 'Conflicting', 141.

[28] The early Cole's communitarian assumptions found him friends in America. See, for example, Alan Ryan's discussion of Cole's American followers in his *John Dewey and the High Tide of American Liberalism* (New York: W. W. Norton, 1995), 309–13.

[29] H. Laski, 'The Basis of Vicarious Liability', *Yale Law Journal*, 26 (1916), 134, and H. Laski to O. W. Holmes, letter dated 22 July 1916, M. de Wolfe Howe (ed.), *The Holmes-Laski Letters: Correspondence of Mr Justice Holmes and Harold J. Laski 1916–1935* (Cambridge, MA: Harvard University Press, 1953), 6–7.

[30] H. Laski, *The Foundations of Sovereignty and Other Essays* (New Haven: Yale University Press, 1921), 246.

[31] See H. Laski, *Authority in the Modern State* (New Haven: Yale University Press, 1919), 55–7.

[32] See H. Laski, 'The Student's Note Book', *Highway*, September 1921, 198.

[33] A separation noted by Laski in a further letter to Holmes, letter dated 28 February 1920, in de Wolfe Howe (ed.), *Holmes-Laski Letters*, 246.

World War that provided the catalyst for the emergence of a new conceptual approach, an approach which, in time, provided the cement of the ideological movement dubbed *socialist* pluralism.[34] These thinkers continued to argue for a vast decrease in the powers of the central state and to connect that programme with a theoretical account of the nature of freedom; but the details of that account began sharply to diverge from those presented by Figgis. That break came, in reaction to the prevailing paradigms of the time— and somewhat paradoxically for a movement known as 'socialist'—when Laski, Cole, and a broad collection of colleagues in both Britain and America rediscovered the appeal of philosophical individualism. With it they would eventually come to a new understanding of the concept of freedom and its consequences.

A New Pluralism: The War on Freedom

When war broke out in Europe in 1914, what had been a steady growth of state authority accelerated at an even greater rate. Through the conflict, the British government became involved in far more areas of everyday life than had ever been the case before. As it did so, it took an increasingly authoritarian line against potential opponents. At the outset of the conflict, the British government introduced the Defence of the Realm Act (DORA), quickly imposing repressive legislation in an attempt to control any radical group that may have been tempted to dissent. DORA was soon followed by legislation conscripting British citizens to fight in an increasingly unpopular conflict. As one American commentator put it, 'the powers of governmental officials and departments' to control the lives of individuals and groups 'were unbelievably broadened and extended'. Beyond conscription, the threat to organized labour was particularly severe. 'Driven by the hard necessity of modern War, to intervene . . . to an unprecedented extent, the State had proved itself . . . a tyrannical master', Cole wrote.[35] Central government limited trade unions' rights to take strike action through the Munitions of War Act in 1915. Many in the grass roots of the union movement responded aggressively. Shop stewards and factory-floor militants turned against the moderate union leaders who had negotiated with government and tried instead to maintain pre-war terms and conditions through radical industrial action. The government responded equally aggressively, forcibly moving

---

[34] The peculiar nature of the connection between the avowedly 'socialist' element of Cole and Laski's project and the pluralist part especially concerned the conception of equality. Discussion of it is resumed in Part III of this book.

[35] O. Tead, 'The Development of the Guild Idea', *Intercollegiate Socialist*, 6 (1918), 17. Cole, *World of Labour* (2nd edn), p. xxvi.

ringleaders from one city to another in a desperate attempt to break their hold on union organization.[36] As the war drew on, Harold Laski confided his fears to Graham Wallas that with state 'centralisation run amok' trade union independence was 'suffering a severe setback'.[37]

Both Laski and Cole swiftly turned to analyse the impact of these developments on the philosophical foundations of state-centred politics. The connection, they both argued, between idealist-style reasoning and the form of state oppression that Britain was enduring was unquestionable. Indeed, Laski claimed that the attempted justification of *all* of the wartime government's repressive measures was to be found in an appeal to the underlying centrality of social unity that idealists and Fabians had popularized in the preceding generations. Even the 'case for conscription' was made in these terms, Laski argued. In order 'to be made whole', Laski contended, the government and its supporters argued that all citizens 'must give the deepest that is in themselves to the state. So will they best be themselves, because from that service manhood and strength and determination are bred into the fibre of the people.' 'It is a brilliant argument', Laski concluded, 'yet it is undeniable that to a great and important part of the British people' who rejected the call for conscription, and doubted the moral acceptability of the conflict itself, 'the appeal is largely without meaning'.[38]

The task the young pluralists set themselves was to find 'the cause of this divergence' between the accepted theory and the apparent political reality, and to set it right. The first cause of tension that Laski identified was the classic Figgisian claim that the state-centric theory of idealists and Fabians depended on 'a certain over-simplification of the structure of society'. Those who advocated the argument 'see the nation as one and indivisible'. They further understand 'the nation' to mean 'the state' and thus render 'national service' as 'state service'. In reality, though, 'it is necessary to look a little deeper. Below the One the Many are visible.' If the domestic experience of the war confirmed anything about the nature of politics, Cole and Laski both argued, it was that the social allegiances of individuals were complex rather than singular. At one level, this was the difference of loyalties *between* individuals in any given society. The causes for that disunity lay in associational membership: 'The loyalties of men are so diversified', Cole wrote in 1917, 'because they are members of so many different groups.' As Laski commented, 'if there is a Belgravia, there is also Whitechapel; if there are people who read

[36] For expert contemporary coverage of these developments, see A. Gleason, 'The Shop Stewards and Their Significance', *Survey*, 4 January 1919, 417–22. A latterday overview is C. Wrigley, 'Trade Unions and Politics in the First World War' in C. Cook and B. Pimlott (eds.), *Trade Unions in British Politics: The First 250 Years* (Harlow: Longmans, 1991), 69–84.

[37] H. Laski to G. Wallas, letter dated 27 June 1918, British Library of Political Science, London, The G. Wallas Papers, 1/61/32.

[38] H. Laski, 'The Case for Conscription', *New Republic*, 6 November 1915, 22. See too G. D. H. Cole, *The British Labour Movement* (London: National Guilds League, 1915), 5.

the *Times*, there are also people who do not read the *Times*.'[39] Nations were marked more by difference than similarity, more by disunity than unity.[40]

Little in these arguments was new to the pluralism of Figgis, and indeed Cole emphasized the continuity: 'The actual '[e]xperience of State intervention has doubled my assurance that . . . [e]verything that was said against the Collectivist solution before the War seems to me to need saying with double emphasis to-day.'[41] This was not, however, a time for simply reiterating the vision of the past decade. For despite the close similarities between Cole and Laski's early work and that of Figgis, the seeds of a break with their mentors were sown in their wartime pluralist writings. The origins of that break lay in an argument that the depth of associational diversity opened up the possibility of conflict of allegiance *within* each individual as well as *between* different individuals. Laski argued that each and every individual in modern society 'shall find again and again that [his] allegiance is *divided* between the different groups to which [he] belong[s]'.[42] Each individual was not socialized in a single community; rather, individuals developed characteristics in a vast array of various differing associations simultaneously. As a result, no individual could be said to possess one, single and exclusive, social character. Instead, people incorporated many diverse goals and opinions, views and viewpoints, ideals and ideas. Each individual, Cole likewise concluded, possesses 'bundles of conflicting aims'.[43]

Both young theorists also stressed that there was no single means of resolving the competition between allegiances that would inevitably be thrown up. Various individuals ranked the importance of their associational connections in a wide variety of ways. In order to illustrate these, Cole began frequently to evoke the following example: two individuals, Mr Jones and Mr Brown, may even be members of the same groups, an industrial company and a social club for example, but one may value vocational solidarity more highly than leisure, whilst the other may sense a deep commitment to the social networks of private life in comparison with the hard labour involved in membership of the company. Through such examples, it became clear to the young pluralists that as there was no common set of substantial desires even between members of the same association, there was essential variety in the goals each and every individual would wish to pursue. In this way, Cole and Laski began to recognize that an individual is a potentially unique mixed bag of desires and allegiances. What R. H. Tawney was later to call the 'infinite diversities' of individuals was established.[44]

---

[39] Laski, 'Case for Conscription', 22.

[40] G. D. H. Cole, *Self-Government in Industry* (London: G. Bell, 1917), 177. See too H. Laski, *Studies in the Problem of Sovereignty* (New Haven: Yale University Press, 1917), 10–13.

[41] Cole, *World of Labour* (2nd edn.), pp. xxvi–xxvii.   [42] Laski, *Studies*, 15.

[43] Cole, *Self-Government*, 177.

[44] R. H. Tawney, *Equality* (London: George Allen and Unwin, 1938), 208.

Pluralism and individualism

Initially, at least to the theorists themselves, this claim established little distance between Cole and Laski and the pluralists of the Figgis school.[45] Its recognition did, however, set the young theorists thinking. In the last few months of the war and in the years immediately after it, new questions began to arise, questions that challenged all the fundamental assumptions underlying the idealist conceptual approach. In particular, given their insistence on the inevitability of complex and competing allegiances within each individual, it became increasingly difficult for the young pluralists to claim that anyone could know with any certainty the nature of another individual's values, allegiances, or obligations. Individuals became, to a significant extent, opaque. Such an observation was troubling for the quasi-idealist conception of liberty that the young pluralists had espoused. If, after all, different individuals have different packages of social allegiances, and rank the importance of their particular associational memberships differently, who could possibly dictate the details of their own particular perfection, what authority could recognize the content of their 'best self' and aid the development of their true liberty?[46]

The full implications of this set of observations were slow to dawn on the new pluralists; but they were quickly spotted, and spelled out in detail, by their opponents. It was the idealist H. J. W. Hetherington who first noticed the logic of the argument in a paper presented to the Aristotelian Society in 1917. Hetherington emphasized that just as Figgis had denied that the national community is the sole location of an individual's socialization to argue that the state cannot demand unlimited loyalty, so Cole was required to insist that no one particular locality, vocational group, or social club could be thought to be so privileged. Hetherington's account of the position outlined by the young Cole recognized that it was the '*individual* as a single conscious centre' that must be the 'centre of [Cole's] outlook'.[47] Cole's obsession with complex and competing social allegiances, Hetherington worried, meant that he 'underestimates all that is implied' in the theory that human character 'is achieved only by participation in the interests of a social world'.[48] In Hetherington's view, an element of individualism was returning. If Hetherington's intention in this paper was to frighten Cole and Laski back into the idealist fold, he could not have failed more spectacularly. For in

---

[45] Nor necessarily should it have. Figgis and Maitland had often recognized the role that a wide variety of groups played in each individual's lives. See Figgis, *Churches*, 88–9; J. Burrow, *Whigs and Liberals: Continuity and Change in English Political Thought* (Oxford: Oxford University Press, 1988), 137.

[46] Harold Laski asks these questions explicitly in his *Foundations*, 169.

[47] H. J. W. Hetherington, 'The Conception of a Unitary Social Order', *Proceedings of the Aristotelian Society*, 18 (1918), 309 (emphasis added).

[48] Hetherington, 'Unitary Social Order', 309.

response to this charge, the new pluralists actually enthusiastically embraced and further developed the individualistic aspect of the argument that Hetherington had outlined. Cole and Laski thus moved firmly and explicitly away from Figgis by rejecting the fundamental metaphysical, sociological, and psychological claims regarding the wholly social nature of man. Just as the early pluralists had turned on the idealist claim that an individual could be understood as a creature shaped by socialization in one association, so the later pluralists urged that there was more to the individual and the individual good than even a multiple collection of associational memberships and allegiances. To put that another way, whereas Figgis had followed the idealists in arguing that in the real world the 'isolated individual does not exist', in the later war years and into the early 1920s Cole and Laski began to dissent.

An explicit break came soon enough. In the final year of the war, Laski explicitly separated his own view from that of the idealists, progressives, and Figgisian pluralists. According to the conception those groups shared, an individual 'derives his meaning from his relations'. In the new 'pluralistic theory', however, Laski insisted 'while his relations may be of the deepest significance, it is denied that they are the sole criterion by which a man ought to be judged.'[49] 'The inherently plural character of human personality', he announced, ensures that 'however rich may be the genius of a man for fellowship he also has an inwardness of perception which no association can absorb'.[50] Indeed, individual 'isolation', the sphere of the 'unabsorbed personality', was now at the centre of his account.[51] Cole soon concurred. 'Men and women', he announced in 1919, 'pour a great deal' into 'various forms of association' but similarly 'a great deal of themselves they cannot pour into any association because it is essentially individual'.[52] 'It is of the essence of the individual human soul', he continued, using uncharacteristically religious imagery, 'that it is individual and cannot be absorbed into anything else'.[53] Both Cole and Laski thus began to reconfirm the individual as the focus for their concept of liberty.

At the close of the First World War, then, both Cole and Laski rejected the idealists' communitarian assumptions altogether and replaced them with a view of an individual standing apart from his social allegiances. Connectedly, they also asserted the primacy of individual judgement. In the wake of the recognition of each individual's potentially divided loyalties, Cole and Laski emphasized the central role of individual choice. It was individuals themselves who had to decide between their priorities, join and leave associations, trade one allegiance off against another. While 'of English writers on political

---

[49] Laski, *Studies*, 11.   [50] Laski, *Authority*, 275.
[51] Laski, *Authority*, 65; H. Laski, *A Grammar of Politics* (London: George Allen and Unwin, 1925, 2nd edn 1930), 67.
[52] G. D. H. Cole, 'National Guilds and the State', *Socialist Review*, 16 (1919), 30.
[53] Cole, *Labour in the Commonwealth*, 37.

theory Dr Figgis is unquestionably the first', Laski wrote in July 1917, he ignores 'the simple fact that in the conflict between society and the individual it is usually the individual who suffers.'[54] The consequence was a demand that understandings of the meaning and value of 'individual freedom' had to be radically detached from claims about communal identity, whether national or group-oriented. 'I would urge you', Laski pleaded, 'to place [the] individual at the centre of things.' As the American scholar Lewis Rockow noted, 'while the criticism of sovereignty by Figgis is mainly on behalf of the group', the new pluralists of the Cole and Laski school were 'chiefly solicitous about the individual'.[55]

These new individualist claims quickly gathered adherents amongst many of the theorists who had written for the *New Age* or who had joined the National Guilds League in the early war years. As A. L. Smith noted, 'a new reverence for the individual' permeated the pluralist movement in response to Cole and Laski's claims.[56] In late 1918, a *New Age* commentator, M. W. Robieson, thus tried to convince his readers that any guild project must be founded on the assumption that it was 'the enormous variation from one individual to another' which entailed that any 'insistence of uniformity is impossible'.[57] An anonymous book reviewer in the NGL's *Guildsman* journal similarly took up the cause against Figgisian assumptions that 'all sides of the individual can be suitably expressed in a group'.[58] Cole's undergraduate friend and fellow founder member of the NGL, Ivor Brown, moved in a similar direction. Throughout the war years, Brown penned a series of articles for both the *New Age* and the *Guildsman* that explicitly attempted to establish distance between guild philosophy and Figgisian pluralism. By the close of 1919, Brown was prone to become publicly enraged at the suggestion that Figgis's political theory possessed any resemblance to the new pluralism. As Brown interpreted it, Figgis's theory was 'authoritarian'. The theologian was, on this account, a 'disliker of individual freedom'. 'Either freedom exists in and for individuals', Brown insisted, 'or it doesn't exist at all.'[59] Beyond the immediate confines of the NGL, there were more influential converts too. Bertrand Russell's *Principles of Social Reconstruction*, published in 1916, was

[54] H. Laski, 'Lecture on Political Freedom', *Fabian News*, December 1925, 51, and *Grammar*, 143.

[55] L. Rockow, *Contemporary Political Thought in England* (London: Leonard Parsons, 1925), 135. See too anon., 'Labour in the Commonwealth', *Nation (NY)*, 24 January 1920, 112–13.

[56] A. L. Smith, 'New Ideals' (London, 1918), Balliol College, Oxford, The A. L. Smith Papers, II/C/6/x. See too M. Freeden, *Liberalism Divided: A Study in British Political Thought, 1914–1939* (Oxford: Oxford University Press, 1986), 18–45.

[57] M. W. Robieson, 'On Certain First Principles', *New Age*, 25 July 1918, 197–8. See too Robieson's stinging critique of idealism in his 'Hegelian Politics', *New Age*, 28 November 1918, 55–6.

[58] 'Hussein', 'The Sign of the Book', *Guildsman*, July 1920, 8–9. As Hugh Gaitskell recalled of a large number of left leaning students of the time, 'we were. . . suspicious of general ideas, especially when they involved some mystical, collective, common good. We preferred the happiness of the individual'. H. Gaitskell, 'At Oxford in the Twenties', in A. Briggs and J. Saville (eds), *Essays in Labour History* (London: Macmillan, 1967), 7.

[59] I. Brown, 'Freedom and Dr Figgis', *Guildsman*, December 1919, 7.

probably the first text explicitly to marry a concern with pluralist demands for associational independence with a clearly individualist inclination.[60] More notable even than Russell was the eventual allegiance of Richard H. Tawney, who had been separated initially from the founding of the NGL by his involvement in front-line fighting in the war. Tawney joined the fold immediately at the war's end. By 1918, he was a regular in NGL meetings and journals, and was to be found emphasizing the necessity of shaping a political theory in opposition to idealism and Fabianism that would stress 'the right of men to live their *own* lives and express their *own* personalities'.[61]

A new conception of liberty

The result of this new brand of individualism was, of course, an almost total rejection of the idealist approach to freedom even as it had been modified by the Figgisian pluralists. Cole, Laski and their host of new colleagues thus undermined the entirety of the idealist understanding. The first three idealist components—the definition of liberty in terms of the pursuit of perfection independent of internal 'moral' obstacles where perfection was seen in communal terms—were the first to fall by the wayside. The task of distinguishing a selfish desire from an element of perfection became difficult if not impossible; after all, what appeared to be an irrational wish to one individual may well be an integral part of the perfect self to another. The opacity of each individual's nature further made the third idealist claim—the essentially communal nature of perfection—appear far more suspect than it had been to either the idealists or the original pluralists. The recognition that each 'individual is distinct from others' involved the concomitant acceptance that one must believe the account others give of their own interests and goals, whether those accounts be purely individual, sectional, or communal.[62] As Laski would later phrase it, the appreciation that individuals are not 'moulded to a pattern', that individuals are 'too distinct' from one another, entails the near-impossibility of any one individual knowing another's nature or ultimate goals better than that other can know them himself.[63] A primary implication of the new pluralists' individualism, as Cole phrased it in his *Social Theory*, was that 'we can only know what we ourselves know to be good'.[64]

This set of contentions further negated the idealist conception's fourth component that an outside authority could assist freedom by laying down rules and regulations to ensure that individuals pursued perfection. No one,

---

[60] B. Russell, *The Principles of Social Reconstruction* (London: George Allen and Unwin, 1916), 44–76.

[61] R. H. Tawney, *The Commonplace Book* (Cambridge: Cambridge University Press, 1972), 47 (emphasis added).

[62] G. D. H. Cole, *Social Theory* (London: Methuen, 1920), 92.

[63] H. Laski, 'Nietzsche's Religion: Review of Figgis', *New Republic*, 28 July 1917, 364.

[64] Cole, *Social Theory*, 93. See too Laski, *Foundations*, 237.

however benign, was likely to be able to empathize fully with the wide variety of goals being pursued by the wide variety of individuals. Anyone who claimed in any society to wish to give assistance to an individual's search for 'perfection' by directing that individual's behaviour would be led almost arbitrarily to encourage and enable the pursuit of some goods and to prevent the pursuit of others.[65] The new pluralists' rejection of this aspect of the idealist approach to liberty was further enhanced by a conviction that 'in the process of politics what broadly gets registered . . . is the will of those who operate the machine'.[66] When idealists, Fabians, and nationalist progressives vested power in the state, or when the early Figgisian pluralists authorized an association to determine the nature of its members' perfection, they were in fact granting power to a group of potentially selfish individual agents: the extent of wartime repression had shown that this was true even in democracies.[67] It was, Laski held, an 'incurable defect of the idealist hypothesis that it makes abstractions of these real persons by whom our destiny is controlled'.[68] Neither the state nor any other association could be allowed to exert dominance in the name of freedom over the particular desires of the people in whose membership they consisted. The central claims of the idealist conception all fell away.

As the idealist conception of freedom was rejected, so a new conception had to replace it. As Laski understood it, what this new form of pluralism essentially 'required' was a new 'theory of the nature of liberty'.[69] Such a theory was grounded, despite all the stress on the potentially 'infinite diversity' of individuals, in a claim regarding a universal aspect of human nature. Cole and Laski thus argued that, however unique they are in other ways, all individuals possessed one identical interest. As Cole contended, all humans 'want to have an opportunity of expressing', pursuing, or developing all the many and various component parts of their own 'desire-set', of what might now be called their 'conceptions of the good life'.[70] On this account, all men have an inherent interest in obtaining and protecting 'the maximum opportunity for . . . self-expression'.[71] This is not to say the humans will by necessity 'use those opportunities all the time' but simply that they desire to be 'able to use them when [they] want to'.[72]

---

[65] See Laski, *Authority*, 38.

[66] Laski, *Authority*, 37. For Cole's concurrence see, *Social Theory*, 181.

[67] See Laski, *Authority*, 29–30, and 'The State in the New Social Order', *Fabian Tract* 200 (London: Fabian Society, 1922), 4 and 7. Laski also noted that a government 'confined to the middle class' will, on such an account, 'reflect the purposes and aptitudes of that class': *Foundations*, 63. It is worth noting that Laski expressed this opinion well before his belated conversion to a form of Marxism in the wake of the Great Depression.

[68] H. Laski, 'Rousseau', *New Republic*, 16 July 1919, 364.

[69] H. Laski, 'The Pluralistic State', *Journal of Philosophy*, 16 (1919), 718.

[70] G. D. H. Cole, 'Guild Socialism', *Fabian Tract* 192 (London: Fabian Society, 1920), 16.

[71] G. D. H. Cole, *Guild Socialism Restated* (London: Leonard Parsons, 1920), 13.

[72] Cole, 'Guild Socialism', 16.

It was here that the basis of the socialist pluralists' shared approach to liberty was to be found. It was a seemingly unreconstructed traditional, individualist liberal perspective: as every human wishes to express or pursue all the various elements of his set of desires, every human has an interest in guaranteeing opportunities will be available for him to be able to do so. Liberty provided that guarantee. Freedom, for Cole, Laski, and their colleagues, consisted not in the attainment of a communal perfection but in the possibility of expression of the diverse contents of the wills of diverse people. Employing language unthinkable to idealists, Fabians, nationalist progressives, or Figgisian pluralists, Ivor Brown thus insisted that 'we are free when our desires and our doings run unimpeded on their way'.[73]

The Institutions of Pluralism

By the end of the First World War, Cole, Laski, and their colleagues had sought to demonstrate that, as far as liberty is concerned, individuals, as the most reliable interpreters of their own values and goods, should be protected from the intervention of others.[74] Individuals should be allowed to decide which goals to pursue, how to pursue them, and whether and when to change their minds. In terms of direct political practice, the new pluralists' individualism augured well for an institutional system based upon a stringent system of negative individual rights. As Laski himself insisted, as 'rights . . . are necessary to freedom . . . we have put them outside the power of the state to traverse'.[75] But such a reconnection of liberty with a system of individual rights casts doubt on the centrality of the connection between liberty and associations that had been so vital to the earlier Figgisian pluralism. For if the key to protecting freedom is guaranteeing individual rights, then the connection between the position of associations vis-à-vis the state and the protection of individual liberty may seem to be of dubious importance. The question that remains then is this: if Cole, Laski and their colleagues resurrected a conception of liberty grounded in a strong individualism, in what sense did they remain *pluralists*?[76]

An initial response would be that the theorists simply *had* to continue to

[73] I. Brown, 'Aspects of the Guild Idea', *New Age*, 24 June 1915, 175.

[74] It is, of course, quite possible that the pluralists could have urged restriction of individual activity on grounds other than liberty: that is, they may have prioritized some other concept above freedom and thus demanded freedom-restricting political programmes. Discussion of this theme is resumed in Part III.   [75] Laski, *Foundations*, 246.

[76] For a contemporary response to this question, see N. Wilde, 'The Problem of Liberty', *International Journal of Ethics*, 33 (1923), 291–306. More recently, Avigail Eisenberg asks this of Harold Laski in her *Reconstructing Political Pluralism* (Albany: State University of New York, 1995), 81–3.

concern themselves with the position of associations. The early pluralists' observation that social groupings were very much an observable feature of human life continued to hold sway; Cole himself was still willing to acknowledge that all individuals are unavoidably 'flung into a social environment' and Laski and other colleagues concurred.[77] Furthermore, the political environment of the time concentrated attention on the role of voluntary associations. The early pluralists had, as the historian Jose Harris has argued, successfully 'captured a wider cultural mood' whereby 'civil society was seen as the highest sphere of human existence'.[78] Similarly, of course, the pluralism of G. D. H. Cole and, even if to a slightly lesser extent, of Harold Laski, Bertrand Russell, and Ivor Brown, was closely wound up with the trade union movement in general and the demand for national guilds in particular. Important as these political and cultural contingencies were, though, the new pluralists tried hard to reconcile their observations concerning the realities of social and political life with their theoretical outlook. Despite, therefore, the new socialist pluralists' rhetorical tendency to play down associations in comparison with their Figgisian predecessors, a dedication to associational independence remained part of their practical programme. A refined version of the doctrine of group autonomy had, therefore, to remain an essential element of their theoretical understanding. As Ivor Brown was at pains to express, 'the individualism' of the socialist pluralists 'differs from the individualism of the last century' precisely as a result of its 'particular acceptance of the group'.[79] The 'old concept of individualism', Harold Laski agreed, was to be made 'to fit new forms'.[80]

The basis of association

The pluralists offered two initial arguments as to why their individualistic rendition of freedom demanded a widespread acceptance of associational independence. The first substantive response was the synthesis of the experience of war and a set of claims inherited from Alexis de Tocqueville.[81] With war proving that the 'effete legalism' of methods like the 'swaddling clothes of the Fourteenth amendment' would fail to protect individuals from an ebullient central state, this argument emphasized the capacity of groups to protect

---

[77] Cole, *Social Theory*, 1; Laski, *Foundations*, 139; R. H. Tawney, *The Acquisitive Society* (London: G. Bell, 1921), 54.

[78] Quoted in J. Stapleton, *Englishness and the Study of Politics: The Social and Political Thought of Ernest Barker* (Cambridge: Cambridge University Press, 1995), 68. As Laski said at the time, the early twentieth century was 'an age predominantly associational in character': 'Basis of Vicarious Liability', 134.   [79] I. Brown, *English Political Theory* (London: Methuen, 1920), 164.

[80] H. Laski, 'Church and State', *New Republic*, 30 November 1918, 142.

[81] See Laski, *Foundations*, 85, and H. Laski to O. W. Holmes, letter dated 5 July 1918, in de Wolfe Howe (ed.), *Holmes-Laski Letters*, 159–60.

the individual from the growing interference of the central state. Men 'kept asunder' are far more vulnerable to the direction of a powerful central authority than those who regularly associate with others. As Laski's undergraduate tutor at Oxford, Ernest Barker, wisely noted, 'the problem of resistance is in actual life always a problem of groups . . . theorists may set limits to the State in the name of the individual' but 'practical resistance' always requires more than an individual standing alone.[82] Indeed, the force of associative action now looked like the only effective way of asserting rights. As Laski put it, 'the individual is lost . . . unless there are fellowships to guard him'.[83] The first answer to the question 'how are we to re-establish the individual in his fundamental rights?' was that groups and organizations ranging from churches to 'the British labour movement' are 'the greatest security we possess'. [84]

The second argument was essentially similar although its force lay in the longer term. It began as an observation that the 'vastness of modern states' led to 'the helplessness of individuals in the grip of enormous organisation'.[85] The argument then led to an insistence that 'if the individual is not to be a mere pigmy in the hands of a colossal' government machine 'there must be such a division of social powers as will preserve individual freedom'. Powers must be balanced one 'against another that the individual may still count'.[86] There were previous models to consider emulating in this regard and, as such, the geographically organized federalism of the United States combined with the separation of powers was widely admired by the new pluralists. Ultimately, though, Cole and Laski rejected this American model as a guide for British debates. 'There can be no solution to the problem . . . by a division of legislative and executive powers', Laski wrote, because such a division failed to go far enough in breaking up the powers of distinct groups and classes. A fundamental question for these new pluralists, then, was how 'to realize . . . the benefits of the separation of powers' without relying upon the American model. A thoroughgoing doctrine of associational independence was, or at least was part of, the answer. 'A great deal could be done', Russell insisted, by 'giving more autonomy to professions, trades and interests'.[87] Cole was equally clear, stressing that 'if the individual is not to be merely an insignificant part of a society' then the

---

[82] Barker, 'Discredited State', 110.

[83] H. Laski, 'A Wrong Kind of Textbook', *New Republic*, 1 July 1916, 232. For Laski's direct debt to Tocqueville, see H. Laski to O. W. Holmes, letter dated 5 July 1918, in de Wolfe Howe (ed.), *Holmes-Laski Letters*, 159–60. For Tocqueville's more general influence on British political thought in this period see Burrow, *Whigs and Liberals*, 101–25.

[84] G. D. H. Cole, 'National Guilds and the Division of Powers', *New Age*, 14 December 1916, 153, and H. Laski, 'The Aims of Labor', *New Republic*, 8 June 1918, 179.

[85] B. Russell, 'Why I am a Guildsman', *Guildsman* September 1919, 3. See too anon., 'Mr Bertrand Russell's Socialism', *New Statesman*, 24 November 1923, 220.

[86] G. D. H. Cole, 'National Guilds and the Balance of Powers', *New Age*, 16 November 1916, 58–9.

[87] B. Russell, 'State and its External Relations', *Proceedings of the Aristotelian Society*, 16 (1916), 309. See too C. D. Burns, 'Principles of Social Reconstruction', *International Journal of Ethics*, 27 (1917), 384–7.

powers in that 'society must be divided in such a way as to make the individual the link between its autonomous but interdependent parts.'[88] Only in a situation where power was dispersed between differing groups, Laski concluded, could 'the centre of importance [be] . . . referred back to the individual'.[89] In the immediate post-war years, then, the new pluralists offered two protective arguments for the 'pluralistic state'. '[L]iberty', Laski summarized, 'results from a division of forces, and the organization of a contingent system of resistances is the only way in which it can be preserved.'[90]

Important as these arguments were, though, they did not exhaust the new pluralist repertoire. In the early 1920s, Cole led Laski and colleagues in producing a more constructive argument that urged a re-examination of the connection between associations and individual freedom.[91] The argument was presented at its clearest in Cole's most abstract book, *Social Theory*, which, as the London *Nation*'s review summarized, sought to illustrate how the new pluralists should reconcile the claim that 'man himself, the individual, is the central fact' with the recognition 'he cannot continue by himself alone [but] must form associations'.[92] The detailed argument began with an acknowledgement that not all the component parts of an individual's desire-set are the same. As Cole put it, 'some desires are of a simple character and only require a simple translation into . . . action for their fulfilment . . . But very many other wants are complex, and require for their fulfilment not a single act of will or action but a whole course of action sustained by a continuing purpose'. It was in these cases that 'the need for organisation may arise'.[93] Cole then stressed that such organization may at first be provided by simple personal planning. An individual may try and pursue some complex and detailed goal by setting himself a personal timetable or following a particular, personally formulated, programme; but Cole also recognized that occasionally the intricate or multifarious nature of the desire before the individual may have other, rather more important, consequences. In such cases, 'the individual may find that the purpose before him . . . can only . . . be furthered by his acting in common with other individuals and undertaking in common with them a course of action which, he hopes, will lead to the satisfaction of the want which he is conscious in himself . . . This consciousness of a want requiring co-operative action for its satisfaction is the basis of association.'[94]

---

[88] Cole, *Self-Government*, 91–2. See too Laski, *Foundations*, 86.

[89] H. Laski, 'Industrial Self-Government', *New Republic*, 27 April 1918, 391.

[90] Laski, 'Pluralistic State', 718.

[91] For Laski's debt to Cole in this regard see the similarity in his formulation in *Grammar*, 71–2.

[92] Anon., 'Society and the Guilds', *Nation*, 15 May 1920, 212. See too T. R. Powell, 'The Functional Organization of Society', *Nation (NY)*, 13 October 1920, 413–4.

[93] Cole, *Social Theory*, 33.

[94] Cole, *Social Theory*, 34. The range of desires to which Cole took this to be connected was immense. On the simplest level, Cole was aware that some desires required coordinated action over the long term to reach fruition. On the more complex level, he was willing to note that some desires include a consideration of the situation and behaviour of others. Cole was aware that often individuals wish to interact with each other and, indeed, see others behave in a particular way.

An individual's goods, although potentially unique and deriving from an 'unabsorbed personality', may well require collective action in the form of a common acceptance of certain rules, regulations, and modes of behaviour. Liberty, even when reconsidered in individualist terms, still required associations. In forming associations, men were understood to be cooperating voluntarily in order to pursue their own ends. As Cole succinctly put it, they may begin to 'act together' but they remain 'acting for themselves'.[95]

On this account, associations had to be independent, free from outside interference, in order successfully to enable their members to pursue or express certain parts of their own individual will. This argument translated into a demand that associations generally be relieved of interference by the state, other associations, or outside individuals. The details of the case proceeded in two stages. First, and most straightforwardly, on the new pluralists' account it was up to the members of the association themselves to decide upon the purpose and nature of the association. It was certainly not for judges or other state officials to dictate what constituted a legitimate union activity. The debates over trade unions' political engagement which began with the Osborne judgement and continued with the arguments over some unions' decision to employ programmes of 'direct action' for ends deemed by others to be 'political' rather than 'industrial' brought the debate very firmly into the public arena. Cole and Laski lined up behind the Miners' Federation leader Robert Smilie's claim that it was for trade unionists themselves to choose where 'political questions end and trade union questions begin'.[96] Cole emphasized the point quite clearly: 'if men have formed an association for one purpose' then neither the state nor any other agency can 'properly tell them that its function is to do something quite different'.[97] Second, and more importantly, on this account all associations aided individual freedom only in so far as they further a particular individual will. If a man wishes to play football, he may form or join an association of other football-lovers in order to facilitate a good game; if he wishes to express a religious conviction he may join a church; or if he wishes to seek improvements in his position at work he may found a trade union. Associations may also further decide upon and implement rules and regulations in order to make their operation possible: the football club will need a set of rules of play to facilitate a good game. Those rules are legitimate only in so far as they are closely connected with the wills and desires of the individuals who came together in order to pursue some particular end.

This formula of legitimate association raised serious questions as to the role of the state, both in its ideal and in its institutional form. In so far as the

---

[95] G. D. H. Cole and W. Mellor, *The Meaning of Industrial Freedom* (London: George Allen and Unwin, 1918), 4.

[96] See the debate on 'Trade Unions and Direct Action' in Labour Party, *19th Annual Conference Report of the Labour Party* (London: 1919), 116–23.   [97] Cole, *Social Theory*, 53–4.

existing state could be described as an association at all, it was all-encompassing, compulsory, and, to a considerable extent, pre-eminent. Cole and Laski, therefore, attempted to reconstruct the state to fit into this model of the legitimate association. 'The state', Cole contended, should be understood as 'the national geographical grouping, and as such can claim to represent those elements in the common life which are best represented on a geographical basis.'[98] 'As a territorial or geographical association,' he continued, 'the state is clearly marked out as the instrument of those purposes which men have in common by reason of neighborhood.'[99] This reasoning, of course, denied the state pre-eminence over other associations. On the socialist pluralists' account, the state was simply one association—a national, geographical association—among others, and each association was to be 'the ultimate authority in its own sphere'.[100] If competing associational loyalties pulled their members in different directions, it was contended, it would be up to individual members of these associations to decide upon their loyalties in each particular case. As each individual 'was linked to a variety of associations', he should decide which one to lend his support to. The connection between liberty, in its new individualist conception, and associational independence was thus re-established. Even after the concept of liberty had been made consonant with the socialist pluralists' radical individualism, it was still seen to require that associations be able to operate free from the hindrance of the central state.[101] Individualism and pluralism were reconciled.

Associational governance: democracy

If this were all that there was to the new pluralists' institutional programme, then it may appear that the Figgisian pluralists and the new socialist pluralists merely took different theoretical paths to legitimize the same practical objective: a different conception of freedom justified the same set of institutional guidelines. In fact, however, the socialist pluralists' theoretical revision of their earlier mentors' conceptual position also resulted in some substantial alteration in the political programme associated with pluralism. The primary difference between the new pluralists and the old lay in the observation that, unlike their predecessors, the socialist pluralists accepted associational independence as a *necessary* but far from a *sufficient* condition for the protection and enhancement of individual liberty. To put that another way: whereas on the Figgis model it was plausible to argue that associations themselves should be able to determine the nature of the goods their members should pursue,

---

[98] Cole, 'Conflicting Social Obligations', 152.

[99] Cole, *Self-Government*, 7–79. See too Laski, *Foundations*, 70.

[100] Cole, *Self-Government*, 85.

[101] This, of course, leaves open the question of whether there was *any* role left for the state, for which see Chapters 5, 6, and 7.

the new socialist pluralists considered that the individualist building blocks of their conception potentially placed associations and individuals in direct conflict. Scholars are simply misguided when they assert that neither Cole nor Laski was aware that sometimes 'groups may be the oppressors'.[102] Both theorists explicitly recognized that it is quite possible that an 'association may so trammel' an individual 'as to leave him no range for free choice or personal self-expression'. Their colleagues and friends were even more insistent. As Ivor Brown put it, the new pluralists were concerned that a 'group may itself be a rigid and tyrannous institution, as bad as Leviathan itself':[103] the 'evils of an absolute state' could not be cured 'by the multiplication of absolutes'.[104] The result of such an observation was that, in order to be conducive to freedom, associations had to be of a very particular sort. Figgis had frequently rejected calls for a reconstruction of the internal structure of associations. Claiming that only each association collectively could choose the form of its internal construction and composition, Figgis insisted that each independent association was 'to rule itself and have its own laws'.[105] The socialist pluralists, however, were not so retiring; associations were to be free from external interference only so long as they were internally structured in a particular way.

The first concrete aspect of the divergence between this new pluralism and the old thus centred on a limitation of what associations could expect of their members. For the socialist pluralists, associations deserved to remain unhindered only in so far as they assisted the individuals who comprised them to pursue the fulfilment of their own personal desires.[106] These associations may have rules and regulations to assist them in their daily operation, they may impose some restrictions on individual behaviour in order to make the associations' goals achievable; but those regulations had to be connected directly to the purpose for which the association was formed. This worry combined with Cole and Laski's observation that an individual's will is not monolithic or unitary but consists of a collection of many different desires or inclinations. As a result, one individual may wish to be a member of many different associations, each affiliation with the aim of assisting him to pursue the fulfilment of one particular desire. As Cole expressed it, 'the position of the individual as the source and sustaining spirit is clear, and the associations show plainly as only partial expressions . . . of the will of the individual . . . they [thus] have no superiority over him and their claim is limited to what he surrenders to them for the performance of their functions'.[107] The sanctions which any association can apply to its members must be either totally confined to their particular sphere

---

[102] A. Vincent, *Theories of the State* (Oxford: Basil Blackwell, 1993), 216.

[103] Cole, *Social Theory*, 181, and I. Brown, 'Freedom and Dr Figgis (continued)', *Guildsman*, February 1920, 7. See too Brown, *English Political Theory*, 166–7.

[104] M. Cohen, 'Communal Ghosts and Other Perils in Social Philosophy', *Journal of Philosophy*, 16 (1919), 689.   [105] Figgis, *Churches*, 261. See too Nicholls, *Pluralist State*, 32.

[106] See Cole, *Labour in the Commonwealth*, 200.   [107] Cole, *Social Theory*, 191.

of interest or have a very limited effect on their members' lives beyond the association. The associational regulation cannot have a seriously adverse effect on a
member's life beyond the association.[108]

It also followed from these pluralist assumptions that entry and exit
requirements should be made as lax as they possibly could be. In particular,
it demanded that the individual's formal and effective right to exit the association, if he feels dissatisfied with it, should be absolutely guaranteed. In
order to ensure that associations do not 'crush' the individual, Russell
insisted, 'membership of an organisation ought to be voluntary'.[109] Tawney
emphasized the importance of this issue as early as 1914, insisting that each
and every industrial association 'must be entered freely'.[110] Likewise, Cole
promised with regard to his proposed industrial associations, freedom
required that 'there will be easy transference from guild to guild'.[111]

More significant still, from the years immediately prior to the First World
War to those immediately after, Cole, Laski, Tawney, and colleagues were
committed to the idea that *democratic* mechanisms were essential in 'any and
every form' of association.[112] Whereas democracy in local and national
government had been continuously extended throughout the decades previous to the emergence of pluralism, the vast majority of non-governmental
industrial and social associations retained the hierarchical structures of old.
The pluralists of the Figgis school had often celebrated such traditional structures, understanding them as an integral part of the self-determination of
associations. Figgis frequently insisted that his pluralism 'recognizes head-
ship, inequality and rules'.[113] No such sympathy, however, was found in the
newer brand of pluralism. There the asymmetry between the politics of
government and the politics of associations was fiercely rejected.

This is not to claim that Cole, Laski and their colleagues wished to encourage an extension of Westminster-style representative elections into industrial
and social associations. The argument went far further than that.[114] These
theorists demanded far more than a democratic system designed to make officials accountable by the processes of infrequent election. Instead, the theorists uniformly urged the construction of a system that would enable the
'fullest participation' of every individual in the associations of which he was
a member.[115] Indeed the commitment to democracy went further still, for all
the socialist pluralists were not only convinced that organizations needed

---

[108] See Cole, *Social Theory*, 36 and, for a clear summary exposition of Laski and Cole's views on
the issue, N. Wilde, 'Plural Sovereignty', *Journal of Philosophy* 16 (1919), 658–65.

[109] Russell, *Principles*, 139.   [110] Tawney, *Commonplace*, 74.

[111] Cole, *Self-Government*, 292.   [112] Cole, *Guild Socialism Restated*, 12.

[113] Figgis, *Will*, 289 and *Gospel*, 51–5.

[114] See H. Laski, 'Can Political Democracy Survive?', *Fabian News*, November 1923, 42–3. In this
way they differed from some left-liberal theorists of the time. See the brief discussion in Freeden,
Liberalism Divided, 59.

[115] Cole, *Social Theory*, 114.

democratic restructuring but they were equally determined that there should be a vast increase in each individual's *proclivity* to participate in those structures. Members of democratized associations must initially develop an inclination to involve themselves in oversight, to remain 'alert and keenly critical' of their officials' activities. Eventually, 'the largest number of persons' had to be passing 'effective judgement' in the day-to-day operation of their associations.[116] Participation in the politics of associations had to be not 'passive but active in character'.[117]

Despite the continuous assertion that 'self-government is good in *every* sphere', as with associational independence it was the industrial realm which received the most attention.[118] The primary 'defect' of modern economic organization was tied carefully in to the new pluralists' account of a legitimate association. Although, that is, 'economic organisations, such as railway companies, subsist for a purpose', at the present 'this purpose need only actually exist in those who direct the organisation; the ordinary wage earner need have no purpose beyond earning his wages'.[119] Workers laboured within industrial associations, they were formally members, but they did not necessarily share the ideals or purposes of the associations. Their associational membership, therefore, did nothing directly to enhance their freedom; indeed, in so far as the association's rules placed restrictions on their lives their freedom was impaired.[120] It was simply unacceptable, as Tawney so often phrased it, that an individual 'politically can be a citizen' whilst in industrial associations 'he is neither a citizen nor a partner but a hand'.[121] In the new industrial groups, the guilds of a guild socialist utopia, 'responsibility for the maintenance of the service should rest upon the shoulders of those, from organiser and scientist to labourer, by whom, in effect, the work is carried out'.[122]

Radical as they now sound, the popularity of these demands for industrial democracy was not confined to these theorists. Industrial democracy was an astoundingly popular cry as plans for social reconstruction were drawn up during and after the war. Indeed it was common throughout the British left to understand trade union militancy as reflecting the desire of working people to democratize industry. Many held that it was 'men's exclusion from control over the organisation and apparatus' of industry which lay at the root 'of all their discontent'.[123] The Labour Party's wartime leader Arthur Henderson

---

[116] Cole, *Social Theory*, 191.

[117] Laski, *Foundations*, 88. See too G. D. H. Cole, 'Democracy and the Guilds', *New Age*, 4 February 1915, 370–1; Cole, *Guild Socialism Restated*, 12; Tawney, *Acquisitive Society*, 66.

[118] G. D. H. Cole, 'Guild Socialism', *Fabian News*, November 1914, 83 (emphasis added).

[119] Russell, *Principles*, 37.

[120] See R. H. Tawney, 'The Conditions of Economic Liberty' (1918), reprinted in R. Hinden (ed.), *The Radical Tradition: Twelve Essays on Politics, Education, and Literature* (London: George Allen and Unwin, 1964), 101–2.   [121] Tawney, 'Conditions', 104.

[122] Tawney, *Acquisitive*, 111.

[123] Tawney, 'Conditions', 102. See too L. Olds, 'The Temper of British Labor', *Nation (NY)*, 19 April 1919, 601–3.

insisted likewise that the wave of strikes which crossed Britain at the end of the war was not 'concerned solely with material or economic ends' but was the result of a frustrated demand from the workers 'to take a larger share in the control of industry'.[124] An extensive number of motions at the British Trade Union Congress seemed to illustrate the point.[125] Such democratizing opinion even penetrated governmental circles. Responding to wartime industrial unrest, the government established a commission to investigate management of the coal industry—the Sankey Coal Commission—and set up a series of compulsory joint consultative committees of workers and management in a number of troubled industries—the so-called Whitely Councils.[126] Such developments provided concrete, if partial, illustrations of the British establishment's conviction that there was significant popular demand for widespread democratization. They were also widely celebrated.[127] Frank Hodges of the British Miners' Federation, who became involved in pluralist circles through his friendship with Cole, observed in 1920 that 'any discussion of the control of industry by the men actually engaged in it is now beyond the academic stage'.[128]

For all the socialist pluralists, however, the popularity of these proposals was not the central issue. The justification for industrial democracy had again to be found in the individualist conception of freedom; it had to be demonstrated, as Tawney put it, that it 'is the condition . . . of freedom that men should not be ruled by an authority which they cannot control'.[129] The task of connecting liberty and democracy was, however, far from easy. Those who advocated extended democracy in the early twentieth century often relied upon an idealist-style conception of freedom. As such, many of the pluralists' contemporaries were absolutely convinced that if democracy could be argued for in terms of freedom at all, it would have to be through use of an idealist or quasi-idealist conception. Laski's undergraduate tutor, Ernest Barker, emphasized the point with great earnestness in 1914. 'One defends democracy', Barker urged, 'not as a form of government but as a mode of spiritual expression.' Democracy is 'an eliciting and enlisting force, which draws from us energies of thought and

---

[124] A. Henderson, 'The Industrial Unrest: A New Policy Required', *Contemporary Review*, 115 (1919), 361.

[125] See for examples, the debates in Trades Union Congress, *53 Annual Conference Report* (1921), 80, and *54 Annual Conference Reports* (1922), 63 respectively.

[126] See Justice Sankey, *Report of the 1919 Royal Commission into the Coal Industry* (1919), reprinted in F. Hodges, *Nationalisation of the Mines* (London: Leonard Parsons, 1920), 133–50, and the *Report on the Establishment and Progress of Joint Industrial Control* (London: HMSO, 1923). See too N. Ridell, 'The Age of Cole? G. D. H. Cole and the British Labour Movement, 1929–1933', *Historical Journal*, 38 (1995), 936.

[127] Although they were, of course, not radical enough fully to satisfy Cole, Laski, or Tawney. See *National Guilds or Whitely Councils?*, anonymous and undated pamphlet in Nuffield College, Oxford, The National Guilds League pamphlet collection. [128] Hodges, *Nationalisation*, 113.

[129] Tawney, *Acquisitive*, 8.

of will which we should not otherwise expend'.[130] Even those guildsmen who still clung to a quasi-idealist, Figgisian vision also understood the role of democracy in these terms. S. G. Hobson, for example, distinguished between a quasi-idealist justification for democracy in terms of shaping a 'spiritual life' and an individualist one that celebrated 'selfish interests, vaulting ambition, or arrogant pretension'.[131] If democracy were to be justified in terms of liberty, then the latter concept would have to be defined in a manner which appealed to such noble values.

The socialist pluralist movement, however, had emerged in direct opposition to such a conceptual understanding. As Ivor Brown insisted, these new pluralists were committed to 'deny the right . . . of the Webbs or of the COS brigade to go round telling people what they really want'. Whereas a theorist equipped with an idealist conception of freedom could insist 'that he knows better than Richard Roe what Richard Roe really wants', to the new pluralists such a claim was 'the final and supreme poppycock'.[132] Freedom involved allowing diverse individuals to pursue diverse life-styles in diverse associations. If the socialist pluralists were convincingly to urge the existence of an affinity between the concepts of liberty and democracy, therefore, they needed to search and argue for a connection which would not violate the individualistic basis of their own conception of freedom.

Many contemporaries considered such a task impossible. In prolonged debate with Ivor Brown, the Figgis-inspired guildsman A. E. Randall argued that 'if he really does deny the right of himself or anybody else to "go round telling people what they really want" I cannot see any justification for his propaganda of *democratic* guilds'.[133] One of the leading American commentators on British pluralism, Kung Hsiao, agreed, insisting that 'Mr Cole's contention that politics can deal only with the actual wills of individuals . . . is to surrender all arguments for democracy'.[134] Many latterday commentators have reached the same conclusions. Andrew Vincent argues that Laski's conception of freedom had, in the end, to be reliant upon an 'idealist formula' even though Laski had 'rejected the entire substratum upon which that formula rests'.[135] Tony Wright likewise charges that Cole's 'treatment of the relationship between democracy and freedom was . . . unsatisfactory' because his individualist conception of freedom could not have done the theoretical work which was demanded of it.[136]

---

[130] Barker, 'Discredited State', 116.

[131] S. G. Hobson, 'Guilds and their Critics: Nation, State and Government', *New Age*, 13 June 1918, 101. See too R. de Maeztu, 'Not Happiness', *New Age*, 8 July 1915, 225–6, and 'On Liberty and Organisation', *New Age*, 19 August 1915, 377–8.

[132] I. Brown, 'Democracy and the Guilds', *New Age*, 18 February 1915, 436–7.

[133] A. E. Randall, 'Autocracy and the Guilds', *New Age*, 11 February 1915, 408.

[134] K. Hsiao, *Political Pluralism: A Study in Contemporary Political Theory* (London: Kegan Paul, 1921), 158–60 and 152.   [135] Vincent, *Theories of the State*, 197–8.

[136] A. Wright, *G. D. H. Cole and Socialist Democracy* (Oxford: Oxford University Press, 1979), 68.

Defending democracy

The socialist pluralists did, though, initially try to present a defence of their democratic ambitious within the bounds of their new individualist conception of freedom. They did so by proffering a set of contentions based upon an argument from John Stuart Mill's *Considerations on Representative Government*.[137] On Mill's account, public involvement in state-level politics is necessary in order to prevent the government of the day overstepping the boundaries created by individual rights. The best security for the protection of freedom comes from a population prepared and able enough to defend its rights.[138] Aware of what Walt Whitman described as the 'never-ending audacity' of officials, the socialist pluralists argued that rights are most likely to be respected when authorities bent on interference are mindful that the 'invasion of those rights will result in protest, and if need be, resistance'.[139] On such an account, a democratically involved populace would be more likely to recognize the intervening presence of a government or an administrative elite than an apathetic one. An active citizen body would also be able and organized enough to 'compel [the] repudiation' of an interfering administration if such action became necessary.[140] As a result administrations in associations overseen by an active citizenry are unlikely even to attempt to overstep their boundaries, aware as they are that such actions would invoke a fierce and negative response. Participation on this model, then, simply ensures the fulfilment of the promise of protection offered by restrictive rights.

To Cole, Laski, and Tawney, the argument from protection applied equally well to the work-place as they did to the political organs of the state. The rules and regulations of work officials were, after all, as likely to block some individuals' pursuit of their own goals as were the interventions of government. Nondemocratic industrial organizations, after all, rarely have to 'take into account' the wills and desires of 'those who work in them'; and non-democratic social organizations may include officials determined to take the association in a direction directly antithetical to the interests of their members.[141] Charters of rights were just as useless in industry as in politics unless backed up with the effective means of protection provided by participation. Indeed, democracy in the work-place could also overcome the initial vagueness of industrial rights. Democratic forums would enable workers to describe the sorts of practices that they felt seriously threatened their ability to pursue their own conceptions of the good in their daily working lives.

This argument most obviously offered a counterbalance to the prevailing

---

[137] See D. Thompson, *John Stuart Mill and Representative Government* (Princeton: Princeton University Press, 1976) for an invaluable modern introduction.

[138] See R. H. Tawney, 'Lecture on Freedom', British Library of Political Science, The Tawney Papers, 19/1/20.   [139] Laski, *Grammar*, 144.

[140] Laski, *Grammar*, 152.   [141] H. Laski, 'State in the New Social Order', 4.

behaviour of unelected and unaccountable leaders of industry. It was on these lines that Cole's friend and ally, deputy leader of the Miners' Federation Frank Hodges, argued that the whole issue of industrial democracy could be understood as 'the struggle to shake off the imposition of external wills because the instruments of production are owned by such wills'.[142] The socialist pluralist theorists, though, did not restrict their worries merely to the interventions of managers, shareholders, or plutocrats. Cole, Tawney, and Laski drew heavily on their understanding of the behaviour of trade union leaders in making their case for expanding democracy into industry. In the wake of the wartime shop-stewards movement, tensions between grass-roots union membership and union officials grew apace. 'Events during the War', Cole concluded, 'have shown time after time how little the official machinery of trade unionism effectively represents the active will of the members.'[143] Experience of industrial disputes in the aftermath of the war continued to demonstrate that at best 'officials and executives [are] prone to lose touch with the feeling of their members' and, at worst, that 'there are tendencies on the part of trade union leaders to substitute their wills for those of their members'.[144] As such, increased democracy, Cole argued, was the 'only machinery which will make the will of the members effective'.[145] Participation would not only act as a deterrent to potentially malign political or economic administrations. Widespread participation would also limit the empathy problem that often lay at the heart of more well-meaning but nonetheless excessive interference. Officials who were continually exposed to the opinions and desires of their constituents were less likely to make the mistake of confusing their own ends and purposes with the ends and purposes of others. The new pluralists also believed that an increase in the level of involvement would decrease the inclination of more altruistic officials to interfere. Administrators who were made constantly aware of the wide diversity of human nature via the democratic process would not be so conceited as to presume they could assist in universal human development by restricting the pursuit of certain goals and promoting the attainment of others.[146]

Cole took this set of arguments further than his colleagues did. He pushed the case perhaps to its logical extreme by compounding this particular call for participation with an advanced theoretical concern regarding the nature of representation. Such was the level of Cole's explicit philosophic individualism that he saw *all* forms of representation, heavily scrutinized or not, as

---

[142] Hodges, *Nationalisation*, p. x.   [143] Cole, *Self-Government*, 22–3.

[144] G. D. H. Cole, 'Trade Unions and Democracy', *New Statesman*, 30 October 1920, 97–9

[145] See G. D. H. Cole, 'The Gun That Did Not Go Off', *New Statesman*, 23 April 1921, 67–8, and Laski as reported in K. Martin, *Harold Laski: A Biographical Memoir* (London: Gollancz, 1953), 66.

[146] This was an argument the pluralists continued to emphasize throughout the period. See, for example, Laski, *Foundations*, 43; 'More of the Adams', *Nation*, 6 August 1921, 687; *Grammar*, 71. Again it owed something to Mill: see A. Gutmann and D. Thompson, *Democracy and Disagreement* (London: Belknap Press, 1996), 42.

necessarily entailing a perversion of an individual's goals. Even if officials were duly elected and constantly examined, Cole was convinced that 'distortion and substitution of the will of the representor for that of the represented' would continue to exist.[147] Individuals, on Cole's scheme, are so diverse that, even in associations where members share a particular interest or goal, their individual outlooks on the nature of that goal, the ways to achieve it, or the priority it is given are always likely to differ. However much individuals need collective action to pursue their own desires, in joining any association an individual is necessarily forced into making a compromise; the individual is required to alter the exact nature of his desire, to make it susceptible to pursuit with others. As Cole stated it, although associational allegiance 'makes possible in one way a vast expansion of the field of self-expression . . . it also in another way distorts that expression and makes it not completely the individual's own'.[148] The fullest amount of participation possible was advocated, therefore, in an attempt to limit that distortion to its smallest level. It was for this reasons that Cole thought individuals not only needed to be involved in a continual process of scrutiny over officials but must also partake in the decision-making process itself. If an individual is actually able himself to shape the policies and regulations of an association, it was argued, then his ability to maintain an opportunity for the fullest expression of his particular desire is significantly enhanced. For Cole, the more an individual can shape an association's approach himself the more his particular understanding of the shared desire is likely to be enacted or enabled. Likewise, the more personally engineered the compromises he has to make in order to accommodate the desires of others are, the more they are likely to satisfy his own ordering of priorities, his own fundamental concerns. As one latterday advocate of this position has claimed, 'the only way that I can maximise my freedom is to ensure that the choices, and hence the actions, of the association are in accord with my own choices. And the only way to ensure that is to control the association's decision-making processes.'[149]

Despite the claims of contemporary critics and latterday interpreters, the importance of participation was thus, initially at least, explicitly and fiercely defended on grounds consistent with the particularity of the individual. No recourse to quasi-idealist claims regarding the fundamental moral worth of participation was explicitly made, and neither were there initially any claims regarding the possible valuable instrumental effects of increased democratization on individual character development.[150] Even where recourse to the

---

[147] Cole, *Labour in the Commonwealth*, 190. See too, *Guild Socialism Restated*, 14.

[148] Cole, *Social Theory*, 186.

[149] R. Archer, *Economic Democracy: The Politics of Feasible Socialism* (Oxford: Oxford University Press, 1996), 26.

[150] Paul Hirst claims in his *Associative Democracy: New Forms of Social and Economic Governance* (Cambridge: Polity Press, 1994) that the pluralist argument for associational democratization

idealist-style conception of freedom would have been easier, the socialist pluralists worked hard, and against the contemporary grain, to demonstrate that 'democracy is, in its philosophical essence, an individualist theory'.[151]

Revisiting perfection for democracy

For all its sophistication, however, this pluralist advocacy of democratic involvement was not without its critics. It was, these critics contended, an argument that held only if individuals, workers, and citizens themselves were insisting on the need for democratic institutions. If, on the other hand, individuals simply do not *want* to participate in the management of their own association's affairs then the pluralists' whole case would collapse.[152] Liberty, in the socialist pluralists' sense, was defined in terms of the possibility of the fulfilment of individual desire. Yet, as individuals, on the socialist pluralists' own account, possess radically diverse natures, then it must be the case that some would choose to pursue ends which do not involve active engagement in decision-making. Such involvement could then, for some, be a distraction from the pursuit of their own desires. Worse still, it could easily be assumed that the goals of many individuals may entail a life of quiet contemplation or consist in the actual avoidance of political activity. In this case it would seem that Cole, Laski, and their supporters were contending that liberty sometimes entailed commanding an individual to pursue an end he had specifically rejected. It needed to be resolved, therefore, how and why the socialist pluralists continued to perceive encouraged democratic involvement in a plethora of associations as essential to liberty, even as it would seem to be, on the socialist pluralists' very understanding of the concept, at least occasionally antithetical to it.

This dilemma seriously concerned the socialist pluralists, particularly as its solution appeared to be ascertainable only by once again examining the fundamentals of the concept of liberty itself. The socialist pluralists' arguments thus went through many permutations as they continuously sought to resolve this potential problem. Laski, in particular, continued to seek a resolution throughout the early 1920s. He penned a series of articles and tracts—most notably *Socialism and Freedom* and *The State in the New Social*

---

required recourse to a belief in, and advocacy of, a 'spontaneous and natural . . . spirit of fellowship in all human beings' (45) which he describes as a 'loose and careless piece of anthropology' (46). The above, though, should demonstrate that the socialist pluralists advanced no such claim. Cole, Laski, and Tawney certainly did believe that a greater sense of communality would follow the development of their form of 'associative democracy'; but they were clear that while fellowship may be a *result* of associational democracy it was neither a *cause* nor a primary *justification* of its development. See, for example, Cole, *Social Theory*, 35–7 and 79–80. Discussion of this theme is resumed later.

[151] Brown, *English Political Theory*, 163.

[152] See E. Pease, 'Self-Government in Industry', *Fabian News*, February 1918, 11–12, and G. Field, *Guild Socialism: A Critical Examination* (London: W. Gardner, Darton and Co., 1920), 90–4.

Order—considering the topic, and he returned to it most thoroughly in his first major post-war book, *A Grammar of Politics*, which he began to compose in 1921 and completed in 1925. Understanding that what was needed was a conceptual approach that was capable of challenging individuals' own accounts of their desires without presenting a fully 'perfectionist' theory on the idealist model, Laski decided to reconsider the detail of his opposition to each of the idealist contentions. His eventual solution began by agreeing with the idealists and their supporters that 'freedom' should be understood to consist *not* in the effective opportunity to pursue one's each and every desire but in the pursuit of the life of 'enrichment', pursuit of, that is, one's 'best self'.[153]

Critics instantly thought that this involved capitulation; but, despite their accusations, Laski persisted. Where it was actually essential to disagree with the idealists, he continued, was in their description of human nature and thus of human perfection. The nature of the 'best self' suggested by Laski continued to differ vastly from that posited by idealists, Fabians, and nationalist progressives. Most importantly, Laski insisted that the nature of the 'best self' was always unknowable: the goals, ends, and dispositions that would characterize it were not predictable. Laski's philosophic individualism and commitment to diversity remained, ensuring that to him it was futile to attempt to describe the component parts of human perfection. He held, in other words, that it was impossible to try to dictate 'what it is worth while to do or enjoy'.[154] Laski indeed took this claim even further. He was not only convinced that an individual's 'best self' was unknowable to others, but that it was not even a priori recognizable by the individual himself. On such a view, no individual can immediately perceive the goals he is 'best' able to follow, the ends that will give him the most satisfaction, the capacities it would be in his interests to develop, or the roles he is 'best' suited to fill. As such, an individual's 'best self' can be discovered only through a lengthy process of 'personal experimentation'.[155] In order to reveal the goals which are 'best' suited to his unique character, an individual must engage in a 'bewildering variety of acts' trying and testing various pursuits to see which collection provides the pathway to the attainment of a peculiarly personal perfection.[156] Experimentation is not a necessary component of everybody's perfection, but it is an essential means to its discovery.

With the admission that each person's 'best self' was unknowable to others and even a priori to himself, all attempts to predict the results of the human pursuit of perfection became futile. The contention that a common good would result from the attainment of each human end thus fell by the wayside. For Laski, there was simply no reason to presume that such coherence or unity would exist; it might, but it might not. Similarly, with the necessity for personal

---

[153] Laski, *Grammar*, 142–3.   [154] Laski, *Authority*, 55.   [155] Laski, *Grammar*, 95.
[156] Laski, *Liberty*, 26.

experimentation recognized, it remained implausible for the socialist pluralist to define liberty as the *attainment* of perfection rather than simply in terms of the *pursuit* of that end. Laski was indeed often willing to admit that perfection may never be reached, or at least that individuals may not know when they have reached it.[157] He was most certainly aware that, given the individual nature of 'best selves', it would be impossible for individuals to judge the level of each others' attainment. The concept of liberty for Laski, therefore, was understood as the possibility of engaging in the personal experimentation necessary to the discovery and pursuit of personal perfection. Freedom is respected, men are at liberty, when the opportunities required to engage in such experimentation are available and when individuals are not restricted from exploring their own natures and pursuing their own 'best' goals. Each man, Laski informed his audience, ultimately desires to 'be himself at his best' and 'freedom is the system of conditions which make that purpose effectively possible'.[158]

According to Laski, then, the conditions of liberty entailed the actual possibility of personal experimentation, and that experimentation demanded not only the absence of governmental interference but also the existence, in each individual, of an 'active mind'.[159] In order for any person to be able to engage in experimentation, to be able to reflect upon his own nature and goals, he must be given to 'the habit of thought'.[160] To be able to so experiment, an individual must be creative, willing to take intellectual risks, and prepared to explore new avenues of possibility. Such activity obviously demands a considerable degree of imaginative ability and intellectual commitment. Again, this was not to suggest that every individual's 'best self' contains a contemplative or intellectual element, nor was it even to claim that the exact process of discovery is always the same. It was, however, to contend that in order to discover the nature of the 'best self' each and every individual must be in a position to investigate the various possible forms that 'self' could take. Individuals, on Laski's account, must, therefore, be ready and able to investigate the nature of their own ends if they are to be effectively able to pursue their own full development.

It was this conception that was then used to defend the necessity of democratic involvement. Laski linked the two together by forcefully arguing

---

[157] It may be asked, of course, that if one could never know if one had reached perfection, what the point was of trying to find it in the first place, especially as perfection for some may reside away from the uncertain world of creative experimentation. In response, it could be suggested that what Laski was trying to do—with admittedly mixed success—was to find a justification strong enough to allow him to insist that everyone had creatively to engage with his own ends without concomitantly involving him in an insistence that experimentation itself was a necessary component of everyone's perfection. He wanted, that is, to urge experimentation without having to contradict the strongly individualist—and thus non-prescriptive—premises of his own argument. John Stuart Mill utilized a similar strategy in the face of the same dilemma of trying to justify his encouragement of 'experiments in living' without invoking a prescriptive account of each individual's nature. For a full account of this approach, see J. Gray, *Mill On Liberty: A Defence* (London: Routledge, 1996), 80–6.

[158] H. Laski, 'Socialism and Freedom', *Fabian Tract* 216 (London: Fabian Society, 1925), 8.

[159] Laski, *Grammar*, 143.   [160] Ibid.

that the experience of living in a non-democratic state or working in an authoritarian industry necessarily stifles the development of creative independence. Individuals who live in autocratic associations, who live, as he put it, 'at the behest of other men', become unable effectively to reflect on their own ends or to examine their own personalities.[161] On this view, if individuals are forced daily to follow rules and regulations shaped by others, a 'routine [fixed] from without', they become little more than 'animate tools' unable to think for themselves.[162] As one of Laski's cited sources for these ideas, Matthew Arnold, eloquently phrased it, the process of being 'heavily overshadowed' which is intrinsic to non-democratic societies has a 'depressing and benumbing effect' on an individual's ability to reflect and experiment.[163] Living under a non-responsive governmental regime, working within an undemocratic industrial organization, spending leisure time in a hierarchical social association would, Laski argued, result in an incapacity to develop individual thoughts and to shape one's own destiny. If individuals knew that their opinions did not matter, that they could not influence the decisions which shaped the direction of their own lives, they would necessarily begin to doubt their own value. Yet self-value, Laski concluded, was a necessary precursor to the intellectual effort, to the creativity, necessary for experimentation.

Based on these arguments, the solution to the dilemma of the defence of democracy was straightforward. Individuals had to be encouraged to participate even if they had an initial antipathy towards doing so because this was one sure means of guaranteeing the creative experimentation that lay at the heart of true freedom. A participatory democracy would release individuals from the psychological restraints which prevented experimentation; it would enable the development of the 'habit of thought' which liberty demanded. It did not even necessarily matter, in this regard, whether citizens and workers *actually* did exert any real influence in the decision making-process. What mattered was that the *felt* as if they did. Individuals who believed they were listened to, who thought their opinions were respected, would be willing to engage in the process of developing their own ideas and would thus acquire the capacity and the aptitude critically to engage with their own ends. In order to be free individuals had to feel free. To feel free they had to participate.

Conclusion

In offering this conceptual programme, Laski offered his fullest defence of the central contentions of socialist pluralist thought. A conception of liberty

---

[161] Laski, *Grammar*, 148.   [162] Ibid.
[163] M. Arnold, 'Democracy' (1861), in S. Collini (ed.), *Matthew Arnold: Culture and Anarchy and Other Essays* (Cambridge: Cambridge University Press, 1994), 6.

infused with a strong sense of philosophic individualism thus provided the basis of a demand for the radical decentralization and democratization of political, social, and economic power. Although Laski's formulation was new in the *Grammar*, the ideas themselves were present throughout the socialist pluralist movement. The emphasis on creative experimentation, on individual discovery, on active participation was shared throughout Cole, Laski, and Tawney's works. As the American commentator Harry Laidler noted, the idea that a non-democratic industrial system 'produced a slave state of mind, which the worker carried over with him into his social and political life' was a commonplace in socialist pluralist literature.[164] All of the socialist pluralists suggestions for institutional reform, moreover, were dependent on an insistence on the importance of protecting the distinctiveness of individuals. Associations were to be largely independent of state control because this helped individuals resist the incursions of government, and associations were to be internally democratic because this helped individuals resist the direction of associational elites. As Laski insisted, his commitment to individualism ensured that '[t]he will of a group ought not to be transformed into a mystical transcendent of the wills of its several members; it is surely better to admit that at bottom we are dealing with wills each one of which is at bottom unique' and which coalesce only 'in the common object after which they strive'.[165]

All of these arguments, however, could not have been much further removed from those suggested by the nationalist progressives in the United States between 1909 and 1914. Where Croly, Lippmann, and Weyl had accepted and radicalized the idealist conception, Laski, Cole, Tawney, and colleagues rejected it in its entirety. Furthermore, where the nationalist progressives had sought to strengthen a weak and divided system of governance, the socialist pluralists attempted to divide and even dismantle a relatively strong set of governmental institutions. Even in areas where the groups agreed, such as the endorsement of participatory democratic mechanisms, their supporting arguments were almost mirror opposites. For whereas the nationalist progressives argued that democratic participation was to be welcomed because it helped replace the selfishness of individualism with the desire to perform collective sacrifice, the socialist pluralists insisted that its benefits were to be found in the protection and assertion of individual difference. And yet, distinct as they were, the positions were far from static. As the war impacted on the domestic politics of the United States in much the same way as it impacted on Britain, even the most nationalistic, state-centric of American reformers began to reconsider their position. As they did so, these thinkers found Harold J. Laski in their midst. Having left England in the midst

[164] H. Laidler, *A History of Socialist Thought* (London: Constable and Co., 1927), 401.
[165] H. Laski, 'The New State', *New Republic*, 8 February 1919, 61.

of the turmoil of the First World War to work first in Canada and then in the United States, Laski spent his first few years arguing there that 'nothing is more greatly needed in America than critical analysis' of the kind that he had helped to develop in Britain.[166] To what extent his new American hosts listened and responded, and to what extent the perspective of the critic himself was affected by the response, are the questions with which Part II of this book begins.

---

[166] H. Laski, 'Labor and the State', *New Republic*, 1 June 1918, 152. For biographical details of Laski's time in the United States, see I. Kramnick and B. Sheerman, *Harold Laski: A Life on the Left* (London: Hamish Hamilton, 1992), 80–152.

II
DEBATE

4

From Nationalism to Pluralism

Introduction

Looking on into Britain in 1914, Herbert Croly, Walter Lippmann, and Walter Weyl paid relatively little attention to the early pluralist stirrings of Cole and Laski. During the early years of the war, it remained the theorists of the Fabian Society and their allies on the left of the New Liberal movement who provided the most enticing conceptual and political agenda overseas. These British thinkers, Croly and colleagues believed, shared essentially the same view of liberty and of community as the nationalist progressives. Furthermore, these groups also increasingly appeared able to translate those ideals into a viable political strategy. Both Fabians and New Liberals justifiably laid claim to having provided the inspiration for radical elements of the reform programme promoted by the Liberal government elected in 1906: a programme that observers believed had transformed the British government from a laggard into an extensive and active state machine. Even though some British radicals discounted the Liberal governments as excessively eager to compromise with conservative critics, the nationalist progressives could only dream of pursuing such a programme in the United States. In this regard, at least, Croly, Lippmann, Weyl and their allies all strove to make the United States more like Britain.

This pattern of allegiance was, however, destined to come under significant strain as the United States entered the First World War. Although the nationalist progressives were initially optimistic that the United States' entry into the war could precipitate a series of constructive domestic reforms, the political forces the conflict unleashed were far from conducive to progressive ideals. While the nationalist progressives looked for reconstruction and reform on a Fabian model, the United States instead lurched into reaction and repression. Nor did the end of hostilities assist. In 1920, as Warren Harding was elected to the presidency condemning government intervention and institutional innovation, the ambitions of nationalist progressivism appeared more unrealistic than ever. Personal crises and traumas compounded the disillusionment. The year 1918 witnessed the deaths of the *New Republic*'s benign proprietor, Willard Straight, and of one of its most noted columnists, Randolph Bourne. A year later, Walter Weyl, one of the journal's three found-ing editors and a theorist at the peak of his powers, died at the age of only 46.[1] The loss placed great strains on those who remained. In the early post-war years, Walter Lippmann and Herbert Croly argued continuously about the direction the *New Republic* should take, and Lippmann eventually departed from his permanent position on the journal's staff in 1921.[2] The strain was beginning to show.

Reflecting on all of these tensions and disappointments, most latterday observers have suggested that the nationalist progressive movement suffered a blow of 'sledgehammer finality' in the aftermath of the war. To these inter-preters, the nationalist progressive moment was over by the early 1920s.[3] Such an interpretation is, however, a substantial oversimplification of developments within nationalist progressivism during and in the immediate aftermath of the war. Rather than simply abandoning their beliefs and rejecting their previous aspirations, the nationalist progressives sought continually to reshape their ideological system in line with the new political demands. These efforts prompted a significant—if now all too often overlooked—outpouring from the leaders of the nationalist progressive movement. Walter Weyl completed *The End of the War* in the year before he died, and worked also on *The Concert of the Classes*, extracts of which were published posthumously in 1921. Walter Lippmann similarly analysed the challenges of the period in *Public Opinion* (1920), a text which radically challenged many essential ideals of the progres-sive past but which nonetheless remained firmly within the general tradition. Herbert Croly laboured simultaneously on *The Breach of Civilization*, and although he failed to complete it the manuscript was circulated amongst friends in 1921. Croly withheld it from the press as he remained unsure as to its conclusions. He was certain, however, as were his colleagues, that the war's greatest intellectual legacy should not be the abandonment of progressive ideals but a thoroughgoing 'reconsideration of former assumptions'.[4]

This chapter examines this reconsideration. It argues, in particular, that throughout these years academic and practical developments in Britain

---

[1] See Editors, 'Walter E. Weyl, 1873–1919.' *New Republic,* 19 November 1919, 335.

[2] See E. Stettner, *Shaping Modern Liberalism: Herbert Croly and Progressive Thought* (Lawrence: Kansas University Press, 1994), 161.

[3] S. I. Rochester, *American Liberal Disillusionment in the Wake of World War I* (University Park, Pennsylvania: Pennsylvania State University Press, 1977), 103. See too B. D. Karl, *The Uneasy State: The United States from 1915 to 1945* (Chicago: University of Chicago Press, 1983), esp. 33. A welcome counterblast is J. Thompson, *Reformers and War: Progressive Publicists and the First World War* (Cambridge: Cambridge University Press, 1987).

[4] H. Croly, 'The Breach of Civilization: Why Liberalism Fails' (1921), draft MS in Felix Frankfurter Papers (Frederick MD: University Publications of America, 1986), Reel 136, 2. This is not to deny that some abandoned ship entirely. For a light-hearted commentary on those who used the war as an opportunity to adopt a more conservative perspective, see W. Weyl, *Tired Radicals and Other Essays* (New York: B. W. Huebsch, 1921), 9.

continued to offer hope for American nationalist reformers even in the aftermath of the First World War. What changed was the nature and focus of the nationalist progressives' interest. Joining together with a new generation of progressive activists, Croly and Lippmann temporarily abandoned their search for convergence with British Fabianism and became directly embroiled instead with the Fabians' greatest British critics: the socialist pluralists. The experience of the war, it will be argued, did not just undermine the *possibility* of the nationalist progressives' reform agenda but threw into question the *desirability* of their fundamental ideals. In responding to this challenge, the nationalist progressives turned directly to the arguments of Cole, Laski, and Tawney, seeking to understand whether the conceptual approaches these socialist pluralists offered could avoid the pitfalls that had beset nationalist progressivism.

The chapter traces the evolution of this inquiry and assess its impact. It explores the emergence of this transatlantic dialogue between the progressives and the pluralists and analyses its initial consequences for the fundamental philosophical claims of the nationalist progressive movement itself. In so doing, it traces the detailed contours of academic exchange, exploring the evolution of the nationalist progressives' theoretical arguments and tracing their implications for their overall political recommendations. The chapter concentrates, therefore, on the reworking of these progressives' ideological system as directed by a continual exchange with the ideas of the socialist pluralists. It is necessary to begin, however, not with rarefied philosophizing or academic debate but with the stark realities of an event whose impact was dramatic enough to push state-centric nationalist progressives into the arms of those staunch opponents of the state, the British socialist pluralists. That event, of course, was the First World War.

The War on Nationalist Progressivism

Croly, Lippmann, and Weyl's enthusiasm for the apparent political viability of British Fabianism and New Liberalism during the earliest of the war years was perfectly understandable. For despite building up an impressive theoretical framework and academic following in the years prior to 1914, the political arm of the 'New Nationalist' movement had signally failed to achieve much in the way of real success. While appearing to promise so much, Theodore Roosevelt's 'Bull Moose' campaign for the presidency in 1912 eventually came to nothing. Indeed, although Roosevelt gave the Republican Party genuine cause for concern, his participation in the election ultimately only made the victory of Democrat Woodrow Wilson all the more clear-cut. As Wilson advanced an agenda of economic and political decentralization, concerned nationalist theorists were left to predict the return to the localized politics of the past.[5] Even more difficult than defeat itself, though, was the loss of the leader. For shortly after the campaign, Roosevelt began to drift away from the genuinely radical elements of the Progressive platform and moved back to the conservative militarism of his own past; and the political figurehead of nationalist progressivism was lost to the movement for ever.[6] The Progressive Party he had spawned, moreover, effectively collapsed as soon as it had an electoral battle to face without the assistance of its erstwhile leader.[7] Although Croly, Lippmann, and Weyl's *The New Republic* continued to garner plaudits, its renown came from its ability to stimulate intellectual debate rather than to influence politics. As Europe entered the war, the political agenda that Croly, Lippmann, and Weyl had outlined still lay resolutely dormant.

It was from this vantage point that these theorists witnessed the outbreak of war in Europe. Horrified as they undoubtedly were by the savagery of modern military conflict, Croly, Lippmann, and Weyl were struck by the practical opportunities for radical reform the war presented in Britain. As the war intensified, the editors of the *New Republic* enthused, the British public was increasingly becoming aware of the 'need for and benefit of organization' of exactly the sorts the Fabians and their allies offered.[8] American observers quickly expected the British government to be pushed into even greater concrete programmes of reform than the peacetime Liberal government had attempted. When those programmes indeed came, with the government seizing effective control of key industries and expanding the social benefit programmes of the previous decade, the nationalist progressives offered them all a warm welcome. 'To the editor or the politician who regards widows' pensions as socialism' Britain now 'must be a strange spectacle', a characteristic *New Republic* editorial thus ran. This most 'conservative of empires' was adopting policies once dismissed as 'the wildest theories of the most scatterbrained visionaries', and it was doing so 'in swift gulps'.[9]

As events rapidly progressed it was not long before the nationalists began to believe that the outbreak of the European war might provide them with more than just an opportunity to admire from afar. Although Croly, Lippmann, Weyl, and colleagues were certainly not anxious to involve the United States directly in the military struggle, at least at first, they were undeniably enthusiastic about the prospect of duplicating the domestic side effects

---

[5] See H. Croly, *Progressive Democracy* (New York: Macmillan, 1914), 16–18 and W. Lippmann, *Drift and Mastery: An Attempt to Diagnose the Current Unrest* (New York: M. Kennerley, 1914), 136–9.

[6] See G. Gerstle, 'Theodore Roosevelt and the Divided Character of American Nationalism', *Journal of American History*, 86 (1999), 1280–307.

[7] See L. Hand to W. Lippmann, letter dated 10 June 1914, Harvard Law Library, Harvard University, Cambridge, Mass., The L. Hand Papers, 106/15.

[8] S. K. Ratcliffe, 'Enrolling the English Nation', *New Republic*, 15 September 1915, 207.

[9] Editors, 'Landslide into Collectivism', *New Republic*, 16 April 1915, 249.

of the conflict.[10] As conservative forces began to campaign for military 'preparedness' in early 1916, the nationalist progressives instantly attempted to drag it in a reformist direction. Here was an excellent opportunity to convince even the most sceptical of opponents of the need for radical change. Even the *New Republic*'s most clearly Germanophile correspondent, Randolph Bourne, believed by that June that the war in Europe could be used to 'set hosts of Americans to thinking out for the first time what a real national strength and readiness would mean'.[11] The 'system of moral training' that such an united effort would require, the *New Republic* editors agreed, should be used to promote 'a sense of public responsibility and a disposition to make personal sacrifices'. For a while it seemed as if preparedness could thus be a means to bring about all the changes needed for an enhancement of social and individual life. To the more optimistic of the nationalist progressives, the list of possibilities was almost endless: 'vocational competence, livelier human sympathies, intellectual alertness, adaptability and tenacity, and an imperturbable faith in the great democratic enterprise of indefinite individual and social improvement': all were to be by-products of the preparation for military struggle.[12]

When preparedness actually gave way to the United States' entry into the war itself in April 1917, the trajectory these thinkers travelled was almost identical: another brief period of shock was once again quickly followed by an optimistic expectation that the travails of international conflict would provide a still further opportunity to advance the cause of national progressive improvement. Such a prediction was boosted immediately by the leadership of President Wilson. Having abandoned his commitment to keep America out of the war, Wilson also left far behind any pre-war dedication to political and economic decentralization. Faced with a demand to reorganize governance on an unprecedented scale, Wilson increasingly drew on the advice of men like the former progressive campaigner Colonel Edward House, figures who urged the President to follow the institutional ideas of the nationalist progressives almost to the letter.[13] Wilson acted swiftly. Recognizing the need for an immensely expanded federal bureaucracy, he created a string of new executive agencies and boards, covering almost all aspects of American life. Most importantly, the federal government was charged for the first time with proactively pursuing economic stability, with providing social services, and with building a sense of national loyalty among the whole American

---

[10] Attitudes to the war itself are well documented in C. Forcey, *The Crossroads of Liberalism: Croly, Weyl, Lippmann, and the Progressive Era* (New York: Oxford University Press, 1967), 222–72.

[11] R. Bourne, 'A Moral Equivalent for Universal Military Service', *New Republic*, 1 July 1916, 217. See too A. F. Davis, 'Welfare, Reform, and World War One', *American Quarterly*, 19 (1967), 516–33 and J. A. Nuechterlein, 'The Dream of Scientific Liberalism: The New Republic and American Progressive Thought, 1914–1920', *Review of Politics*, 42 (1980), esp. 177–8.

[12] Editors, 'The Newer Nationalism', *New Republic*, 29 January 1916, 321.

[13] For Wilson and House, see R. Steel, *Walter Lippmann and the American Century* (London: Bodley Head, 1980), esp. 107–11.

people. Within six months, almost 20 executive boards had been designed to deal with industrial relations alone. As this remarkable feat of state-building got under way, the relationship between American nationalist progressives and their British counterparts even appeared temporarily to be reversed. Watching from afar as Wilson took Washington in hand, the British Fabian Graham Wallas wrote to the progressive jurist Learned Hand to congratulate the United States on the construction of the 'intellectually serious' and 'centralised Democratic State' for which 'The New Republic pleads'.[14]

As the business of governing a large-scale central state in wartime began in earnest, the American reformers' cause enjoyed a further boost as the need for professionals to staff these new agencies led to progressive personnel being swept into Washington. Felix Frankfurter led the way, leaving the Harvard Law School to head the War Labor Policies Board that would advise a government on how to use its new powers to 'seize factories and draft workers'.[15] Walter Lippmann's wartime position in Washington was even more elevated. Still only 27 years old, Lippmann struggled hard to avoid a military posting but when he did manage to avoid the front he was drafted instead into 'the Inquiry', a secretive governmental committee charged with providing the ideas and the information required to draw up the United States' war aims.[16] As Lippmann helped compose Wilson's 'Fourteen Points' for an eventual peace treaty, his place in world history was assured and with it the progressives' occupation of the centre of American politics seemed secure also. There were conservatives and businessmen in the new administration, of course, but at the start it was the progressives' opportunities that somehow appeared more central. And this was a judgement widely shared. Leading conservatives believed that progressives overwhelmingly dominated the war government: the 'radicals are so thick in Washington', one complained, 'that you cannot help but stumble over them'.[17]

With the capacity of the federal government dramatically enhanced and nationalist progressive personnel in key positions within the new structures, key progressive programmes found their way onto the immediate political agenda in a manner inconceivable prior to the war. The reform of industrial relations was of especial import. Even the most committed advocate of laissez faire or 'pure and simple' unionism had to recognize the force of the demands for change. The combination of an overwhelming demand for production and the loss of a fifth of the labour force to the armed services entailed that radical moves simply had to be made to entice the American worker into

[14] G. Wallas to L. Hand, letter dated 2 September 1916, L. Hand Papers, 44/16.
[15] See D. Montgomery, The Fall of the House of Labor: The Workplace, the State, and American Labor Activism, 1865–1925 (Cambridge: Cambridge University Press, 1987), esp. 374.
[16] For Lippmann's wartime activities, see Steel, Walter Lippmann, esp. 128–40.
[17] W. H. Barr, cited in J. Haydu, Making American Industry Safe for Democracy: Comparative Perspectives on the State and Employee Representation in the Era of World War One (Chicago: University of Illinois Press, 1997), 171.

greater productive effort. Nationalist progressives claimed to possess the solution and for a while at least they were taken at their word. The leadership of Wilson's newly established National War Labor Board was handed over to progressive lawyer Frank P. Walsh, who was determined to cajole sceptical businesses into introducing the form of carefully regulated 'industrial democracy' for which Croly and colleagues had long argued. Significant early successes were reported: collective bargaining rights began to be guaranteed, trade union membership soared, and an increasing number of large corporations agreed to establish consultative committees with their workers. Before the end of 1917, many progressive activists grew ever more optimistic. With industry now widely understood as a legitimate sphere of government intervention, the prospects for a complete transformation of the American economic system appeared better than ever. Intoxicated by their own success, some nationalists began to push for the complete nationalization of certain key industries, including railroads, steel, and coal mining.[18] The mechanisms coherently to plan and centrally to direct the economy in the common interest, for which nationalist progressives had always called, were finally destined, or so they believed, to become a reality.

Complementing these concrete economic reforms, the Wilson administration also exhibited an express dedication to encouraging the psychology of collective sacrifice that lay at the heart of the nationalist progressive project. Wilson, that is, was explicitly committed not just to mechanistic reform but to reform that reached into the heart and soul of each American citizen. To that end, he established a Committee for Public Information, headed by one-time progressive journalist George Creel. Determined to weld American citizens into 'one white-hot mass', Creel argued that as Americans struggled against a common enemy 'fraternity, devotion, courage, and deathless determination' would become the central characteristics of every citizen of the nation. Others quickly endorsed the ideal. Directly echoing Herbert Croly's dedication in *The Promise of American Life*, the Postmaster General Albert Burleson, another Wilson appointee, suggested that the time had come for every member of a 'minority' to become as 'one with the majority'.[19] Even the President himself joined the collectivist chorus. Once derided by the *New Republic* for desiring 'a revival of Jeffersonian individualism', the wartime Wilson warmly embraced the communitarian goals of nationalist progressivism.[20] '[S]ome day', he predicted, 'historians will remember these momentous years as the years which made a single person of the great body of those who call themselves Americans.'[21]

---

[18] See J. A. McCartin, *Labor's Great War: The Struggle for Industrial Democracy and the Origins of Modern American Labor Relations* (Chapel Hill: University of North Carolina Press, 1997).

[19] Albert Burleson, cited in R. Schaffer, *America in the Great War: The Rise of the War Welfare State* (New York: Oxford University Press, 1991), 15.   [20] Croly, *Progressive Democracy*, 16.

[21] G. Creel and W. Wilson, cited in Schaeffer, *America in the Great War*, 5, 6–7.

In its first few months, therefore, war was sweet for the nationalist progressives. Having reached an apparent political impasse in the early 1910s, the United States had been suddenly led by an unexpected war in a direction that the nationalist progressives themselves could justifiably claim to have mapped out. New centralized institutions were being created to direct the economy and the federal government was making a concerted effort to shape the attitudes of a whole nation. These gains also appeared to guarantee substantial future success. Although it was military conflict rather than domestic reform that was binding Americans of all sorts together, Walter Weyl contended, such a rich sense of 'solidarity, once gained, can never again be surrendered'. As 'rich man, poor man, beggar-man, thief' seemed 'to be fused' together for the first time in modern American history, nationalist progressives openly wondered if a moment of prophetic fulfilment was near. With the arrival of the war, perhaps even the *Promise of American Life* was about to be attained.[22]

From reform to repression

The cause for optimism was, however, not to last, for underneath the appearance of progressive success there lurked a darker side to the expansion of the American government in the war, far darker than that which the Munitions Act and the Defence of the Realm Act had revealed in Britain. Thinkers and activists who expressed scepticism about America's role in the conflict were swiftly and dramatically repressed. Such repression, moreover, was carefully orchestrated by the same administration that had seemed to promise progressives so much. In June 1917, at Woodrow Wilson's personal bequest, Congress rushed through an Espionage Act and followed it within the year with a Sedition Act. Executive officials, whether of conservative or progressive pedigree, employed these new legislative instruments to the full. Albert Burleson used the powers granted to him to prohibit dissenting journals from entering the US mail. At various times in the war, he impounded the communist *Masses*, the more moderate *Intercollegiate Socialist*, the liberal *Nation*, and even threatened the *New Republic* itself if it refused to follow editorial advice from the government.[23] More worryingly still, the Sedition Act enabled the United States Justice Department to pursue and arrest almost any political dissident that its officials feared could hinder the war effort. In the most celebrated case, the American Socialist Party leader Eugene Debs was tried and eventually imprisoned for urging non-compliance with military conscription, with the blessing of the Supreme Court—even of Justice Holmes. And Debs was just

---

[22] W. Weyl, *The End of the War* (New York: Macmillan, 1918), 159, 303–4.
[23] See D. Levy, *Herbert Croly of the New Republic: The Life and Thought of an American Progressive* (Princeton: Princeton University Press, 1985), 254.

the tip of the iceberg. The Justice Department relentlessly pursued many more activists, reporters, and thinkers throughout the war. By 1918, it had prosecuted over 2,000 radicals and secured convictions in over half of the cases it brought. As the war came to its close, the Department's officials had managed to imprison almost a third of the Socialist Party of America's National Executive Committee.[24]

In the wake of these systematic centrally directed attacks on dissenters came a trawl of even more restrictive activities conducted at a lower level. The overworked Justice Department happily devolved the responsibility for repression to local authorities and even directly to members of the American public themselves. As even the most far-fetched of reactionary arguments as to the necessities of war gained credence in Washington, it was easy to spread concern in the localities. In 1917, the Department encouraged the formation of the American Protective League, an organization which employed a quarter of a million patriots, mainly but not exclusively from small rural communities, to track down dissenters, to harry potential German-sympathizers, and to denounce draft-dodgers to the authorities. Both psychologically and politically empowered by its new-found status, the League and its allies then seized the opportunity to complement federal acts with more localized prohibitions on a host of lifestyles and life-choices of which they had long disapproved. Immigrant communities were especially harshly targeted. The relatively benign attempts at 'Americanizing' the incoming groups that characterized pre-war progressive-led efforts at affecting cultural integration rapidly shifted into ferocious attacks on the remnants of 'alien' cultures. Any sign that the primary national loyalties of these groups lay anywhere other than in the United States was fiercely denounced. Immigrants, it was argued, had to be and be seen to be '100% American'.[25]

It was not long before this general atmosphere of intolerance began to infuse the administration's broader political agenda. The swing from progressive reform to repressive reaction was particularly severe in industry and industrial relations. During the optimistic moments at the war's outset, the leader of the American Federation of Labor, Samuel Gompers, already closely connected to Wilson's Democratic Party, had initially exercised considerable

---

[24] For full details of the Justice Department's behaviour in the war, see D. M. Kennedy, *Over Here: The First World War and American Society* (New York: Oxford University Press, 1980), esp. 45–92, and Schaffer, *America in the Great War*, esp. 14–29. It is important to recall, however, that despite the continual attacks on the left, the Socialist Party's vote rose rather than fell during the war itself. In one particularly high-profile campaign for the New York mayoralty, the leading socialist activist and theoretician, Morris Hillquit received over 20% of the popular vote. Indeed some contemporary commentators detected a connection between Hillquit's success and the extent of federal repression by suggesting that the Socialist candidates collected liberal and anti-establishment votes that would in other circumstances have gone elsewhere. See J. Weinstein, *The Decline of Socialism in America, 1912–1925* (New Brunswick: Rutgers University Press, 1984), 119–26

[25] See D. King, *Making Americans: Immigration, Race, and the Origins of the Diverse Democracy* (London: Harvard University Press, 2000), esp. 85–126.

influence. He negotiated a voluntary no-strike deal in exchange for promises of greater union recognition. The deal, however, was a failure. Where most observers had expected industrial calm and compliance, industrial chaos swept through the United States. Shocked both by the economic privations of wartime—with rampant inflation combined with stagnant wages—and by the political consequences and opportunities of expanding state power, main-stream American labour mobilized as never before. There were an unprece-dented number of strikes—3,000 in the first six months of America's participation in the war—and they were of unprecedented volume, with 6,285,519 workdays lost in the same half-year.[26]

The Wilson administration's response to the unrest was to abandon the carrot of progressive reforms and to turn instead to the more traditional stick of industrial repression. It was the International Workers of the World (IWW) who bore the brunt of the attack. Manifold efforts were made all across the country forcibly to disband the 'Wobblies'. In one remarkable incident, over a thousand striking copper-miners in Bisbee, Arizona, were summarily deported out of the State; the miners were carted from town to town by vigi-lantes and eventually abandoned in the New Mexico desert. The legal author-ities clamped down on individual ringleaders even more dramatically. In Chicago, the leader of the IWW, 'Big' Bill Heywood, was sentenced to 20 years' imprisonment, a sentence he escaped only by fleeing to the Soviet Union.[27] Indeed, so worried was Washington about the influence of the IWW that the American State Department even prevented delegations from the British Trades Union Congress from sailing to the United States. Having apparently lost almost any sense of reality, the Wilson administration feared that these generally moderate British trade unionists would persuade their American counterparts to adopt the radical courses of political and industrial action advocated by the anarchists and the syndicalists of the IWW.[28]

When the war finally came to a close, it was the reactionary and not the reformist side of the Wilson administration that triumphed. In 1919, Wilson set about dismantling almost all of the progressive government machinery constructed during the war. As he did so, many large-scale corporations, now relieved of state regulation, began to abandon their wartime commitments. Organized labour responded with an enormous outburst of unrest. Industry once again became a battleground; the strikes of 1919 outdid even those of the war years in their ferocity. In an attempt to bring capital and labour together again, Wilson called two industrial conferences in Washington, but the result was only greater chaos and failure. As the balance of delegates was

---

[26] For an exceptional account of these developments see McCartin, *Labor's Great War, passim.*

[27] The story is recounted with great zeal in P. Renshaw, *The Wobblies: The Story of Syndicalism in the United States* (London: Eyre and Spottiswood, 1967), 213–42.

[28] See P. Kellogg to F. Frankfurter, letter dated 20 June 1918, Social-Welfare History Archive, University of Minnesota, Survey Associate Records, 75/588.

consciously biased in business's favour, even Samuel Gompers walked out in disgust. Progressives left the capital in droves, leaving the conservative leaders of business more firmly entrenched than ever. Beyond the industrial realm, the '100% American' movement expanded to stretch beyond immigrant cultures to questions of political allegiance as well.[29] Across the nation, great efforts were made to root out radicals of all sorts from public life. Combining the attacks on immigrants with those on radicals, Attorney General A. Mitchell Palmer, another progressive Wilson appointee, orchestrated the infamous 'Palmer raids'. Employing a motley collection of Justice Department officials, Protective League activists, and disgruntled informers, Palmer arrested hundreds of left-leaning politicians, thinkers, and organizers, all of foreign birth, and summarily deported them from the country.[30] Looking on it horror, it was not reform and economic solidarity that appeared to Weyl and colleagues, but reaction and repression.[31]

The initial response

Eager to distance themselves from the repression of the wartime government, most nationalist progressives argued that their reform agenda had been imperfectly implemented by the Wilson administration. There was, they initially argued, no reason to question nationalist philosophical essentials but only to regret the inadequate way in which they had been pursued. The central problem with the wartime state, on Croly and colleagues' first analysis, was therefore its tendency to allow unscrupulous politicians and bureaucrats to skew it away from serving the 'general' interest. Having finally been put into a position to regulate industry, for example, the American federal government was presented with an unparalleled opportunity to detect and to serve the common good, yet in exercising its new powers the incumbent administration consistently behaved 'less [as] a nationalist state' and more as 'a middle class institution'. 'The business men of the country became for the period of the war the licensed agents of the government', the *New Republic* complained, and they continuously abused their position.[32] It was in this way that the American government was unable justifiably to command 'the exclusive loyalties of men'.[33] Croly, Lippmann, and Weyl constantly employed the administration's failure to halt industrial unrest as the most powerful illustration of just this shortcoming. The central cause of the wave of strikes, the *New*

---

[29] See King, *Making Americans*, 100–7.

[30] For a contemporary perspective, see L. Post, *The Deportations Delirium of Nineteen-Twenty: A Personal Narrative of an Historic Official Experience* (Chicago: C. H. Kerr and Co., 1923).

[31] The literature on wartime and post-war repression is voluminous. For an excellent overall summary of these developments, see A. Dawley, *Struggles for Justice: Social Responsibility and the Liberal State* (Cambridge, MA: Belknap Press, 1991), 172–217.

[32] Editors, 'The Passing of Sectionalism', *New Republic*, 15 June 1921, 61.

[33] Editors, 'The Supremacy of the State: A Reply', *New Republic*, 15 June 1921, 192.

Republic insisted, was not the unwillingness of workers to make reasonable sacrifices for the good of the nation, but the willingness of the federal government uncritically to acquiesce to the demands of employers. For all the good work done by the National War Industries Board and for all Wilson's protestations of treating each side equally, the nationalists thus claimed, the Democratic administration was essentially unwilling to challenge the balance of industrial power. The result was an industrial policy that only very super-ficially resembled that of the nationalists; it was a policy that served to 'sharpen rather than to assuage the criticism of the industrially disfran-chised'.[34] For all of his dynamic ability to construct new governmental mech-anisms, Wilson left the economy unsettled and society divided.

The same story of lost opportunities and of misused institutional innova-tions characterized nationalist accounts of other elements of the wartime administration's behaviour. Wilson's Sedition and Espionage Acts, it was sometimes charged, were not mistaken in and of themselves, but they had been employed disastrously by short-sighted officials. Similarly, the idea of encouraging American citizens to do all they could for the war effort was not itself a bad one; but the small-town activists of the American Protective League had never been interested in building a genuine ethic of national soli-darity. Rather, Walter Weyl complained, they had sought to abuse their new-found position of authority to pursue their own sectional goals. It was peculiar and particular religious and traditional loyalties that lurked behind their activity and that explained their desire not to affect genuine cultural exchange and social integration but rather to force the end of 'gambling, whisky drinking, of beer drinking, of opium smoking, of horse racing'.[35]

This argument was, however, very difficult to sustain, whatever means were used to accuse the 'forces of conservatism' of misinterpreting national-ist ideals. Despite all their efforts to maintain the conceptual commitments of old, the very real consequences of the wartime experience were far too damaging. Even the most optimistic of the nationalist progressives was aware that it was simply not convincing to argue that all the problems of wartime repression were the result of the wrong people being in charge of the right mechanisms. Many of those who were directly implicated in the censorship and control of dissenting groups had, after all, possessed impec-cable progressive credentials. The nationalist progressives had all initially celebrated the appointments of Creel, Burleson, and Palmer.[36] Such embar-rassment was even more acute in industry. For those who had crafted the Wilson government's initial industrial strategy had often done so in a manner directly correspondent to the suggestions of key progressive thinkers.

---

[34] H. Croly, 'The Future of the State', *New Republic*, 15 September 1917, 181.

[35] W. Weyl, 'The Illusion of Progress' (1921), Special Collections, Rutgers University Library, The W. Weyl Papers, 2/24/3.

[36] See S. Cobden, *A. Mitchell Palmer, Politician* (New York: Columbia University Press, 1963).

The nationalist progressives had, therefore, to admit that the causes of the difficulties were far more deeply entrenched. And as such, the *New Republic's* editors began to worry that there was something intrinsic in the structure of the federal government, and not just in its personnel, that explained why for all his efforts Wilson had failed 'to provide an improved machinery for carrying out the collective purposes of the American people'.[37] Key parts of the state machine itself, at least as currently constituted, simply could not be trusted. It was as such that the nationalists marked out the first conceptual casualty of the war. Their belief in the essential reliability of the organs of the central state, unshakeable before 1914, even before 1917, was now at an end. From late 1918 onwards, these progressives' reflections on the central state were far more frequently negative than positive. If industrial peace was to return, and genuine social harmony to be reached, the post-war nationalists began to argue, the federal government would have to 'consent to a diminution and a redistribution of authority', at least for the time being.[38] Similarly, Walter Weyl contended that the 'wave of repression' that the conflict had introduced should not just be blamed on individual judges or advocates, but should be taken as an illustration of the 'utterly intolerable evils of our age of absolute states'.[39] The new generation of nationalist progressives was often to be found putting the matter even more bluntly. In late 1918, the *New Republic's* new industrial correspondent, Ordway Tead, argued that the pre-war conceptual approach would have to be rethought. It had, he insisted, placed 'the integrity of an abstract State ahead of the integrity of the individuals who comprise it'; and although Croly, Lippmann, and colleagues had only intended good when they had done so the result was that they had elevated the state as 'an abstraction, an unreal philosophical notion, into a fetish and drag[ged] down human personality into a place of comparative insignificance'. 'Today', Tead concluded, 'we can have none of it.'[40]

Tead's vigour opened the way for a more dramatic questioning of the essential efficacy and equity of the state machine. It even initiated an investigation into the idea's conceptual underpinnings. As the post-war years progressed, many leading nationalist progressives reconsidered the value of national communal unity itself. Whereas previously an enhanced sense of national belonging and solidarity had been described as the secret for individual fulfilment, now it too looked much more like a mixed blessing. During the war, the federal government had urged, just as the nationalist progressives had always done previously, that each and every citizen should prioritize the

---

[37] Editors, 'The Passing of Sectionalism', 61.

[38] Croly, 'Future of the State', 181. For an excellent summary of all of these arguments see N. Wilde, *The Ethical Basis of the State* (Princeton: Princeton University Press, 1924).

[39] Weyl, 'Illusion of Progress', 3 and R. MacIver, 'The Supremacy of the State', *New Republic*, 13 October 1917, 304.

[40] O. Tead, 'Labor Unions in a Democratic State', *Good Government*, 9 September 1918, 133.

common good over his personal interests. It had also made continual and conscious efforts to ensure that clear standard patriotic patterns of behaviour were set and that these ideals were realized. As such, the propaganda efforts of war, the *New Republic*'s editors noted, brought about 'the increasing standardization of American opinions, habits, and objects of popular consumption'.[41] But although on the surface this was a standardization for which the new nationalists had always longed, when it actually arrived it appeared far less desirable than had in theory. It was, after all, the people themselves as much as any agent of the administration who, in coming together in a solid, patriotic uniformity, would brook no disagreement. It was the American public, or at least a significant section of it, that eagerly lent support to the repressive initiatives of Palmer and Burleson and who often actively took the vigorous pursuit of a narrow and restrictive form of patriotism into their own hands. This led Croly and colleagues into a sharp reassessment of American national culture. Far from being overly individualistic, overly eager to hang on to individual difference at the expense of collective sacrifice, as the nationalists had always bemoaned, the 'average American' now actually appeared rather excessively 'suggestible', preferring not to resist reactionary incursions by the state but, at best, 'to sail with the wind' and, at worst, to imitate the most extreme measures of repression.[42] And as the problem changed, so too did the solution. The answer to America's problems was not more solidarity, but less, not more conformity, but greater diversity.

Taken together, then, these reflections on the problems of American wartime experience had damning consequences for the nationalist ideological system in general and for the conception of liberty and personal development that the progressives had inherited from the idealists in particular. In the wake of excessive, ill-focused state activity, the idea of liberty as consisting in the attainment by each individual of a communal perfection under the guidance of a centralized state was increasingly discredited in the United States, just as it had been several years earlier in Britain. As repressive act followed repressive act, and as the political centre gave credence to them all, the governmental involvement which had once seemed freedom's guarantor now appeared to entail that 'personal liberty' was actually coming to 'an end'.[43] The vast majority of progressive personnel experienced what Croly was to call a remarkable 'deflation of expectation'. The progressives' 'fixed beliefs', one *New Republic* correspondent declared, were 'shocked into disintegration'.[44] A conceptual approach that had once seem to be rivetingly modern now appeared to belong 'to a world . . . outgrown'.[45] Nor did this look like a short-lived phenomenon. The failures of the old system now

[41] Editors, 'Passing of Sectionalism', 61.   [42] Ibid.
[43] Editors, 'Economic Dictatorship after the War', *New Republic*, 12 May 1917, 37.
[44] J. Dewey, 'A New Social Science', *New Republic*, 6 April 1918, 292
[45] MacIver, 'Supremacy of the State', 304.

appeared not as much a contingent feature of wartime politics as a necessary flaw in the nationalist progressives' conceptual scheme. At the war's close, Croly himself, the father of nationalist progressivism, argued that the movement had fallen 'into a mistake from which the liberal tradition should have protected it' when it considered the 'democratic state or any other unbalanced centre of political power as a wise, patient and trustworthy servant of human liberation'.[46] As the federal government and State authorities turned on dissidents, on unionizing workers, and on immigrants, all in the name of protecting and enhancing national unity, the *New Republic*'s editors and correspondents moved away. '[I]f this is solidarity', the journal's editors concluded in a remarkably candid turn away from their previous position, then 'give us the old chaos and the old diversity'.[47]

Beyond Disillusion: The Birth of a Progressive Pluralism

Reflecting on this conjunction of political struggle and ideational disillusionment, it is easy to understand why so many contemporary commentators and latterday historians saw the war as the final blow to nationalist progressive expectations. Yet the theorists did not abandon the search for a workable reform programme. Rather, they began the tasks of reconsidering their previous arguments and developing the ideological commitments anew. Within a year of the end of the war, each of the surviving nationalist progressive theorists had begun a wholesale reconsideration of his ideals and his practical suggestions. 'We are living in . . . a revolutionary world', Walter Lippmann thus contended, and such a world demanded not surrender but that the approaches to political concepts derived before the war began should be 'reexamined as fearlessly as religious dogmas were in the nineteenth century.'[48] Croly, Lippmann, and colleagues were further joined in this belief by a new generation of theorists who had been intellectually reared on *The Promise of American Life*, *A Preface to Politics*, and *The New Democracy*, and who were ready to develop the theories still further. Ordway Tead and Arthur Gleason, both regular *New Republic* contributors, led this group. Having seen the failures of the Progressive Party, Tead and Gleason had more sympathy with the American Socialist Party than their predecessors had, but they were both determined to ensure that the essence of the nationalist progressive vision survived and they were committed to playing a direct personal role in the reformist politics in the new world order. Working together this new generation and the survivors from the old searched for an alternative conceptual

---

[46] Croly, 'Breach of Civilization', 14.   [47] Editors, 'Landslide into Collectivism', 250.
[48] W. Lippmann, 'A Clue', *New Republic*, 14 April 1917, 317.

approach with which to replace the elements that had been discredited by the experience of the war. It was also a quest that briefly, at least, appeared successful. By 1922, the *New Republic* was happy to proclaim that 'progressivism is reborn'.[49]

As these theorists reconsidered their position, it was once again to Britain that they first turned. They looked there after the war, however, for substantially different ideological reasons than they had before. Whereas previously Britain had been lauded as a country capable of taking bold steps towards adopting a more interventionist state, it was now to be celebrated as a 'nation which respects individual liberty and protects it as we in America do not yet do'.[50] The wartime developments on the British left, and especially the arrival of socialist pluralism, seemed exactly to meet the requirements of the new situation. As they began, many of those developments were already being widely discussed across the whole ideological spectrum of American reformist politics. The form of socialist pluralism known as British guild socialism was first celebrated by the theorists of the American Socialist Party, whose repression throughout the war made the British pluralists especially notable for their 'inspiring' and 'glorious' 'defense of individual liberty'. 'From every point of view the principles of Guild Socialism bid fair to be incorporated in American theory and practice', America's leading socialist theoretician, Jessie Hughan proclaimed as the war ended.[51] Keen to hear more directly from the movement itself, the *American Labor Year Book*, produced by the socialist adult education Rand School in New York, gave ample space over to G. D. H. Cole and separately to his wife Margaret to explain their strand of guild and pluralist thinking in more detail. American socialists even opened a bookshop, 'The Sunwise Turn', in New York's Greenwich Village specifically to propagate the pluralist message.[52] Surveying developments on the left in 1920, the liberal social commentator John Graham Brooks concluded that 'Cole's books are eagerly read by thousands of students in the United States'.[53]

Enthusiasm for Cole's form of radical British pluralism quickly moved out of the relatively small circles of American socialism and reached the mainstream. On that journey it was the moderate organ of progressive social work, *The Survey*, which first broadcast the message to a liberal American audience. Throughout the years from 1917 to 1920 *The Survey*'s editor, Paul Kellogg, insistently argued that the pluralists' time had come. Arthur Gleason joined Kellogg in compiling two well-received books—*Inside the British Isles* and

---

[49] Editors, 'Progressivism Reborn', *New Republic*, 13 December 1922, 56–7.

[50] Weyl, *Tired Radicals*, 121–2.

[51] J. W. Hughan, 'Guildsmen and American Socialism', *Intercollegiate Socialist*, 7 (1918), 20–3. See too O. Tead, 'Guilds for America', *Intercollegiate Socialist*, 7 (1919), 31–3.

[52] See R. H. C., 'Readers and Writers', *New Age*, 12 September 1918, 320.

[53] J. G. Brooks, *Labor's Challenge to the Social Order: Democracy its Own Critic and Educator* (New York: Macmillan, 1920), 403.

British Labour and the War—extolling the movement's virtues.[54] 'The whole recent impulse and forward thrust of labor', they reported, 'was in the theories and proposed practices of guild socialism. The future lay with the ideas of 'guild socialism, of industrial unionism, of producers' share in control, of pluralistic sovereignties, of the federal principle', Gleason contended. 'It is time that our statesmen, our social experts, our writers and our industrial leaders begin to study' socialist pluralism, Gleason concluded, for soon 'they will be forced to accept it.'[55]

It was not a long step from *The Survey* to the more self-consciously academic *New Republic* itself. Soon the leading British socialist pluralists appeared in print more frequently there than anywhere else in the United States. As this enthusiasm took hold, Lippmann may have recalled his earlier contact with Cole. The two had met during Lippmann's tour of radical political groups in Britain in 1914, and Cole had subsequently tried to make use of his connection in the United States by asking Lippmann to publish his work in the *New Republic*.[56] But while these initial pre-war attempts had been rebuffed, at the end of the war an invitation was forthcoming. Cole then contributed a string of articles for the journal chronicling events in Britain and outlining their theoretical implications. So vast were the implications of the pluralist revolution taken to be that he was quickly joined by other leading pluralists, R. H. Tawney chief amongst them.[57] Despite Cole and Tawney's success at finding an American audience, the ideals of the pluralist movement were predominantly represented in the United States by the other leading member of the trio, Harold J. Laski.

Having departed from Britain in 1916, first for McGill University in Montreal and then for Harvard, Laski was already firmly ensconced in the American university system by the time of United States' entry into the war. A relentless and remarkably successful self-publicist, he reached new levels of prominence as progressive theorists seeking a theoretical grounding in these new approaches turned to him for guidance and instruction. Laski's distinct advantage was that whilst his work dealt 'with the issues that lie at the very centre of guild socialism' he himself was not directly associated with the potentially parochial concerns of the British trade union movement, as many of the guild socialists appeared to be. Rather, he was a reputed professor of political science and public law at the country's leading university, more than capable of extracting the generalizable lessons from the British experience in

---

[54] A. Gleason, *Inside the British Isles* (New York: Century Co., 1917) and A. Gleason and P. Kellogg, *British Labor and the War: Reconstructors of a New World* (New York: Boni and Liveright, 1919).

[55] A. Gleason to P. Kellogg, letter dated 7 July 1919, Survey Associates Records, 77/575, and A. Gleason, 'The Discovery', *Survey*, 19 May 1917, 159.

[56] See G. D. H. Cole to W. Lippmann, letter dated 9 November 1914, Yale University Library, The W. Lippmann Papers, 326/1/6/269.

[57] See, for example, R. Bourne, 'The Guild Idyl', *New Republic*, 2 March 1918, 151–2; G. D. H. Cole, 'British Labor in Wartime', *New Republic*, 1 June 1918, 142–3.

a manner understandable to Americans. Here was a British pluralist on American soil, popular with the leading progressive intelligentsia, and enthusiastically willing to write widely in reputable journals of opinion. He was soon to make himself 'invaluable'.[58] With prodigious talent and an uncanny gift for addressing almost any audience on its own terms, Laski's success was almost guaranteed.

Important as his personality was, the response that Laski's work received in American progressive circles reflected more than the pleasures of his affability and journalistic availability. His pluralist ideas themselves seized the imagination of progressives of all colours. Already by 1917, the New Republic was congratulating Laski on opening 'up new and attractive possibilities for the future'.[59] Three years later, the New York Nation wrote that Laski's work was of such import that 'no student of politics, law or sociology can afford to leave [it] unread and unmastered'.[60] By 1925, Roscoe Pound, the Dean of Harvard Law School and a powerful influence on progressives everywhere, was to go even further. Laski's 'influence', Pound argued, 'is to be seen in almost everything which is written in English on politics or jurisprudence today'.[61] With such a reputation, Laski moved effortlessly from the pages of the New Republic's book reviews to its pages of comment and editorial. For Lippmann and for his colleagues, it was Laski who 'produced the most elaborate and sustained criticism' of nationalist ideas, and in so doing it was Laski who became 'invaluable'.[62]

Laski's great intellectual advantage was that he spoke directly to the nationalist progressives' concerns. His work constantly demonstrated that while he shared a detailed knowledge of the Americans' intellectual starting points—idealism, pragmatism, social psychology, and Fabianism—he vigorously disagreed with their conclusions. In this way, Laski took advantage of leading columns in the nationalist progressives' own journal to address head-on the very conceptual debate that had initially divided these two movements. He continually revisited, that is, the idealist conception of liberty, its related theory of human development, and the political consequences that the nationalists had taken to be derived from them. He was similarly unstinting in his praise of socialist pluralist developments in Britain. He bluntly informed his American audience that a renewed discussion of the 'very essence of liberty' was progressing in Britain and insisted that they needed to take heed of it. '[I]n England', he insisted, 'nothing is so much debated as the evils of a centralized state; nothing so much desired as adequate methods of decentralization.' Surveying the scene in the United States, of course, Laski

[58] W. Lippmann, 'Authority in the Modern State', New Republic, 31 May 1919, 148.
[59] L. K. 'The One and the Many', New Republic, 5 May 1918, 25.
[60] Anon., 'The State in Transition', Nation (NY), 5 July 1919, 21.
[61] R. Pound, letter dated 14 December 1925, Harvard Law Library, Harvard University, Cambridge, R. Pound Papers.   [62] Lippmann, 'Authority', 148.

found the very opposite appeared to have been the case and he lay the blame partially with the nationalist progressives themselves. Since 1909 and the publication of *The Promise of American Life*, Laski surmised, nationalist progressives had sought to 'make Washington a kind of Hegelian harmonization' where Congress and President should be capable of transcending the differences between the States and between competing groups in society with careful use of 'federal statute'.[63] The experience of war, Laski continued, should have demonstrated that it was time to reject this 'ancient and false worship of unity' and to abandon any trust in 'an undivided sovereignty as the panacea for our ills'. The United States of America, Laski patronizingly instructed his audience, had been the birthplace of the decentralized ideal, and Americans should accept that a revived division of powers was now, just as in revolutionary times, the only genuine guarantee of liberty.[64] 'It would be tragic', Laski concluded with a characteristic final rhetorical flourish, if this ideal of decentralization was neglected in America just 'at the very moment it begins to bear fruit in foreign lands.'[65]

In reconsidering their positions in the face of the challenge of war, the nationalist progressives appeared willing to heed this advice in a way totally inconceivable prior to the conflict. By the close of 1918, the search for the right pattern of 'division of power between the state and groups' as shaped in British pluralism was announced to be the central issue in American progressive political thought. As Lippmann put it, this was the 'intellectual problem' that was 'certain to preoccupy the thinking of the next generation'.[66] Such a search, moreover, was explicitly held to be fundamental to politics precisely because therein lay the political prescriptions that would guarantee 'liberty', just as had been suggested in the British case.[67] The connection between freedom and the need to guarantee the independence of groups and organizations from the authority of the state thus emerged in the United States, and it came, paradoxically enough, from the country previously celebrated for its political centralization and its cultural homogeneity. It came, that is, from Britain.

Patterns of convergence? An American pluralism

Shaken as they were by the strength of the challenge emanating from Britain, the former nationalist progressives soon found new pluralist champions of their own. As early as June 1918, Harold Laski noted that there were many

---

[63] H. Laski, 'Sovereignty and Centralization', *New Republic*, 16 December 1916, 176.

[64] See H. Laski on Cole in 'Industrial Self-Government', *New Republic*, 27 April 1918, 392, and H. Laski, *Studies in The Problem of Sovereignty* (New Haven: Yale University Press, 1917), 273–4.

[65] H. Laski, 'Federal Power', *New Republic*, 23 November 1918, 109.

[66] See H. A. Overstreet, 'The New State', *Journal of Philosophy*, 16 (1919), 582–5, and Lippmann, 'A Clue', 316.

[67] See Editors, 'A Clue', New Republic, 17 September 1917, 192, and Tead, 'Labor Unions', 136.

'students in America' who 'realize that we have been driven back to the fundamental notions of the state' and who were trying to find alternative conceptual strategies for understanding the meaning and implications of the idealist view of liberty and human development as a result.[68] Leading the way were two theorists of very different backgrounds, John Dewey and Mary Parker Follett.

Described by Walter Lippmann as the 'finest and most powerful intellect devoted to the future of American civilization', John Dewey had been contributing to the *New Republic* on and off since the journal's launch. For most of that time his work combined a brand of pragmatism with Hegelian idealism, and he had used this initially surprising philosophical starting point to provide a forceful justification for a vigorously democratic form of the new nationalism.[69] During the war, Dewey went through the same sense of excitement and anticipation followed by deep despair at the conflict's domestic developments as his colleagues on the *New Republic* staff. During this time, he read the work of Cole extensively, and was quickly attracted to many of the ideas he found there.[70] While Dewey already carried significant weight before the war, Mary Parker Follett, in contrast, was a relative newcomer to the academic scene in the United States. Educated both in Cambridge, Massachusetts and in Cambridge, England, Follett had a solid grounding in the academic study of politics. Her earliest publication was a short study of the speaker of the House of Representatives which urged American progressives to take the British House of Commons as their model for institutional reform: a position essentially the same as that advanced by Croly's *Promise of American Life*.[71] What brought Follett dramatically to the forefront of the nationalist progressive imagination, however, was her knowledge of British pluralism, in both its academic and its more distinctly political manifestations, and her dedication to adapting it to American conditions. This central conviction was shared with Dewey; and both theorists pursued it relentlessly in their respective post-war masterpieces, Follett's *The New State*, published in 1919, and Dewey's *Human Nature and Conduct* and *Reconstruction in Philosophy*, released two years later.

The initial similarities between the arguments of Dewey and Follett and

---

[68] H. Laski, 'Labor and the State', *New Republic*, 1 June 1918, 152.

[69] Compare J. Dewey, 'The Ethics of Democracy' (1888), reprinted in *John Dewey: The Early Works* (Carbondale: Southern Illinois University Press, 1988) with W. Lippmann, 'The Hope of Democracy', *New Republic*, 1 July 1916, 231. See also M. Cohen, 'John Dewey's Philosophy', *New Republic*, 2 June 1916, 118–19.

[70] See A. Cywar, 'John Dewey in World War One', *American Quarterly*, 21 (1969), 578–94, and A. Ryan, *John Dewey and the High Tide of American Liberalism* (New York: W. W. Norton, 1997), 154–99.

[71] For more biographical information, see P. Graham (ed.), *Mary Parker Follett–Prophet of Management: A Celebration of her Writings from the 1920s* (Cambridge, MA: Harvard Business School Press, 1995) and K. Mattson, *Creating a Democratic Public: The Struggle for Urban Participatory Democracy in the Progressive Era* (University Park, Pennsylvania: Pennsylvania State University Press, 1998), esp. 88–104.

those of the British socialist pluralists were striking. 'The unified state is now discredited', Follett outlined, emphasizing that such a failure should take its place as the centrepiece of a new political theory. Dewey willingly concurred. The 'demoralization of war', he argued, was fundamentally a result of forcing the 'State into an abnormally supreme position'.[72] As the diagnosis of the problem shared pluralist overtones, so the solution too appeared to match that of Laski, Cole, and Tawney. The centralized state had to be replaced by a new institutional order that placed multiple groups at the centre of its organization: the 'ever-increasing multiple groups of life to-day must be recognized and given a responsible place in politics.'[73]

As Follett and Dewey provided more detail for these arguments, it became clear that the foundations of these American pluralists' conceptual arguments were arranged around two essential pluralist themes. The first emphasized, just as the British had, the inevitable plurality of everyday life in an advanced society. Theorists in the post-war world, Dewey argued, had to accept a 'plurality of changing, moving, individualized goods and ends'.[74] The days of certainty when social leaders could expect all their citizens to share a set of identifiable single goods was over. Difference and disagreement, especially as to the essential ends of life, was an inevitable feature of existence in the modern world. 'Variety is more than the spice of life; it is largely of its essence', Dewey summarized.[75] Turning more directly to politics, Dewey and Follett then related this recognition of 'the fact of pluralism' to a normative acceptance of the place of manifold groups and group allegiances within society. The fact of pluralism, Dewey thus insisted, 'demands a modification of hierarchical and monistic theory'.[76] Follett employed a homespun style to emphasize the point with more clarity than Dewey could muster. As diversity is an inevitable part of 'the game of life', Follett suggested, 'men have many loyalties . . . I may have to say the collective I or we first of my basket-ball team, next of my trade-union, then of my church club or citizens; league or neighborhood association, and the lines may cross and recross many times.' And yet the welcome Follett and Dewey gave to groups and group allegiances was far from grudging. They did not dismiss these multiple allegiances as inevitable *irritants* in the body politic as the nationalist progressives may have appeared to do. Rather, non-state groups and associations were now to be enthusiastically endorsed. 'Every combination of human forces', Dewey insisted, has 'its own unique and ultimate worth.' No group should 'be degraded into a means to glorify the State.'[77] This was true both of groups

---

[72] M. Follett, *The New State: Group Organization the Solution of Popular Government* (New York: Longmans Green and Co., 1918), 258. J. Dewey, *Reconstruction in Philosophy* (London: University of London Press, 1921), 204.   [73] Follett, *New State*, 245.

[74] Dewey, *Reconstruction*, 163.

[75] J. Dewey, *Human Nature and Conduct* (New York: The Modern Library, 1922, 2nd edn 1930), 308. See also 210–37.   [76] Dewey, *Human Nature*, 290.

[77] J. Dewey, *Reconstruction*, 204.

united by their place in the economic and social order and of immigrant groups too. No longer would national communal harmony entail the rejection of cultural difference or competing allegiances. 'The theory of the Melting Pot', Dewey now admitted, 'always gave me rather a pang. To maintain that all the constituent elements, geographical, racial and cultural, in the United States should be put in the same pot and turned into a uniform and unchanging product is distasteful.'[78]

These claims brought Dewey and Follett extremely close to the position that had been outlined by Cole and Laski. Diversity, they argued, was inevitable, and its recognition entailed an acceptance of a wide range of group loyalties and allegiances. Indeed, Dewey and Follett went even further than this. They also suggested that group organization was essential not only because it reflected certain phenomena in society but also because it was the fundamental means of ensuring the protection and enhancement of the *freedom* of the individuals who composed them. Each individual, Follett insisted, 'gains his true freedom only through the group'.[79] It was, Dewey argued, the existence of a wide range of independent groups each allowed to operate largely independently within its own sphere that essentially makes for the 'difference between the free and the enslaved' society. As a 'free man would rather take his chance in an open world' than be cosseted 'in a closed world', Dewey contended, so every citizen must rightly welcome a proliferation of different organizational units.[80]

Among the leading nationalist progressives, the post-war arguments of Follett and Dewey were seized upon instantly. Surveying the political and social landscape in 1918, Herbert Croly cited Follett in arguing that individuals are becoming 'increasingly attached to centers of allegiance and social activity other than the state'. There are 'within nations', he wrote, many 'class, trade, and professional associations [all of] which will compete with the state for the loyalty of its citizens'.[81] 'We have learned to note many selves, and to be a little less ready to issue judgement upon them', Walter Lippmann summarized.[82] Moreover, the editors of the *New Republic* no longer presented such divided loyalties as largely undesirable characteristics of modern life. Although they continued to emphasize that this form of '[s]ectionalism has no doubt frequently hampered the American people in realizing their desirable common purposes', they also accepted that their old responses to it were no longer viable. The war had demonstrated beyond doubt that any efforts at a straightforward nationalization of the sort progressives had previously demanded would 'degenerate into centralization'. The American people, the

---

[78] J. Dewey, 'The Principle of Nationality' (1917), reprinted in J. A. Boydston (ed.), *The Collected Works of John Dewey: The Middle Works*, x (Carbondale: Southern Illinois Press, 1980), 289.

[79] Follett, *New State*, 6.   [80] J. Dewey, *Human Nature*, 311.

[81] Croly, 'Future of the State', 181.

[82] W. Lippmann, *Public Opinion* (New York: MacMillan, 1922), 174.

chief proponents of nationalist progressivism thus now argued, 'need to be aroused, not as formerly for accelerating' the work of this form of nationalization 'but for the purpose of checking it'.[83] As one leading commentator noticed, 'one penetrating figure after another' was falling for the attractions of the pluralist ideal.[84] The central contentions of socialist pluralism, it appeared, had established themselves in the most unlikely section of the United States.

Continual conflict: liberty, individuals, and community

It may easily thus appear that transatlantic conceptual agreement was quickly reached and without great controversy; the American pluralists demanded a radical decentralization of authority and they defended that demand on the basis of claims regarding the essential diversity of human society. A fundamental distinction, however, remained between the British socialist pluralists and their counterparts in the United States. The core of British socialist pluralism was a rendering of the concept of freedom in distinctly individualist terms. For the British socialist pluralists, an individual's freedom 'lies more in getting his own way, in making his own will count, than in the wisdom of his way, or the quality of his will; for he is just as free, just as much himself, in imposing a narrow sectional interest on himself and others as in standing for the larger and more social view'.[85] But for all of the convergence between British socialist pluralists and their American successors there was none on this issue; this was the breaking point, and that break was explicit.

In *Reconstruction in Philosophy*, John Dewey exclaimed that according to the British socialist pluralists' 'conception of the individual self' the 'individual is regarded as something *given*, something already there'. In Dewey's view, though, although it was important to recognize that 'social arrangements, laws, institutions are made for man', as the British pluralists always insisted, it was just as important to note that 'they are *not* means for obtaining something for individuals' as Cole and Laski had claimed. Rather, and most crucially, Dewey insisted, they are really 'means of *creating* individuals'.[86] 'Only in the physical sense of physical bodies that to the senses are separate is individuality an original datum', Dewey explained. 'Individuality in a social and a moral sense is something to be wrought out', not something preordained.[87] Institutional reorganization should not, then, be intended better to satisfy the desires, demands, and preferences of given individuals but rather to forge different sorts of characters, or to 'educate every individual into the full stature of his possibility'.[88]

[83] Editors, 'Passing of Sectionalism', 61.   [84] Overstreet, 'New State', 585.
[85] H. J. W. Hetherington, 'The Conception of a Unitary Social Order', *Proceedings of the Aristotelian Society*, 18 (1918), 310.
[86] Dewey, *Reconstruction*, 194.   [87] Ibid.   [88] Dewey, *Reconstruction*, 186.

In making this claim, the perfectionist element of the idealist conception of freedom that had been so welcomed by the original nationalist progressives returned into full view. And as it did, Dewey also insisted on a further element of the idealist interpretation: the idea that the obstacles to true freedom included the very sorts of mental, emotional, psychological constraints that had concerned the idealists and nationalist progressives in the pre-war generation. 'Freedom', Dewey thus insisted, is 'that release of capacity from *whatever* hems it in.'[89] Nor was he alone in this claim. Mary Follett was even more convinced of the necessity of rejecting what she saw as the 'passive' understanding of freedom advanced by the British pluralists. Freedom, she argued, 'is not caprice or whim or a partial wish or a momentary desire. On the contrary freedom means exactly the liberation from the tyranny of such . . . impulses'.[90] In a sentiment that owed nothing to Cole's wartime brand of pluralism and everything to Walter Lippmann's *Drift and Mastery*, Follett concluded by insisting that freedom was to be found in a reordering of men's desires. 'Men follow their passions and should do,' she insisted, just as Lippmann had, 'but they must purify their passions, educate them, discipline and direct them.'[91]

As the idea of liberty as a 'formative' endeavour, a perfectionist concept free from 'internal' as well as 'external' obstacles remained from the progressivism of old, so even more tellingly did the idea that such perfection was essentially communal in character. The 'fallacy of pluralism is not its pluralism but that it is based on an outside individual', Follett argued, for the 'outside individual is a pluralist myth'.[92] As such there was no glory in the isolation or introspection that was at the heart of Laski and Cole's thesis. 'Moral independence for the adult means arrest of growth,' Dewey concluded, 'isolation means induration'.[93] As Follett expressed it, 'the activity which produces the true individual is at the same time interweaving him and others into a real whole'.[94] Even the language was reminiscent of the nationalist progressivism of the pre-war world. 'Individuality', Follett argued in an almost direct quotation from Croly, 'is the capacity for union'. 'The measure of individuality', she continued, 'is the depth and breadth of true relations. I am an individual not as far as I am apart from, but as far as I am a part of other men . . . Our definition of individuality must now be "finding my place in the whole".'[95] For Dewey and Follett, then, any persuasive account of human freedom had to recognize that 'we are fundamentally members of a society and the actions that separate us from, or antagonize our fellows are actions that bring us finally to real contradiction with ourselves and frustrate our true natures'.[96] Within this form of American pluralism, just as much as in nationalist progressivism, freedom was still unmistakably a social construct.

---

[89] Dewey, *Reconstruction*, 208.
[91] Follett, *New State*, 340.
[93] Dewey, *Reconstruction*, 185.
[95] Follett, *New State*, 62.

[90] Follett, *New State*, 69.
[92] Follett, *New State*, 16.
[94] Follett, *New State*, 7.
[96] Wilde, *Ethical Basis*, 107.

The most remarkable conceptual continuity with the nationalist progressivism of the pre-war era, though, was still to come. It lay in the fact that for both Dewey and Follett the locus of the community itself remained the *nation* itself. This was not even British pluralism in the Figgisian sense, the sense that the very young Cole and Laski had endorsed, where *groups* smaller than the nation itself provided individuals with their communal perfection. Such a view was again explicitly dismissed for being 'as entirely particularistic as the old individualistic theories' only with 'the particularism merely transferred from the individual to the group'.[97] Instead, this American form of pluralism was distinctly designed as a better means of building a supra-group, a national community. For Follett and Dewey, cooperation was a psychological goal to be learnt at a local or group level and then transferred to the nation. As Dewey continued, the 'multiplying of all kinds and varieties of associations' which in British pluralist thought 'looks like a movement toward individualism' was conceived in the American version as 'the cultivation of every conceivable interest that men have in common'.[98] 'Our multiple group life is the fact we have to reckon with; unity is the aim of all our seeking.'[99] The reason to celebrate difference was so that each separate group could bring 'its own diversifications to contribute to American life'.[100]

Such a commitment pervaded everything and these American pluralists made continual efforts to illustrate that it was not incompatible with their commitment to allowing group allegiances to flourish. Seeking to explain the phenomena of politicians who privileged local loyalties over national ones, for example, Follett did not attribute blame to an inevitable, all-pervading parochialism but rather to a psychological immaturity that was itself born of individualism and *not* of sectionalism. 'When we watch men in the lobbies at Washington working for their state and their town as against the interests of the United States, do we sometimes think, "these men have learnt loyalty and service to a small unity, but not yet to a large one"?', she asked. The answer was clear, if unconvincing: 'If this thought does come to us, we are probably doing them more than justice. It is not because America is too big for him to think of that he might perhaps think of Ohio or Millfield, it is just because he *cannot* think of Ohio and Millfield ... the man who works hardest for Millfield and Ohio will probably when he comes to Washington work most truly for the interests not of Millfield and Ohio but of the United States, because he has learned the first lesson of life—to think in wholes.'[101]

All these similarities with the nationalism of the past were shocking to those who expected the war to have forced a more radical break. For to those

[97] Follett, *New State*, 10.   [98] Dewey, *Reconstruction*, 203.
[99] Follett, *New State*, 310. Follett drew on the work of Felix Adler in this regard. See F. Adler, *An Ethical Philosophy of Life* (New York: D. Appleton and Co., 1918), esp. 305–19.
[100] Dewey, 'Nationality', 288.
[101] Follett, *New State*, 80.

looking at these aspects of Dewey and Follett's work, it appeared as if the British socialist pluralists had actually had no impact at all. For, after all, the individualist rejection of an idealist conception of freedom had been right at the core of the earlier disagreements and it seemed to remain so still. In order to emphasize the differences, therefore, both Dewey and Follett presented themselves as still diverging from the theorists of the earlier nationalist movement in significant ways. Somewhat disingenuously they argued that the difference came in the understanding of the nature of national community. As Norman Wilde summarized, Follett and Dewey presented 'community, not as an actual fact, but as a task to be accomplished and accomplished not by compromise, but by a real transformation and integration of wills'. For them, Dewey and Follet argued, this sense of community was a goal to be achieved rather than as a preordained actuality. It could not be found in the admiration of entrenched national traditions or by the maintenance of established patterns of social interaction. The means to promote social harmony would have to be flexible, even fluid.[102] Reassured that this separated nationalist progressive aspirations from the conservative repression of the war years, Croly took this idea up instantly. The development of a true communal spirit in the United States, he argued, would have to be 'slow, painful, deliberate and purposive'.[103]

The actual conceptual difference with past positions was nonetheless fairly small. In offering a criticism of idealism back in the late nineteenth century, pragmatists like William James had long argued that progressives needed to approach their pursuit of the social ideal in a forward-looking, flexible, pragmatic manner rather than by extolling the virtues either of established traditions or of deistic unity.[104] And, in this regard if not in others, James's words had been consistently heeded in nationalist progressive circles. Indeed, in parts of *Drift and Mastery*, Lippmann had outlined a remarkably similar argument to the one that Dewey and Follett presented. 'Men are bound together by common interests', he had argued, and thus it 'is the union, the trade association, the grange, the club and the party' that initially 'command allegiance' rather than the nation state.[105] Indeed, G. D. H. Cole had underlined, presumably with warm approval, that very section in his own copy of Lippmann's text two years before America entered the war.[106] Croly too had staked out much of this territory before the conflict. In a classic formulation in *Progressive Democracy*, he suggested that a nation was 'made up of an innumerable number of smaller societies' but that this fact should not be taken as

---

[102] N. Wilde, 'The Attack on the State', *International Journal of Ethics*, 30 (1920), 370.
[103] Croly, 'Breach of Civilization', Frankfurter Papers, 19.   [104] See Chapter 1.
[105] Lippmann, *Drift*, 161.
[106] See Cole's copy of *Drift and Mastery*, Nuffield College, Oxford University, The Cole Collection, HN.57.L.

an endorsement of group autonomy. Rather these societies should 'seek some form of mutual accommodation'. It was out 'of these joint responsibilities and common purposes', Croly had long contended, just as Follett and Dewey suggested, that 'a social ideal gradually emerges'.[107]

Much, then, if not most, remained from the past. And it was partly no doubt due to these remarkable similarities that the previous exponents of the 'new nationalism', Croly and Lippmann, so warmly received the Dewey and Follett project. Indeed, in many conceptual essentials there was never really a break from the nationalism of old. Appropriately, it fell to Herbert Croly best to summarize the real limits to the ideological distance travelled by progressives in the immediate aftermath of the war. Reflecting on the suggestions of, in turn, the original nationalist progressives and the British socialist pluralists, Croly was still in no doubt where he stood. 'If democracy were confined to an exclusive choice between an indivisible state and a dismembered society', he wrote, 'I would accept the former as the alternative which probably would allow a larger measure of human development.' The glory of the work of Follett and Dewey, though, was that it appeared to illustrate that democracy 'is not confined to such a choice'.[108] As a later *New Republic* editorial held, the recommendations and conceptual arguments of the American brand of pluralism showed that 'American citizens need new political and social convictions not as a substitute for [their] discordant activities but as a necessary precondition for pulling their activities together'.[109] American pluralism had saved the place of the perfection of communal nationalism in the nationalist progressives' conception of liberty. The essential goals of the movement thus remained the same.

The New Progressive Politics

Despite all the disappointments of the war and the flirtation with British-style socialist pluralism that those disappointments caused, the basic conceptual building blocks of nationalist progressive philosophy survived into the early 1920s. The commitment to an ideal of communal nationalism where individual freedom was understood in terms of making oneself a better part of the whole remained relatively unchanged. That does not mean, however, that the whole nationalist programme stayed unaltered. For although their underlying

[107] Croly, *Progressive Democracy*, 197.
[108] Croly, 'Future of the State', 183. Dewey himself put it more philosophically: 'This is no Bergsonian plea for dividing the universe into two portions, one all of fixed, recurrent habits, and the other all spontaneity of flux. Only in such a universe would reason in morals have to take its choice between absolute fixity and absolute looseness.' *Human Nature*, 245.
[109] Editors, 'The Making of an American Nation', *New Republic*, 31 October 1923, 243.

goals remained the same, the movement's approach to realizing them may have changed substantially. The general *political* agenda of the nationalist progressives, that is, may have been restructured far more dramatically than their essential conceptual commitments. The grandiose state-building plans of the past, after all, appeared far less plausible and desirable in the early 1920s than they had in the early 1910s. It is possible that the nationalist progressives' wartime experience led to a thoroughgoing process of political reconsideration.

In line with such a view, many commentators, both recent and contemporary, have argued that the nationalist progressives and their allies abandoned politics almost entirely in the early 1920s. In examining the general outline of progressive political proposals in the post-war age, they have argued that Follett and Dewey actually chose to overlook the need for significant institutional reform, preferring instead to concentrate on low-key educational endeavours and neighbourhood civic movements in the belief that the attitudes and behaviour of individual citizens could be effectively shaped without the need for major political reform. Eldon Eisenach has even contended that these post-war American pluralists constructed a conception of the state itself with which to excuse the absence of a more hard-headed political programme. For Follett and Dewey, Eisenach charges, 'the state' was to be understood as '"located" in the good citizen, who, in whatever role and location, spontaneously acts according to the consciously held and shared ideas of the public good'. 'Where is the state?', Eisenach asks. For Dewey and Follett, he answers, it is '*wherever* good citizens gather, organize, and act'.[110]

While this interpretation rightly emphasizes the importance both of these American pluralists gave to the attitudes and behaviour of American citizens, it nonetheless does these authors a grave disservice. Neither of them rejected the need for wholesale political reform. Follett and Dewey were convinced that although their own activities might be best suited to local, educational endeavours, the reform of the formal political institutions of the United States remained an essentially prerequisite for the achievement of their longer-term goals. 'Exhortation to good citizenship is useless' by itself, Follett clearly insisted, because we only 'get good citizenship by creating those forms within which good citizenship can operate'.[111] And it was not just Dewey and Follett who emphasized the need for significant reform. All the theorists concerned with the remnants of the nationalist project maintained their faith in the essential desirability, indeed the practical *necessity*, of far-reaching institutional change. For Croly and Lippmann in the post-war years, just as for Dewey and Follett, the essential problems of politics still required significant institutional innovation. As they continued to seek

---

[110] E. Eisenach, *The Lost Promise of Progressivism* (Lawrence: Kansas University Press, 1994), 132 (emphasis added).   [111] Follett, *New State*, 339.

means to foster communal sentiments amongst citizens of the nation and to detect and pursue the genuine, objective realities of communal life, they remained convinced that without an alteration in the structure of society and the economy and in the fabric of the formal governmental machine then there simply could be no significant attitudinal or behavioural reform.

Yet what remains to be seen is whether the general nature of the proposed institutional reforms had significantly changed from the pre-war years, and especially whether their programme remained as sympathetic to an expansion of state power as it had before the war. An initial inspection of this often-overlooked aspect of progressive literature is not particularly revealing. At a cursory glance very little seems to have changed at all. The old targets of criticism appear to remain just as clearly delineated in the post-war texts as the pre-war ones. Despite all of pluralist protestations, for example, the separation of powers in the federal government was just as violently attacked by the post-war generation as by the pre-war one. '[O]ur system of checks and balances gave no real power to any department', Mary Follett thus complained, and a 'condition of chaos was the result'.[112] Judicial review by the Supreme Court of federal or State legislation was likewise considered no more favourably than it had been before. The Supreme Court itself was not the enemy it had once been, but that was because the Court itself had changed, not because the nationalist progressives or the successors had altered their position. Both Dewey and Follett, for example, warmly welcomed the Court's move away from its previous interpretations of the fifth and fourteenth amendments. Under the tutelage of Pound and Frankfurter in academia and Holmes and Brandeis on the Court itself, Follett argued, 'particularistic law is giving way to a legal theory based on a sound theory of inter-relationship'. The doctrine of 'individual rights' that the Court previously upheld was, she contended, now 'long outgrown'. 'Our future law is to serve neither classes nor individuals, but the community.'[113]

Some things had altered, however, and once these texts are investigated closely enough those changes can be seen to mark out a new nationalist progressive approach to politics itself. Whereas before the war the conceptual arguments of the nationalist progressives had resulted in fairly unmitigated argument for state centralization, the situation in the post-war world could not be so clear-cut. The issue was summarized most clearly by John Dewey's co-author, the political philosopher J. H. Tufts. Nationalist progressives continued to hold, Tufts argued, that a 'real public opinion—an opinion better and larger than the opinion of any one of us—must be created, built up by joint effort . . . a social will must be brought into being'. But they now realized that the efforts to construct such a 'social will' had to begin lower down.

---

[112] Follett, *New State*, 166.
[113] Follett, *New State*, 56 and 126. See also Dewey, *Human Nature*, 239–40.

'In expanding the national state' during the war 'our political life has not kept pace with our political machinery.' The result was that 'we must turn back to the local unit again for the vitalizing springs'. The question, however, was how such a notion could be reconciled with the continuing commitment to the construction of bolder national sentiment. The answer lay, at least in part, in an adaptation once again of British practice. The progressives of the *New Republic* sought to find a means of combining the socialist pluralists' 'valuable plea for administrative decentralization' with their rejection of the fundamentally individualistic basis of the 'philosophic theory of a pluralistic state'.[114]

Reconciling the irreconcilable: guild socialism and a strong state

The fundamental practical lesson of the pluralist movement as Herbert Croly saw it was a recognition of the need to grant 'the immense number of voluntary associations' which 'breed and flourish in the soil of every progressive society' a significant place in the effective government of the nation.[115] All of the nationalist progressives working after the war insisted that groups were to play two essential roles, mirroring the objective and the subjective elements of their commitment to communal endeavour. First of all, groups would offer essential advice to those in central government often tempted to mistake their own prejudices for reasoned judgements. Drawing on groups in this way 'would allow us to escape from the intolerable and unworkable fiction that each of us must acquire a competent opinion about all public affairs'.[116] Second, the groups would offer an invaluable education in communal behaviour. They would induct citizens into the habit of behaving communally. As Follett argued, the 'chief need of society to-day is an enlightened, progressive and organized public opinion, and the first step towards an enlightened and organized public opinion is an enlightened and organized group opinion. When public opinion becomes conscious of itself, it will have a justified confidence in itself. Then the "people", born of associated life, will truly govern. Then shall we at last really have America.'[117] '[W]e are ready for membership in a larger group', she contended, 'only by experience first in the smaller group.'[118]

These advisory and educative functions were in part to be achieved by political decentralization. The war, the *New Republic*'s editors argued, had rendered 'it more and more evident that the business of government has to be distributed over a vast area of groups'.[119] A 'true Hegelianism', Follett concluded, 'finds its actualized form in federalism'.[120] A revivified federalism,

---

[114] N. Wilde, 'Foundations of Sovereignty', *International Journal of Ethics*, 32 (1924), 444.
[115] H. Croly, 'A School for Social Research', *New Republic*, 8 June 1918, 169
[116] Lippmann, *Public Opinion*, 31.   [117] Follett, *New State*, 226.
[118] Follett, *New State*, 249.   [119] Editors, 'A Clue', 192.
[120] Follett, *New State*, 267.

then, was to be an essential characteristic of the new political order. But as the guild socialists had contended in Britain, the progressives continually argued that such a federalism would have to include the devolution of political power to various economic, social, and cultural groups, as well as, or often instead of, to the local territorial units of States and municipalities.[121] And, again as in Britain, by far the most importance was given to industrial affairs in general and industrial relations in particular. In this arena, many among the new generation of nationalist progressives, led by the *New Republic*'s Ordway Tead, argued for a programme of industrial democracy that was at least superficially similar to that demanded in Britain by the guild socialists. 'We seek to-day the extension of representative government, not only into politics but into industry', Tead argued, so that 'throughout the whole fabric of American life, our common efforts shall contribute to the rearing of a great community wherein shall dwell a happy people disciplined for the fullness of freedom.'[122] Tead lent qualified support to G. D. H. Cole's ideal, as he understood it, that in industry 'each body is awarded jurisdiction over those matters concerning it, and it alone'.[123] On such a view, 'the actual technique of production must be left in the hands of the people with experience in producing'.[124] As Tead concluded, 'in order to secure maximum production labor's voice must become increasingly dominant where chiefly its interests are affected'.[125]

The American reformers nonetheless remained unwilling to accept all of the pluralists' recommendations. The remaining nationalist progressives insisted that there were severe limitations to the 'guild socialist' programme's ability to meet the exacting criteria of enhancing both the subjective sensation and the objective reality of communal harmony. The objective pattern provided the clearest set of problems. First, a thoroughgoing commitment to absolute associational independence appeared unable to tackle the problems of expertise. People 'live in grooves, are shut in among their own affairs, barred out of larger affairs, meet few people of their own sort, read little', Lippmann argued.[126] And as such it was difficult to grant them full power over industrial decision-making. Croly wholeheartedly agreed, arguing the 'success' of guild-style organization was always going to be 'impaired for want of ... trustworthy information'.[127] The 'real environment', Lippmann suggested, 'is altogether too big, too complex, and too fleeting for direct acquaintance'.[128] Second, there was the issue of the interrelationship between

---

[121] See Lippmann, 'A Clue', 317.
[122] O. Tead, 'The New Place of Labor' (1918), Labor-Management Documentation Center, Cornell University, Ithaca, The O. Tead Papers, 5, 185.
[123] O. Tead, 'National Organization by Industries: England', *New Republic*, 8 February 1919, 49.
[124] O. Tead, 'National Control of Railroads', *Intercollegiate Socialist*, 6 (1918), 4.
[125] O. Tead, 'Productivity and Reconstruction', *The Public*, 16 March 1918, 334.
[126] Lippmann, *Public Opinion*, 48.   [127] Croly, 'School for Social Research', 169.
[128] Lippmann, *Public Opinion*, 16.

different elements of the industrial system. The many, small 'economic units' in the United States 'are so dependent upon others', Dewey argued, that the idea that it would be possible to endow each of them with its own 'sovereignty' is necessarily a 'pious fiction'.[129] 'All our functions must be expressed, but somewhere must come that coordination which will give them their real effectiveness.'[130] Walter Weyl was all the more clear. 'Our whole industrial society is interdependent', he argued, and you 'cannot remove' or hinder 'one wheel without bringing the whole machinery to a stop.'[131]

As a result, throughout the early 1920s these progressives remained unwilling to accept that democratic industrial associations should be wholly responsible for the direction of their own affairs, operating within an otherwise open market. Especially with regard to staple industries, the progressives were insistent that careful, centralized regulation of production should be maintained and, indeed, enhanced. The editors of the *New Republic* were categorical in their defence of the necessity of some form of centralized economic control. '[U]nless there is team work in planning and centralized control of production', they argued, 'unless all heads of divisions and departments awake to the realization that the government is confronted by a single production programme and act accordingly, we shall repeat the disaster of the headless days.'[132] Even Ordway Tead, the commentator usually most sympathetic to the British guild ideal, argued that there was a real need for 'increased coordination' between industries. It was vital, Tead contended, to seek 'really scientific control of production in the public interest—a control for the purpose of assuring that the real demand shall be supplied, no more and no less, and that the supply shall be of honest goods and sensibly distributed'.[133] Democratic mechanisms within industries were useful, therefore, but they had their limitations. Workers would thus be allowed a say 'in how production took place and under what conditions'; but when it came to considering 'what was produced, how much, the quality and the price' such a decision would have to lie elsewhere. Indeed, Taylorite scientific management, with its claim that such questions could be answered objectively in the common interest if only experts were able to examine them hard enough, retained a remarkable hold on the imaginations of most nationalist progressives. 'The problem is to study scientifically how production can be carried on in close relation to needs and demands and to modify the present mechanism in order to provide in a more intelligent way for the conduct of certain functions which are not now recognized as necessary or are unintelligently or uneconomically administered.'[134]

[129] Dewey, 'Nationality', 290.   [130] Follett, *New State*, 321.
[131] Weyl, *Tired Radicals*, 43.
[132] Editors, 'Causes of Industrial Unrest', *New Republic*, 30 March 1918, 252.
[133] Tead, 'National Organization', 51.
[134] O. Tead, 'The World Tomorrow', *The World Tomorrow*, March 1921, 88.

In such regards, it was, Tead contended, 'the consumer' who 'was the indispensable party' in any economic system.[135] But, as before, the interests of these consumers were to be represented not only indirectly through the mechanisms of the market but also directly and consciously through the organs of the state. In so far as Britain provided a model here, it was not the guild socialist vision but rather the Fabian ideal as represented by the Webbs and by Ramsay MacDonald that was clearly and explicitly endorsed. There was, as Tead himself admitted, a continual need for 'a resolute, and I believe unanswerable, stand in behalf of the efficacy of political institutions as the fundamentally necessary expression of public opinion and judgment'.[136] It was 'for the community of consumers and citizens' as best represented by a democratic central state and 'not for any producer, or association of producers' to decide 'what shall be produced, and where and when; in what kinds, what quantities, what qualities; and also, seeing that process determines cost, by what process and at what price'.[137] Borrowing almost directly from the Fabians, Tead concluded that 'production must, in other words, be carried on in direct, avowed, and measured relation to a demand dictated primarily by considerations of national and international welfare'.[138]

The political implications of this concern were dramatic. For the nationalist progressives and their Fabian counterparts in Britain, one of the central failings of the market system was its inability effectively to allocate labour. In an unregulated market, in these progressives' view, individual workers were often to be found pursing occupations or vocations to which they were ill-suited or for which there was no genuine social need. Drawing heavily on the recommendations of Frederick W. Taylor's Scientific Management movement, the nationalist progressives railed after the war, just as before it, against the 'chaos' and lack of order they saw as characteristic of the modern economy.[139] In particular, many nationalist progressives determined that individual workers should be allowed significantly less flexibility when it came to choosing both their place of work and the manner in which it should be conducted than either the free market allowed or the pluralist and guild socialist alternative envisioned. The nationalists' admirers in Britain spelt out the implications distinctly. Echoing clearly F. W. Taylor's insistence on the central importance of the 'scientific selection of the workman', the Fabian Sidney Webb argued that 'the only justification for the claim to enter any vocation can be the public need for the service

[135] O. Tead, 'Contemporary Social Theory' (1920), The Tead Papers, 5, 418.
[136] Tead, 'Contemporary Social Theory', 418.
[137] S. and B. Webb, The Consumers Co-operative Movement (London: Longmans, Green and Co., 1921), 482.   [138] Tead, 'Productivity', 333.
[139] See Editors, 'Democratic Control of Scientific Management', New Republic, 23 December 1916, 204–5.

and the producer's capacity to render it'.[140] 'The price' that workers are 'called upon to pay for the privilege of living' in a society of economic and social stability, the Webbs continued, consisted in the performance of useful work, the precise nature of which was not to be 'determined' by 'what the producer chooses' but by the organized community itself.[141] Absolutely no doubt was left as to the implications of this point. 'All appointments' must be 'centralised and systematically scrutinised.'[142] In 1915, the *New Republic* had argued that a proper industrial bureaucracy using 'the power of scientific management' could effectively 'assign tasks appropriate to any degree of will power or acquired skill'.[143] Even in the aftermath of the war, the ideal that a reformed centralized authority should be charged 'systematically to think out the function that each person has to perform and the relation in which each must stand to others and to the whole' remained at the very centre of their reforming vision.[144]

The problems with guild socialist suggestions were not confined to the identification and meeting of objective criteria of industrial production. For despite all of Follett and Dewey's hope that an energized group life would be the ideal training ground for a supra-group communal loyalty a suspicion remained that some, perhaps many, groups would retain 'merely particularist purposes' the pursuit of which would 'threaten the integrity of both individual and social life'.[145] Given that many groups tended to maintain fairly isolated existences, it had to be asked 'how do great numbers of people each feeling so privately . . . develop any common will?'[146] Tead, too, worried that a pluralist political order would not provide the 'conditions through which' the 'spirit of public service' could realistically be expected to emerge.[147] The result of these anxieties was again a call, however initially timid, for the return of some role for the central state in shaping the collective sentiments of the nation. Trying to have their pluralist cake and eat it too, the *New Republic* argued that the 'American nation must seek and find some different and better way of redistributing political and economic power which will preserve it chiefly in the hands of individuals, locations and voluntary associations of the people and yet which will manage to keep them on friendly terms with one another and with society as a whole.'[148]

---

[140] S. and B. Webb, *The Constitution of the Socialist Commonwealth of Great Britain* (London: Longmans, Green and Co., 1920), 284, and F. W. Taylor, 'On the Principles of Scientific Management', reprinted in E. Boris and N. Lichtenstein (eds.), *Major Problems in the History of American Workers* (Lexington, MA: D. C. Heath, 1991), 322.

[141] S. and B. Webb, *Co-Operative*, 482.

[142] S. Webb, *The Works Manager To-Day: An Address Prepared for a Series of Private Gatherings with Works Managers* (London: Longmans, Green and Co., 1917), 24.

[143] Editors, 'Salvaging the Unemployable', *New Republic*, 2 October 1915, 222.

[144] S. and B. Webb, *Constitution*, 202.   [145] Croly, 'School for Social Research', 168.

[146] Lippmann, *Public Opinion*, 193.

[147] O. Tead, 'The Guild State' (n.d), Tead Papers, 5, 11.

[148] Editors, 'The Making of an American Nation', *New Republic*, 31 October 1923, 244.

Although groups were to be granted a degree of autonomy, all the nationalist progressives insisted that a significant role for the state in directing associational life would have to remain, even if scaled down from the ambitions of the past. A central organization with a final say was required to act as a 'regulator and adjuster among them; defining the limits of their action, preventing and settling conflicts' and to set 'the industrial stage in an orderly and statesmanlike fashion'.[149] Even a commitment to the nationalization of industry survived the pluralist turn.[150] Certain as to the benefits nationalization would bring in terms of systematic industrial planning but anxious as to the potential costs in terms of innovation and economic freedom, the *New Republic* attempted to draw up detailed criteria for the nationalization of certain key industries.[151] Thorstein Veblen thus argued that any large-scale industry 'which has reached such a state of routine, mechanical systematization, or automatic articulation that it is possible for it to be habitually managed from an office by methods of accountancy' was suitable for nationalization.[152] Of the leading nationalist progressives of old, the argument was most clearly articulated by Walter Weyl. In his last year of life, Weyl argued that such a strategy would rightfully legitimize the nationalization of both the railroads and the mining industry. Indeed, Weyl wished to push this argument as far as it would possibly go: 'The government should progressively extend its power over all basic industries', he concluded, 'with the double intention of effecting unity and of securing profits.'[153]

This general outline of a political programme illustrates that the nationalist progressives sought to strike a very difficult compromise in the early postwar age; they wanted enough pluralism to keep the all-powerful state at bay, while allowing enough integration both to enable the nation collectively to respond to shared problems and to encourage the development of a substantial shared sense of common identity. As Follett concluded, group 'differences must be integrated, not annihilated, nor absorbed. Anarchy means unorganized, unrelated difference; coordinated, unified difference belongs to our ideal of a perfect social order.'[154] 'One would always prefer this to be a movement from below up rather than from above down', Follett suggested, 'but it is not impossible for the two movements to go on at the same time.'[155] Even John Dewey, generally the most enthusiastic supporter of decentralization, was willing to go so far as to assert the essential supremacy of the state over other associations. As he did, he even employed that age-old organicist image

---

[149] Dewey, *Reconstruction*, 203, and O. Tead, 'Trade Unions and Efficiency', *American Journal of Sociology*, 22 (1916), 34.

[150] See Editors, 'The Railroads and the Nation', *New Republic*, 21 November 1914, 11–12.

[151] On Hobson's reception in America, see J. L. Hammond, 'The New Outlook in Industry', *New Republic*, 7 March 1923, 50–1.

[152] T. Veblen, 'A Policy of Reconstruction', *New Republic*, 13 April 1918, 320

[153] Weyl, *End of the War*, 307.   [154] Follett, *New State*, 39.

[155] Follett, *New State*, 248.

of the central government as working in society as a 'conductor of an orches-
tra'.[156] The exact nature of that conductor role remained to be seen, of
course. It was a lesson to be learnt through pragmatism, by the process of trial
and error. Walter Lippmann responded to this pragmatic injunction. The
correct balance between 'centralization' and 'political anarchy' would 'have
to be pieced together', he argued, through analysis, invention, and
research.[157] But whatever the imprecision on detail, there was certainty on
the general principle. Not only did the progressive ideal of a national communal perfection remain central to their conceptual programme, the position of
the central state as the final guarantor of communal harmony also remained
an undiminished part of the institutional settlement required to promote it.

Building bridges: class and the state

That state itself, however, would have to be reformed. If the American federal
government, in particular, was to play a significant part in enabling the
progressives to attain their goals it needed to be reconstructed. At the heart of
this reformed state, the nationalist progressives argued, was the need for a
more prominent role for carefully selected expertise. This charge was the
centrepiece of Lippmann's first significant post-war work, *Public Opinion*. 'The
lesson' of the wartime experience, Lippmann charged, 'is a fairly clear one'.
The American public overlooked the genuine 'common interests' of the
nation and were led into reaction partly by their own intellectual and
emotional shortcomings and partly by the mismanagement of the nation by
a conservative political elite. What was required, therefore, was a programme
of reform which would enable state affairs to be directed of by a well-intentioned and well-informed elite: 'a specialized class whose personal interests
reach beyond locality'.[158] For all her apparent pluralism, Follett differed not
at all here, arguing that 'efficient government by the employment of experts
and the concentration of administrative authority' was a prerequisite for a
politics of reform.[159] The role of progressive personnel in Washington during
the war was interpreted as a strength rather than a weakness. The willingness,
as Follett saw it, of progressive intellectuals to 'sacrifice business and personal
interests . . . to pour out their all for the great stake of democracy' was one of
the more creditable legacies of the conflict.[160]

Yet despite such optimistic assertions, a more pervasive worry had entered
progressive thought in the post-war world. None of the nationalist progressives could deny, that however well staffed by progressive expertise, the state
could no longer straightforwardly be trusted to pursue the common good.

---

[156] Dewey, *Reconstruction* 203.   [157] Lippmann, *Public Opinion*, 397.
[158] Lippmann, *Public Opinion*, 310.   [159] Follett, *New State*, 175.
[160] Follett, *New State*, 338.

However hard Felix Frankfurter, Walter Lippmann, and Frank Walsh had tried, their efforts in the Wilson administration had amounted to very little. Indeed, the behaviour of most agencies of the federal government had worsened rather than improved. Such problems were particularly severe in economic management as industrial conflict during the war had continued to grow with the result of a great enhancement of class tension. Such a problem, moreover, struck right to the heart of the nationalist vision and the theorists were quick to identify it: 'Human society as a composite whole, whose continuity depends upon the preservation of a flexible balance among its parts, is in danger of being torn to pieces by irreconcilable class enmities', Croly contended in late 1918.[161]

What this implied was the need thoroughly to reconsider the relationship between citizens, and especially working-class citizens, and the state itself. The extent of the wartime clash between classes threw 'the foundation for [the state's] legitimate authority and for the allegiance of its citizens' entirely into question.[162] Unless people feel that they are related directly to the state, Walter Weyl argued, they may be unwilling to 'accept the state as their natural representative'.[163] Social harmony and economic order could be established only by an active state; but an active state had to offer a programme that all citizens could accept as a true reflection of their own essential interests and needs. There is an 'essential evil', Croly contended, from the attribution of 'moral sovereignty to physically powerful states *without* any significant assurance of the power for genuinely social purposes'.[164] The resolution to this problem was not, however, the pluralist solution of debunking the state entirely. Rather, it was to find some means of ensuring that the state was more responsive to the demands of those groups and sections of society currently excluded. Such responsiveness was dependent in turn 'upon the ability of the masses of the community politically to control' the government machine.[165]

This worry led directly to the most dramatic of all of the nationalist progressives' new institutional commitments to emerge from the war. From 1918 and throughout the early 1920s, the *New Republic* progressives dedicated themselves to constructing an effective political party in the United States that encompassed organized labour. Without direct representation for labour, a democratic state 'is capable of using its power as intolerantly, as oppressively, and as indifferently to human liberty as the autocratic state'.[166] Borrowing not from the socialist pluralists but once again from the Fabians, the nationalist progressives argued that the only way to ensure that the legislative and executive branches appreciated the needs of the workers was

[161] Croly, 'School for Social Research', 168.
[162] Croly, 'Future of the State', 183.
[163] Weyl, *New Democracy*, 283.
[164] Croly, 'Future of the State', 181.
[165] Weyl, *End of the War*, 308.
[166] Croly, 'Breach of Civilization', 13.

by 'attaching to labor unionism political methods and outlook'.[167] The great value of a genuinely democratic society, Croly insisted, consists in the development of 'resolute disposition to seek the realization of social objects through the agency of political methods, a frank confidence in the good faith of the political establishment'.[168] Empowering working people in general, and trade unions in particular, to involve themselves in politics could provide just such an assurance. '[T]he time has come', these American progressive intellectuals insisted, for the American trade unions 'to go into politics'.[169] 'The most effective safeguard ... against a deplorable class warfare', the editors of the *New Republic* continued, consists in the formation of a party of workers whose programme would be 'as radical as the proposed program of the British Labour party'.[170] This demand found its apotheosis in the response accorded to the British Labour Party's first real manifesto, *Labour and the New Social Order*, published in November 1918. The formation of 'a party which seeks a commonwealth of, by, and for the working people of all kinds', the *New Republic* explained, 'would escape the bondage of a class prejudice and the necessity of an exclusive class policy'.[171] The idea 'struck fire' in the 'progressive imagination' because it offered the only way to 'approach the future from the standpoint of the community as a whole'.[172]

The advantages of involving workers directly in the political process also stretched beyond the taming of the state. The *New Republic* also argued that it would lead unions themselves to temper their demands and commit them to finding socially desirable solutions to otherwise intractable sectional disputes. Encouraging workers to form their own political party, it was continually argued, would lead them to 'assume the responsibility for adapting their class program and needs to those of the other classes and to that of the community as a whole'.[173] The process of active negotiation and coalition building essential in politics would lead unions away from their dedication to conflict to a more moderate position, one complementary to the demands of other sections of society. Two essential tasks—making the state more truly representative of the common interest and moving workers themselves from sectionalism to communalism—could, thus, both be met by enabling the mobilization of the trade union movement behind a single political party; a

---

[167] Editors, 'Towards Industrial Democracy', *New Republic*, 1 September 1917, 123.

[168] H. Croly, 'The Obligation of the Vote', *New Republic*, 9 October 1915, 8. See too, O. Tead, 'A National Labor Policy', *New Republic*, 17 November 1917, 67–9.

[169] Editors, 'Labor in Politics', *New Republic*, 19 November 1919, 336.

[170] Editors, 'British and American Labor', *New Republic*, 16 February 1918, 69–71.

[171] Editors, 'The Nationalism of the British Labour Party', *New Republic*, 17 August 1918, 64. See also J. A. Fitch, 'Labor and Politics', *Survey*, 8 June 1918, 287–9.

[172] Gleason and Kellogg, *British Labour*, 125. For an almost identical formulation, see Follett, *New State*, 120–1.

[173] Editors, 'Labour in Politics', *New Republic*, 19 November 1919, 336. See also 'Why a Labor Party?', *New Republic*, 26 April 1919, 399, and 'A New National Party', *New Republic*, 4 March 1920, 108–11, and Tead, 'National Labor Policy', 67–9.

party that they believed would have the further advantage of being directed not by class-conscious workers but by removed, impartial experts. Combining the arguments into one, Mary Follett argued that what organized workers need is 'leaders who are alive not to the needs of labor, but to the needs of the whole state: then it will be seen as a corollary how labor fits in, what the state needs from labor, what labor needs from the state, what part labor is to have *in* the state.'[174]

Disappointed that they should take such a view, Harold Laski campaigned vigorously against the idea that the nationalist progressives should pursue the creation of a Labor Party. Addressing the 1919 Academy of Political Science conference in New York, he urged that Americans had very little to learn from the Fabians' experience in Britain. The 'very special' nature of the British Labour party's connection to its 'peculiar environment', Laski insisted, entailed that 'to attempt its application, either in outline or detail, to the . . . problems of American reconstruction would certainly be mistaken and possibly disastrous'.[175] Although most neutral observers agreed with Laski's reasoning, the desire to construct an American Labor Party was not entirely confined to the realm of philosophical fantasy. A series of convention resolutions from the United Mine Workers of America lent support to almost the entire programme of the British Labour Party, inspiring the nationalist progressives and encouraging them to seek wider practical support for the idea throughout the immediate post-war years.[176] Indeed, success appeared to beckon in November 1918 when, in an explicit challenge to the continued formal apolitical stance of Samuel Gompers' American Federation of Labor (AFL), the Chicago Federation of Labor attempted to establish a local Labor Party. That party grew a year later into a National Labor Party which 'frankly admit[ted] its kinship to the British Labour Party'.[177] But despite high-level progressive expectations that such an organization would have 'an excellent chance of capturing the White House', the sceptics quickly turned out to be right. The party failed to make any significant headway.[178] Unsuccessful in its attempt to persuade the progressive Senator Robert La Follette to stand as its candidate for the presidency, it ran in 1920 as a Farmer-Labor party with the relatively unknown attorney Parley Parker Christensen at its head. Its performance was dismal. It polled only 290,000 votes, less than half the amount

[174] Follett, *New State*, 330.

[175] H. Laski, 'British Reconstruction Proposals and the American Attitude', *Proceedings of the Academy of Political Science*, 8 (1919), 193. Compare with a more moderate assertion of difference: S. Webb, 'The Inter-Allied Labor Conference', *New Republic*, 23 March 1918, 225–7.

[176] See D. Montgomery, 'Industrial Democracy or Democracy in Industry?', in N. Lichtenstein and H. J. Harris (eds), *Industrial Democracy in America: The Ambiguous Promise* (Cambridge: Cambridge University Press, 1996), 36–7.

[177] Editors, 'The Labor Party', *Survey*, 13 November 1919, 229. See also Editors, 'Independent Labor Party Launched', *Survey*, 30 November 1918, 264–5, and 'Growing Support for a Labor Party', *Survey*, 14 December 1918, 354.

[178] Frank P. Walsh cited in McCartin, *Labor's Great War*, 197.

that Eugene Debs won for the American Socialist Party, and far fewer than the progressives themselves had enjoyed when fighting under the banner of Theodore Roosevelt.[179] In the aftermath of the 1920 election, as the AFL's leadership put increasing pressure on local unions to disaffiliate from the movement, this American Labor Party grew progressively weaker. Four years later, it was eventually the sad but not unexpected victim of a communist takeover, the inevitable victim of insurmountable institutional obstacles and unhelpful social cleavages.[180] The most grandiose of the nationalist progressives' new political ideals fell at the first hurdle.

Conclusion

No matter how unsuccessful the efforts at partisan reconstruction were, they demonstrated one thing very clearly: the power of the nationalist progressives' dedication to communal loyalty remained undimmed after the war. Even Walter Weyl's *The End of the War*, a book infused with pluralist rhetoric and concerns about an all-powerful central state, still suggested that human progress could not be guaranteed 'until the separate interests within each nation are completely extinguished'.[181] The 'child of intelligent social readjustment', the *New Republic* likewise insisted, must still be 'national unity'.[182] In the aftermath of the conflict, however, this position was inherently unstable. It gave credence to bold political programmes which were even more unrealistic than those that had preceded them and it involved these thinkers in a balancing act which was increasingly difficult to strike. It was no surprise, therefore, when it began to break down. By 1925, Walter Lippmann's loyalties to the nationalist progressive cause, whether in its new or its old form, began to waver dramatically. In his next major work after *Public Opinion*, *The Phantom Public*, he explicitly denied not only the value but also the possibility of a genuinely progressive national communal unity, and even rejected his own accusations against 'the pluralistic theory' as 'grossly exaggerated'.[183]

Nonetheless, in the immediate aftermath of the First World War something dramatic had happened. The nationalist progressives turned to British socialist pluralism for advice. After that discussion had concluded its initial stage,

---

[179] See C. Merz, 'Enter: The Labor Party', *New Republic*, 10 December 1919, 53–5.

[180] The story of the collapse of the Labor Party movement is expertly told in Weinstein, *Decline of Socialism*, 272–4. See also N. Fine, *Labor and Farmer Parties in the United States, 1828–1928* (New York: Russell and Russell, 1961). Progressive exasperation at the communist take over is shown in R. Lovett, 'The Farmer-Labor Fiasco at Chicago', *New Republic*, 18 July 1923, 198–200.

[181] Weyl, *End of the War*, 311.

[182] Editors, 'Nationalism of the British Labour Party', 65.

[183] W. Lippmann, *The Phantom Public: A Sequel to 'Public Opinion'* (New York: MacMillan, 1925), 161. For more details, see the Epilogue.

an important gulf remained between the British socialist pluralists and the American progressives both on the central philosophical issues of freedom and human development and on the key institutional arguments concerning the place and role of the central state. Reviewing Mary Follett's *The New State* for the *New Republic*, Harold Laski demarcated the line of division clearly for both his contemporaries and for posterity. He could not accept that 'liberty is to consist in making myself one with the community . . . for there is in each soul certain recesses where no other can penetrate'.[184] 'Miss Follett knows her Hegel, her Duguit, her James, her Roscoe Pound, her Harold Laski. She knows her particularism, her syndicalism, her guild socialism her dualism, her pluralism', a *Political Science Quarterly* reviewer complained. 'But she does not know human nature.'[185] It was a view with which Laski agreed entirely. Working through Lippmann, he urged the nationalist progressives to accept this opinion also. They should not to take Follett and her allies' version of pluralism seriously, he argued; rather they should recognize the philosophical desirability of the essentially individualistic, British pluralist vision instead. But all to no avail.[186] How Laski and the other British socialist pluralists responded to the nationalist progressives' refusal to accept his lead, and how they adapted their own programmes as a result, is the subject of the next chapter.

[184] H. Laski, 'The New State', *New Republic*, 8 February 1919, 61.
[185] H. L. McBain, 'The New State', *Political Science Quarterly*, 34 (1919), 170.
[186] See H. Laski to W. Lippmann, letter dated 14 April 1919, Yale University Library, New Haven, The W. Lippmann Papers, 326/1/17/688.

5

From Pluralism to Community

Introduction

Despite the great degree of interest it provoked, the British socialist pluralists' ideological system was eventually rejected by its American admirers. The pluralists' unapologetic individualism and their practical dedication to a vigorous idea of associational independence, although attractive in the immediate aftermath of war, was ultimately dismissed as creating too many possibilities for anarchic reaction and for further dividing the allegiances of an already diverse citizen body. Ordway Tead thus worried that British socialist pluralism would allow 'self-regarding impulses' to 'gain ascendancy'.[1] Mary Follett was even more decisive in her dismissal. 'The present plans for guild socialism', she argued, 'while they may point to a possible future development, and while they may be a step on the way, as a scheme of political organization have many weak points.' Chief among those was the likelihood that their institutional recommendations would 'give way' both to 'individual self-ishness' and 'group selfishness'. 'From such experiments', she concluded, 'we shall learn much, but the new ship of state cannot ride of such turbulent waters.'[2]

The British socialist pluralists themselves were undeniably taken aback by the astringency of this attack, especially as it was joined by an assault from within Britain itself conducted along largely the same lines. The pluralists' Fabian contemporaries, indeed, were even more severe in their judgement than the Americans had been. To them, the theoretical overview presented by Cole, Laski, Tawney, and colleagues opened the door to 'sheer chaotic anarchy'.[3] Even radical British Liberals like L. T. Hobhouse and J. A. Hobson argued that the socialist pluralists simply did not have the necessary 'feeling for the unity of the common life'. The concentration on the 'diversity' of individuals and associations, Hobhouse continued, obscured the 'essential

---

[1] O. Tead, 'The Bases of Social Theory', *The Freeman*, 7 June 1920, 406.
[2] M. Follett, *The New State: Group Organization the Solution of Popular Government* (New York: Longmans Green and Co., 1918), 330.
[3] Anon., 'The Quest for Freedom', *New Statesman*, 11 January 1919, 305.

interconnections' of modern existence.[4] As Laski himself noted, the pluralists' critics, in the United States and in Britain, were characterized by a 'continuous insistence upon the well-being of the community as a whole against the specialised interest of competing groups'.[5] 'No criticism', Tawney likewise complained, was 'more common.'[6]

This widespread theoretical critique took a distinctly practical form as an attack on pluralist industrial and economic policy in general and as a reaction against the pluralists' perceived sympathy for radical trade unionism in particular. Despite all the difficulties unions had faced during the war, Thorstein Veblen argued in the *New Republic*, they still had no right 'to exercise an unlimited sabotage in order to gain a private end regardless of the community'.[7] American nationalist progressives thus joined with leading theorists in the Fabian Society in Britain in articulating a concern that Cole, Laski, and Tawney's habitual expression of contempt for the 'omnicompetent state', however admirable in itself, would lead to a severe and unhealthy restriction on necessary regulatory authority. In any economic system characterized by a strict doctrine of associational independence, these critics warned, strong industrial associations would be able to dominate all other groupings. Associations 'powerful enough and prepared enough to enforce their demands' could exert tremendous and unwarranted influence; independent industrial associations or unregulated trade unions could restrict output and drive up prices if it suited their own narrow interpretation of their own interests.[8] The more confident workers become of 'their place in the industrial system', Walter Lippmann contended, 'the smaller becomes the majority which can paralyze that system'.[9] As Lippmann continued, the pluralists' critics were not willing to contemplate the consequences of such a development; they would not 'tolerate forever great suffering because of a deadlocked dispute . . . in an industry producing immediate necessities'.[10] In Britain, Sidney Webb agreed. He warned of 'organised brigandage by strongly combined and momentarily indispensable people' and insisted that the 'only ultimate safeguard' was a countervailing 'regard for community and its real interests'.[11] Associations could not be allowed to hold an entire nation to ransom.

---

[4] L. T. Hobhouse, 'A Ground Plan for Socialism', *Manchester Guardian*, 21 September 1920.

[5] H. Laski, 'Mr Wallas as a Social Analyst', *Nation*, 9 April 1921, 60.

[6] R. H. Tawney, 'The Case for the Consumer', *Guildsman*, December 1919, 3. See also G. D. H. Cole, *Self-Government in Industry* (London: G. Bell, 1917), 226.

[7] T. Veblen, 'A Policy of Reconstruction', *New Republic*, 13 April 1918, 319.

[8] See G. Field, *Guild Socialism: A Critical Examination* (London: W. Gardner, Darton and Co., 1920), 101. See also H. Vivian, 'National Guilds and the State', *Economic Journal*, 30 (1920), 233–7.

[9] W. Lippmann, 'Can the Strike be Abandoned?', *New Republic*, 21 January 1920, 224.

[10] Lippmann, 'Strike be Abandoned?', 226.

[11] S. Webb, 'The Living Wage', *Fabian News*, January 1913, 15.

The solidity of this critique impressed Cole, Laski, and Tawney. Especially as the post-war era was increasingly marked by bitter industrial disputes, the pluralists found it difficult to ignore concerns about the effects of an unreconstructed doctrine of associational independence. By the early 1920s, they were frequently insisting that they were fully aware that even the most intimate of internal associational actions could seriously and negatively impact upon the well-being of other associations and the members. Our critics 'are unquestionably right', Laski accepted in 1922, 'in their insistence that no vocation can ever be left the complete control of its function'.[12] Tawney concurred, declaring that an 'unfettered freedom' in associational interrelations could result in the emergence of 'something in the nature of private war'.[13] Even Cole, probably the socialist pluralist most dedicated to the idea of associational independence, was willing to concede that all associations should be obliged to abide by some 'definite standard' in their relations with others.[14] Just as they were conceptually united in proposing a new conception of freedom during the war, so these theorists were agreed as to the necessity of some compromise with their critics in the post-war age. It came as no surprise, therefore, when Laski used his major post-war work, *A Grammar of Politics*, to plead that his form of pluralism was concerned 'not with the defence of anarchy but with the conditions of its avoidance'.[15]

This search for compromise entailed that there had to be some way of discriminating between the actions which independent groups ought to be allowed to pursue and those in need of regulation. In order to discover a set of criteria by which to do so, Cole, Laski, and Tawney all returned once again to examine the concept of 'community'. In the immediate post-war period, all of the major socialist pluralists steadfastly denied that their ideological system inevitably overlooked the demands of 'the whole'.[16] Rather, the socialist pluralists contended that there was a place for the richly communitarian discourse of the British left within the pluralist scheme. Cole, Laski and Tawney even went so far as to argue that they, rather than Fabians or nationalists, were the true heirs to the ideological commitments of communitarian utopians like as Robert Owen and William Morris, just as they were the genuine successors to liberal individualists such as John Stuart Mill. The theorists' post-war articles were thus at least rhetorically as eager to respond to the potential 'oneness of humanity' as they were simultaneously willing to deny the possibility of any meaningful 'social unity'.[17]

This move was frequently mocked. As Ordway Tead argued in a review of

---

[12] H. Laski, 'The Co-operative Movement', *New Republic*, 14 June 1922, 81.

[13] R. H. Tawney, *The Acquisitive Society* (London: G. Bell, 1921), 33 and 54.

[14] G. D. H. Cole, *Social Theory* (London: Methuen, 1920), 52.

[15] H. Laski, *A Grammar of Politics*, (London: George Allen and Unwin, 1925, 2nd edn 1930), 100.

[16] See the excellent discussion in J. A. C. Pemberton, 'James and the Early Laski: The Ambiguous Legacy of Pragmatism', *History of Political Thought*, 19 (1998), esp. 284.

[17] H. Laski, 'Rousseau', *New Republic*, 16 July 1919, 364.

Cole's post-war collection of essays *Chaos and Order in Industry*, when the pluralists attempted to speak the language of 'community' their critics began to 'cry inconsistency or compromise'.[18] They did so with serious effect, as shall be seen later in this chapter, and they have continued to do so ever since. Latterday commentators on the pluralists have similarly dismissed this post-war emphasis on a pluralist view of 'community'. David Nicholls argues that the 'trouble began' for G. D. H. Cole 'when [he] tried to put forward some theory about the relationship which should obtain among . . . and between groups' and more recent readers such as David Runciman have agreed.[19]

As contemporary observers like Ordway Tead himself knew, however, so harsh an evaluation is hard to maintain without a detailed conceptual account of the pluralists' approach to the idea of community and its consequences, and it is just such an account that is all too often missing from the critics' work.[20] This chapter provides the fuller analysis necessary by offering a detailed examination of the socialist pluralists' response to their post-war critics and by carefully examining the philosophical basis of their conception of 'community' and its apparent political consequences. The chapter asks, in particular, whether Cole, Tawney, and Laski were willing to see the only constraints upon associations' behaviour as either self-imposed or imposed by unavoidable and unalterable physical, psychological, or even market-economic 'realities', or, alternatively, whether their conception of community allowed them to support some, as yet indistinct, form of consciously imposed associational regulation. Such a discussion both reveals the ideological creativity of the socialist pluralists and opens the door to a reinvigorated discussion of their actual plans for the reconstruction of Britain's political, social, and economic system.

Recasting Community and Building a Functional Society

On the nationalist progressives' model, even as adapted in the aftermath of the war, industrial associations, however internally democratic, were still ultimately to be directed by the demands of the community as a whole, either indirectly through centralized regulation or directly through national ownership. This, of course, implied that, had they the power to do so, the nationalist progressives would have been willing to use the central state to impose

---

[18] O. Tead, 'Self-Government in Industry', *The Freeman*, 9 February 1921, 525.

[19] D. Nicholls, *The Pluralist State: The Political Ideas of J. N. Figgis and his Contemporaries* (London: St Martin's Press, 1994), 87, and D. Runciman, *Pluralism and the Personality of the State* (Cambridge: Cambridge University Press, 1997), 170–3.

[20] Tead argued that the criticisms were generally based only on a 'superficial' reading of Cole's text. See Tead, 'Self-Government', 525.

significant limitations on the behaviour of associations, especially industrial associations. Associations would be able to make recommendations to the central state and to compete in a generally open marketplace, but if their activities were thought to conflict with some greater public good, then, in the final instance, their decision-making role was to be restricted. Such a view was defended by continuous reference to the central importance of the interests of the 'national community' in comparison with the demands of sectional interests or of particular individuals.

The socialist pluralists rejected every aspect of this argument. They were committed to the view that the irreducible diversity of individual opinion ensured that it was simply impossible to identify any thick 'national community' interest. As Laski put it, 'from any survey of the facts, the main thing that emerges is the inevitable variety of views by which we are confronted'.[21] 'The relation of the parts' in a modern nation state, Laski argued, is 'unified in neither aim nor method.' 'Because men are varied they move in a varied direction', he continued, 'their effort is different and their interpretations of life refuse reduction to a single scheme.'[22] As the pluralist fellow-traveller Bertrand Russell insisted, 'I have no wish to deny men often aim at something which they believe to be the "public good." But their conception of what constitutes the public good is a product of their own impulses and passions, a subjective thing.'[23] Any approach to the idea of 'community' that considered otherwise, G. D. H. Cole concluded, was 'essentially false'.[24]

The search for a socialist pluralist conception of 'community' with which to counter the criticisms of their rivals began, therefore, rather unpromisingly with a rejection of the possibility of detecting any substantive common goal. In constructing their alternative vision, the socialist pluralists could have no recourse to any claims regarding a substantial 'shared good' or 'common end'. The socialist pluralist thinkers were not willing, as Laski so clearly insisted, to try to 'hack their way to an artificial unity'.[25] A conception of community had to be developed which could somehow accommodate an insistence on difference. Furthermore, if Cole, Laski, and Tawney were to integrate a conception of community into their ideological scheme it would have to be compatible with their individualistic rendering of the idea of liberty and with the essential voluntarism of the pluralists' understanding of the purpose and legitimacy of associations. The industrial recommendations of the nationalist progressives, and especially the restriction of occupational mobility implicit, often even explicit, in their advocacy of a form of state-centred Taylorism

---

[21] H. Laski, 'The Temper of the Present Time', New Republic, 18 February 1920, 335.

[22] H. Laski, The Foundations of Sovereignty and Other Essays (New Haven: Yale University Press, 1921), 28, and H. Laski, Authority in the Modern State (New Haven: Yale University Press, 1919), 166.

[23] B. Russell, 'The State and its External Relations', Proceedings of the Aristotelian Society, 16 (1916), 302.

[24] G. D. H. Cole, Labour in the Commonwealth: A Book for a Younger Generation (London: Headley Bros, 1918), 37.   [25] Laski, 'Temper', 335.

simply violated this constraint. All the pluralists had long distanced themselves from the idea that individuals owed the community a duty to perform any particular form of labour. Even after Laski's acceptance of the perfectionist element of the idealist conception of liberty, the socialist pluralists' dedication to the individual's pursuit of his or her initially unrecognizable 'best self' included a commitment to the possibility that such a self could be discovered through pursuits in industrial associations of the individual's own choosing. Cole was thus insistent that any 'guilds' of the future must 'not be closed corporations, but open associations which any man may join'.[26]

This is not, of course, to imply that the pluralists sought to allow everyone to pursue exactly the career they chose. As Cole continued, an interest in openness 'does not mean . . . that any person will be able to claim admission as an absolute right . . . In many occupations, there will be preliminary training . . . and tests of fitness to pass . . . [But] he will have free choice . . . of the available openings'.[27] The personal experimentation that was at the core of the pluralist conception of liberty demanded that each and every individual be able to try out a wide variety of occupations and, to as great an extent as possible, pursue them in a wide variety of ways.[28] Any system of centralized appointment and industrial direction on the Fabian or nationalist progressive model would appear certain to curtail such experimentation. For Cole, all of these fantasies of state-directed scientific management sought only to train 'man to be the best possible machine'.[29] As Laski more directly phrased it, the socialist pluralists were dedicated to ensuring that industrial activity offered 'avenues for experimentation on a much wider scale' than the nationalist progressives were willing to accept.[30]

As other commentators have noted, this argument also revealed a fundamental difference in the pluralists' and their critics' attitude to work itself.[31] For many progressives, it appeared that work was necessarily to be understood as involving a considerable disutility. Industrial labour was an unpleasant duty that the worker must perform in order to enable the consumer to enjoy the fruits of industrial cooperation. The nationalist progressives and their allies did not just ignore the unpleasantness of work, however, for in addition to offering workers a more equitable distribution of the product of industry they promised that the weight of the industrial burden would be lightened by carefully considered industrial coordination. As the *Nation* phrased it, reformers should be disposed 'to measure the future advance of civilisation by the diminishing part which industry should play in human

[26] G. D. H. Cole, *Guild Socialism Restated* (London: Leonard Parsons, 1920), 75.
[27] Cole, *Guild Socialism Restated*, 75.   [28] See Laski, *Grammar*, 95.
[29] G. D. H. Cole, *The World of Labour: A Discussion of the Present and the Future of Trade Unionism*, 2nd edn (London: G. Bell, 1913), 326.   [30] Laski, 'The Co-operative Movement', 81.
[31] See, for example, A. Wright, *G. D. H. Cole and Socialist Democracy* (Oxford: Oxford University Press, 1979), 62–6, and P. Beilharz, *Labour's Utopias: Bolshevism, Fabianism, Social Democracy* (London: Routledge, 1992), 72–3. I thank John Burrow for bringing this point to my attention.

life' rather than by the expansion of enjoyment in work itself.[32] As J. A. Hobson continued, the ideal vision was of a society 'which gives less and less of its total fund of time, energy, thought and feeling to those tasks of production which we call industrial' and which enables individuals to enjoy an expanded and better resourced leisure time.[33] Effectively coordinated industrial effort would release more time and create more resources which, when equitably distributed, would enrich individuals' lives. There was no doubt for theorists in the nationalist tradition that workers should 'not live to work, but work to live'.[34]

This view, however, was again specifically and consistently rejected by Cole, Laski, Tawney, and their colleagues. As these theorists had collectively shaped a conception of liberty that emphasized individual diversity, so too were they unified in insisting that the workplace must be a positive centre of individual experience. There was little value, Ivor Brown argued, in the tendency to avoid talking 'about making work better, but only making it shorter'.[35] The socialist pluralists were all aware that for the vast majority of labourers the nature of day-to-day work itself was always likely to be unpleasant. Laski, indeed, was willing to argue that 'the centre of importance for most men . . . will be the period of leisure rather than the period of work'.[36] But they were also convinced that a sense of significance at work played a large role in determining whether he was capable of 'experimenting with the best of himself', even in his leisure time. Such a sense of significance, the socialist pluralists all held, was undermined by any system that denied individuals the opportunity to employ their initiative in the choice of their occupation or to deny them the substantial right to direct the operations of their work-place. An industrial system which directed individuals towards particular occupations which were themselves significantly directed by the state would result, Tawney argued, in 'an exasperating' sense of 'paralysis', of insignificance, which would in effect deny the possibility of meaningful psychological experimentation.[37] 'We must, of course, produce in order to live', Cole insisted, 'but is it essential that we inculcate a slave mentality in the producer?'[38] Allowing individuals to choose their own work and democratically to direct the bulk of their industrial associations' operations, as Laski saw it, would not stop the average worker from being 'a tender of machines' but it would 'make the worker' *feel* as if he 'count[ed] in the world'.[39] Whereas

---

[32] Anon., 'What Sort of Democracy?', *Nation*, 4 January 1919, 639.

[33] J. A. Hobson, 'The New Industrial Revolution', *Contemporary Review*, 118 (1920), 643.

[34] S. Webb, *The Works Manager To-Day: An Address Prepared for a Series of Private Gatherings with Works Managers* (London: Longmans, Green and Co., 1917), 11.

[35] I. Brown, 'Aspects of the Guild Idea', *New Age*, 6 May 1915, 7.

[36] H. Laski, 'The State in the New Social Order', *Fabian Tract* 200 (London: Fabian Society, 1922), 5.

[37] R. H. Tawney, 'Industry and the Expert', *Guildsman*, June 1921, 5.

[38] G. D. H. Cole, 'Slave Virtues and Other Virtues', *New Statesman*, 14 January 1922, 414.

[39] Laski, *Authority*, 91.

the nationalist progressives clearly believed it possible to combine the 'central authority of the state' in the 'co-ordination of production and distribution' with the 'rebellious spirit of freedom of thought and action' necessary for experimentation, the socialist pluralists did not.[40] They took F. W. Taylor at his word when he suggested that, according to the doctrines of scientific management that nationalist progressives wished to adapt, 'one of the very first requirements for a man who is fit to handle pig iron as a regular occupation is that he should be so stupid and phlegmatic that he more nearly resembles an ox than any other type'.[41] The socialist pluralists' dedication to ensuring workers were offered as great a degree of individual choice and flexibility as possible continued to throw the potential compatibility of their doctrine with and any notion of regulatory authority into doubt.

The principle of function

Despite their resolute critique of the nationalist progressives' regulatory principles, Cole, Laski, and Tawney all insisted that they were well aware of the need for *some* form of regulatory principle; associations could not always be left to act just as they thought fit. To this end, all three leading pluralists argued that they possessed a 'definite standard' with which to assess associational activity. That standard was to be found in a principle of 'function'. Associations, that is, were to be assessed both according to whether they provided a 'socially useful service'—where that term is yet to be defined—and whether they provided that service in a manner compatible with the goods of other associations and the well-being of the generality of individuals. This was not an easy standard. Laski, Cole, and Tawney did not view function, as some of their laissez-faire contemporaries did, as an almost inevitable feature of the practical operations of societal interactions.[42] The socialist pluralists all insisted that 'an association does not automatically . . . fulfil a function' simply 'by pursuing the interests of its members'.[43] Indeed, almost all associations were held to be failing to fulfil their necessary functions. It was the existing capitalistic order, and not the tenets of socialist pluralism, that wrongly 'assured' some 'men that there are no ends other than their own ends . . . no limit than what they think advisable.'[44]

Throughout the early 1920s, the pluralists' critics on both sides of the Atlantic puzzled over this response to their criticisms, eventually dismissing them almost out of hand. First, they argued that the pluralists' principle of

---

[40] J. R. MacDonald, *Socialism After the War* (Manchester: National Labour Press, 1918), 20 and 17.
[41] Taylor, cited in H. F. May, *The End of American Innocence: A Study in the First Years of Our Time, 1912–1917* (New York: Columbia University Press, 1992), 133.
[42] See the discussion is S. den Otter, *British Idealism and Social Explanation: A Study in Late Victorian Thought* (Oxford: Oxford University Press, 1996), 189–95.
[43] Cole, *Social Theory*, 52.
[44] Tawney, *Acquisitive Society*, 33.

function, and the conception of community on which it had to be based, involved the very sort of presumptions that the pluralists had so aggressively rejected. In reviewing the discussion of function in Cole's *Social Theory*, L. T. Hobhouse thought he detected a considerable anomaly. In talking of society as a 'federation of functions', Hobhouse contended, Cole had tried covertly to smuggle in an acceptance of the communitarian, even organicist, premises he dismissed elsewhere. Cole's theory of function, Hobhouse argued, relied upon an 'idea of what I should like (and he would very much dislike) to call the organic structure of society'.[45] Any principle of function, Hobhouse concluded, necessarily involved reference both to a unified community interest and to an understanding of interdependent parts assisting the work of each other. To be 'functional', on such an account, associations would have to perform specific roles for the benefit of an agreed general end. In the United States, Lippmann agreed wholeheartedly with Hobhouse's critique. To understand 'function' any other way, he charged in *Public Opinion*, was illegitimately to 'play' with the word to make it serve one's own end.[46]

The second response of contemporary critics regarded the practical implications of the functional principle. Here critics contended that for all the pluralists' bombastic anti-statism, the principle of function entailed support for a vital regulatory authority identical to the role of the state advanced by nationalist progressives and their supporters. In making this point, the Cambridge economist D. H. Robertson again chose Cole as his target. Asking 'who is to co-ordinate' functions in Cole's model society, Robertson considered that the pluralist must have expected the job to fall to 'the old state writ large'.[47] In allowing a principle of function to be used to test the performance of associations, the socialist pluralist appeared to have 'expelled the state by the door only to re-admit it through the window'.[48] In the United States, Lippmann combined this charge with the previous one. If 'you are going to have government define functions', he argued, then the 'premise of the [pluralist] argument disappears'.[49] The same point struck the Harvard jurist, T. R. Powell, who argued that although Cole may call his 'new agencies of political authority' by 'other names', the individuals who ran them would still 'chuckle *l'état c'est moi*'.[50]

These criticisms were, however, distinctly unfair. Although there was substantial ambiguity in many of the pluralists' texts, Cole, Laski, and

[45] L. T. Hobhouse, 'The New Democracy', *Manchester Guardian*, 19 April 1920.

[46] W. Lippmann, *Public Opinion* (New York: Macmillan, 1922), 231.

[47] D. H. Robertson, 'Social Theory', *Economic Journal*, 31 (1920), 231.

[48] Robertson, 'Social Theory', 231.

[49] Lippmann, *Public Opinion*, 308.

[50] T. R. Powell, 'The Functional Organization of Society', *Nation (NY)*, 13 October 1920, 414. More recent critics have agreed. See A. Gutmann, *Liberal Equality* (Cambridge: Cambridge University Press, 1982), 82–4; Runciman, *Pluralism*, 173–4; A. Wright, *R. H. Tawney* (Manchester: Manchester University Press, 1982), 58–60.

Tawney's approach to function did not begin with any organicist or statist conviction. Instead, it was rooted in a particular economic debate prevalent in the early 1920s. From the very outset of that decade, the major pluralist theorists abandoned their faith in an entirely unregulated system of industrial associational independence as they joined with a large number of contemporary commentators, from across the political spectrum, in a worry about the very future of British industrial production. Spurred by the substantial decline in output in the heavy industries caused at least in part by the large number of potentially productive days lost to industrial action, it was commonplace in post-war economic speculation to consider that Britain was unable to maintain the high levels of output believed necessary to compete in the world market. 'Almost everyone is agreed', the economist Henry Vernon wrote in 1921, that decline in output is 'a very serious danger to economic prosperity in this country.'[51] The British Trades Union Congress hotly debated the issue of production at its 1919 conference, with many delegates worrying that decline was so sharp that it threatened the provision of the very 'necessities of life'.[52] Indeed in that year, as industrial unrest reached unprecedented levels of intensity, the progressive press in Britain drifted into near panic. 'Industry', the London *Nation* complained, is 'paralysed'.[53] A year later, the situation seemed, if anything, to have worsened. 'Once [British] capitalism was associated with ... a guaranteed and continually increased output of resources', a later editorial ran, 'but it has become inefficient as a method of production' with the result that the country 'has been set groping for its secure means of livelihood'.[54]

All of the leading socialist pluralists shared these concerns, and they often expressed them with even greater passion. Cole, for example, warned in 1920 that if you 'get a manufacturer to speak to you without reserve, almost any of them will tell you that the normal standard of production has gone down by 50% or more' and that 'the general curve of production is going steadily downwards'.[55] Tawney's *Acquisitive Society*, published in 1921, was premised on a similar assumption that the prevailing industrial system 'no longer secures ever-increasing output of wealth'.[56] Laski too insisted that the 'very conditions of the system' resulted in limited output.[57] Even when industrial unrest lessened, these concerns continued to be aired right throughout the

---

[51] H. Vernon, *Industrial Fatigue and Efficiency* (London: G. Routledge and Sons, 1921), 118. For figures on these trends, see B. R. Mitchell, *Abstract of British Historical Statistics* (Cambridge: Cambridge University Press, 1971), 130.

[52] See Trades Union Congress, *51st Annual Conference Report* (London: 1919), 211–16.

[53] Anon., 'To Save the Commonwealth', *Nation*, 9 August 1919, 550–2.

[54] Anon., 'A New Start for Liberalism', *Nation*, 15 May 1920, 192.

[55] G. D. H. Cole, 'Lecture at the South Place Institute' (1920), Nuffield College, Oxford, The Cole Papers, A1/50. See also G. D. H. Cole, 'The Consumer Pays', *New Statesman*, 20 March 1920, 700.

[56] Tawney, *Acquisitive*, 174.

[57] H. Laski, 'Socialism and Freedom', *Fabian Tract* 216 (London: Fabian Society, 1925), 10.

1920s. As unemployment in Britain rose in the early 1920s, encompassing over 14 per cent of the labour force by 1923, it contributed further to the same concern. The 'real cost' of the unemployed lies 'not in the doles', Cole argued, but 'in the loss of the products that could [be] made and the deterioration of . . . productive capacity'.[58] Nor was the importance of this theme lost on the pluralists' critics. Although the nationalist progressive were far from sure as to the veracity of the pluralists' economic analysis, the *New Republic* nonetheless recognized the importance of the decline in productive capacity. Fundamental to the socialist pluralists' view of function, Alvin Johnson thus reported, was their belief that the prevailing industrial system 'is already as good as dead' and that the cause of that death was a spiralling decline in the level of production.[59]

The existing industrial system was thus held to be simply incapable of producing the level of goods and services that a society consisting of a collection of free, experimenting, individuals would require. If production levels continued to decline, the pluralists urged, then the effective liberty of the majority of citizens would be unnecessarily and avoidably restricted. 'Any institution which thwarts or encumbers' the production of goods was thus open to severe rebuke.[60] Many in the pluralist and guild socialist movement lined up in support of this position. The first underlying assumption that unified these thinkers' view of function was quite straightforward: a functional system of organization was one which ensured the 'continuity of supply'.[61] The 'object' or function 'of industry', as Tawney so often insisted, was simply 'to produce goods'.[62] Abandoning any previous sense of bias on the side of producers, the British socialist pluralists thus took a distinct and unambiguously consumerist approach to the problem of production.

Beyond the economic crisis, one reason why Cole, Laski, and Tawney adopted this understanding of 'function' was, of course, that an interest in generic productivity was entirely consistent with the heavily individuated account of personality that they had developed elsewhere. 'Output is wanted by the worker', a National Guilds League (NGL) supporter announced, because no matter what his outlook on life 'his standard of living directly depends on it.'[63] Indeed, it can clearly be argued that, despite the apparent tension between the principle of function and the pluralists' other recommendations,

---

[58] G. D. H. Cole, 'The One Thing Needed', *New Statesman*, 24 November 1923, 201–3. See also G. D. H. Cole, 'The Industrial Outlook', *New Statesman*, 18 August 1923, 538–9, and J. A. Hobson, 'The Cry for Productivity', *Nation (NY)*, 18 March 1925, 291. For a discussion of the same theme in the United States, see A. Brinkley, *Liberalism and its Discontents* (Cambridge, MA: Harvard University Press, 1998), esp. 88–90.

[59] A. Johnson, 'Revolutionary Reconstruction', *New Republic*, 15 December 1920, 80. See also O. Tead, 'Productivity and Reconstruction', *The Public*, 16 March 1918, 332.

[60] Tawney, *Acquisitive*, 96.   [61] Laski, *Grammar*, 488.

[62] Tawney, *Acquisitive*, 179.

[63] C. Stevenson, 'The Demand for Output', *Guildsman*, November 1919, 5. See also G. D. H. Cole, 'A Wasting Asset of Industry', *New Statesman* 20 December 1919, 342.

the principle's initial theoretical underpinning was located in the pluralists' dedication to protecting and enhancing their very own individualistic rendering of freedom. Whatever way of life people value or desire they are likely to require material resources to allow them to pursue their goals, and the greater the level of material scarcity than more difficult that pursuit will be. As if to illustrate this point further, Arthur Penty, a guildsman more prone to communitarian moralizing than his pluralist contemporaries, explicitly condemned his colleagues for 'apparently consider[ing]' the question of *what* is produced 'a matter of complete indifference'.[64]

Penty was wrong, however, to imply that Cole, Laski, and Tawney worried *only* about the level, or quantity, of production. They also expressed concern with the quality of that which was being produced. This qualitative concern took two forms. First, there was the doubt that the goods produced by the existing economic system were unnecessarily shoddy. In examining a series of industries, Cole noted, for example, that it was clearly possible to 'improve notably the quality as well as the quantity' of the goods produced.[65] It seemed to the socialist pluralists, that capitalism produced goods that were not of the highest possible quality, nor even of the quality necessary for everyday use; capitalist firms were willing to produce commodities unfit for the uses for which they were required if doing so would reduce costs and increase profit.[66] The second qualitative concern regarded the sorts of products that capitalism made available. The pluralists argued that somehow 'the wrong commodities' were being produced.[67] As Laski phrased it, empirical evidence demonstrated that the prevailing economic system resulted in the building of 'picture palaces when we need houses' and spending on 'battleships when what is needed is schools.'[68] The goods produced by privately owned and autocratically run associations competing in a marketplace were not the goods actually required.

This second qualitative concern was potentially more problematic than either the quantitative or the first qualitative worry as it is here that the spectre of a communitarian, organicist metaphor emerged most clearly. It might well be remarked that a market system could be said to produce the wrong sorts of goods only if one had a conception of the right sorts of goods that was independent of, or even antithetical to, existing consumer choice and individual preference. This was clearly the position shared by both British Fabians and American nationalist progressives. L. T. Hobhouse suggested that 'a sound economic system is to secure work that is good and useful to society, not work that is pretentious or bad' and Walter Weyl argued that it was

[64] A. Penty, 'Can Our Industrial System Survive?', *Guildsman*, May 1921, 9.

[65] G. D. H. Cole, 'The Building Guilds', *New Statesman*, 25 February 1922, 585.

[66] See G. D. H. Cole, 'Lecture at Mortimer Hall', (1921), Cole Papers, A1/50; Cole, *Social Theory*, 56–8; Laski, *Grammar*, 488–9.   [67] Laski, *Grammar*, 175.

[68] Ibid. See also Tawney, *Acquisitive*, 40–2.

American 'ultra-individualism' that led directly to patterns of 'unwise and anti-social consumption'.[69] On such an account, Laski may be presented as criticizing the construction of 'picture palaces' on the grounds that individuals, for some as yet unspecified reason, should not wish or, as the idealists would have had it, do not 'really' wish to have such facilities at their command. There may have been a claim, following a tendency displayed by many contemporary social researchers, that 'picture palaces' degraded their customers' moral character. It is clear that R. H. Tawney's occasional indulgence in Christian moralizing could have lent some support to such an interpretation. D. H. Robertson likewise argued that Cole too brought a rather puritanical disposition to his assessment of the sorts of goods and services that capitalism tended to produce.[70] On this interpretation, the 'functional' production of goods would concentrate on providing those goods identified by some, as yet anonymous, agency as in the 'overall community interest' or in the idealistic 'real' individual interest rather than serving the actual wills and desires of diverse, choosing, market-based consumers. As a result, Cole, Laski, and Tawney's vision would differ little in its implicit assumptions from the communitarian organicism that they had so vigorously rejected elsewhere.

This interpretation is nonetheless seriously misleading. Cole, Laski, and Tawney's primary concern with regard to the sorts of goods provided by the economic system was distinctly not with the 'moral' impact of the products available. Rather, they all worried about the negative effects the production of those goods had on the continued provision of other goods which were perceived to be essential to the process of individual experimentation. Laski's concern, however rhetorically phrased to appeal to those with a more clearly moralizing agenda, was that the production of 'picture palaces' and 'battleships' rather than the provision of housing or education implied that certain sections of society would be left without the fundamental resources required for experimentation. Such a situation could not be endorsed even if those associations were internally democratic and externally independent because it was the interest in individual experimentation itself that justified the dedication to associational independence in the first place.[71] If the pluralists' system of economic and social organization was to be designed to maximize the liberty of the individual, it must ensure that the resources necessary to the process of experimentation were available to everybody. The socialist pluralists' critique of the level and quality of production was not, therefore, dependent upon any organicist-style, thick theory of an independently existing society or upon any notion of individuals' 'real interests' beyond that of

---

[69] L. T. Hobhouse, 'The Right to a Living Wage', in W. Temple (ed.), *The Industrial Unrest and the Living Wage* (London: Collegium, 1913), 68, and W. Weyl, *The New Democracy: An Essay on Certain Political and Economic Tendencies in the United States* (New York: Macmillan, 1912), 330.

[70] See D. H. Robertson, 'Mr Cole's Social Theories', *Economic Journal*, 31 (1920), esp. 537–9.

[71] See Laski, *Grammar*, 184.

experimentation. The conceptual definition of function the pluralists offered was consistent with the theoretical underpinnings of the rest of their ideological project.

Protecting the functional: identifying a regulatory authority

It is still not evident, however, whether the principle of function fell foul to the second criticism levelled at it by both contemporary and latterday commentators. It is not yet clear, that is, whether it is correct to assume that the principle of function involved a dedication to the sort of centralized regulation and direction of the productive process that was directly contrary to the pluralists' commitment to industrial self-government. This view is lent some credence when it is recalled that the socialist pluralists' critique of productive shortcomings was consciously aimed not only at the prevailing capitalist economy but also at its utopian self-governing alternative. In the early 1920s, Laski publicly concurred with the Webbs in their worry that an unregulated system of self-government might endanger the supply of resources.[72] As a result, Laski was convinced that a system of self-government would have to be regulated in such a way as to ensure that general productivity increased to a position where it was capable of providing individuals with the resources their experimentation required. Even Cole, the socialist pluralist most dedicated to associational independence, admitted the potential threat an unconstrained market of self-governing associations posed to the availability of resources. In a *New Republic* article directed squarely at his American critics in 1919, he admitted that a self-governing coal industry could display a lack of concern with 'the interest of the coal consumer'. Indeed, he warned, with more than a little understatement, that if a dispute were to arise in a guild society between coal producers and the rest of industry, then the coal consumer could be in for 'an unpleasant time'.[73] All the socialist pluralists appeared sure, therefore, that for the sake of maintaining production the activities of associations would have to be at least partially regulated.

This position did not, however, mark a substantial political convergence with either American nationalist progressivism or British Fabianism. As far as Cole, Laski, and Tawney were concerned, the level of production was not a *pre-eminent* goal but rather an instrumental condition for widespread experimentation. The means of promoting an increase would, therefore, have to be very carefully monitored. If it was demonstrated that a decrease in the level of industrial democracy, for example, such as the granting of increase powers to a technocratic elite would lead to an increase in the quantity and quality

---

[72] Laski, 'The Co-operative Movement', 81.
[73] G. D. H. Cole, 'The Coal Question in Great Britain', *New Republic*, 10 September 1919, 172.

of production, the socialist pluralists would not be automatically committed to such a measure. A balance would have to be struck between a means of maintaining high productive capacity and the preservation of other liberty-enhancing measures. Tawney was absolutely clear on this point. He was dedicated to maximizing the resources available only 'so long as' that maximization 'does not conflict with some still more important purpose'.[74] Cole was equally committed to this compromise. 'We need', he suggested, 'to satisfy the producers' demand for responsibility and self-government' at the same time as guaranteeing 'a full provision of the goods and services which [each individual] justly requires.'[75]

In such a situation the theorists were inevitably drawn into a difficult, perhaps impossible, process of balancing and measuring the various different effects. One such balancing act is clearly identifiable in their work. Whereas the pluralists accepted the need for some form of regulation to ensure the maintenance of production, they were always determined that such regulation should not have the effect of coercing individuals into taking employment or pursuing productive exercises that were not, to a considerable extent, a direct result of their own choice. Although the consequence of the argument about 'function' was to place a duty on individuals and their industrial associations to contribute to general production, the form that provision took was to be decided to the greatest possible extent by the individuals themselves. Cole committed himself to such a position as early as 1916 when he insisted that 'the state has not the right to compel a man to perform a particular act' even though it 'may still have the right to demand of him some equivalent service to which no . . . objection can be raised'.[76] Four years on, the claim remained largely the same, with Cole recognizing 'if men have formed an association for one purpose we cannot properly tell them its function is to do something quite different'.[77] This insistence remained well into the mid-1920s when Laski stressed that although one was required to serve in some way it was not to be the government's decision whether one contributed productively 'by being a bricklayer or an artist or a mathematician'.[78]

Causing and curing productive failure: the question of motivation

The balancing acts the pluralists had to perform in order to achieve these goals were not easy. Most importantly, Cole, Laski, and Tawney had to determine what sorts of regulations or restrictions were required to promote and

---

[74] Tawney, *Acquisitive*, 96
[75] Cole, *Self-Government*, 109.
[76] G. D. H. Cole, 'The State and its External Relations', *Proceedings of the Aristotelian Society*, 16 (1916), 323.
[77] Cole, *Social Theory*, 53.
[78] Laski, *Grammar*, 94.

protect production. Critics have often presumed that such regulation must, almost by definition, have taken a Fabian form. There was, though, no a priori reason to make such an assumption, as before the regulatory methods could be identified it was necessary to establish more clearly what caused the undesirably low levels and quality of production.

Faced with a concern at the level of production, most early twentieth century left-leaning political thinkers turned to the central state to conduct a programme of economic rationalization or reorganization.[79] The founders of the British Labour Party such as the Webbs and MacDonald expressed the need for 'a dominant plan', and nationalist progressives like Croly and the young Lippmann essentially agreed that what the economy required was a greater emphasis on specialized appointments and expert management at both a micro- and a macro-level. [80] All three of the leading socialist pluralists, however, initially looked elsewhere, arguing that it was perfectly possible to find a solution to the problem of production that did not threaten their dedication to personal experimentation. If, after all, the statist solution could be dismissed as inefficient as well as directly detrimental to individual freedom, then the conceptual battle would be easier won. In the years prior to the British general strike of 1926, none of the major pluralist thinkers cited the lack of planned coordination between industrial associations as the primary reason for the perceived general decline in the level of production. 'Great as are the technical deficiencies of the present organisation', R. H. Tawney remarked with reference to output in the coal industry, 'it is not in these that the centre of the problem is to be found.'[81]

In searching for an alternative explanation for the declining levels of production, all three leading socialist pluralists turned instead to ideas developed in the United States in the late nineteenth and early twentieth centuries, and especially to the work from the infant discipline of industrial psychology. Adopting a position developed originally by those on the edge of the American nationalist progressive movement, including Simon Nelson Patten, Robert Valentine, Ordway Tead, and Thorstein Veblen, Laski argued that 'the main problem' of production was a 'psychological one'.[82] Laski was far from alone in this position. In 1920, he wrote to Graham Wallas that Tawney too was willing to admit that 'most of the current economic problems are at bottom psychological'.[83] Tawney confirmed and clarified the

---

[79] See N. Thompson, *Political Economy and the Labour Party: The Economics of Democratic Socialism, 1884–1995* (London: University College London Press, 1996), 15–25 and 35–46.

[80] S. and B. Webb, *The Principles of the Labour Party* (London: Labour Party, 1918), 4. See also Chapter 1.

[81] R. H. Tawney, *The Nationalisation of the Coal Industry* (London: Labour Party, 1919), 31. See also R. H. Tawney, 'The Coal Industry and the Consumer', *Contemporary Review*, 116 (1919), 152.

[82] Laski, *Grammar*, 211.

[83] H. Laski, letter to Graham Wallas dated 2 May 1920, in British Library of Political Science, London, The G. Wallas Papers, 1/64/91.

assessment, writing a year later that the failure of output was primarily 'the failure of the customary stimuli to evoke their customary response in human effort'.[84] Cole was equally insistent. Ordway Tead himself recognized that Cole's *Guild Socialism Restated* should be a work of great interest to Americans because its whole thesis was dependent on the results of psychological investigation into 'the limits of competition as the basis of economic motive'.[85] As ever, the pluralists' acolytes were also agreed. The essential element in explaining productive failure for Ivor Brown was 'working-class psychology' and for the Miners' Federation's deputy leader Frank Hodges it was again 'psychology' which explained the 'ruinous' levels of 'low production'.[86]

In searching for a reason why capitalism seemed unable to produce the level or quality of goods individuals required for their personal experimentation, all three of the major socialist pluralists looked to the sorts of incentives to which the prevailing economic system appealed. This was a position that many in the United States had already taken. The notion that it was essential to enlist the willing 'co-operation of the workers' in order to improve their productivity was a commonplace among the more liberal advocates of scientific management. The idea's leading American advocate, Robert Valentine, briefly had the ear of Theodore Roosevelt, and even F. W. Taylor himself was prepared to accept that there was a place for psychological factors in a rounded explanation for poor productive performance.[87] For the nationalist progressives in the United States, though, the psychological aspect was just one of many; it was a factor to add to the Fabian-style analysis of industrial failure, not to replace it. Yet a difference emerged here, for the British socialist pluralists understood the psychological factors not as single players in a larger picture but as the very root cause of the deterioration of productive capacity. Britain's relative economic failure, that is, lay in the failure of 'the motives we have hitherto relied upon to secure the application of effort to the task of production'.[88] 'The question of motives', Cole declared, 'is fundamental.'[89]

Capitalism, as all three leading socialist pluralists understood it, attempted to motivate individuals to produce goods either with the lure of personal financial gain, a motive described as 'greed', or by the threat of personal

---

[84] Tawney, *Acquisitive*, 173.

[85] O. Tead, 'Partners and Citizens in Industry', *New Republic*, 22 March 1922, 118.

[86] I. Brown, 'Aspects of the Guild Idea', *New Age*, 6 May 1915, 54, and F. Hodges, *Nationalisation of the Mines* (London: Leonard Parsons, 1920), 81.

[87] See L. Hand to R. Valentine, letter dated 26 March 1913, Harvard Law School Library, Harvard University, The L. Hand Papers, 44/1; F. W. Taylor, 'On the Principles of Scientific Management' (1916), reprinted in E. Boris and N. Lichtenstein (eds.), *Major Problems in the History of American Workers* (Lexington, MA: D. C. Heath, 1991), 322; J. Dewey, 'Creative Industry', *New Republic*, 2 November 1918, 20–2; R. Wiebe, *The Search for Order, 1877–1920* (New York: Hill and Wang, 1967), 151.

[88] G. D. H. Cole, 'Motives in Industry', *The Venturer*, 1 (1920), 201.

[89] Cole, 'Lecture at Mortimer Hall', 5.

financial ruin, a motive tagged 'fear'.[90] 'Greed', it was held, was what led entrepreneurs to invest their time, capital, and talent on the promise that, if they did so, they might be able to achieve great personal riches. 'Fear', on the other hand, enabled these capitalists to urge workers to labour on a principle of 'needs must where the devil drives'. Workers were led to believe the only way they could 'get food for themselves, their wives and children' was by labouring.[91] For the socialist pluralists, however, both these motives were insufficient and increasingly inoperable. Each of the socialist pluralists gave different detailed reasons why they believed that greed, the motivation of the prospect of 'pecuniary gain', was a contributory factor to productive failure. In the detailed debates of the Sankey Coal Commission's inquiry into the British coal industry, Tawney accused private coal firms of 'working only the coal which is at present most profitable' in a manner which was, at the very least, 'a crime against posterity'.[92] More generally, Cole rhetorically asked in 1920: 'If a capitalist ring can make a higher profit from restricting output, will it not usually restrict output and pat itself on the back? . . . If a manufacturer can make a higher profit by producing luxuries than producing necessaries, will he not in almost all cases produce luxuries with an untroubled conscience?'[93] Harold Laski likewise endorsed this concern, but gave it his own twist. He differed from his two contemporaries by not decrying the temptations of profit but rather criticizing the current system for emphasizing an incentive that simply failed to provoke effort. With a benign naivety more notable now than in the 1920s, Laski doubted whether a large enough number of individuals were ever motivated to develop technology or involve themselves in directing economic affairs by the desire for simple personal financial benefit. The 'importance of profit-making as a motive has been greatly exaggerated', he argued, as most men do not seek 'monetary wealth', he continued, but 'find their rewards' in other areas.[94]

More damning still was the critique of the second capitalistic motivation, that of 'fear'. This motivation, as the pluralists understood it, was believed to be successful only when workers were unable to see an alternative to the prevailing economic system. When workers were convinced that there was another viable way by which to relieve their 'hunger and their misery', the pluralists believed, they would no longer work for the capitalists but turn their efforts to overturning the existing economic order.[95] As the socialist pluralists saw it, two developments of the early twentieth century made such

---

[90] See Cole, *Labour in the Commonwealth*, 218–19; Laski, 'The Co-operative Movement', 81; and *Grammar*, 211–15; Tawney, 'The Case for the Consumer', 3.

[91] G. D. H. Cole, 'The New Spirit in Industry', *New Statesman*, 1 January 1922, 390.

[92] Tawney, *Nationalisation*, 16–17.   [93] Cole, 'Motives in Industry', 203.

[94] Laski, 'State in the New Social Order', 14 and Laski, *Grammar*, 198.

[95] See Johnson, 'Revolutionary', 80.

a development all but inevitable. As Tawney put it, both 'education and experience have destroyed the passivity' of the workers.[96] The first cause, then, was the growth of workers' education, a movement in which all the socialist pluralists played a part.[97] Education, as the pluralists perceived it, had convinced the workers of the inadequacies of the capitalist system of industrial organisation. In particular, it had convinced them that an economic system could allow a far greater role for worker input in the direction and management of everyday affairs and that it could allow them a greater share in dividends and profits, that is, in the economic results of their own labour. The workers were now thought to be aware that there were not only alternatives available to capitalism but more attractive ones also. This widespread faith in the desirability of a new economic system was joined by a new hope that such a system was also now realizable. In the early post-war years, the growth in the trade union movement was widely held to have empowered workers to transform the economic structure of society. 'The huge extension of trade union organisation', Cole emphasized, had 'fundamentally altered' the economic position. Workers now had a 'greatly increased self-confidence' that they themselves could being about drastic change in prevailing economic institutions.[98] When the workers were aware of the possibility of other better economic systems and of the strength of their 'own organised power' then they would no longer be capable of being motivated by fear.[99]

The combination of education and confidence in trade union action appeared to be leading many workers consciously to refuse to labour. Indeed, in protest at capitalism's injustice, the socialist pluralists held, there were already purposive 'limitations on output, ca'canny, strike upon strike'.[100] Even in industries without a tradition of union militancy the old motivations failed to generate productive energy. For Tawney, the signs of 'irritation and apathy' were evident almost everywhere.[101] Other commentators concurred that 'even without a deliberate policy of ca'canny by anybody' worker effort and output were seriously diminished.[102] The general decline of trade union activity in the mid-1920s did not weaken the pluralist conviction that workers had ceased to labour effectively.[103] Writing in the *New Statesman* in 1925, Cole insisted that workers 'unable to

---

[96] Tawney, *Acquisitive*, 178.   [97] See Chapter 6.
[98] Cole, 'Motives in Industry', 204.
[99] G. D. H. Cole, 'The Unity of Trade Unionism', *New Statesman*, 22 April 1922, 59.
[100] Johnson, 'Revolutionary', *New Republic*. See also F. J. C. Hearn Shaw, *Democracy and Labour* (London: Macmillan, 1924), 231–4, for the view from the right of the political spectrum.
[101] R. H. Tawney, 'Recent Thoughts on Government in Industry', in P. Alden (ed.), *Labour and Industry* (Manchester: Manchester University Press, 1920), 193.
[102] Anon., 'The Responsibility of Labour', *Nation*, 13 September 1919, 692. See also J. Brooks, *Labour's Challenges to the Social Order: Democracy its Own Critic and Educator* (New York: MacMillan, 1920), 401.
[103] For the decline, see P. Renshaw, 'The Depression Years, 1918–1931', in B. Pimlott and C. Cook (eds), *Trade Unions and British Politics: The First 250 Years* (Harlow: Longmans, 1991).

resist' as a result of the decline in union power had nonetheless 'grown sullen' and were thus still unwilling to produce 'either more or better output'.[104] Throughout the 1920s, then, the socialist pluralists were convinced that British production would continue to decline in both quantity and quality. Through all of this time, Tawney insisted, the 'single greatest economic loss is the dissatisfaction which pervades the majority of those engaged in it'.[105]

As they were united in diagnosing the problem, the socialist pluralists were again agreed in proposing a solution. Laski, Cole, and Tawney were convinced that new incentives and motivations were necessary. Such motivations were to be found in the 'ideal of service'.[106] On this account, individuals would pursue productive activity, contribute their time and effort to the process of producing goods of a satisfactory standard, not out of fear of insecurity or out of a desire to satisfy their material wants but because they consciously wished to 'render a service to the community'.[107] As Tawney saw it, this change in motive implied that an individual would work not 'for personal gain or to gratify himself' but to fulfil a self-recognized social responsibility.[108] Laski phrased the same idea in much the same way, describing the transformation as 'the replacement of the spirit of acquisitiveness by the spirit of service'.[109] As a result, workers would produce at a level they were failing to be persuaded to attain by either of the motives of greed and fear. The pluralists set their sights high. Once industry was democratized and removed from the directive influence of either the state or the capitalist, the motive of social service would evoke 'cordial and constructive co-operation on the part of the workers' which would do more to increase output than would 'a generation of scientific invention'.[110]

The continuous assertion of this claim also indicated something of a stronger dedication. Indeed, by the early 1920s it was apparent that the major socialist pluralist writers sought a change in motivation for reasons that stretched beyond the desired instrumental effect of increasing productivity. Cole was perhaps most explicit in his dedication—the new motives, he insisted, were 'the best instead of the meanest'—but Laski and Tawney concurred.[111] What lay behind this substantial dedication was a conviction as to the essential desirability of fostering a 'spirit' or 'sentiment' of community. The socialist pluralists were all convinced that the sorts of sentimental attachments that should

---

[104] G. D. H. Cole, 'The Case for Higher Wages', *New Statesman*, 14 February 1925, 525–6.
[105] Tawney, *Nationalisation*, 143.   [106] Cole, 'Lecture at South Place Institute'.
[107] G. D. H. Cole, 'Guild Socialism: A Lecture at Kingsway Hall' (1920), Cole Papers, A1/50/10.
[108] Tawney, *Acquisitive*, 9.   [109] Laski, 'State in the New Social Order', 14.
[110] Tawney, 'Coal Industry Commission', 152.
[111] G. D. H. Cole, 'A Mining Guild', *New Age*, 8 May 1919, 23. See also Laski, *Grammar*, 217, and Tawney, *Acquisitive*, 18.

prevail between individuals, even individuals of sharply differing associational allegiances, were the sentiments of 'fellowship'. The motive of 'social
service' would be both a result and a contributory cause of the development
of this broader sense of community. The motives to which an industrial association appealed in order to persuade its labourers to labour had to be ones
which were compatible with the encouragement of a certain sort of sentimental attachment between individuals and across associations.

The motives of 'fear' and 'greed' were thus non-functional not only
because they failed to encourage people to produce but also because they set
individuals sentimentally apart from one another. As Laski phrased it, once
motives based upon the promise of financial reward were removed, then the
motivations of work are no longer ones which 'breed' a 'feverish envy' which
sets men against each other.[112] Workers encouraged to work for the sake of
'common service' ensure that a broader sense of 'fellowship becomes possible'.[113] Cole was similarly clear. He insisted that profit as a motive was to be
rejected not only because it impairs the productive process but also because it
has the tendency to 'stir up bad blood'.[114] When workers are set against
consumers in the search for monetary reward, Cole insisted, it is difficult to
develop a widespread 'sense' of 'social brotherhood'.[115] The dedication to the
motive of 'social service' was, therefore, demonstrative of a fundamental
theoretical conviction above and beyond a concern with increasing production. The pluralists all shared a commitment to the development of a 'spirit
of community' as an intrinsic as well as an instrumental good.

This was, however, still a substantially different conception of community
and its place in individual development from that offered by the Fabians or
the nationalist progressives. For the socialist pluralists, the development of
community was not dependent upon the pursuit of one particular set of
goods or ends, nor was it dependent upon the widespread theoretical acceptance of the notion of community as possessed of an independent existence.
Connectedly, it did not depend upon individuals conceiving of their identity
as to any great extent constituted by their communal or societal attachments
and as such it was capable of avoiding the overly prescriptive tendencies associated with the idealist approach. Indeed, Cole was convinced that one of the
greatest expressions of communality, in his sense, came about when one individual labourer provided another who possessed different aims and values
with the resources that other required to pursue his own goals. The theoretical commitment behind the pluralists' principle of function was independent
of both an organicist conception and an idealist theory of a deep-rooted
essential social interconnection.

To begin with, at least, this conception of community as a sentimental

---

[112] Laski, *Grammar*, 217.   [113] Ibid.   [114] Cole, *Social Theory*, 61.
[115] Cole, *Social Theory*, 48.

attachment between otherwise different individuals was also explicitly intended to rule out the Fabian and nationalist progressives' practical recommendations. For whereas these groups had insisted that a centralized state was required to act as the key 'social instrument', as the fundamental agency for overseeing social evolution, Cole and colleagues used their conception of community to establish an argument against central control. Cole argued that as, on his conception, community 'is not an institution or a formal association but a centre of feeling', it 'does not necessarily involve any particular form of social organisation'.[116] Indeed, he went even further by insisting that the 'spirit of community' was always expected to 'escape formal organisation'.[117] The sentimental attachments which the pluralists believed constituted a living community could easily be deadened by any overly legalistic attempt to inculcate them. Individuals had either to be let alone to develop these attachments or to be encouraged indirectly by means of more subtle policy instruments lest they be driven apart by the frustrations imposed by centralized regulation. It was in this way that a new conception of community—one which described 'community' simply in terms of sentimental attachment—was forged.

The Return of the State

The socialist pluralists' response to their critics was constructed in three stages. First, they outlined a conception of 'function' which stated that industrial associations should be encouraged to produce as much as possible, as this was the best means to ensure that every citizen's resource requirements were met. Second, they argued that production levels could best be maximized by releasing workers from the 'fear' and 'greed' inspired by the incentive structures of a capitalist economy. Third, they contended that the new motivations of 'social service' were based on a set of 'sentimental attachments' between diverse citizens and workers which were valuable in and of themselves. There was, it seemed, no need for a 'thick' conception of community or national interest and no need for a powerful central regulatory agency. All of this, of course, appeared hopelessly utopian to the pluralists' critics. Defending his insistence on proper regulatory authority, the British Liberal J. A. Hobson suggested that the pluralists' suggestions would 'disappear before any rigorous analysis'.[118] Graham Wallas agreed, arguing that Tawney, in particular, was prone to 'exaggerate the degree to which' it was safe to rely on the 'public spirit of the producer'.[119] Such a response from British critics was

---

[116] Cole, *Social Theory*, 28.   [117] Cole, *Guild Socialism Restated*, 158.
[118] J. A. Hobson, *Incentives in the New Industrial Order* (London: Leonard Parsons, 1922), 159.
[119] G. Wallas, 'The Acquisitive Society', *Nation*, 11 June 1921, 401.

expected but, given that the basic psychological insights had come from the United States, the pluralists might have hoped for a better reception there. It was not to come. Considering the pluralists' arguments concerning economic motivations, the *New Republic*'s Alvin Johnson remarked that 'it is harder to think of great masses of labour ... functioning so smoothly to the end of public service as great masses of capital ... have worked to the end of private enrichment'.[120] Walter Lippmann was more critical still. All the theory demonstrated to him was the 'lengths to which a clever man will sometimes go in order to escape a full recognition' of the necessary 'role of force' in regulating society.[121] Worst of all was the judgement of Ordway Tead, one of the very industrial psychologists on the basis of whose evidence the pluralists had attempted to build. In reviewing Cole's *Social Theory*, Tead complained that 'nowhere in the book does he buttress what seem to be essentially deductive arguments by evidence of the genuinely inductive character as supplied by psychology'. 'In a word', Tead concluded, Cole 'fails' properly to consider 'the basic problem as to whether human nature is so constituted that it will flourish best' under the institutions that Cole and his colleagues desired to construct.[122]

Cole, Laski, and Tawney were thus challenged to give a detailed account of how the new motivations and sentimental attachments were to take hold. Their initial hope appears to have been that the spirit of social service would emerge almost as soon as industry was effectively democratized. Workers in such a system, it was suggested, would labour to produce for their fellows an unprecedented level and quality of material goods. This faith was based upon a number of thoughts. The first, and most shockingly naive, was expressed predominantly by G. D. H. Cole. In the early 1920s, Cole frequently advanced a conviction that despite their diversity all human beings possessed a natural proclivity to support and sustain all other humans. All people, on such an account, have 'a sense within themselves' which calls for their meaningful contribution to the well-being of others.[123] As Cole was to claim even in later years, 'men are fundamentally decent' and will willingly perform genuine service for others 'if they are given the chance'.[124] This vision, borrowed and developed explicitly from Rousseau's account of *pitié*, further entailed that such a chance arrives when individuals no longer have to worry about the frequent frustration of their own wills and desires by authority or by an unnecessary limitation of material resources.[125] When freedom in this sense is attained, Cole's 'personal hope and conviction' was that men would seek to

[120] Johnson, 'Revolutionary', 82.   [121] Lippmann, *Public Opinion*, 296.

[122] O. Tead, 'Bases of Social Theory', *The Freeman*, 7 July 1920, 406.

[123] G. D. H. Cole, *Incentives under Socialism* (Girard, Kansas: Haldeman-Julius, 1931), 8.

[124] G. D. H. Cole, 'Why I am a Socialist', *Adelphi*, December 1932, 183.

[125] See Cole's 'Introduction' to G. D. H. Cole (ed.), *Jean Jacques Rousseau: The Social Contract and the Discourses* (London: Everyman, 1913), esp. pp. liv–lv.

find a 'social significance', to 'provide a social service'.[126] 'Set me free', he concluded, 'and they will turn by instinct to the making of good things well.'[127]

Although Cole was not entirely alone in this dedication—the ever-supportive Ivor Brown remarked that 'the desire to serve the community' is 'as common to man as the desire to eat, drink, and marry a wife'[128]—even he was aware that the claim was not likely to be entirely persuasive. Indeed, the issue was at the very centre of one of the most heated exchanges at the Royal Commission established by the post-war Lloyd George government to investigate new ways of running the coal industry in 1919. Cole, claiming to have evidence that a large number of coal miners would be inspired by 'that motive of public service' if only the industry were democratized, was asked by the Commission's Chair, Justice Sankey, 'to return to the Commission with the names' of those he had surveyed. Cole, seemingly unabashed, was, of course, unable to do so.[129] It is unsurprising in this light that although Laski and Tawney were equally convinced that motivation provided the key to the issue, they offered little public support to the suggestion that a concern for 'social service' would flow naturally as soon as individuals were 'set free'. 'Ideally', Laski summarized, workers would be voluntarily willing to 'give of their best for their fellows' but it was unlikely that a situation would straightforwardly emerge. As such, the success of the new incentives and motivations would have to be won 'by the sweat of our brow'.[130]

Tawney and Laski thus developed a more detailed account of the fundamental structural and institutional changes that were needed to encourage workers to feel as if they wanted to provide a 'social service'. As both of them regularly declared, while eliciting the sense of 'social service' did not involve an impossible 'change in human nature', it did require an 'emphasis' on 'elements in human nature that are now ignored'.[131] The particular difficulty, of course, was to find a way to extend individuals' loyalties beyond the confinements of their own associations. After all, the pluralists had turned to the concept of function in the first place because the trade unions upon whom their reform programme depended had 'tended to foster sectional loyalties . . . at the expense of any wider loyalty' to the 'whole'.[132] Critics eager to dismiss the pluralists' approach seized on their apparent inability to address this central dilemma. In his extended critique of guild socialism, Guy Field noted that although 'the sentiment of Guild patriotism' would 'almost

---

[126] Cole, *Labour in the Commonwealth*, 220, and 'Guild Socialism', 10.

[127] Cole, *Labour in the Commonwealth*, 221.

[128] I. Brown, 'Aspects of the Guild Idea', *New Age*, 20 May 1915, 55.

[129] See A. Gleason, *What the Workers Want: A Study of British Labour* (London: George Allen and Unwin 1920), 419–21.   [130] Laski, *Grammar*, 200–1.

[131] Laski, *Grammar*, 213, and Tawney, *Acquisitive*, 185.

[132] G. D. H. Cole, 'The Unity of Trade Unionism', *New Statesman*, 22 April 1922, 59.

certainly very strongly developed under this system . . . this sentiment might express itself in a resolve, not to do their best for the members of other guilds, but to get all they could from the other guilds with the least possible trouble for themselves'. The sorts of solidarities built up in internally democratic and externally independent guilds could easily 'degenerate into guild jingo-ism'.[133] The London *Nation* agreed, arguing that labour already suffered from the fact that its 'ideal of loyalty was too narrow in scope' and suggesting that such difficulties would be exacerbated rather than resolved if industries were independently and democratically run by their workers.[134]

Unless one adhered to the controversial claim that humans have a natural proclivity to communality and, as such, a natural desire to try to provide mate-rial resources for their fellow humans, then it was clear that the pluralists were without a straightforward case. The pluralists' response to this ongoing critique was guarded. Tawney recognized that the objections were 'plausible' but also dismissed them as 'short-sighted'.[135] Cole, too, frequently grumbled about his critics' lack of 'trust'; his guild system might be a 'leap in the dark' but it was one worth taking.[136] Laski, though, was more hard-headed than his colleagues and was perfectly willing to admit openly that more than a combi-nation of associational independence and internal industrial democracy was required. In order to ensure that the 'minds of men are turned towards the qualities' which characterized a motivation of 'social service', he insisted, a whole range of policy options had to be considered.[137] In practice, Cole and Tawney joined him in accepting that more had to be done.

Reconsidering state legitimacy

From the critics' perspective, however, none of this fully resolved the ques-tion of the role of regulatory authority. Even if the cause of productive failure was one of motivation rather than of organizational incompetence, clearly some authority still had to be charged with ensuring that this failure was overcome. If the motive of social service was to operate, sentimental attach-ments had to be developed, and all the socialist pluralists were eventually willing to concede that such a development required more than just the free play of independent associations. And even if Cole was right in claiming that this would not been a difficulty in a society characterized by liberty, then *prac-tical* problems would still undoubtedly arise. The principle of function, after all, did not just require the creation of the right subjective sensations. It also entailed the achievement of actual objective results. The production of goods

---

[133] G. Field, *Guild Socialism: A Critical Examination* (London: W. Gardner, Darton and Co., 1920), 54.

[134] Anon., 'The Future of the Labour Party', *Nation*, 15 November 1919, 226–7.

[135] Tawney, *Acquisitive*, 187.

[136] G. D. H. Cole, 'The Leach Gatherer', *Socialist Review*, 21 (1923), 265–70; 'Motives in Industry', 206; *Guild Socialism* (London: Fabian Society, 1920), *passim*.   [137] Laski, *Grammar*, 215.

had to increase. And even if sentimental attachments were widespread, conflicts between industrial associations or between associations of producers and of consumers could still feasibly occur over matters of empirical judgement about which even the most altruistic of individuals would disagree. There was surely a need for some form of regulatory authority to resolve such disputes.

Initially, the pluralists' answer to this question hinged on their very precise understanding of associational legitimacy. The socialist pluralists were committed to a doctrine of associational independence which guaranteed each association 'ultimate authority in its own sphere'.[138] The state, in this schema, was just a geographical association 'clearly marked out as the instrument for the execution of those purposes which men have in common by reason of neighbourhood', which, for rather unclear reasons, the pluralists associated with consumption.[139] The state, that is, represented 'men as users of . . . goods'.[140] Further, on this model, if competing associational loyalties pulled their members in different directions, it was up to the individual as a member of these associations to decide upon his loyalties in each particular case. If there was an industrial dispute where different groups disagreed, therefore, no one group—neither state nor non-state, neither consumers nor producers—would have automatic priority. They would resolve their disagreements through consultation and debate. Cole developed a whole range of programmes and schemes intended to allow the various associations to resolve disputes through consultation, including an idealized Joint Committee of Producers and Consumers.[141] It would further help, Cole frequently remarked, that as each individual was both a producer and a consumer he would likely chose the sensible option in each case of conflict. 'As all guildsmen would be members of the state' and 'at least most' citizens 'members of a guild', Cole expected 'a great deal of cross-voting, resulting in a majority for one side or the other.'[142]

There were, of course, huge problems with this account, all of which made Tawney and Laski rather more circumspect about entirely negating the position of some form of central authority. Although they were in substantial conceptual agreement with Cole as to the nature of 'function' and 'community', to them these concepts required that there should be at least some residual role for a central body of governance. 'I am probably a heretic', Tawney wrote in 1920, but 'I do not agree with what I understand to be Cole's view . . . that the consumer can be left to take care of himself.'[143] As the 1920s progressed, all of the socialist pluralists' approach began to change. Laski

---

[138] Cole, *Self-Government*, 85.   [139] Cole, *Self-Government*, 78–9.
[140] Laski, *Authority*, 83.   [141] See Cole, *Guild Socialism Restated*, 117–38.
[142] G. D. H. Cole, 'National Guilds and the State', *Socialist Review*, 16 (1919), 29.
[143] R. H. Tawney, 'Socialism', British Library of Political Science, London, The R. H. Tawney Papers, 19/7/7.

continued to see the state as a geographical association necessarily concerned only with those interests men have in common as a result of geographical proximity. What began to shift, however, was his detailed understanding of those interests; and by the early 1922 he was willing to accept that 'there are many functions' with which an 'undivided communal organ' was legitimately concerned. These included 'the provision of law and justice, the national health, the provision of public education'.[144] The role accorded to the state was increasing.

The issue was dealt with again, with even greater sophistication, three years later in *A Grammar of Politics*. Here Laski continued to employ the original socialist pluralist analytical framework, arguing that in order to be legitimate associations must explicitly 'exist to fulfil purposes which a group of men have in common', but he once again changed his definition of those purposes.[145] In the *Grammar*, Laski insisted that the relevant 'purpose' was that of individual qua individual rather than the individual qua associational member. Confusingly intermingling the language of 'purpose' with that of 'will', Laski argued that each individual possesses essentially two kinds of 'will'. 'There is the will of the individual as the member of some special association, seeking, through its means, to fulfil some definite purpose' but there is also 'the will of the individual himself as a final unit.'[146] The state, in Laski's revised view, could be best associated with this aspect. On this account, Laski was able to charge the state with ensuring the provision of the resources required to enable individuals to choose freely between associations and lifestyles, to experiment with the 'best of themselves'. Moreover, as the individual himself 'as a final unit' must always 'stand over and above' his day-to-day allegiances, judging the acts of his associations and contemplating changes in loyalty or in life-plan, so the association charged with representing this idea of the 'final unit' should rightly stand to some extent above other forms of association.[147] 'Clearly a function of this kind', Laski concluded, 'involves a pre-eminence over other functions ... To satisfy common needs, it must control other associations to the degree that it secures from them the services such needs require.'[148] Among other things, this revised state theory provided a means of charging the mechanisms of the state with the task of ensuring that industrial associations really did perform their productive functions.

This was not, however, a straightforward story of capitulation to a Fabian-style statism. Rather, Laski account of the state's acceptable role remained grounded in his conceptions of liberty as experimentation and of community as sentiment. Contemporary reviewers of the *Grammar of Politics* were thus in doubt that he remained a 'pluralist' who did not believe in the 'omnipotent,

---

[144] Laski, 'State in the New Social Order', 12.
[146] Laski, *Grammar*, 69.   [147] Ibid.
[145] Laski, *Grammar*, 67.
[148] Laski, *Grammar*, 70.

omnicompetent nation-state'.[149] Laski's renewed account of state legitimacy did not commit him to adopting the state-centric vision outlined by Fabians or nationalist progressives, partly because the conceptual arguments that underpinned it remained very different, and partly because the precise description of state authority was still to be outlined. This last concern was crucial; interesting as the story of the abstract theoretical evolution is, it alone cannot provide a full account of the pluralists' attitudes to the state's role in political life. The devil, then, lay in the detail.

The state and transition

One particularly important omission from a solely theoretical examination is that it does not provide a full account of the theorists' approach to the role of the state in the process of transition from a capitalist society to a socialist pluralist one. The question remained as how society was to move from one stage of development to the next. In moving from one society—a capitalistic one centred on 'fear' and 'greed'—to another one—a socialist pluralist commonwealth based on a dedication to 'social service' and sentimental attachment—there was going to have to be a significant alteration in a wide range of political, social, and economic arenas. It is, though, not as yet obvious who Cole, Laski, and Tawney believed was to direct that process of change. Before the end of the war, there had been no doubt in pluralist circles that there was little use in seeking support from state, in the form of the central government, in this respect. 'It is no use . . . to look to the state for salvation', Cole argued in 1917.[150] Instead, the favoured method in the war years had been what became known as 'encroaching control'. On this view, trade unions 'must be transformed from a negative into a positive power . . . instead of having only the brake in their hands, the trade unions must assume control of the steering-wheel'.[151] Unions should start to demand as much power as they possibly can, stretching from the appointment of their own foremen up to having a considerable say in management structures. As such, over time, capitalists would be driven from industry and, as political power would likely follow economic power, society could begin to be reconstructed. Nor was Cole alone in advocating such a strategy. Even R. H. Tawney, the least rhetorically anti-statist of the pluralists, talked of 'encroaching control' as the primary means of transitional politics, hoping 'to see workers in large scale industries undermining the place of the capitalist by encroachment that will make his position untenable'.[152]

However widespread these ideas had been, the post-war years threw up

---

[149] W. A. Robson, 'A Grammar of Politics', *Fabian News*, September 1925, 38.
[150] Cole, *Self-Government*, 16.   [151] Cole, *Guild Socialism Restated*, 20.
[152] Tawney, 'Socialism', 14.

difficulties which cast severe doubts upon the method. Although the unions appeared to be developing a programme of 'direct action' up until the early 1920s, militancy did not last as long as Cole and his colleagues hoped. Indeed, in early 1921, British trade union activity collapsed dramatically, especially as the so-called Triple Alliance failed in April. Cole recognized that the time of trade unions being able to exert any significant influence had passed. 'The last few months have produced a compelling demonstration of the limits of successful industrial action', he told his *New Statesman* readership in July of 1921, 'high hopes were raised which are now only being completely dissipated.'[153] In the wake of these failures, the socialist pluralists turned instead towards far more mainstream political approaches to social change. Throughout the early 1920s, it was through an idealized vision of the British Labour Party that they sought the fulfilment of their hopes, just as the nationalist progressives had. The collapse of union power in industry, Cole insisted, made it 'manifestly necessary' that 'Labour should achieve parliamentary power'.[154] Cole, Laski, and Tawney all thus attempted to exert influence within the party itself and campaigned hard for a Labour victory. Their partisan loyalty even stretched to lending support to former opponents. 'We are not always in agreement with Mr Ramsay MacDonald', Cole admitted of the Fabian-inspired Labour leader, 'but his skill as a parliamentary tactician is undoubted.'[155]

This support should not be taken to mean that the socialist pluralists abandoned their fundamental ideological positions in the early 1920s, or that they were left in a position indistinguishable from the Fabians' or nationalist progressives'. Rather, the socialist pluralists began to adopt a distinctly pragmatic approach to the mechanisms of the central state. While Cole, Laski, and Tawney all preferred to look to non-state bodies to provide the impetus for reform, they were all intelligent enough to note that, in certain circumstances and acting in certain ways, the state could aid rather than hinder the pursuit of their essential goals. In particular, the three thinkers were all agreed that carefully directed governmental provision in some fields could, at least to a limited extent, positively shape the psychology of the population. Tawney often argued that some governmental reforms could assist in the creation of that 'industrial conscience and morale' necessary in any transitional period.[156] 'If', Tawney continued, the socialist pluralist 'conception of industry . . . is to be effective it must . . . be a spirit working within it and not merely a body of rules imposed by an outside authority . . . But in the revolution needed to make the development of that spirit a possibility, the state can, if it pleases, play a considerable part.'[157] As

[153] G. D. H. Cole, 'The Swing of the Pendulum', *New Statesman*, 16 July 1921, 406–7.

[154] Cole, 'Swing', 407.

[155] G. D. H. Cole, 'Labour in the First Session', *New Statesman*, 23 December 1922, 349–50.

[156] R. H. Tawney, 'The Minimum Wage in Britain', *New Republic*, 28 June 1922, 126.

[157] R. H. Tawney, 'The Conditions of Economic Liberty' (1918), reprinted in R. Hinden (ed.), *The Radical Tradition: Twelve Essays on Politics, Education, and Literature* (London: George Allen and Unwin, 1964), 114.

Cole himself noted in his guild socialist journal *New Standards*, it was perfectly possible for a socialist pluralist to expect that a 'government' with the requisite 'will' and 'imagination' could 'foster instead of stifle the will to power among the workers'.[158] The fact that in the pluralists' eyes the legislative programmes of the pre-war and wartime governments had not managed to achieve this end now implied only that those governments had pursued the wrong aims or utilized the wrong means. It did not entail that any form of helpful and positive state action was impossible. '[T]he state being with us', Laski intoned, 'we must make the best of it.'[159] None of this necessarily implied any theoretical inconsistency or dramatic compromise. But it certainly did mean that the socialist pluralist attitude to the role of the state was rather more complex than it had first appeared.

Conclusion

In the early post-war years, Cole, Laski, and Tawney shaped and shared a conception of community rooted in a broad collection of normative commitments and empirical observations. Developing from a concern over the future of British production and the threat such a decline posed to the provision of resources for experimentation, the theorists devised a principle of function and moved on to establish a distinct approach to community itself. That concept was understood in such a way as to avoid the criticisms they had levied at their opponents, whether British or American in origin. They conceived of community in terms of widespread sentimental attachments of fellowship between otherwise diverse individuals rather than as an organic entity that provided the essential shape and purpose to individuals' lives. As far as a prescriptive standard was concerned, however, such a conception still provided a guide to associational behaviour. Groups were to be shaped and regulated in such a way as to ensure that the essential pluralist goals were achieved; the direct freedom of internal democracy, of industrial self-government, would be compromised in order to ensure the availability of the resources necessary for widespread individual experimentation and in order to develop a feeling of mutual attachment between individuals in the whole variety of society's associations.

This argument, however, reasserted the need to consider once again the role of the mechanisms of the central state. For what had once seemed inherently hostile now appeared as a potential agency of positive reform. This in itself created the possibility of a positive, constructive, and continual dialogue

---

[158] G. D. H. Cole, 'The Labour Government and Workers' Control', *New Standards*, October 1924, 361.   [159] Laski, 'State in the New Social Order', 8.

with the nationalist progressives. For although important philosophical differences still separated the two movements they both found themselves in the early post-war years returning to examine the possibilities of state-led reform, despite a continuing scepticism about the current make-up of the state machine. That dialogue was facilitated even further by the recognition that both movements identified two areas of public policy as central to their immediate reformist endeavours. The first of these areas was education, and especially the education of adults. Both the socialist pluralists and the nationalist progressives had high expectations of the potential of education successfully to kick-start the process of reform. They were captivated by 'a new sense of the significance of education', openly pinning their hopes on the 'combination of intellectual and moral training' that it could provide.[160] The second area concerned the distribution of material resources, income, and wealth. Again, it was hoped that immediate improvements here might mark the beginning of a far wider reformist movement. Providing workers with a 'safeguarded against unfairness in the distribution of the product' was one of the first steps in instilling within them the ambition to build a new social order.[161] The precise ways in which these arguments developed, and the ways in which they brought these two movements still closer together, is the focus of Part III.

[160] Laski, 'State in the New Social Order', 4; Tawney, *Acquisitive*, 198.
[161] Laski, 'Socialism and Freedom', 10.

III
CONVERGENCE

6

Education as Politics

Introduction

As the nationalist progressives and the socialist pluralists entered the post-war era they faced serious political difficulties. Although both movements had been widely celebrated in domestic and international academic communities, their prospects in terms of real politics appeared far more seriously circumscribed. In the United States, the nationalist progressives were faced with both a political elite and a population at large that seemed determined to resist significant state-led reform, especially in the economy and industrial relations. The election of Warren Harding to the presidency in 1920 coincided with an almost hysterical fear of Bolshevism and radicalism, shocking progressives of all forms. The constant inflexibility of a two-party system that resolutely refused to give way to radical alternatives, be they Progressive, Socialist, or Labor, further augured sharply ill for any form of nationalist progressive revival; dreams of an American Labor Party sweeping to power and instituting a programme of European-style collectivism remained just idle fantasy. In Britain, meanwhile, political developments appeared similarly ill-suited to the pluralists' aspirations. After the war, party politics appeared dominated by the polarized alternatives of laissez-faire Conservatism and statist, bureaucratic Fabianism and New Liberalism. In the mainstream left, popular policy initiatives still focused on the growth of the central bureaucratic apparatus, the provision of social welfare by the state, and the nationalization of industry. There seemed little room in such an environment for a radical political movement based upon a combination of decentralization and democratization. The programmes the nationalist progressives and socialist pluralists were outlining simply seemed out of place in their own societies.

In this climate adult education, especially the education of manual workers, began to exert a remarkable hold on the political imagination of both movements. Here was an arena where small but eager political activists might actually be able to wield an influence which might eventually reap considerable rewards. The decade following the outbreak of the First World War in particular was an era in which discussions about the provision of education for working adults occupied a central place in the deliberations of a wide range of political parties, policy-making bodies, and ideological movements. Such discussions stretched far beyond straightforward pedagogical concerns to encompass recommendations for the building of a better society. A successful educational movement could begin the process of transforming the political ideals of the public from below. In the aftermath of the First World War, it seemed not only perfectly possible to argue that a renewed system of adult education was 'capable of stimulating and satisfying the demand for popular education'; it also appeared reasonable to suggest that it offered the key to the development of individual potential, the means to forge a new sense of national solidarity, and a solution to the problems of the malfunctioning democracies of Britain and the United States.[1] The movement for adult education, moreover, was dependent neither on the prevailing political elite nor on the structure of party politics. The evolution of adult education, therefore, appeared to offer a political opportunity of unrivalled possibility, and both socialist pluralists and nationalist progressives wanted to control it.

In 1925, the British *New Statesman* noted the efforts that the socialist pluralists and nationalist progressives were making and suggested that 'the educational movements among workers on both sides of the Atlantic are well deserving of a comparative study'.[2] Such a study, it continued, could do much to reveal whether the differences between efforts in Britain and the United States were due to contrasting ideological convictions, to institutional, social, and cultural circumstances, or to a combination of the two. The task of comparing the two movements may not be quite as straightforward as the *New Statesman* implied but the journal was nonetheless right in asserting that workers' education provides a perfect forum for exploring the theorists' attempts to transform their two distinct sets of conceptual commitments into practical reforms. In pursuit of this goal, this chapter proceeds in three sections. First, it introduces the development of the adult education movement in both countries and challenges the prevailing scholarly orthodoxy that asserts that the pluralists and progressives engaged in educational activities in a 'non-ideological' and 'non-partisan' way. Second, it proceeds to analyse the manifold ways in which the pluralists and progressives employed their contrasting sets of ideals in constructing their accounts of the essential goals of educational reform. It identifies the goals that each movement was trying to achieve through its intervention in educational endeavours, seeking as it does so to understand the complexities of its evolving ideological programme. Finally, it examines the role that the different political environments of Britain and United States played in encouraging the two movements to reformulate their ideals. It analyses the movements' changing proposals of

---

[1] A. Zimmern, *Why Should University Students Join the WEA?* (London: WEA, 1919), 2. See also anon., 'What Does Labor Want?', *Nation*, 1 February 1919, 505–6, and C. S. Golden, 'The Workers Educate Themselves', *Labor Age*, 4 April 1922, 1.

[2] Anon., 'Workers Education in England and the United States', *New Statesman*, 7 April 1925, 330.

reform and illustrates the complex ways in which the groups' solutions to difficult political dilemmas drew them steadily closer together. Looked at as a whole, these three sections will illustrate that this engagement was a story neither of fundamental ideological convergence nor of overly expedient search for compromise. Rather, it shall be seen that both groups began by attempting to build adult education movements which directly reflected their own, very different, ideological programmes. What drew socialist pluralists and nationalist progressives paradoxically together was not any fundamental convergence of ideals but, rather, the need intelligently to respond to the very different social and political environments in which they found themselves. It was, as will be shown, the process of practically implementing two theoretical systems, of seeking to make the philosophical the possible, in two distinctive political contexts, which led these groups to espouse strikingly similar practical programmes.

Education as Politics

The British adult education movement developed initially in the last few decades of the nineteenth century, beginning with the offering of 'extension classes' from the Universities of Oxford, Cambridge, and London. In 1899 the movement took residential form in the shape of Oxford's Ruskin College, founded with the help of the American radical historian, Charles Beard. Ruskin aimed to provide an introduction to the benefits of university education for working men drawn largely from the trade union movement. The popularity of the college's work among educational reformers and students alike led swiftly to the construction of a larger institutional body that intended to extend the availability of Ruskin-style classes to those workers unable to leave their jobs and travel to Oxford. The Workers' Educational Association (WEA) was thus conceived in 1903 to work in conjunction with the extra-mural departments of Oxford and other universities in bringing university tutors in direct contact with working-class students in their own home towns.[3] In the first three years of its existence, the WEA established 13 nationwide branches, largely in the north and Midlands of England, and served around 2,000 long-term students. By 1923, it had grown to 419 branches stretching right across the United Kingdom; 24,360 long-term students were then engaged in weekly tutorial classes, and roughly the same number again participated in less frequent tuition each year.[4] Over 8,000 of

[3] The abbreviation WEA is used throughout this chapter to refer to the Workers' Educational Association and its attendant organizations in the extra-mural departments of the universities.

[4] For a thorough introduction, see B. Jennings, *Knowledge is Power: A Short History of the W.E.A* (Hull: University of Hull, 1979).

these students also received the WEA's monthly magazine, *The Highway*, a journal that formed a necessary component of most university libraries and quickly became a forum for both educational and wider political debate.[5]

Word of the WEA rapidly spread to the United States as British political commentators started a drive for the idea's export almost as soon as it began. By the war years, many advocates were to be found describing the new developments in British workers' education as the twentieth century's 'greatest discovery in civic techniques'.[6] With many American progressives already well-disposed to the idea, the wider progressive movement quickly took the bait. In 1921, Arthur Gleason, British correspondent of the *Survey* and the *New Republic*, argued that the spread of British workers' education had already resulted in broad range of unparalleled social improvements in Britain and was continually forging ever greater opportunities for reform. Through the work of the WEA, Gleason contended, 'a large and dominant minority of British labour' had become 'readers of books, students of modern economics, instructed co-operators, attendants in classes and at lectures'.[7]

Inspired by what they read, American nationalist progressives quickly sought to emulate the success of the British movement. Two major initiatives especially caught the attention. In the first effort, Herbert Croly joined together with Charles Beard and James Harvey Robinson, both disgruntled with the lack of freedom of expression allowed professors in post-war Columbia University, to establish the New School for Social Research in New York in 1918. Initially conceived as something of a mixture of the London School of Economics with its dedication to the 'scientific' training of bureaucrats, social scientists, and social workers, and of Ruskin College with its commitment to educating the officials of organized labour, the New School's first cohort of students was a rather peculiar combination of already well-educated professionals and workers with little previous educational experience at all.[8] This problematic balance was quickly resolved and in 1922 the School revised its focus under the new directorship of another *New Republic* editor, Alvin Johnson, who refashioned it explicitly as centre for adult education.[9] The second major initiative was an emulation of British innovations

---

[5] For details of the development of the *Highway*, see the uncatalogued papers of The Workers Educational Association, Temple House, London, WEA Papers, The General Purpose Committee, 1919.

[6] H. Laski, 'The Workers as Citizens', *New Republic*, 11 February 1920, 322.

[7] A. Gleason, 'Workers' Education in Britain', *New Republic*, 20 April 1921, 237.

[8] See A. Johnson, 'The New School for Social Research', in S. Hook and M. R. Konovitz (eds), *Freedom and Experience: Essays Presented to Horace M. Kallen* (Ithaca: Cornell University Press, 1947), pp. xi–xii.

[9] At the end of the first year of the New School's existence, there were 549 students, 317 of whom had a record of significant previous academic experience. See E. J. Putnam, 'The New School for Social Research', *New Republic*, 4 February 1920, 294. For the redevelopment of the School under Alvin Johnson, see the wonderful account in A. Johnson, *Pioneer's Progress: An Autobiography* (New York: Viking Press, 1952), 271–88, and M. Rutkoff and W. B. Scott, *New School: A History of the New School for Social Research* (New York: Free Press, 1986), 19–42.

even closer than the New School. It occurred in 1921, when a series of progressive thinkers, labour activists, and educationalists gathered at the New School to form the Workers' Education Bureau of America (WEB), explicitly on the model of the British WEA. Although the WEB failed to engage directly in teaching itself, preferring to act as a centre of coordination and assistance to a wide range of individual educational endeavours, within a year of its foundation it was assisting in the provision of over 40 tutorial classes across the country, indirectly serving approximately 7,000 students.[10] 'From a movement of practically no significance', the *New Republic* reported in 1921, the WEB's programme of workers' education was growing 'so rapidly that it is a matter of only a few years before every important industrial city in the country will have its own classes.'[11] Looking on from afar, the British were delighted by this 'new ferment' for adult, and especially workers', education in the United States.[12]

To the more discerning of contemporary commentators, this particular American enthusiasm for things British may have come as something of a surprise. For education in general and of adults in particular was perhaps the single most significant area of which public provision in the United States outstripped that of the United Kingdom in the early twentieth century. In Britain, the arrival of the WEA could quite easily be explained as a reaction to the absolute failure of the 'national educational system' to meet the demands of the working class for further and higher education; indeed, almost no public educational provision was available to most working people beyond elementary schooling.[13] In the United States, however, the general picture was much more positive prior to the arrival of the WEB. At the close of the nineteenth century, 32 American cities already provided publicly supported evening schools for those over 15 years old, and many of them were free of tuition charges or at least offered substantial financial assistance. In 1900, New York City alone possessed 43 municipally funded schools for adults and Philadelphia had 54. Indeed, so thorough was the coverage available in the United States that early efforts to construct university extension classes on the model of those offered by Oxford and Cambridge collapsed due to lack of demand.[14]

Despite all this, many American progressives were convinced that there was something qualitatively different about the British WEA which demanded attention. That difference lay primarily in the ability of the theorists themselves

[10] Anon., 'Workers' Education in the United States', *American Labor Year Book 1921–1922* (New York: Rand School of Social Science, 1922), 202–3.

[11] Editors, 'Workers' Education', *New Republic*, 12 October 1921, 173.

[12] Anon., 'Workers' Education', *New Statesman*, 19 March 1921, 712.

[13] See A. Gleason, *Workers' Education: American and Foreign Experiments* (New York: Bureau of Industrial Research, 1921), 39.

[14] See L. Goldman, *Dons and Workers: Oxford and Adult Education Since 1850* (Oxford: Oxford University Press, 1995), 307–8.

directly to shape developments in the organization. Unlike the extant American adult education movement, which was led primarily by municipal leaders or philanthropic businessmen, in Britain it was radical political theorists and activists who clearly exercised the most sway. Their domination of British adult education was not aggressive—it was not continually re-asserted by dogmatic insistence or protective controls—but it was nonetheless roundly pervasive. It was this sense of *control*, the apparent possibility of shaping society through shaping the education of its adults, that the nationalist progressives sought to emulate when they began to build their system for workers' education in the United States.

Yet despite this pursuit of control, the leaders of both the WEA and the WEB were extremely anxious to be seen as standing apart from the many divisive social, economic, and political debates of the early twentieth century.[15] They continually stressed the impartiality of the education their organizations offered. Despite their designation as 'workers' educational organizations, both the WEA and the WEB consistently presented themselves as devoid of any rigid class bias. Both were eager to note that socio-economic classes do not, and should not be expected to, adhere to any singular political position. As 'a very real conflict of ideals exists' within each socio-economic class, the WEA's *Highway* journal argued, disagreements should be aired within each lecture circle and tutorial class as well.[16] Likewise, in their self-image the WEA and the WEB were also devoid of any party political propaganda—they were officially 'non-party in politics'—and indeed of any distinct doctrinal orientation. The WEA's official spokesmen thus celebrated its refusal to 'ram . . . opinions down students' throats' and the WEB 'emphatically' stated that 'education is as fundamentally and functionally different from propaganda as is the real from the false'.[17] In taking this stance, the

---

[15] Most latterday observers have emphasized this aspect. Lawrence Goldman draws on Ross McKibbin in making the former argument. See his *Dons and Workers*, 184–5. See also B. Harrison, 'Oxford and the Labour Movement', *Twentieth Century British History*, 3 (1991), 236. For the other view, see B. Simon, 'The Struggle for Hegemony, 1920–1926', in B. Simon (ed.), *The Search for Enlightenment: The Working Class and Adult Education in the Twentieth Century* (London: Lawrence and Wishart, 1990), esp. 22; S. Rowbotham, 'Travellers in a Strange Country: Responses of Working-Class Students to the University Extension Movement, 1873–1910', *History Workshop Journal*, 12 (1981), 88; R. Fieldhouse, 'The Liberal Tradition in Adult Education', in R. Taylor, K. Rockhill, and R. Fieldhouse (eds), *University Adult Education in England and the USA: A Reappraisal of the Liberal Tradition* (Beckenham: Croom Helm, 1985), 21. Marxists have always criticized the WEA for its commitment to 'impartiality'. In the 1920s, the Plebs' League urged that the pursuit of such goals was necessarily spurious: that the 'objective' position was an ideological smokescreen for bourgeois values. Latterly, critics have urged that the WEA necessarily distracted workers from the 'real' industrial and political struggle. For the former perspective, see The National Council for Labour Colleges, *N.C.L.C.: History, Report and Directory* (London: NCLC, 1924), and for the latter see A. Phillips and T. Putnam, 'Education for Emancipation: The Movement for Independent Working Class Education, 1908–1928', *Capital and Class*, 10 (1980), 18–32.

[16] M. Matson, 'Correspondence', *Highway*, February 1919, 47, and Editors, 'The Object of Workers' Education', *New Republic*, 25 April 1923, 239.

[17] For WEA, Goldman, *Dons and Workers*, 163–90, and for WEB, S. Miller, 'The Promise of

WEA and the WEB consistently and publicly rejected the educational approach of rival organizations, in particular the Marxist National Council of Labour Colleges (NCLC) in London and the Rand School of Social Science in New York, organizations which both professed an explicit class, partisan, and doctrinal identity.[18] As it appeared to activists in both the WEA and the WEB, the NCLC and the Rand School offered not a genuine education but rather the inculcation of 'mere slogans and dogmas'.[19]

Despite these assertions, however, the socialist pluralists and the nationalist progressives undeniably gained an ideological advantage from their control of the WEA and the WEB. Such influence was most obviously established in terms of personnel. Pluralist and progressive theorists did not just advise adult educators but were deeply involved in the direct provision of adult education. The list of lecturers at early workers' education classes in both countries, indeed, reads like a roll-call of these two ideological movements. R. H. Tawney directed the very first tutorial group of the WEA in Rochdale, northern England. G. D. H. Cole was similarly ever-present in the developing WEA. His 1922 appointment as Staff Tutor for the London University Joint Committee was recognized by the WEA's *Annual Report* with a note on the 'special importance and significance' of his work for adult education.[20] Cole's students would later recall that, in addition to being a 'very fine chap', he was the summer school tutor who 'undoubtedly . . . made the greatest impact' with his 'electric energy and razor like brain'.[21] In the United States, the nationalist progressives initially worried that they could not quite reach this level of achievement. 'American colleges', Arthur Gleason complained, were not producing the 'humble-minded' scholars with the 'democratic personality' needed effectively to serve in workers' classes.[22] Gleason's worries may have appeared to be confirmed when the progressive economist Thorstein Veblen so failed to engage his adult students at the New School that he was forced to resign as a result.[23] It was not too long, however, before more successful volunteers were rounded up. The first classes at the New School for Social Research were led by an exceptional collection of

Workers' Education', in *Report of the 43rd Convention of the American Federation of Labor* (Washington, DC: 1924), 3. See also Editors, 'Workers' Education', *New Republic*, 12 October 1921, 174.

[18] For a full historical account of the debate between the WEA and the NCLC, see Simon, 'Struggle', *passim*. For the NCLC's following in America, see M. Starr, 'More About Education with a Punch', *Labor Age*, October 1924, 10–11.

[19] C. T. Cramp, 'What Education Means', *Highway*, February 1927, 92, and Johnson, *Pioneer's Progress*, 275.

[20] See WEA, *Annual Report* (1922), Bodleian Library, Oxford University Archive, DES/RP/11/15, 133.

[21] G. Hodgkinson, 'Letters from Oxford', letter dated 25 January 1920, in Ruskin College Archive, uncatalogued; H. Pollins, *The History of Ruskin College* (Oxford: Ruskin College, 1984), 38; and J. Brown, *I was a Tramp*, undated and uncatalogued text, Ruskin College Archive, 238.

[22] A. Gleason, 'Workers' Education', in A. Gleason and S. Miller (eds), *Workers' Education* (New York: Workers Education Bureau, 1921), 14.

[23] On Veblen, see J. A. Hobson, *Veblen* (London: Chapman and Hall, 1936), 20.

progressive theorists—Felix Frankfurter, Alvin Johnson, Walter Lippmann, and John Dewey among them—and they all agreed to provide WEB-sponsored classes in addition to their more formal work at the School.[24] Harold Laski, as ever, bestrode both groups, seemingly equally at home in the New School, where he lectured on 'Representative Government', as in his WEA-sponsored tutorial classes on 'democracy' in Northumbria.[25] Throughout the 1920s, Laski thus brought direct advice from the WEA's early experiments in Britain to the Americans and then returned the favour after he re-established himself on British soil by importing lessons learnt at the New School back to the WEA and to the British Institute of Adult Education that he helped to found in 1923.[26]

Personnel alone, however, was not enough to guarantee serious ideological influence in and of itself. In order to assert actual control, these thinkers would have carefully to craft the details of WEA and WEB syllabuses and course schedules. The socialist pluralists were initially rather cautious in shaping the curriculum; Tawney's very early WEA syllabuses were remarkably balanced, covering a wide range of material and sources. But by the early 1920s, a large number of courses had become more heavily skewed towards topics and approaches that suited the concerns of pluralists and progressives. Despite his claims to 'impartiality', G. D. H. Cole's 1920 London University Extension course on 'Social Theory' used as its main text Cole's own *Social Theory*, hardly an impartial guide to the complexities of the debate.[27] The topics chosen for WEA summer schools also closely mirrored pluralist concerns. In 1919 the students studied 'Problems of Democracy', the highlight of which was a discussion with J. H. Whitley on the future of workers' control in 'Industrial Councils'. In 1920 the students similarly analysed 'Modern Tendencies in Politics and Industry' and even 1921's topic of 'Ancient Rome' allowed room for some classical lessons in 'the efficiency and control of industry'. In the United States, this level of influence was more than matched. The New School's very first programme included a class by progressive philosopher Horace M. Kallen on 'Theories of the State', which introduced students, among other things, to a critical evaluation of the 'speculations of Guild Socialism'.[28]

Yet despite these signs of overt proselytizing, neither movement's efforts could be fairly characterized as propaganda. Many classes only touched on

---

[24] See J. Jordan, *Machine Age Ideology: Social Engineering and American Liberalism, 1911–1939* (Chapel Hill: University of North Carolina Press, 1994), 104.

[25] See E. Smith, 'The New School for Social Research: Preliminary Lectures', *New Republic*, 18 January 1918, 350.

[26] See I. Kramnick and B. Sheerman, *Harold Laski: A Life on the Left* (London: Hamish Hamilton, 1992), 180–3.

[27] See Secretary's Reports to the Tutorial Classes Committee 1919, 1920, and 1921, Oxford University Archive, DES/M/1/5-6.

[28] New School advertisement, *New Republic*, 15 March 1922.

political concerns tangentially, and even when direct sessions were held on the movements' texts or ideas they did not present their own detailed, substantive, and comprehensive positions in the classroom or summer school as an unarguable truth. More important than the straightforward advocacy of a policy programme was the overall *reason* for educating adults, and especially working-class adults, and, connectedly, a distinct understanding of the *way* in which that education ought to be provided. The frequently stated objective of WEA education was to equip students 'not so much with positive knowledge of any subject, as with a method of thought . . . which they can apply . . . in their daily life'. Accordingly, as Cole noted in 1922, 'it does not matter much what you teach people, it is *how* you teach them'.[29] Pluralists and progressives developed their own distinct understanding of what adult education was for and this interpretation resulted in a very particular view of how the classes of the WEA and the WEB should be organized.[30] Cole was thus able to argue that a WEA 'education, without any inculcation of doctrine' would still result in the creation of 'a state of mind most unfavourable to the continuance of our present' social and political arrangements and favourable to pluralist ones.[31] To theorists on both sides of the Atlantic, the overall goals of adult education and, connectedly, the means of education were what mattered; and those goals, moreover, were directly shaped by the underlying conceptual commitments that structured socialist pluralist and nationalist progressive political philosophy more generally, with their particular approaches to the concepts of liberty and community to the fore.

Competing Ideologies, Divergent Aims

An identical task faced the socialist pluralists and the nationalist progressives as they commenced their work in adult education: they both needed to construct an educational agenda out of their ideological commitments. They had to find a way to mould their abstract, occasionally utopian, often vague ideals into a clear agenda for the direction of the education of adults. Such a task was no doubt daunting but it provided one of the best means possible of realizing their ideological goals in societies that appeared sceptical of them. Both movements were this determined that the programme they would offer

---

[29] G. D. H. Cole, 'The Doubtful Value of Lectures', *New Statesman*, 7 October 1922, 9 (emphasis added).

[30] As Laski insisted, 'the subject matter of all true education is whatever leads to a deeper grasp of life'. See G. D. H. Cole, 'The After School Period', address in *The British Institute of Adult Education 4th Annual Conference* (London: 1925); H. Laski, 'Knowledge as Civic Discipline', in O. Stanley (ed.), *The Way Out: Essays on the Meaning and Purpose of Adult Education* (Oxford: Oxford University Press, 1925), 55.

[31] G. D. H. Cole, 'Slave Virtues' and Other Virtues', *New Statesman*, 14 January 1922, 413.

would not only be true to the spirit of their philosophy but actually mirror it as precisely as it could.

Educating for freedom: contrasts and comparisons

Every aspect of the British socialist pluralists' approach to the education of adults was imbued with their dedication to enhancing individual freedom. The precise nature of the contribution adult education was to play in this regard was broken down into three interrelated categories. First, education would provide each individual with the mental agility necessary to be able to 'interpret his own experience'.[32] Educated individuals would possess the ability to understand, reflect upon, and consider their responses to the experiences of their daily lives. Without such an education, the pluralists feared, workers would go through life continually told what to do and what to think until their reactions to events were shaped not by 'thought, but by dumb inertia'.[33] Second, the pluralists also believed that adult education would enable individuals to go beyond this interpretive stage and enable them to begin to question their previously held commitments and beliefs. Engagement in tutorial classes would enable individuals to develop the 'keen and critical spirit' necessary to reflect on their own goals and, if necessary, to reconsider them. Adult education could thus confer 'the ability to be sceptical' necessary to any process of experimentation.[34] Third, education would promote individuals' motivation to expand their horizons, pursue new lifestyles, and to seek their 'best selves'. After engaging in the inspiring process of education, the pluralists thus hoped, individuals would no longer be satisfied with their everyday lives but rather would employ their new-found critical skills and seek to 'become better human beings'.[35] As Harold Laski proudly declared, the WEA would wrest people out of their complacency and enable 'a complete devotion to the best in life'.[36] G. D. H. Cole insisted that 'no man who goes through a course of WEA tutorial classes can come out from them quite as he went in'.[37] By combining these three elements adult education could provide both the means and the motivation to personal freedom. It would both 'encourage and equip' individuals to 'think for themselves and make up their own minds'.[38] Individuals would

---

[32] R. H. Tawney, *The Educational Needs of Democracy* (Leeds: Yorkshire WEA, 1919), 8.

[33] Laski, 'Knowledge', 49.

[34] H. Laski, 'The Philosophy of Adult Education', *Journal of Adult Education*, September 1926, 16.

[35] R. H. Tawney, 'Education and Social Progress', address to the Manchester Co-operative Society (1912), WEA Papers, 6–7.

[36] Laski, 'Knowledge', 54. Cole agreed, arguing that education would stir 'the spiritual sense of our people'. See G. D. H. Cole, 'Socialism and Education' (n.d.), Nuffield College, Oxford, The Cole Papers, B2/16/2/23–5.

[37] G. D. H. Cole, 'An Oxford Summer School', *The Blue Book* 5 (1913), 14.

[38] G. D. H. Cole, 'Cross-Roads in Adult Education', *New Statesman*, 29 August 1925, 542.

thus 'rise to the full height of [their] personality' through the processes of 'creative experiment'.[39]

This socialist pluralist desire to promote independence of mind directly shaped their approach to the internal structure of WEA educational provision. Most importantly, on Laski, Cole, and Tawney's scheme, WEA classes were to be almost wholly focused on participatory 'class discussion'.[40] Whereas much early extension work had centred on lectures by the learned, the pluralists' tutorial classes were to promote free-ranging discussions and to encourage the expression of a wide variety of views. In order to teach the necessary sceptical and critical spirit, the pluralists believed, WEA classes had to expose individuals to as many diverse perspectives on as wide a range of issues as possible. Only in so far as adult education enabled individuals to be exposed to a host of positions could it challenge prejudices and intellectual laziness and thus contribute to the individual student's liberty. The successful WEA class was thus said to provide 'opportunities, abundant and inspiring, for developing . . . powers of judgement, of reflection and of criticism'.[41] Furthermore, this aspiration was picked up and advocated by a whole host of attendant organizations and sympathetic commentators. Indeed, all the major elements of liberty as experimentation were to be found throughout the WEA. The WEA laid stress on developing each student's capacity for criticism, on the contribution adult education would make to the processes of self-discovery, and, most fundamentally, on the importance of the individual as the fundamental unit and source of value. One interested observer, the Independent Labour Party's Jim Lawson, himself a student at Ruskin, noted in the *Highway* that adult education's primary mission must be to develop the worker student's facilities for developing his own 'power of reason and judgement' so that he could choose his own direction in life.[42] The government-appointed Ministry of Reconstruction's Adult Education Committee's *Interim Report*, which was signed by a host of WEA notables including the Master of Balliol College, Oxford, A. L. Smith, the WEA's founder, Albert Mansbridge, and even the trade union leader Ernest Bevin, similarly remarked that workers' education 'is based on a claim for the recognition of human personality'.[43] The WEA's own *Annual Report* of 1920 was even more explicit. In direct contrast to the dominant collectivism of the Fabian left, it noted that 'the attitude of the Association to education is that the primary purpose of all education should be to develop individual capacity, judgement and personality'.[44]

---

[39] H. Laski, *A Grammar of Politics* (London: George Allen and Unwin, 1925, 2nd edn, 1930), 78.
[40] Cole, 'Cross-Roads', 541.
[41] A. Zimmern, 'Report to the Board of Education on the WEA', Bodleian Library Oxford, A. E. Zimmern Papers, MS 118, 68.   [42] J. Lawson, 'Editorial', *Highway*, February 1922, 76.
[43] *The Interim Report of the Adult Education Committee of the Ministry of Reconstruction* (London: HMSO), 54   [44] WEA, *Annual Report* (London: 1920), 189.

Mansbridge summarized it all with a characteristically straightforward turn of phrase, declaring that 'the assertion of the right of individuality is the root of the whole matter'.[45]

In the United States, the nationalist progressives also strove to ensure that the new initiatives in adult education were infused with their own commitment to individual liberty and personal development. They interpreted those ideals themselves, however, very differently from the socialist pluralists. When liberty was discussed as a goal for adult and workers' education in the United States it was the communalistic form of that ideal that clearly triumphed, while the pluralists' brand of individual, creative experimentation received very little attention. Indeed, the very ideal of positioning such individualistic improvement as a fundamental educational ideal was often pointedly rejected. Asking whether the 'purpose' of workers' education was to 'benefit the worker as the individual', the WEB's introductory volume, *Workers' Education in the United States*, declared that while there is 'no doubt that every student in our classes does get some benefit from their work' that was distinctly not 'what we are aiming at'.[46]

This rejection of the pluralists' individualistic educational ambitions would have come as no surprise to those familiar with the pre-war nationalist progressive writings. In *The Promise of American Life*, Croly argued that 'an individual's education' should consist 'primarily in the discipline which he undergoes to fit him both for fruitful association with his fellows and for his own special work'.[47] More surprising, perhaps, was the fact that such a dedication survived the shocks of war completely intact. Indeed, if anything, the class conflict that characterized American society at the end of the war allowed the reassertion of an essentially communal direction for educational provision. 'Americans are losing their innocent faith in the immunity of their commonwealth from [social] disintegration', the *New Republic* argued in 1919, and as such 'they want to know what plans [for] education' can be adopted to 'secure the moral unity of the American nation.'[48] Four years later the message was almost identical. An extensive programme of education for all ages was required dedicated to the idea that the 'liberation and enhancement of [the] individual' could be realized only through their immersion in 'social life as a whole'. Without such a programme, the *New Republic*'s editors concluded, 'modern civilization' will 'perish through the warfare' of 'special interests' and 'classes'.[49] 'We repeat over and over', John Dewey insisted in his post-war masterpiece

---

[45] A. Mansbridge, 'Freedom in Adult Education', address to the 5th BIAE Annual Conference 1928, 80.

[46] A. Lee, 'Methods of Mass Education', in S. Miller (ed.), *Workers Education in the United States* (New York: Workers Education Bureau, 1921), 112–13.

[47] H. Croly, *The Promise of American Life* (New York: Macmillan, 1909), 403.

[48] Editors, 'Americanism in Education', *New Republic*, 10 May 1919, 38.

[49] Editors, 'The Object of Workers' Education', *New Republic*, 25 April 1923, 239.

Reconstruction in Philosophy, 'that man is a social animal' and that 'the heart of the sociality of man is education.'[50]

As ever, the nationalist progressives detected two elements to this task of preparing individuals to play their communal role: an objective one and a subjective one. The objective role was to prepare individuals to function effectively in their lives as workers. John Dewey may have agreed with his British pluralist contemporaries that adult education should strive to provide individual students with the opportunity for the 'awakening and movement of the mind', but he equally stridently argued that such an 'awakening' was desirable only in so far as it was essential for the full and effective functioning of the overall community. Educators needed to equip their students 'with trained imagination and resourceful skill' so that they could be prepared to provide 'expert action in a complex society'.[51] What was required, Dewey concluded, was a continual programme of 'instruction' that prepares individuals to flourish in their 'social dependencies and interdependencies'. Such a programme was 'as important for the adult as for the child'.[52] The psychological aspect was also crucial. As Dewey argued, when education for 'social efficiency' is confined to training for the provision of 'overt acts' its 'chief constituent is omitted' and that chief constituent was 'intelligent sympathy or good will'.[53] The primary need, the *New Republic*'s editors thus insisted, was for a 'system of adult education adapted to stimulate a sense of public responsibility and to bestow on the American citizen some kind of moral cohesion'.[54] Through such an education, as a WEB student himself reported, 'the prevailing individualistic psychology ceases in the mind of the student. He begins to think and act guided by the knowledge of the need of solidarity'.[55] Insofar as the nationalist progressives and their allies could control it, American workers' education was, then, to be firmly focused on the centrality of 'civic duties and responsibilities'.[56] It was in this way that adult education was to lead the way to social change. The 'inertia of individualistic thinking', as one WEB tutorial class leader concluded, will be 'overcome by the momentum of our socialized thinking'.[57]

This fundamental difference in justificatory emphasis was far from a purely academic dispute. These commitments structured the form of the education

---

[50] J. Dewey, *Reconstruction in Philosophy* (London: University of London Press, 1921), 185.

[51] J. Dewey, 'Address to Local No. 5, American Federation of Teachers' (1928), Labor-Management Documentation Center, Cornell University, Ithaca, A. J. Muste Papers (Microform), and J. Dewey, 'Vocational Education', *New Republic*, 11 March 1916, 159.

[52] Dewey, *Reconstruction*, 185.

[53] J. Dewey, *Democracy and Education* (New York: Macmillan, 1922), 121.

[54] Editors, 'The Newer Nationalism', *New Republic*, 29 January 1916, 321.

[55] C. Sproger, 'The Value of Workers' Education', in Miller (ed.), *Workers' Education in the United States*, 85.

[56] J. Frey, 'The Ideals in the American Labor Movement', *International Journal of Ethics*, 27 (1918) 492.

[57] C. J. Hendley, 'Obstacles in the Way of Labor Education' in Miller (ed.), *Workers' Education in the United States*, 108.

that the theorists sought to provide. Most notably, the British pluralists' commitment to enhancing liberty as individual experimentation was taken to demand a specifically non-vocational form of education in the British WEA, while liberty as communal participation allowed a much more ambiguous relationship to the demands of vocation to emerge in the United States. In Britain, that is, although Laski, Cole, and Tawney were well aware of defi-ciencies in the skill and efficiency of the post-war work-force, they were all simultaneously convinced that the education provided by the WEA should be essentially non-technical in orientation.[58] Vocational adult education would, these thinkers all held, enable individuals merely to become a more effective 'cog in the machine' of industry as any emphasis on training people to respond better to the demands of the workplace 'ran the risk of reducing men to mere instruments of machine technology'.[59] As Laski pointedly instructed his audience in the *New Republic*, there is no advantage in seeking to make 'the whole world a vast polytechnic' for 'vocational education is in the end no more than the handmaid of a system that is already in decay'.[60] In Cole, Tawney, and Laski's view adult education was not to be designed to benefit employers, 'the profit-making of the world', nor for that matter was it to aid the job of the 'Fabian bureaucrat', but rather it was to enable 'the develop-ment of the will, understanding and initiative' of each individual indepen-dently of the position that individual might occupy in the occupational structure.[61]

The position for the progressives in the United States was, as previous scholars have noted, very different.[62] There it was study of the humanities and the encouragement of abstract introspection that were disparaged, and vocational practices when properly organized that formed the basis of ideal instruction. This was partly no doubt because they were already well served by the substantial municipal and philanthropic adult education movement. The pursuit of 'culture', one WEB spokesman concluded, could be left in the United States to 'the public and high school system, the universities and their extensions, and the various philanthropic agencies', all of which were far more fully developed than they were in Britain.[63] This difference in educa-tional emphasis was also, however, the result of clear ideological commit-ment. The central purpose of workers' education, the *New Republic* editors

---

[58] See Chapter 5.

[59] *Interim Report*, 78, and H. Laski, 'Surveying the Wreck', *Nation*, 23 April 1921, 133–4.

[60] H. Laski, 'Adult Education', *New Republic*, 20 March 1919, 283.

[61] G. D. H. Cole and A. Freeman, 'Why the Workers Should Demand Education', *WEA Year Book, 1918*, WEA Papers, 56. See also G. D. H. Cole, 'Cross-Roads', 542.

[62] See K. Rockhill, 'Ideological Solidification of Liberalism in University Adult Education: Confrontation over Workers' Education in the USA', in K. Rockhill, R. Fieldhouse, and R. Taylor (eds), *University Adult Education in England and the USA* (London: Croom Helm, 1985), 175–220.

[63] A. Lee, 'Methods of Mass Education', in Miller (ed.), *Workers' Education in the United States*, 112–13.

argued, was to offer 'organized training in [those] practical arts' which are 'fundamental to the life of the community'.[64] What that required, in turn, was knowledge of a wide range of practically, that is to say 'vocationally', useful subjects. If, after all, students were equipped with a wide range of practical skills then their employment was more likely to be both personal fulfilling and more beneficial to society in general. In response to these demands, the very first meeting of the WEB established a special committee to investigate the desirable scope and focus of vocational education. The recommended curriculum that emerged from these discussions covered topics ranging from the social sciences—mastery of which was deemed necessary for the social engineers of tomorrow—through the mechanisms of 'industrial management' to precise and detailed training in 'industrial technique'.[65]

The depth of this transatlantic disagreement on the aims and the subject matter of workers' education led some of the American progressives occasionally to question the usefulness of using the British experience as a base. Even such a staunch anglophile as Arthur Gleason wondered whether the 'salty individualism of the British' movement rendered its 'untidy' and 'casual[ly] unprogrammed adventure into the universe' of adult education of less use to American educators than some continental European experiments.[66] Croly even occasionally thought that the German experience might be a more helpful guide given that the *Volkshochschule* of post-war Germany placed more emphasis on the 'moral and social' dimensions of adult education than the British WEA appeared to do.[67] But more often, the American nationalist progressives attempted to play down the difference between their approach and that of the British pluralists. Although John Dewey was probably the most vociferous advocate of vocational and communal education, he worked particularly hard to ensure that his British audience knew that he was well aware of the potential difficulties. Dewey sought always to ensure that the aim of workers' education was 'industrial intelligence, rather than technical trade efficiency'. There was, Dewey held, no simple contradiction between vocational and liberal education: the former need not just produce 'efficient workmen in an industrial machine' and the latter did not always provide 'for free-functioning citizens in a democracy'. If, he continued, tutorial classes in vocational subjects were properly organized they could forge

[64] Editors, 'Education for Work', *New Republic*, 11 March 1916, 146.

[65] See F. Cohn, 'Report and Recommendation of the Organizing Committee' (1921), Labor-Management Documentation Centre, Cornell University, Ithaca, WEB Records, 1/10; Editors, 'Education for Work', *New Republic*, 11 March 1916, 146; J. R. Copenhaber, 'What Subjects are of the Most practical Value to the Workers', in Miller (ed), *Workers' Education in the United States*, 81. Those who held out against the vocational emphasis were exactly those who had found the most to support in British pluralism and guild socialism generally. See J. Hughan, 'Cultural vs. Vocational Training', *Intercollegiate Socialist*, 7 (1918), 25.

[66] A. Gleason and S. Miller, *Workers Education* (New York: Workers Education Bureau of America, 1921), 7–8.   [67] H. Croly, 'Education for Grown-Ups', *New Republic*, 12 December 1923, 60.

workers 'ready, like the energetic and professional man, to affect the standards and endeavors of his profession and the community life'.[68] 'Why', Dewey continually asked, 'should it be thought that one must take his choice between sacrificing himself to doing useful service for others or sacrificing them to the pursuit of his own exclusive ends, whether the saving of his own soul or the building of an inner spiritual life and personality?'[69] Phrasing the issue in terms of such a stark choice, Dewey insisted, was entirely misleading. Indeed 'the contrast' such a position 'assumed' between education for either 'social dependence' or 'social independence' always 'does harm'. An education which prepared workers for 'a genuine vocation' would, the *New Republic* agreed, imply 'neither a life devoted to thought' nor training for a 'dull mechanistic job to which personal and artistic intellectual interests are mere trimmings'. Rather, it would embrace elements of both. The WEB and its related institutions should aim to train a generation of manual workers capable of enjoying 'a life as genuinely professional as the lawyer and doctor and engineer'.[70]

Education for governing: preparation for associational democracy

Noble as this effort at reconciliation was, it failed entirely to bridge the gaps between the two movements; there was still a lurking suspicion in Britain that the American approach concentrated too distinctly on 'fitting' individuals in to a pre-existing industrial and social order rather than allowing them to find their own way in a free-flowing complex of associations. And yet whatever their other differences, there was one more concrete area in which both groups did agree. Since the end of the war, both movements had firmly asserted the necessity for far greater control to be devolved to non-state associations, and both wanted, in particular, industry to be subject to greater democratic decision-making on the part of workers themselves. As they agreed on that goal, so both groups also saw adult education as a perfect way to lay the foundations for such a role. If voluntary organizations were to be run successfully, they would have to be run by people who had at least a rudimentary training in the direction and management of human affairs. 'No adequate educational agency has as yet been provided', Herbert Croly complained, to train those who will 'engineer and man' these newly empowered associations.[71] John Dewey spelt out the consequences even more clearly: 'only as modern society has at command individuals who are trained by experience in the control of industrial activities and relationships, can we achieve industrial democracy, the autonomous management of each line of

---

[68] H. Douglas, 'Apprenticeships and Industrial Education', *American Labor Year Book 1917–1918* (New York: Rand School of Social Science, 1918), 203, and Editors, 'The Issue in Vocational Education', *New Republic*, 26 June 1915, 192.   [69] Dewey, *Democracy and Education*, 123.

[70] Editors, 'The Issue in Vocational Education', *New Republic*, 26 June 1915, 191–2.

[71] H. Croly, 'A School of Social Research', *New Republic*, 8 June 1918, 169.

productive work by those directly engaged in it.'[72] Both the WEA and the WEB recognized this preparation as an essential part of their role. As the WEA's 1920 *Annual Report* phrased it, training was required 'for equipping [individuals] to share in the most effective way in the activities of the various organisations of which they are members'.[73] As the dedication to some form of associational democracy had provided the basis for some, admittedly limited, convergence at an ideological level, it offered the basis for a form of convergence in the educational arena too.

Whatever the potential for agreement, however, any hopes for straightforward and substantial agreement that the movements might have shared were quickly shattered. For the educational emphasis of pluralists and progressives differed in important ways even here. For British socialist pluralists, training for associational democracy was initially understood in terms of training students in the independence of mind and scepticism necessary not only to challenge their own convictions—to engage in personal experimentation—but also to cast doubt on the positions of others, and especially of those in authority. The WEA thus saw its role as encouraging 'the rank and file' to be no longer 'content to accept the opinions put forward by accepted leaders'.[74] Students could develop the essential skills of criticism and analysis simply through the experience of discussing a wide range of themes. In learning how to 'diagnose, criticise and add to' the views of their tutors and classmates, students would be ready to engage in debate and discussion in their places of work.[75] Worker students would then be able sceptically to watch over those who were involved in day-to-day operational management. If such an education could spread, it would end the situation which 'train[ed] the few to power and the many to subordination' and allow everyone to influence and attempt to control the operations of the associations in which they engaged.[76]

For the nationalist progressives, though, this often appeared simply blind utopianism. Although they welcomed the WEA's dedication to creating an 'environment of discussion and cooperation' they also continually reiterated their dedication to technical training.[77] Technical efficiency simply had to occupy a central place in the curriculum. James H. Maurer, the first president of the WEB, worried that although 'we hear a lot of talk among some well-meaning people that the workers will run things; that we are going to democratize industry' no such changes could be forthcoming unless those

---

[72] J. Dewey, 'Creative Industry', *New Republic*, 2 November 1918, 23.

[73] WEA, *Annual Report* (1920), 190. See also *Interim Report*, 54.

[74] J. MacTavish, 'The WEA', in *WEA Yearbook* (1918), WEA Papers, 331.

[75] A. Mansbridge, *University Tutorial Classes: A Study in the Development of Higher Education among Working Men and Women* (London: Longmans, Green and Co., 1913), 15.

[76] Cole and Freeman, 'Workers Should Demand', 57.

[77] Editors, 'Extending the University', *New Republic*, 6 January 1917, 260.

sympathetic to change demonstrate that they 'are prepared to make a better job than those who are running things now'. Unless the WEB and other organizations could ensure that the workers' were 'properly prepared', Maurer thus concluded, they 'will make just as big and possibly a greater mess out of things than what the present managers are guilty of doing'.[78] What was required, therefore, was a 'middle way between the ponderous text-book methods' that characterized traditional training in industrial and managerial methods 'and the smattering and superficiality of "popularized knowledge"' that the open-ended abstract discussions of humanistic themes in the WEA appeared to encourage. [79]

Even the British socialist pluralists' continual scepticism of authority could not blind them to the fact that there might be something in this critique. Cole, Laski, and Tawney all saw that the students' democratic experience had both to teach workers to criticize the proposals of others *and* to construct reasonable alternatives of their own.[80] Indeed, it was not only critics from abroad who made the case for a more practical focus to workers' education. As the post-war world aged, the WEA's students themselves began to demand a clearer focus to their work. One student, as recorded by Albert Mansbridge, argued that what was required were more courses which 'help towards a real understanding of labour problems'.[81] Leading British trade unionists joined the demand that the Association concentrate more energy on providing students with ways of dealing with 'the practical difficulties that must inevitably arise' as society took the first, tentative steps towards full-blown industrial democracy.[82] In 1921, a Trades Union Congress Educational Enquiry Committee similarly urged that adult education should be redesigned so as to provide workers with 'a wide range of knowledge germane to economic and political problems' in order to enable effective 'direct participation of trade unions in management'.[83] Eventually, the WEA fell somewhat into line and began to organize classes on these more practical, rather

[78] J. Maurer, 'The Pressing Need for Labor Education', in Miller (ed.), *Workers' Education in the United States*, 76.

[79] Editors, 'Extending the University', *New Republic*, 6 January 1917, 260.

[80] See G. D. H. Cole, 'The Origins of Working-Class Education in Britain' (n.d.), Nuffield College, Oxford, The Cole Papers, GDHC/A1/24/12, 7.

[81] Mansbridge, *University Tutorial Classes*, 107. See also the comments of those WEA members surveyed by the St Philip's Settlement Education and Economics Research Society in their quantitative and qualitative survey of working class attitudes in their *The Equipment of the Workers: An Enquiry* (London: George Allen and Unwin, 1919), esp. 132–67.

[82] MacTavish, 'WEA', 330. This did not hold only for industrial involvement but for involvement in a whole host of other associations. As Laski wrote to Holmes, he wanted 'the working man to grasp how England is governed before he goes out to discover how it ought to be governed'. Letter dated 27 January 1925 in M. de Wolfe Howe (ed.), *The Holmes-Laski Letters: Correspondence of Mr Justice Holmes and Harold J. Laski 1916–1935* (Cambridge, MA: Harvard University Press, 1953), 703.

[83] Trade Union Educational Enquiry Committee Report (1921), reprinted in J. Corfield, *Epoch in Workers' Education: A History of the Workers' Educational Trade Union Committee* (London: WEA, 1969), 211.

than abstractly uplifting, themes. By 1923, there were 81 WEA classes in aspects of economics. Cole himself led a London University tutorial class on 'Social and Economic Reconstruction', which in addition to some reasonably high economic theory also considered more immediate issues, including the effects of particular government acts on the everyday operations of trade unions.[84] Some limited form of practical, even vocational, training entered the world of British workers' education.

Constructing communal attachments

Reflecting on these developments, Tawney moved the British pluralists even closer to the position of their American counterparts, arguing that 'if organisations are to work successfully we will have to find the means of cultivating the intellectual *and* moral qualities which will enable men to participate' in them.[85] This emphasis on the more generally *moral* role of educational training brought the pluralists back to the accusations that progressives had always levelled at their plans for social and political reconstruction. Not only would democratic associations need to avoid practical errors but they must also restrain themselves from making specifically ethical mistakes, falling into sectionalism or selfishness. Even Cole was conscious that without alteration the 'feeling among trade unionists will still be purely sectional', whatever his faith in a distant utopian future.[86] Workers, it was claimed, had to become aware of their responsibilities generally considered. In addition to equipping and promoting democracy, adult education was, even for the socialist pluralists, also a means of domesticating it.[87]

Many noted a dichotomy or a contradiction here, wondering whether the socialist pluralists had abandoned their individualistic position and moved more dramatically towards accepting the propriety of 'function'. Many later historians have thus postulated a stark division amongst adult educators between those who 'felt education was necessary to prevent the working class *misusing* . . . power, and those who wanted them to be educated in order to *obtain* power', and castigated the socialist pluralists for seeming to be intent on blurring the line.[88] Amongst the socialist pluralists, though, both positions were advocated, not through any inconsistency but because the two positions were both essential elements within the same political ambition

---

[84] See Syllabus in Cole Papers, GDHC/E2/1/26. See also Mary Stocks' account of Cole's commitment to providing the 'education necessary for the proper discharge of the responsibilities which lay ahead of the Labour Movement', in M. Stocks, *The Workers' Educational Association: The First Fifty Years* (London: George Allen and Unwin, 1953), 81–2.

[85] R. H. Tawney, 'Adult Education in the History of the Nation', address in *The British Institute of Adult Education 5th Annual Conference* (London: 1926), 18–19 (emphasis added).

[86] Cole, 'Socialism and Education', 27.

[87] See, too R. H. Tawney, *The Acquisitive Society* (London: G. Bell, 1921), 196.

[88] Rowbotham, 'Travellers', 87 (emphases added).

and conceptual framework. The dual role for education in this regard reflected the important conceptual balance the pluralists had wished to strike ever since their first ideological engagement with nationalist progressive critics in the aftermath of the war.

As Chapter 5 illustrated, the pluralists all wanted a substantially unregulated associationalist democracy but they wanted one where citizens were going to behave responsibly, a society in which, in the pluralists' jargon, associations would *function* effectively. The pluralists had to persuade their various progressive critics that their ideal polity would not be run for the sectional interests of those who ran their powerful organizations and well-placed industries but in order to provide goods which could be utilized by other groups and by experimenting individuals. The pluralists wanted 'freedom and responsibility combined' and adult education was an ideal means by which to achieve that aim. In their theoretical works, Laski, Cole, and Tawney were constantly engaged in a balancing act between their dedication, on the one hand, to individual experimentation and, on the other, to fostering a widespread sentiment of fellowship. This conceptual balancing act perfectly replayed itself in the approach to adult education. As an annual report of the WEA phrased it, 'the attitude of the Association is that the primary purpose of all education should be to develop individual . . . personality' but it should always also recognize the necessity of engendering a 'deep sense of responsibility for the well-being of the community'.[89]

Theoretically, as the previous chapter showed, this key conceptual balancing act between freedom and communal responsibility had been struck by relying squarely on the development of vague sentimental attachments between individuals of different associational allegiances and ideals. For the pluralists, 'community' was best understood as a set of 'reciprocal sentiments'.[90] They fiercely resisted both the anti-individualism of any claim to know the 'content of each person's best self' and any organicists' view of society as possessive of an independent existence, both of which they believed to be antithetical to an interest in individual freedom and human diversity.[91] For the pluralists, humans living in the same environment merely had an innate proclivity to 'be bound by ties of sentiment', a proclivity which it was the WEA's duty to recognize and encourage. Again it is evident that this very particular conception informed the socialist pluralists' approach to adult education. The socialist pluralists understood their task as the striving for the creation of an environment capable of stimulating individuals' supposed natural proclivity to behave sympathetically and empathetically. As Cole argued, the role of the WEA in this regard was to attempt to bring about 'a

---

[89] WEA, *Annual Report* (1920), 189.

[90] A phrase borrowed from R. M. MacIver, *Community: A Sociological Study* (London: Macmillan, 1917), 69.

[91] See Chapters 3 and 5.

more natural state of communal feeling'.[92] Tawney understood the project in the same way. For him, adult education should simply aim to generate 'emotional warmth'.[93]

Once again, too, the WEA generally appears to have accepted the pluralists' own definition of the goal. Despite the efforts of some, the WEA's view of its task of fostering community embraced neither the Hegelian metaphysics of idealism nor the organicism of New Liberals and Fabians, ideas which had shaped the whole ideological basis of the nationalist progressives. The pluralists had to seek a means of developing this vague communal spirit without hindering the development of experimental diversity and individuality. Indeed, Laski, Cole, and Tawney all set themselves the task of constructing an adult education system which could encourage and equip individuals to become more independent, critical, 'autonomous', while simultaneously leading them to develop strong sentimental bonds with others whose views of life were very different from their own. To combine freedom with communality in this way, two answers were proposed. First, Cole argued that individuals who were able to express themselves freely or felt released were more likely as a result to be communally spirited. Just as Cole expected communality to bloom once the antagonisms created by frustrated ambitions within industrial life were removed, so he argued that 'the educationalist aims at promoting communal feeling' simply by establishing 'a new educational system allowing free growth to . . . individuality'.[94] The second proposed solution was more thoughtful. Cole, Laski, Tawney, and their WEA colleagues expected sympathies to emerge within the tutorial class as the result of students' experiences of continuous working together. The class would build up loyalties 'in much the same way' as 'co-operative societies, trade unions, political bodies'.[95] A microcosm of 'social solidarity' emerged within the class as soon as the once 'solitary student finds that he is one of a crowd'.[96]

The solution once again lay in the *way* that education was provided rather than in the detail of its content. As students begin to run their own tutorial classes, Cole, Tawney, and Laski all proposed, they also learn to become responsible for that class's success or failure. As a result 'a new attitude is produced'.[97] As soon as a student was able 'to make the laws by which he is governed', even within one association, he would begin to realize the responsibilities which come with power. A WEA workers' education would provide

[92] Cole, 'Socialism and Education', 2.

[93] R. H. Tawney, 'The Future of the WEA', *Highway*, October 1928, 3.

[94] Cole, 'Socialism and Education', 3.

[95] Mansbridge, *University Tutorial Classes*, 53.

[96] R. H. Tawney, 'An Experiment in Democratic Education' (1918), reprinted in R. Hinden (ed.), *The Radical Tradition: Twelve Essays on Politics, Education and Literature* (London: George Allen and Unwin, 1964), 74 and 77.

[97] C. H. C. Osborne, 'Self-Government in Schools', *Guildsman*, October 1921, 4.

the necessary 'civic discipline'.[98] Classes had one further and distinct advantage over many other associations in this regard. In the tutorial class, many people with otherwise very different viewpoints and associational allegiances would meet and mix. As the Ministry of Reconstruction's Adult Education Committee recognized, 'there may be a tendency to narrowness of outlook in groups of people brought together for a specific purpose' but within the WEA this disadvantage is 'overcome by the breadth of teaching and by a leaven of other students'.[99] Within the tutorial class 'all partialities are brought in' and as a result the sectional feelings and antipathies of different groupings are slowly annulled.[100] Not only would different sorts of workers meet in the WEA but also cross-class sympathy was to be developed within the tutorial class and, especially, at the summer schools where working-class adult students would interact with undergraduates from the traditional universities. There it was possible for 'the peer's son [to] rejoice in the fellowship of the miner's son, and the casual labourer in the fellowship of the don'. With such an experience, Laski and colleagues hoped, workers would learn instinctively to behave reasonably when they come to effective power.

For the nationalist progressives this marked progress, but not convergence. To begin with, the goal itself was far too restrictive. What was required, John Dewey argued, was 'something more than a feeling' of communal attachment. 'It is', he continued, 'a cultivated imagination for what men have in common and a rebellion at what unnecessarily divides them' that provided the essential requirements.[101] Moreover, the absence of specific training in communal goods appeared to render the WEA's programme vague and unrealistic. A programme of effectively targeted skills should be developed, even if that meant restricting the appeal of the whole workers' educational programme. Only 'those who are willing to overlook their individual fortunes for the purpose of actively engaging' in communal service were desired by American progressive adult educators.[102] And those who volunteered must, as Croly put it, be 'gradually trained' in the ethics and the practices of 'industrial self-government'. Upon that issue, all nationalist social reform 'must in the long-run depend for its success'.[103] To some, this eminently practical direction reflected 'a phase of anti-intellectualism at work which is short-sighted and dangerous'. To others, it was an inherent part of the process required to lay the essential building blocks of a better society.[104]

---

[98] Osborne, 'Self-Government', 4.

[99] *The Final Report of the Adult Education Committee of the Ministry of Reconstruction* (London: HMSO, 1919), 114.   [100] Tawney, 'Adult Education', 25.

[101] Dewey, *Democracy and Education*, 121.

[102] I. Mufson, 'What Did I Get Out of It?', *Labor Age*, April 1924, 7.

[103] H. Croly, *Progressive Democracy* (New York: Macmillan, 1914), 390.

[104] W. Y. Elliott, *The Pragmatic Revolt in Politics: Syndicalism, Fascism and the Corporate State* (New York: Macmillan, 1928), 37.

Adult Education and the State

Both groups were drawn to education as an issue because they believed that their ideals in this arena were attainable in the present or at least in the very near future. Adult education in its idealized form, that is, was not reliant on the construction of an ideal commonwealth nor was it as unobtainable a goal as the construction of an American Labor Party or a British self-governing system of Guilds. It could be built immediately, and it could be built by the theorists themselves. There was, however, predictable initial disagreement as to the means of building it. For the socialist pluralists in Britain, the body designed to provide the essential service of shaping free yet communal citizens—the WEA—was a specifically voluntary organization. Students were to be under no legal compulsion to attend and they should receive no direct state assistance to do so. There was to be no centralized state agency overlooking the content of the curriculum and the tutors were to be provided with no material remuneration from the state for the huge amounts of time and energy they invested.[105] In the United States, however, the nationalist progressives were initially much more enthusiastic about involving the formal processes of the state. There, adult education was to be part of a project of national renewal, and federal and State governments were to be encouraged both directly to provide and benignly to oversee the development of a new educational order. The roots of this disagreement once again lay in the essentials of the two ideological systems.

Voluntarism and statism in the ideal

For the pluralists, their commitment to liberty understood as individual experimentation required that adult education remain distinct from the realm of state control. The pluralists' central concern in this regard was that a curriculum overseen by the state would negate the flexibility of the tutorial class. Their worry was not so much the traditional liberal concern, exemplified by John Stuart Mill, that 'a general state education is a mere contrivance for moulding people to be exactly like one another'.[106] Rather, the pluralists desired to ensure that the students *felt* as if they themselves possessed control over the education being provided. The psychological development of a sense of independence was at the heart of Cole, Tawney, and Laski's conception of adult education. The desire to promote liberty as experimentation demanded

---

[105] See G. D. H. Cole, *World of Labour* (London: G. Bell, 1913, 2nd edn, 1917), 19 and Laski, 'Present Position', 34.

[106] See J. S. Mill, 'On Liberty', in M. Warnock (ed.), *Utilitarianism, On Liberty, and Essay on Bentham* (London: Fontana, 1979), 239. Bertrand Russell brilliantly criticized this view in his *Principles of Social Reconstruction* (London: George Allen and Unwin, 1916), 143–67.

that 'the business' of WEA education 'is to serve the workers who want education' by 'giving them as far as possible what they want, and not what "supe-
rior" people think they ought to want'.[107] In order to produce creative and
independent students, adult education 'must of necessity be voluntary, elas-
tic, spontaneous and largely self-governing'.[108] Such flexibility could not be
ensured in a state-run system where inspections and assessments were likely
to be the norm. A centralised curriculum would engender a 'dry formalism'
which would stifle creativity.[109] The WEA was 'altogether against' any state
involvement that would entail 'the rigid supervision of educational work . . .
by any bureaucratic body'.[110]

Perhaps more surprisingly, the second of the pluralists' ideological
commitments—their dedication to engendering a sense of communal attachment—was also understood to augur ill for state involvement. The vague and
essentially sentimental nature of the socialist pluralists' conception of
community entailed that WEA classes should be left to take their own decisions and shape their own policies. Even 'well-meaning regulation', Tawney
insisted, could easily 'destroy' the fragile construction of a 'corporate
spirit'.[111] As Cole noted in another context, community spirit 'expresses itself
most freely and completely in those spheres of social life into which organisation enters least'.[112] The pluralists believed that it was generally impossible
for individuals to be coerced into developing sentimental attachments.
Rather, all the pluralists hoped, students would develop widespread sentimental attachments simply from the persistent experience of working
together with various different people within the tutorial class. The 'corporate
enthusiasm, the spirit of mutual helpfulness and co-operation and loyalty'
which all of the pluralists desired could be fostered in this instance only 'by
membership of a voluntary society'.[113]

In the United States, the nationalist progressives had no such ideological
reasons to reject the role of the state in operating workers' education. They
were, after all, committed to crafting a very different institutional ideal, one
in which citizens would be led to develop a strong sense of national communal commitment, understood in both objective and subjective terms, and
abandon their attachment to sectional, particularistic interests and the deeply
entrenched culture of American individualism from which those interests
sprang. For the nationalist progressives, therefore, the formal mechanisms of

---

[107] G. D. H. Cole, 'Recollections of Workers' Education' (1936), Cole Papers, GDHC/A1/24/9, 4.
[108] A. Zimmern, 'The Universities and Public Opinion', WEA Yearbook (1918), 244.
[109] G. D. H. Cole, 'A Coming of Age', New Statesman, 19 July 1924, 433.
[110] G. D. H. Cole, 'University Education', New Statesman, 19 May 1923, 163.
[111] Tawney, 'Adult Education', 24.
[112] G. D. H. Cole, 'What is the State?', Venturer, 1920, 531.
[113] Tawney, 'Future of the WEA', 3. The pluralists' debt to their predecessors in this regard can be
easily noted; see, for example, A. Toynbee, 'Are Radicals Socialists?', in A. Toynbee (ed.), Lectures on
the Industrial Revolution (London: Beacon Press, 1908) .

the state were the obvious place to turn, and, indeed, in the era prior to the United States' entry into the war it was exactly the direction in which nationalist progressives looked. In 1916, the *New Republic* nailed its colours clearly to that mast. One of its most committed educational correspondents, Randolph Bourne, laid out a plan calling for the extension of universal, publicly provided education into adulthood. After graduating from school at 16, he argued, all citizens should be expected to spend two years in some form of educational activity 'organized and administered by the State educational administrations and supervised and subsidized by the national government'. The distinctively public and national focus was held to be essential by Bourne, for only by involving those bodies that represent the whole community in the provision of adult education could 'we begin to organize a true national service which will let all serve creatively towards the toning up of American life'.[114]

Although Bourne's rather grandiose plans almost inevitably came to nothing, the basic ideas were not entirely ignored. Just before the United States entered the war, the State of Massachusetts opened a so-called 'People's University' aimed to put 'at the free disposal of every citizen the intellectual resources of all the various colleges in the State'.[115] The State University of California also began discussions with various interested parties, including the State Federation of Labor, in an attempt to extend its facilities and classes to adults and working-class adults in particular.[116] In Wisconsin, home of Robert La Follette's more moderate brand of progressivism, the State legislature appropriated significant sums to university extension, raising the financing available from $20,000 in 1907 to $225,000 in 1914. All in all, over 30 States offered their working citizens something in the way of publicly funded adult education.[117]

Politics and convergence

But in both cases, political reality strongly shifted prevailing political attitudes. That reality impacted most dramatically on the United States. As the 'Red Scare' took hold in 1918 and 1919, rather that assisting progressive educational programmes, many federal and State agencies of repression began to target left-leaning adult education classes ruthlessly. In 1919 New York State established a Joint Legislative Committee to Investigate Seditious Activities, chaired by red-baiting Senator George Lusk. Openly targeting radical educational institutions, the Committee's agents raided the American

---

[114] R. Bourne, 'A Moral Equivalent for Universal Military Service', *New Republic*, 1 July 1916, 217–19.

[115] Editors, 'Extending the University', *New Republic*, 6 January 1917, 26.

[116] See L. J. Richardson, *1925 Report of the A.F.L. Committee on Workers' Education*, WEB Records, 5277/1/ 44.   [117] See Goldman, *Dons and Workers*, 312.

Socialist Society's Rand School for Social Science, sequestrating its funds, seizing its papers, and damaging its property. Lusk's Committee policy recommendations were also aimed at progressive initiatives. It demanded that all schools and colleges not under the supervision of the State Education Department or maintained by a religious denomination obtain a license from the Board of Regents. The New School for Social Research, surely the most moderate of the American experiments, was then denied an educational charter and had to turn to the District of Columbia instead.[118] In Illinois, the State legislature similarly insisted that all educational establishments should reserve places on their boards for the local business community. To accept such an approach would, most of progressive mind believed, be to 'surrender the control of these schools into the hands of organized capital' and that, in turn would 'mean an educational system would be devised' which may 'make for efficient workmen in an industrial machine but would not make for free-functioning citizens in a democracy'.[119] 'From all parts of the country come hundreds of authentic reports of restrictions put upon professors and teachers', the WEB reported, all due to the 'conservative, if not reactionary' tendencies of public boards of education throughout the nation. Education policy lay in the hands 'almost entirely of influential business and professional men who have a deep-seated fear and hatred of anything that can be construed as encouragement to the labor movement'.[120]

Individual nationalist theorists strove to ignore these developments and to maintain the insistence that state activity should dominate workers' education in the post-war world. The *New Republic*'s H. K. Randall argued that the 'public' nature of American education 'including the publicly-supported university' was 'one of the few achievements of collective enterprise in comparison with private enterprise' and thus it was the job of adult educators to help this publicly funded and run system 'do what it exists to do—give real education to real workers'.[121] But most could not ignore the repressive environment. The realities of post-war politics in the United States rendered any aspirations of benevolent state support hollow. The most that nationalist progressives could do in the face of these difficulties was try to transform the problem into a challenge. Arthur Gleason thus argued that relying on 'public educational funds' had always made many of the workers involved in classes 'suspicious' of the reliability of their tutors. The unavailability of state support thus brought new opportunities as well as difficulties as it would lead the workers' education movement into a closer relationship with the organized

---

[118] See Johnson, *Pioneer's Progress*, 277.

[119] H. Douglas, 'Apprenticeships and Industrial Education', *American Labor Year Book 1917–1918* (New York: Rand School of Social Science, 1918), 203.

[120] James H. Maurer, quoted in R. J. Altenbaugh, *Education for Struggle: The American Labor Colleges of the 1920s and 1930s* (Philadelphia: Temple University Press, 1990), 77.

[121] H. K. Randall, 'Why Workers' Education', *New Republic*, 16 November 1921, 351.

working class itself.[122] The WEB itself went even further in embracing the new era. Its guide on 'How to Start Workers Classes' published in the early 1920s reported that the recruitment of teachers had always lain at 'the heart of the problem'. Even where suitable teachers from state-run schools, colleges, and universities were still easily available, the guide argued, they should be avoided at all costs. Such teachers 'are frequently lacking in knowledge of the labor movement' and are under surveillance of educational authorities predisposed to unthinking conservatism'.[123] One professor of the Rand School even urged committed freethinkers in the United States to 'refrain from sending' their *children* to state-run public schools. Whereas pre-war the movement had been entirely based on state support, now 'voluntarism' became 'one of the ideal standards of our striving'.[124] In the face of these difficulties, financial and administrative resources would have to be found from elsewhere, and here nationalist progressives turned once again to the trade union movement. 'The heart of workers' education', the *New Republic* commentator argued, was 'the class financed on trade union money.'[125]

As it first appears, then, workers' education in both Britain and the United States would be entirely directed by a voluntary organization. It would be run, as far as possible, by its immediate members in their own long-term interests. There was, despite the ideological differences, a transatlantic settlement on the pluralist position. For the British this was the achievement of a long-cherished goal. The WEA was the embodiment of an organization other than the distrusted state which could promote in practice the desired synthesis of the pluralists' own conceptual commitments. It could enable experimentation but also foster a sense of community, all without involving the dubious authority of the centralized state. For the nationalist progressives, it was the unfortunate accident of circumstance.

Even this pattern of convergence, however, is not as straightforward as it may seem. For in some ways, circumstances were such that the roles of the two groups did not just converge but were actually *reversed*. For whatever the internal independence of the British WEA, it was distinctly not antithetical to *some* level of involvement from central government. The WEA fiercely resisted all attempts by the state to dictate the content, means, or goal of its adult education provision. The WEA's General Purpose Committee, on which both Cole and Tawney were represented, met in special session in 1919 when it appeared that local authorities may try to exert a greater degree of control in adult education provision.[126] The WEA did not, however, resist central

---

[122] Gleason, *Workers' Education*, 13–14.
[123] B. Mitchell, *How to Start Workers' Classes* (New York: Workers Education Bureau, 1921), 19.
[124] W. Calhoun, 'Education and the State', *Rand School News and Book Review*, 4 December 1920, 2.
[125] Gleason, *Workers' Education*, 5.
[126] See GPC minutes, special meeting 29 October 1919, Temple House, London, WEA Archive, uncatalogued papers.

state funding. In fact, as Tawney noted, it was difficult in this regard 'to exaggerate the services' which were rendered to WEA-based 'education by public authorities'.[127] In its early days, the WEA preferred not to rely on state funding and concentrated instead on assistance from 'co-operatives, trade unions and other working-class organisations' in the belief that 'where zeal exists material resources will be forthcoming'.[128] Eventually, however, the organization did turn to government and to local authorities for financial aid. By 1919 the vast majority of active WEA branches had a local authority funding their operations. Nor was this reliance on state aid hidden from the WEA's members. The *Annual Report* of 1920, for example, made clear that 'the possibility of securing increased grants from the Treasury is exercising the attention of the central executive of the WEA'.[129] The Board of Education in the Lloyd George government, under H. A. L. Fisher, was generally sympathetic to these requests; and following a national protest in March 1922 even the widespread cuts in public spending known as the 'Geddes Axe' did not affect the WEA's state-funded status.[130] Through the WEA, Cole, Laski, and Tawney attempted to deliver an educational organization which was 'free, independent, yet getting the best' from the established system.[131]

All of this implied a remarkable turn-around. Now British observers of the American scene were not denouncing progressives for their all too pliant reliance on the state but rather commiserating with them for their inability to draw on public resources. Writing for the American *Labor Age*, Arthur Greenwood expressed grave concerns that the WEB had been forced to 'hold aloof from the public system of education'. Such a position entailed, he believed, 'that a valuable means of influencing the whole educational life of the country will have been lost'. For despite its continual emphasis 'upon freedom of teaching and freedom of discussion', Greenwood concluded, the British WEA had always been able to carry on because of 'money provided by the . . . local education authorities and the State'.[132]

What becomes clear from this final set of observations is a further recognition that the politics of pluralism and progressivism was far from straightforward. Although Cole, Tawney, and Laski closely applied their theoretical commitments to fundamental areas of policy, they were not dogmatic in their assertions as to how exactly liberty as experimentation, associational democratization, and community as widespread sentimental attachment could be achieved. The pluralists' key conceptual commitments were to be translated into political reality by, in this instance, an organization which

---

[127] Tawney, 'Adult Education', 20.
[128] GPC minutes, 29 March 1914, 21, WEA Archive; WEA, *Annual Report* (1922).
[129] See WEA, *Annual Report* (1920).
[130] See Mansbridge, *University Tutorial Classes*, pp. vii–ix. See also G. D. H. Cole, 'Education in the New Parliament', *New Statesman*, 8 December 1923, 264–5.
[131] Anon., 'Adult Education', 206.
[132] A. Greenwood, 'The WEA at Work', *Labor Age*, April 1924, 10.

was committed to doctrinal impartiality, which was internally democratic, but which ultimately was financed by the central state. In contradiction to many accounts which characterize Cole and Laski as members of a distinctly and resolutely anti-statist movement, and Croly and his colleagues as supporters of an intransigently statist one, their interest in the position of the state was actually secondary to their interest in furthering their interpretations of liberty and community in their own different political settings. Far from being the utopian idealists that their grand abstract theories suggest, both groups were willing and able to accept that different empirical factors demanded different political responses.

Conclusion

The first arena of public policy to be examined has clearly demonstrated that the practical suggestions of both the socialist pluralists and the nationalist progressives were thoroughly infused with the core conceptual commitments outlined in the first two parts of this book. Not only can this book's new approach to these ideological movements explain the various objectives which the WEA and the WEB pursued in the early years of the inter-war era, but an exploration of the WEA and the WEB also enables a fuller understanding of the ideology itself. This investigation has demonstrated both that the theorists constantly sought to reconcile their fundamental commitments to the demands of the environments in which they found themselves and that they clearly prioritized their interest in the practicality of those commitments over any abstract commitment to any anti- or pro-statist position. For both socialist pluralists and nationalist progressives, commencing from different ideological starting points but finding themselves in different political situations, the state was sometimes to be resisted but sometimes to be embraced.

With these themes in mind, it is possible now to turn to look at another dominant arena of political activity that again presented the two groups with reasons to overcome their clear ideological differences. This arena was one in which the pluralists faced a still more difficult choice between promoting their conceptual commitments and preserving the integrity of their anti-statism and where the nationalist progressives would have to respond to significant public rejection of their state-centred aspirations and be led to discover alternative routes to their overall ideological goal. This arena was provided by the emergence of the welfare state and by the insistent demand for the redistribution of wealth and opportunity. This was an issue which asserted far greater importance in the everyday lives of most working class citizens than the pursuit of education, whether cultural or vocational, individualist or communal, democratic or hierarchical. After all, as Harold Laski informed Oliver Wendell Holmes in a rare moment of modesty, most students of the WEA and the WEB were in far greater need of 'a square meal' than they were of his 'erudition'.[133] How that square meal was to be assured was a central question that faced reformers on both sides of the Atlantic. It is to that it is necessary now to turn.

[133] Laski to Holmes, letter dated 22 December 1919 in de Wolfe Howe (ed.), *Holmes-Laski Letters*, 451.

7

The Politics of Poverty

Introduction

The relief of poverty, whether through the protection of the financial position of workers or through the provision of direct monetary benefits from the state, often takes a place at the very centre of the ideological heritage of the British and American reform traditions. The evolution of poor relief, stretching from the early efforts of cooperatives, trade unions, and friendly societies through to the large-scale state endeavours of Franklin Roosevelt's New Deal and Britain's Beveridge Report thus provides the analytic core of many examinations of British and American political development. Yet despite the general centrality of this theme, the emergence of the welfare state is hardly to be found in the available scholarly accounts of socialist pluralism and nationalist progressivism.[1] Few studies of the work of Croly, Laski, and their colleagues have carefully considered their definitions of poverty or their plans for its alleviation. These thinkers themselves are also largely absent from the broader histories of social policy. A student starting with an interest in the history of social welfare and looking for its intellectual roots would discover quickly that the socialist pluralists or nationalist progressives were not the welfare reformers that their successors of the Beveridge and New Deal eras would become.[2] They did not play any significant personal role in radically restructuring social policy nor were their ideas frequently cited by those who did. Their actual suggestions came to little, their general ideas dismissed by contemporaries and ignored by posterity.

---

[1] In her influential study, Jose Harris specifically apologizes for a lack of discussion of 'the pluralists and guild socialists'. J. Harris, 'Political Thought and the Welfare State', *Past and Present*, 135 (1992), 135. For nationalist progressives, see R. J. Lustig, *Corporate Liberalism: The Origins of Modern American Political Theory, 1890–1920* (Berkeley: University of California Press, 1982), 210; E. Stettner, *Shaping Modern Liberalism: Herbert Croly and Progressive Thought* (Lawrence: Kansas University Press, 1992), 50. J. Thompson, *Reformers and War: American Progressive Publicists and the First World War* (Cambridge: Cambridge University Press, 1987) once again commendably stands out as an exception to this scholarly rule, see esp. 42.

[2] This chapter concerns itself only with monetary remuneration for work or the provision of benefits in cash. It does not examine the provision of benefits in 'kind' such as direct health care, housing, or education.

Scholars attempting to explain these problems have generally argued that the socialist pluralists and nationalist progressives found the whole question of poverty and poverty alleviation exceptionally difficult to address. Available scholarly accounts thus emphasize the ways in which both movements continually sought to redirect the attention of their contemporaries *away* from the redistribution of material resources and on to other concerns.[3] Evidence for such a view is not hard to find. G. D. H. Cole frequently declared that an over-concentration on 'a doctrine of the distribution of income' distracted reformers.[4] Other radicals, Cole argued, 'have fixed their minds too exclusively on the distribution of wealth' and failed, as a result, to consider more fundamental problems.[5] Tawney too argued that 'the fundamental grievance' of modern societies 'is not a mere deficiency of material resources'. 'Hunger and cold cause misery,' he argued, 'but men do not revolt against winter.'[6] The pluralists, moreover, openly encouraged the progressives to take heed of this view. In 1917, Laski wrote to Lippmann to warn him that the Asquith and Lloyd George governments so admired by many radicals in the United States had served only to 'debauch the workers in a vat of social welfare'. 'I hope', Laski continued, that American reformers 'can be persuaded to be less stupid.'[7] The nationalist progressives appear to have required no such lead. 'What the wage-earner needs', Herbert Croly argued, 'is not the equalization of an existing system of privilege, but the construction of a new system which will repair the inadequacies and redress the grievances of the old.'[8] The demand 'for a better distribution of wealth', Walter Lippmann concurred, may be of *some* consequence but 'without a change in the very nature of labor, society will not have achieved the happiness it expects.'[9] None of these arguments was a plea for conservatism. Rather, both movements insisted that a challenge to the whole structure of the 'industrial system' was far more desirable than a mere 'tinkering' with the distribution of income.[10]

Despite these arguments, however, the theme of material allocation did not disappear altogether from the socialist pluralists' and nationalist progressives'

---

[3] A. Wright, *G. D. H. Cole and Socialist Democracy* (Oxford: Oxford University Press, 1979), 74. See too Lustig, *Corporate Liberalism*, 210.

[4] See G. D. H. Cole and W. Mellor, *The Meaning of Industrial Freedom* (London: George Allen and Unwin, 1918), 1–5.

[5] G. D. H. Cole, 'Guild Socialism', *American Labor Year Book 1919–1920* (New York: Rand School of Social Science, 1920), 391.

[6] See R. H. Tawney, 'The Conditions of Economic Liberty' (1918), reprinted in R. Hinden (ed.), *The Radical Tradition: Twelve Essays on Politics, Education, and Literature* (London: George Allen and Unwin, 1964), 102.

[7] H. Laski to W. Lippmann, letter dated 6 October 1917 in Yale University Library, The W. Lippmann Papers, 326/1/17/688.

[8] H. Croly, *Progressive Democracy* (New York: Macmillan, 1914), 119. See also 383.

[9] W. Lippmann, *A Preface to Politics* (New York: M. Kennerley, 1913), 67.

[10] G. D. H. Cole, 'The First Charge upon Industry', *New Statesman*, 15 July 1922, 409. See also L. Olds, 'The Temper of British Labour', *Nation (NY)*, 19 April 1919, 603.

work. For although they frequently criticized the priority other movements accorded the issue, they were still willing to insist that all citizens should have the right to expect decent 'payment in employment and unemployment, in sickness and in health'.[11] Especially in their journalistic works, both movements frequently and vigorously condemned the inequalities of capitalistic resource distribution, and argued that some, as yet indistinct, form of egalitarian ordering would characterize the distribution of resources in their ideal societies.[12] At the very least, Laski insisted, all individuals must be guaranteed 'a reasonable standard of life'.[13] The nationalist progressives agreed. Any desirable programme of reform, Herbert Croly argued, must include realistic suggestions for protecting citizens 'against the accidents of work and life'.[14] All of the people should be assured that the 'vital necessities' of life would be easily and continually available to them.[15]

These thinkers, therefore, appear to have been caught in a contradiction. On the one hand, they were committed to downplaying the importance of the distribution of material resources and to redirecting reformers' attention elsewhere. On the other hand, they were often equally insistent that a wide-scale redistribution of income and wealth was a vital component part of their own reform agenda. Some commentators have argued that this contradiction was the result of short-term political expediency outweighing the demands of ideological integrity. Without offering an immediate solution to the problems of poverty, unemployment, and ill-health, after all, neither socialist pluralism nor nationalist progressivism could have expected to last long as political movements. The depressions of the late nineteenth century and then again of the early 1920s combined with the contemporary explosion of social scientific studies into the distribution of wealth to make it impossible for any serious movement to ignore the question of poverty. Alternatively, other scholars have contended that the groups were unaware of their own inconsistencies. On this view, their pronouncements against an interest in material redistribution were simply, if conveniently, forgotten when they turned directly to consider individual initiatives for poverty relief. The movements sought to 'reform, rescue and transcend' existing economic and social structures 'all at the same time'.[16] Employing either interpretation has enabled commentators to argue that the socialist pluralists' and nationalist progressives' contributions to debates on poverty contained little serious content.[17] It is unsurprising, they contend,

---

[11] I. Brown, 'Trade Unionism without Tears', *New Age*, 11 November 1915, 44.

[12] See R. H. Tawney, *The Acquisitive Society* (London: G. Bell, 1921), 39–40; H. Laski, *A Grammar of Politics* (London: George Allen and Unwin, 1925, 3rd edn 1930), 161; G. D. H. Cole, *Guild Socialism Restated* (London: Leonard Parsons, 1920), 72–3.

[13] H. Laski, 'Socialism and Freedom', *Fabian Tract* 216 (London: Fabian Society, 1925), 8.

[14] Croly, *Progressive Democracy*, 119.

[15] Editors, 'The Meaning of Reconstruction', *New Republic*, 14 December 1918, 183.

[16] See Wright, *Cole*, 207.

[17] Wright, *Cole*, 176. See too Stettner, *Shaping Modern Liberalism*, 72.

that neither contemporaries nor posterity reacted favourably to the socialist pluralist or nationalist progressive considerations of the problems of poverty. Their efforts appeared almost inevitably destined for failure.

These arguments may be factors in an explanation but they present far from the full picture. An alternative interpretation begins with an understanding of the two movements' ideological development as structured primarily by their core conceptual commitments to particular views of liberty and community. Seen in this way, the movements turned to consider the question of poverty and its alleviation but they did so for instrumental rather than intrinsic reasons. Neither group was prepared to accept that the sorts of concerns with material distribution that other reform movements had, such as a Fabian dedication of 'equality of resources', were actually of paramount concern, but they were willing to concede that poverty and its related problems made the realization of their own fundamental ideals more difficult. Harold Laski thus argued that citizens must be 'safeguarded against the pressure of material want' because otherwise 'freedom is impossible'.[18] Walter Weyl made exactly the same connection: 'we shall not advance far in working out our American ideals', he contended, without 'striking hard' against 'inequality of possession, inequality of income, inequality of industrial opportunity.'[19] It was, therefore, a dynamic interaction of ideological commitments and economic, social, and political realities which shaped the groups' often confusing responses to these issues. The tension that they felt between downplaying material concerns and responding to the realities of poverty could be seen, therefore, as a direct consequence of their desire to find compelling ways to ensure the realization of their own fundamental ideals in often difficult circumstances. Here, as in adult education, the movements' practical political efforts reveal *flexibility* rather than inconsistency, pragmatism rather than loss of principle.

This chapter pursues this interpretation in two sections, analysing the ideological and the practical elements of the movements' response. First, it examines the complex ways in which the essential ideological commitments of both the socialist pluralists and the nationalist progressives structured their attitudes to the abstract principles of resource distribution. Second, it analyses both movements' efforts to construct practical mechanisms to ensure the realization of their ideals. Through both levels of analysis it will be seen that neither movement abandoned their ideals when they turned to the issue of poverty, nor did they labour entirely in vain.

---

[18] Laski, 'Socialism and Freedom', 8.
[19] W. Weyl. 'Equality', *New Republic*, 23 January 1915, 14.

The Principles of Distribution

Whatever the theorists' rhetorical protestations to the contrary, the fundamental commitments of both socialist pluralism and nationalist progressivism demanded that they consider the distribution of material resources. The leading members of both movements were aware that they had to identify a set of precise principles to structure the allocation of material resources. As they set out to do so, they inherited two general commitments from their immediate reformist predecessors, especially the British Fabians. The first of those commitments was to the notion of a 'national minimum' standard of life. The second was an insistence that all payment, whether from the state, employers, or workers' guilds, should be conditional on the performance of a 'function'. Neither the socialist pluralists nor the nationalist progressives rejected these ideals, but they did insist on interpreting them in their own distinctive way.

The national minimum

In spelling out their distributive principles, the socialist pluralists and the nationalist progressives both began by insisting on the need to offer every citizen access to a guaranteed 'national minimum' level of economic resources. The 'first item' in any genuinely progressive reform programme, Walter Lippmann argued, 'is to drag the whole population well above the misery line. To create a minimum standard of life below which no human being can fall is the most elementary duty of the democratic state.'[20] Every citizen, Laski similarly demanded, must be provided with the resources necessary to meet his 'primary needs'.[21] This idea of a 'national minimum standard' to ensure that each citizen was guaranteed the 'security, health . . . and remuneration which are necessary to the enjoyment of a wholesome human life' was shared by practically all reform movements in the twentieth century.[22] The reasons for which it was advocated, however, differed dramatically from movement to movement.

At the most general level, the socialist pluralists explained their commitment to the idea as a necessary consequence of their dedication to liberty as personal experimentation. A reliable stream of income, the socialist pluralists all argued, was a prerequisite to the sense of security and stability necessary for individuals to be able to plan their lives in a manner conducive to the large-scale life choices associated with creative experimentation. Individuals,

---

[20] W. Lippmann, *Drift and Mastery: An Attempt to Diagnose the Current Unrest* (New York: M. Kennerley, 1914), 254.   [21] Laski, *Grammar*, 160.
[22] Croly, *Progressive Democracy*, 119.

they insisted, must have access to an adequate range of resources at all times if they are to be able to reflect realistically on their life-choices, reject them if necessary, and effectively choose to pursue various other ways of life. Similarly, the nationalist progressives couched their support for the idea of a national minimum in their own characteristic terms. The commitment to the 'national minimum' was shared with the pluralists but it was interpreted differently. Without the security of a steady income, they contended, individuals become distanced from one another as they are forced to engage in the petty personal squabbling of the competitive struggle for existence, and as such 'low wages prevent the elevation of the national standard of life'.[23] In order to have citizens dedicated to national improvement, Walter Lippmann argued, 'you need a country in which everyone has some stake and some taste of its promise'.[24] The citizen who suffers in neglect and poverty, after all, 'has no reverence for a government under which he starves, or for a social system into which he does not fit'.[25]

While they may have disagreed in their fundamental rationale, both movements also argued that the guarantee of a national minimum was further demanded by their shared commitment to democratization and to associational self-government. Without continual access to a reasonable level of income, both groups insisted, no citizen could be expected to be able to participate properly in democratic governance. Citizens would have to be emancipated from 'apprehension and deprivation' before they could be expected to throw themselves into this business of government.[26] Both movements were also concerned that the current distribution of resources seriously subverted already existing democratic mechanisms. If one section of society holds an inordinately large share of economic assets then they would be effectively able to capture the democratic process for the benefit of their own sectional interests. Any democratic state or individual association characterized by a sharp inequality of income and wealth thus put personal freedom at risk and potentially perverted the course of communal reconstruction.[27] So long as economic resources 'remain in the hands of the few democracy is a sham', Bertrand Russell summarized for the socialist pluralists.[28] 'Poverty, chastity, and obedience', as Walter Lippmann more poetically insisted, 'are not the ideals of a self-governing people.' [29]

The question of distribution could not rest here, however. For despite the straightforwardly egalitarian language of the national minimum, neither

[23] Editors, 'The State's Right to Experiment', *New Republic*, 3 February 1917, 7.

[24] Lippmann, *Drift*, 255.

[25] Editors, 'The Dangerous Classes', *New Republic*, 8 August 1915, 7–8. See also Editors, 'The Labor Board and the Living Wage', *New Republic*, 15 November 1922, 191.

[26] Croly, *Progressive Democracy*, 380.

[27] All these themes are developed in Laski, *Grammar*, 161.

[28] B. Russell, 'Why I am a Guildsman', *Guildsman*, September 1919, 3. Cole, *Guild Socialism Restated*, 14.   [29] Lippmann, *Drift*, 251.

movement believed that each and every individual in society had a claim to precisely the same set of resources. It was the level of 'need satisfaction' that was intended to be equalized, not the quantity of income or wealth. In order to meet the minimum, some individuals would require more resources as a result of being more 'needy' than others. Resource allocation, therefore, should not be 'uniform . . . for all sections, classes, and industrial groups within a country'.[30] Rather, as Laski put it, the minimum is not 'the same for all' as 'while there is an irreducible minimum of human want which each citizen must be able to satisfy, those wants are not identical in all'.[31]

The nationalist progressives began the process of defining the 'national minimum' more precisely by arguing that the 'vital necessities' of life should not be interpreted in any narrow, pseudo-scientific way. As Walter Weyl insisted, the 'economic level' that nationalist progressives sought to guarantee had to be well above the 'poverty line' used by social scientific investigators and calculated on the basis of an assessment of individual biological needs of 'mere physical efficiency'. Neither, though, was the entitlement of each individual to be revealed by reference to the subjective aspirations of particular individuals. Citizens would not be entitled to a larger minimum guarantee solely by virtue of the choices they had made, the aspirations they possessed, or the allegiances they expressed. Such a calculation, after all, could reward the greedy at the expense of the cautious and subsidize the profligate rather than reward the thrifty. In place of these options, the nationalist progressives decided that the necessary level of resources for each individual in society was to be defined by reference to his place within the nation and the social system itself.[32] The settlement of the 'national minimum' in each individual case was, therefore, to be a decidedly communal calculation based upon a 'thoroughly contemporary knowledge of a wholesome standard of living'.[33] In particular, each citizen had to be kept above a level which would allow him to function effectively and adequately to perform his social duties. This level itself was thought to depend 'upon a large group' of changing social factors, including the sort of work for which the individual was best suited.[34] Advocates of this position believed, of course, that their approach would not lead to any callous prioritizing of collective over individual interest; the individual recipient would benefit from such a distribution as much as society at large. On the nationalist progressives' communitarian reading of human development, after all, an individual's needs themselves were actually shaped by his role within the

---

[30] W. Weyl, *The New Democracy: An Essay on Certain Political and Economic Tendencies in the United States* (New York: Macmillan, 1912), 209.

[31] Laski, *Grammar*, 197. 'Want' here is used in the sense that 'in *want* of' is synonymous with 'in *need* of' rather than as a synonym for desire or preference.

[32] Editors, 'Meaning of Reconstruction', 183.

[33] O. Tead and R. Valentine, 'Work and Pay', *Quarterly Journal of Economics*, 31 (1917), 253.

[34] Weyl, *New Democracy*, 209.

industrial and social system. An 'improved fit' of individual to social role would thus increase the 'freedom of action and comfort' of the individual concerned.[35] Hence it was right from the perspective of both individual and social whole that the individual's social function should determine his precise entitlements.

As with many of the nationalist progressives' ideals, this view fell closely in line with the work of British predecessors, especially of Fabians and New Liberals. Sidney and Beatrice Webb had long argued that the 'national minimum' should be determined with reference to 'the interests of the well-being of the whole'.[36] The New Liberals staked out similar territory; Leonard Hobhouse urged that it was necessary to guarantee 'to each man and to each class that . . . which serves to maintain them in the adequate exercise of the function which it is theirs to fulfil in social life'.[37] The socialist pluralists, however, found this strategy extremely difficult to endorse. The socialist pluralists' individualistic philosophical assumptions implied a stark rejection of any attempt to define a person's primary needs by reference to the position occupied within a social or industrial structure.[38] Such a definition would impact negatively upon the possibility of occupational mobility, a possibility which the socialist pluralists conceived as an essential element of personal experimentation.[39] It would also ignore the fact that the pluralists desired experimentation was not entirely a work-bound phenomenon but was intended to extend into the worker's leisure time too. A pluralist definition of the economic resources required for each individual would have to be shaped not only by the conditions necessary for effective work but also by the conditions which affected their use of their spare time.[40] If people were separable from their associational allegiances, then clearly their fundamental needs had to be ascertainable independently of their associational membership.

The socialist pluralists had, therefore, to establish an alternative means of calculating each individual's precise claim on material resources. The starting point, as ever, was the need for creative experimentation; the socialist pluralists were committed to the view that each individual should be guaranteed access to those resources necessary to enable him to enjoy a life of creative experimentation.[41] As Laski put it, the task that faced them was how to identify the range of resources required to 'enable a man to be a man' rather than simply to allow an individual to perform a particular function.[42] This was, of

---

[35] S. Webb, 'The Necessary Basis of Society', *Fabian Tract* 165 (London: Fabian Society, 1906), 4.

[36] Webb, 'Necessary Basis', 8.

[37] L. T. Hobhouse, 'The Right to a Living Wage', in W. Temple (ed.), *The Industrial Unrest and the Living Wage* (London: Collegium, 1913), 69.   [38] See Chapter 3.

[39] See Chapter 5.   [40] See Laski, *Grammar*, 95.

[41] For a more detailed assessment of the theoretical problems involved here, see M. Stears, 'Needs, Welfare and the Limits of Associationalism', *Economy and Society*, 28 (1999), 570–89.

[42] Laski, *Grammar*, 160, and Croly, *Progressive Democracy*, 119. See too W. Weyl, *The End of the War* (New York: Macmillan, 1918), 306–7.

course, a particularly complicated definitional dilemma and it was one that
the socialist pluralists never entirely resolved. Their efforts largely focused on
identifying an agency that could effectively be charged with the task. They
could not allow individual associations to define needs any more than they
could allow the central state or any other organ of the general community to
do so, but the issue had to be resolved somehow. Cole, in particular, continually re-examined the question, outlining and then rejecting a wide series of
positions throughout the war years and into the 1920s. Eventually, in his
most detailed discussion of the issue for the *Socialist Review* in 1924, he fell
back on the same cumbersome compromise that had also characterized his
efforts to resolve the tensions between producers and consumers. He argued
that an independent panel of experts should be constructed to assess the level
of provision necessary for a wide range of social groups, both in and out of
work. Such a panel would be required to hear evidence from all society's
different associational groupings and to consider the opinion of medical and
sociological experts, but in the end it could be called upon to adjudicate
between competing demands and craft a final decision itself.[43] Cole expected
that such an endeavour would combine an element of popular involvement
while also guaranteeing that the final assessment of individuals' needs would
be neither vocationally nor purely subjectively bound. Although it was not a
particularly satisfactory view, inviting at least as many institutional questions
as it resolved theoretical difficulties, it served the socialist pluralists' general
purposes well enough.

The condition: functional payment

However it was to be determined, neither movement believed the actual
receipt of the national minimum should be unconditional. Rather, both
socialist pluralists and nationalist progressives made it perfectly clear that this
right was 'relative to a duty'.[44] There was a condition to be fulfilled before
any individual could expect to receive resources, whether directly from the
state or indirectly through his employers. At its most straightforward, Tawney
presented the condition as the insistence that 'those who render service faith-
fully should be honourably paid, and . . . those who render no service should
not be paid at all'.[45] Similar formulations were to be found throughout the
other pluralists' work. 'There must be a relation between function or service
and the possession of property', was Laski's version of the same claim.[46] The
demand that payment must 'bear some definite relation to service', was Cole's
interpretation.[47] The nationalist progressives were just as insistent. American

---

[43] See G. D. H. Cole, 'The Minimum Wage', *Socialist Review*, 22 (1924), 58–63.
[44] Laski, *Grammar*, 184.   [45] Tawney, *Acquisitive*, 8.
[46] H. Laski, 'Can Political Democracy Survive?', *Fabian News*, October 1923, 43.
[47] G. D. H. Cole, 'The Basis of Wages', *New Statesman*, 17 April 1920, 35.

citizens, the *New Republic* argued, 'should have access' to the necessaries of life only 'by title of the work' that they do.[48] There is no room for 'useless payments', Walter Lippmann pithily asserted, in the nationalist conception of just distribution.[49]

The primary rhetorical target of the functional payment condition for both pluralists and nationalist progressives was the 'idle rich' who lived off the 'unearned wealth' of rents or on inheritance.[50] The condition was not, however, entirely confined to an attack on the wealthy. The 'idle poor' also concerned both the pluralists and the nationalist progressives and both movements insisted continuously on the need to put those who would not labour to work, and there was no sympathy for those who refused. Cole, indeed, explicitly insisted that 'those who are not "genuinely seeking work"' should be 'eliminated' from consideration for poor relief.[51] In so far as was possible, employment should be found for all. Even employment in 'make-work' schemes funded by general taxation was preferable to the provision of 'dole' or benefit.[52] Even the otherwise well-ingrained balanced budget and low taxation orthodoxies were cast aside in the search for productive work. 'If private enterprise can not supply the work', the *New Republic*'s editors argued, 'then the state must.'[53] Cole similarly contended that 'a great national loan' could legitimately be raised for the establishment of public works. All of this was to be pursued even if it meant that 'the taxing power' of the government had to 'be employed to the limit'.[54]

As with the idea of national minimum, there was little new about this functional payment formula itself; it was a mainstay of most radical theories of resource distribution in the early twentieth century.[55] Sidney and Beatrice Webb had enunciated a similar, if all the more harsh, proposition throughout the late nineteenth century and New Liberals like Leonard Hobhouse provided a more detailed defence of the argument throughout the early twentieth century. Despite the surface simplicity, however, once again the socialist pluralists' and the nationalist progressives' understanding and use of the functional principle were far from identical either with each other or with their immediate predecessors' accounts.

For the nationalist progressives, the dedication to functional payment was read off the essential dedication to communal participation and service in

---

[48] Editors, 'Meaning of Reconstruction', 183.   [49] Lippmann, *Drift*, 101.

[50] Ibid.; Laski, *Grammar*, 531; Weyl, *New Democracy*, 266.

[51] G. D. H. Cole, 'Unemployment', *New Statesman*, 14 March 1925, 650.

[52] G. D. H. Cole, 'The Government and the Unemployed', *New Statesman*, 11 November 1922, 166.

[53] Editors, 'Meaning of Reconstruction', 183.

[54] G. D. H. Cole, 'The One Thing Needed', *New Statesman*, 24 November 1923, 201–3, and Editors, 'The Meaning of Reconstruction', 183.

[55] Ross Terrill was simply mistaken when he stated that Tawney was the first British theorist to connect 'function to property'. See R. Terrill, *R. H. Tawney and his Times: Socialism as Fellowship* (Cambridge, MA: Harvard University Press, 1973), 163. For earlier examples, see S. and B. Webb, *English Poor Law Policy* (London: F. Cass, 1st edn 1910, reprinted 1963), 304–7.

both its subjective and its objective senses. To begin with, functional payment was celebrated as a means of instilling the psychological conviction of communal service. By guaranteeing that each citizen was positively rewarded for his work for the common good, the efforts of workers to provide for themselves and to enhance national well-being would dovetail clearly and explicitly for the first time.[56] Seen another way, the functional payment condition would also ruthlessly expose those who failed in their communal duties. 'Every American who has the opportunity of doing faithful and fearless work, and who proves faithless to it', Croly intoned, would be revealed for what they were. They would receive no payment for their lack of commitment to the national project and would be denounced for their desire to 'split the community' instead of unifying it.[57] The avoidance of useful work, moreover, could be taken as a sign of moral weakness, revealing both a lack of communal commitment and an unwillingness to develop the practical skills required for solid communal endeavours.[58] Refusing socially useful employment, Croly argued, 'cheapened the personality' and in so doing 'cheapened the one constituent of national life over which he can exercise most effectual control'. From this there was no comeback, for 'thereafter, no matter how superficially patriotic and well-intentioned he may be, his words and actions are tainted and are in some measure corrupting in social effect'.[59]

Such an argument reminded Croly's readers that functional payment was meant also to have an objective impact on national well-being. It was also intended to be self-reinforcing. If individuals were able to claim a 'national minimum' then the economy needed to be healthy enough to be able to provide the necessary direct financial benefits. The nationalist progressives built this dedication to efficiency and sustainability right into the heart of their defence of functional payment. In *Drift and Mastery*, Lippmann asked 'where is the money' for the meeting of needs to 'come from?' The answer was that it was to be 'made up of all the leaks, the useless payments, the idle demands . . . the extortion and parasitism of industrial life'.[60] Such an argument held for both the top and the bottom of the income and wealth spectrum. At the top, functional payment would ensure that wealthy shareholders and landowners would no longer be entitled to enjoy a large part of the nation's wealth without offering an explicit or a perceptible service.[61] By taxing away 'unearned income' a nationalist progressive state could offer recompense to everybody else. Preventing the diversion of a large part of national product to a small, relatively useless section of society would both improve the distribution of wealth and also aid in the creation of an increased

---

[56] See H. Croly, *The Promise of American Life* (New York: Macmillan, 1909), 207.
[57] Editors, 'The State's Right to Experiment', *New Republic*, 3 February 1917, 7.
[58] Editors, 'The Invisible Republic', *New Republic*, 5 October 1921, 148.
[59] Croly, *Promise*, 431.   [60] Lippmann, *Drift*, 102.
[61] See Weyl, *End of the War*, 306–7.

national wealth.[62] The same was true at the bottom end. For if those who refused or who were unwilling to labour were simply rewarded with unconditional benefits there would once again be a net loss to the nation's wealth. 'To cut off the income of the useless will not impair efficiency', Lippmann thus concluded, 'it will, in fact, compel them to acquire a useful function.'[63]

Although the economic analysis behind these declarations was relatively simplistic, the nationalist progressives all believed that techniques of scientific management could be employed both to fine-tune them and to put them into practice with little delay. If used intelligently by socially conscious businessmen or bureaucrats, it is 'within the power of scientific management to assign tasks appropriate to any degree of will power or acquired skill, however infinitesimal', the *New Republic* thus argued. The well-informed bureaucrat could thus calculate the socially necessary return to capital and tax away the rest. If the state employed proper Taylorite expertise, it could also ensure the provision of useful labour for even the most idle and talentless of citizens and finally 'disembarrass society of the incubus of the work-shy'.[64] The truly 'scientific manager' could take 'the tramp just brought from the roadside or the loafer committed to the slums', set him a task and teach him 'how to perform it'.[65] Anyone who refused work in such an environment on the grounds that he was unsuited to it or unable to conduct it could be unmasked as a fraud and threatened with punitive confinement or merely cut off from any income as a result. The 'slacker and floater' who were parasitical on the work of others in the community would come to be regarded 'with contempt and detestation'.[66] The most recalcitrant 'won't works', those who were immune even to the demands of the functional payment condition, should be sent to 'labor colonies where the enforced habits of regular living, hard work and good food might induce a desire to return to society where he that would eat must work'.[67]

Despite their commitment to functional payment, the socialist pluralists were outraged by such suggestions. They had long been sceptical of the role of scientific management, had vigorously dismissed the notion that any particular individual should be expected to serve any particular social function, and were horrified at the idea that the state could confine individuals who had committed no crime into virtual prisons. They shared the nationalist progressives' conviction that there was both a psychological and a more concretely objective reason to value the functional payment condition but they held that the advantages of each were sharply distinct. The socialist

---

[62] See Weyl, *New Democracy*, 249, and Editors, 'Production and the Cost of Living', *New Republic*, 17 September 1919, 192–3.   [63] Lippmann, *Drift*, 115.
[64] Editors, 'Salvaging the Unemployable', *New Republic*, 2 October 15, 221.
[65] Editors, 'Salvaging the Unemployable', 222.
[66] Editors, 'To Restore the Morale of Labor', *New Republic*, 16 April 1918, 194.
[67] O. Tead, 'The Cure and Prevention of Unemployment' (n.d), The Ordway Tead Papers, 6, 24–5.

pluralists believed that welfare programmes which provided monetary benefit without expecting work in return would actually augur ill for the creative
experimentation that lay at the hear of their ideological programme. Passive
receipt of benefits would, they worried, invoke a level of psychological laziness. As Cole put it, 'doles' encourage not a creative but a 'servile character'.[68]
'Social legislation', Laski concurred, 'has the incurable habit of tending
towards paternalism; and paternalism is the subtlest form of poison to the
democratic state.'[69] Payment without industrial service could remove 'external', resource-based obstacles to experimentation only at the risk of encouraging 'internal', psychological ones. The functional payment condition was
one way to ensure that receipt of economic benefits was conducive to an
'active' instead of a 'passive' character.[70] Here all the pluralists illustrated their
continued interest in the value of workplace interactions in shaping individuals' non-working lives. 'Employment', Cole insisted 'maintains the workers'
spirit.'[71] It 'preserves men from that human ill that is the product of dependent idleness'.[72] All the pluralists thought that working for their money gave
individuals a sense of independence and significance rather than a sense of
dependence and insignificance.[73]

In addition to this role in enabling creative experimentation, the socialist
pluralists also believed that functional payment was an essential means of

[68] G. D. H. Cole, *Labour in the Commonwealth: A Book for a Younger Generation* (London: Headley Bros, 1918), 136.
[69] H. Laski, *The Foundations of Sovereignty and Other Essays* (New Haven: Yale University Press, 1921), 43.
[70] Tawney, *Acquisitive*, 66.
[71] G. D. H. Cole, 'The Cost of Idleness', *New Statesman*, 13 January 1923, 422.
[72] G. D. H. Cole, 'The Question of the Hour', *New Statesman*, 13 October 1923, 5–6.
[73] The pluralists were not alone in proffering this set of contentions in the early 1920s. There was a certain similarity in their claim and in the worries about individual moral 'character' that featured in many idealist investigations into poverty and poor relief. In addition, the growing literature of industrial psychology was prone to reach similar conclusions. The role that workplace existence played in shaping a worker's whole mind-set became an increasingly accepted academic trope. Many trade unionists were also prepared to accept that prolonged periods of unemployment limited the creativity of individuals and the militancy of the movement. A Miners' Federation delegate at the TUC conference in Southport, 1922, described unemployment as a 'hellish manufactory' which turned out 'damaged humans'. On this account, many an unemployed workman became 'a slave, a slimy, creeping slave', unable to resist industrial autocracy and similarly unable to lead a creative personal life. The actual psychological evidence available to latterday commentators is, of course, rather less clear. Some workers certainly did lose a sense of purpose from their lives as they fell into unemployment. They lost contact with friends and former workmates, fell out of union member-ship, and felt as if their position in local society had been considerably devalued. Others, however, felt a certain release from the monotony of industrial production. Modern social historical research has revealed that unemployed workmen remained in close connection with one another and devel-oped a rewarding social and even political life during periods away from work. It is perhaps symp-tomatic of Cole, Tawney, and Laski's overemphasis on the centrality of the industrial realm that they did not see that removing at least some individuals from the workplace allowed them to be more creative, to experiment more broadly, than insisting that they remain within it. See R. McKibbin, *The Ideologies of Class: Social Relations in Britain 1880–1950* (Oxford: Oxford University Press, 1989), 228–58; TUC, *Report of the 1922 Annual Conference* (London: 1922), 343; K. Nicholas, *The Social Effects of Unemployment in Teeside, 1919–1939* (Manchester: Manchester University Press, 1986).

ensuring that industry produced the level of goods and services required to guarantee that the entire British population could have access to the necessaries of life. Tawney expressed the connection between this concern and functional payment at its most straightforward. Individuals, he remarked, may not 'work hard' to 'make necessaries' if they 'see that another obtains ... without working at all', with the result that production levels would fall below their already perilously low level. 'The surest way to encourage production', Tawney then concluded, 'is to make clear that those who do not produce will not consume.'[74] The simplicity of this idea was clearly attractive but it created two immediate difficulties. First, the socialist pluralists could not be seen to endorse the prescription of the nationalist progressives' model. They had long rejected the methods of scientific management and had even more vociferously dismissed the notion that any particular individual should be thought of as having any one particular function to perform. Second, their own definition of 'function' itself, as described in Chapter 5, made the functional payment condition very difficult to employ. On their view, the performance of a 'function' simply involved either some form of contribution to the production of those resources necessary to enable widespread personal experimentation or a productive activity carried out in a manner conducive to the development of widespread sentimental attachments. In 1924, Cole admitted that however attractive such a definition, the functional payment condition offered 'no way' of practically 'measuring service ... known to the wit of man'.[75] A year later, Laski likewise accepted that his view of function rendered it almost 'impossible in any genuine way to measure service'.[76]

The socialist pluralists argued instead, therefore, that, rather than prescribing precisely what individuals ought to be expected to do and rewarding them accordingly, the functional payment condition would play an essential role in *encouraging* workers to involve themselves in the productive process and to do so in a broadly communal manner. The argument behind this claim was somewhat convoluted. It began with an assertion that one of the reasons that workers were unwilling effectively to labour in a capitalist society was that they believed that the distribution of resources was unfair. In the existing economic order, the pluralists argued, workers saw a distribution which, on their own subjective assessment, over-rewarded some and underpaid many. As Cole argued, 'we must persuade the workers that it is worth their while, and their bounden duty to do their best' but 'we cannot do this while we still ask them to work under a system which, from any moral standpoint, is utterly indefensible'.[77] It is 'idle to expect that men will give their best to

---

[74] Tawney, 'Economic Liberty', 115.
[75] G. D. H. Cole, 'Wages: The Relativity Myth', *New Statesman*, 26 March 1924, 57–8.
[76] Laski, *Grammar*, 159.
[77] G. D. H. Cole, *Chaos and Order in Industry* (London: Methuen, 1920), 12.

any system which they do not trust'.[78] As such, an important solution to Britain's poor level of production was to ensure that the remuneration for labour was 'consistent with the sense of justice of those employed under it'.[79] In order to rekindle production, Laski insisted, it was necessary to 'found a theory of wages in the common consent of men'.[80] The socialist pluralists then concluded by arguing that the British workers' analysis of what counted as fair was best codified in the functional payment condition. The idea that monetary benefits should follow from productive contribution stood far closer to prevailing public attitudes to the distribution of economic resources than the existent largely unregulated capitalist one. Under a system regulated by the functional payment condition any inequalities of payment which continued to exist would be 'referable to causes [which are] analysable and intelligible' and, as such, they would not encourage the 'baulked disposition' which interrupted productive energy.[81] Introducing functional payment was, therefore, an important step towards of developing 'the psychological atmosphere in which we can get the best' productive effort from the workers.[82] As Cole expressed the theory in his only book-length treatment of the issue, *The Payment of Wages*: 'the essential characteristics of a satisfactory system of remuneration is . . . that it shall put men in a mood to give of their best.'[83]

Equality

These arguments as to the usefulness of functional payment raised one further question. For it often appeared that the movements may have been willing to employ it not only as a condition for the receipt of the national minimum but also as a justification for payments *over and above* that minimum level. Each movement had to ask, therefore, whether individuals should be entitled to earn more than each other in an ideal society and, if so, to identify some set of criteria by which they should be rewarded.

In seeking to resolve these arguments, some scholars have argued that the functional payment condition itself was an implicit argument for *equality*. 'Since few people perform functions hundreds of times more socially valuable than other people', Ross Terrill has thus argued, 'a system of rewards based on social function is likely to be egalitarian.'[84] There is, however, a clear and powerful objection to this as an explanation of the functional payment condition. If equality was the primary goal of those who upheld functional

---

[78] Tawney, *Acquisitive*, 188.
[79] G. D. H. Cole, *The Payment of Wages: A Study in Payment by Results in the Wage-System* (London: George Allen and Unwin, 1st edn 1918, 2nd edn., 1928), p. xx.
[80] Laski, *Grammar*, 200.
[81] Laski, 'Socialism and Freedom', 11.
[82] H. Laski, 'The State in the New Social Order', *Fabian Tract* 200 (London: Fabian Society, 1922), 14.
[83] Cole, *Payment of Wages*, p. xx.   [84] Terrill, *Tawney*, 167.

payment, it is unclear why they would have to develop the principle rather than straightforwardly to adopt an argument for the more direct equalization of income. After all, at the time George Bernard Shaw's case for absolute income equality was well respected in socialist and progressive circles. It would have been relatively easy for either group to adopt it as its own, adapted if necessary to take into consideration their differing account of needs.[85] But they did not. Shaw indeed had launched a vigorous attack on the idea of functional payment as early as 1913.[86] Advocates of functional payment like the pluralists and nationalist progressives did not, therefore, simply fail to pick up on the possibility of a direct route to an equalized income but flatly rejected it. Terrill's response to this rejection is unimpressive. He argues that a 'dynamically induced equality' through the principle of functional payment was more 'attractive and more realistic than an arithmetically determined equality'.[87] On such a view, Terrill suggests, functional payment was simply a more practicable way of approaching the Shavian ideal.

The theorists' works, both academic and journalistic, give very little succour to Terrill's view. The nationalist progressives, indeed, explicitly argued that a 'large amount of *inequality*' was to be accepted both as a necessary incentive and as a deserved reward for particularly impressive contributions to national well-being.[88] 'It is not an essential part of the conception of the reconstructed state that differences in private fortune be eliminated', the *New Republic* argued at the end of the First World War, nor was it 'essential that the struggle of man for position or power should be abated'.[89] What was important, though, was that this struggle was *fair* and designed for the larger social benefit. Functional payment was thus connected to an ideal of equality of opportunity rather than equality of reward. Conceiving of material rewards 'from a functional point of view', Croly instructed, entailed understanding them in terms of 'an opportunity of achievement rather than as a right of possession'. 'Society is undoubtedly interested in affording everybody an opportunity to win prizes in the race; but it is still more interested in arranging for a fast race, a real contest and an inspiring victory', he tried to explain with his usual metaphorical panache. 'If for the present a large part of the spoils must belong to the victors, it is the more necessary to insist that the victors shall be worthy of the spoils.'[90] Those who enjoy significant material rewards as the result of market or government valuation of the usefulness of their 'natural gifts', Croly thus contended, 'must, for the most part, be

---

[85] Cole did in fact express sympathy for Shaw's position as a potential policy option within the socialist pluralist commonwealth; but he too steadfastly rejected it as a principle during the period of transition. See Cole, *Guild Socialism Restated*, 72–3.

[86] For a brief summary of the debate, see S. Collini, *Liberalism and Sociology: L. T. Hobhouse and Political Argument in England, 1870–1914* (Cambridge: Cambridge University Press, 1979), 134–5.

[87] Terrill, *Tawney*, 169.   [88] Croly, *Progressive Democracy*, 114 (emphasis added).

[89] Editors, 'Meaning of Reconstruction', *New Republic*, 183.

[90] Croly, *Progressive Democracy*, 114–15.

allowed to keep them' as long as they have been 'forced to earn' them.[91] 'Society cannot afford to treat men and women better unless the men and women themselves deserve better treatment', Croly concluded, but if they do then 'society itself ... must take measures to redeem this responsibility.'[92]

Among the socialist pluralists in Britain, the case for absolute equality found a slightly more receptive audience, but even here it was generally accepted that there should be substantial exceptions to an otherwise egalitarian distribution of material goods. Inequalities of reward, on such a view, were justified if they were proportional to increases in production or if they compensated for the disutilities involved in the performance of a particularly unpleasant, but entirely necessary, task. As Laski put it, to those who perform a special sort of service 'relatively speaking a large salary will be paid'.[93] Tawney pursued this theme thoroughly, especially in *The Acquisitive Society*, where he frequently argued for a precise pattern of differing payments for the fulfilment of differing functional activities.[94] Cole also suggested that it was sometimes necessary to grant rewards to the talented; he once insisted, for example, that it is necessary to 'make it worth a man's while to become a skilled workman' by providing some considerable financial reward for skilled labour. He also believed that it was not for the state, or anybody else, to tell independent and democratic associations how to reward their members; guilds should be 'autonomous as regards the determination of the rewards to be paid for work.'[95] Absolute clarity, however, was missing from his contribution to these debates. Occasionally, for example, it appeared that actual productive success was not Cole's overriding concern. As such, a decent system of material reward 'should secure at least an approximate correspondence of earnings to *effort*' rather than to actual *output*.[96] At other times, a more substantial egalitarian consideration appeared to trump his interest in productivity or effort: he rejected programmes of 'profit-sharing' because he considered them incompatible with a 'distribution of national income on the basis of needs' rather than labour contribution.[97] But the one thing which was clear from all this was that the socialist pluralists did not consistently support an egalitarian approach to reward. Rather, both movements considered that it was the cause of the inequalities of prevailing distributive patterns that was at fault, rather than their simple existence. It was '*irrational* inequality'—inequality not related to the provision of service or the performance of a function—rather than the inequalities themselves, or the idea of inequality per se, which the theorists' pointedly attacked.[98]

[91] Croly, *Progressive Democracy*, 114.   [92] Croly, *Progressive Democracy*, 121.
[93] Laski, *Grammar*, 525. See also 198.   [94] See Tawney, *Acquisitive*, esp. 222–3.
[95] O. Tead, 'The Meaning of National Guilds', *The Dial*, 23 August 1919, 151.
[96] G. D. H. Cole, 'Actual Wages', *New Statesman*, 21 March 1925, 684, and G. D. H. Cole, 'On Payment by Results', *New Statesman*, 3 June 1922, 233 (emphasis added).
[97] G. D. H Cole, 'Profit Sharing', *New Statesman*, 8 May 1920, 123.
[98] Tawney, *Acquisitive*, 39.

Identifying the Instrument of Progress

Both socialist pluralists and nationalist progressives were equipped with a set of distributional principles clearly related to their fundamental ideals. They could not rest there, however, for the task of attempting to implement them presented severe problems. As the distribution of resources was taken to be of essentially instrumental rather than intrinsic value, the precise manner in which resources were to be redistributed was of vital importance. If the mechanisms which directed the programmes for remuneration and compensation acted in ways contrary to the demands of the movements' other, more fundamental, commitments, then the very benefit of redistributing them could be lost. The road to the ideal progressive society is 'difficult and long', Weyl argued, and any 'radical economic readjustment' along the way had to be conducive to the general journey.[99] Any 'diffusion of wealth', as such, had to be achieved in a manner which could 'gives us all a foretaste of the civilised life' which intelligent, far-reaching reform could create.[100]

These efforts were further complicated by the particular characteristics of the two polities in which the movements were operative. In Britain, efforts to guarantee citizens some form of material security were well under way by the First World War. The New Liberal government of Herbert Asquith and David Lloyd George secured free school meals and medical checks for needy children, administered a national system of labour exchanges for those looking for work, guaranteed national health and unemployment insurance for a quarter of the working population, oversaw minimum wage boards for those in sweated industries, and directly provided old-age pensions for those unable to work any longer. Even the return of the Conservative Party to office in the aftermath of the war failed to undermine these reforms; indeed, expenditure on 'welfare' programmes expanded rather than contracted in the early 1920s as more workers were brought under the social insurance umbrella.[101] The American case could not have been more different. Despite continual pressure from some local trade unions and many progressive reformers, a host of obstacles prevented the development of any significant innovations in social policy during the period of this study.[102] A sceptical American Federation of Labor, dedicated to maintaining the independence of collective bargaining, also rejected demands for state-provided social insurance, as did an impressively coherent and well-organized business

---

[99] Weyl, 'Equality', 14.   [100] Weyl, New Democracy, 200.

[101] For a detailed introduction, see M. Freeden, The New Liberalism: An Ideology of Social Reform (Oxford: Oxford University Press, 1978).

[102] For detailed accounts of local efforts, see O. S. Halsey, 'Health Insurance', Intercollegiate Socialist 6 (1918), 23–6, and Editors, 'Health Insurance', New Republic, 25 March 1916, 200–1.

lobby. Even when State legislatures or Congress passed reforms ensuring minimum wages or protection against exploitation, obstructive State and federal courts often vehemently opposed them. Although reformers enjoyed some success in guaranteeing workers a right to compensation for industrial injury and in restricting the working hours of women and child workers, there was not one serious federal attempt directly to redress the causes or the consequences of unemployment; and not one single State successfully introduced health or unemployment insurance legislation before the onset of the Great Depression.[103] President Harding himself forcefully insisted that there was to be no 'palliation from the public treasury' for the difficulties of poverty and unemployment as 'the excess of stimulation from that source' was 'reckoned to be a cause of the trouble rather than source of cure'.[104]

As in adult education, the difficulty here, therefore, was one of a severe mismatch between ideological aspiration and political reality. The socialist pluralists, on the one hand, wished to construct alternatives to state-based provision in a society characterized by an apparently ever-expanding state. The nationalist progressives, on the other, looked toward organized public, and preferably national, provision in a society deeply sceptical of government power. The implications of this mismatch structured both of the movements' attempts to design mechanisms of resource redistribution which could be both conducive to the attainment of their ideals and realistically expected to succeed.

Responding to reform

All those in the United States committed to social policy reform were initially extremely impressed by the reforms of the New Liberal government. To the American Association for Labor Legislation and other related pressure groups, it appeared that the British were dramatically leading the way to a better society. In their most optimistic moods, these reformers even believed that the British model would, in time, be exported to the United States without significant alteration. When opponents of any large-scale social reform argued that the very idea itself was inimical to the American way of life, the nationalist progressives retorted that the same had previously been said of Britain. The *New Republic* insisted that state-provided social welfare is 'un-American' only

---

[103] There is a plethora of excellent scholarly literature available on this area. See, for especially fine introductions, M. Katz, *In the Shadow of the Poorhouse: A Social History of Welfare in America* (New York: Basic Books, 1986); D. Levine, *Poverty and Society: The Growth of the American Welfare State in Comparative Perspective* (New Brunswick: Rutgers University Press, 1988); D. Rodgers, *Atlantic Crossings: Social Politics in a Progressive Age* (Cambridge, MA: Belknap Press, 1998); T. Skocpol, *Protecting Soldiers and Mothers: The Political Origins of Social Policy in the United States* (Cambridge, MA: Belknap Press, 1992).

[104] W. Harding, in H. Hoover (ed.), *Report of the President's Committee on Unemployment* (Washington DC: Govt Off., 1921), 27.

'in the sense that it is new to America, as it was new to Great Britain four years ago'.[105] Britain's success also gave succour to the argument that some form of significant redistribution of wealth and opportunity was inevitable in the long run, a 'natural outcome of modern industrialism'. Capitalism, it was argued, produced 'everywhere the same kind of industrial population, without land to maintain or roof to shelter them, with slender reserves for a rainy day, with the mutual-aid groupings of the earlier order shattered, and with health often weakened by urban life and factory strain'.[106] And as the United States was destined to be the capitalist society par excellence, so, the logic continued, there was every 'reason to believe that in a generation we may be attaining results more significant than those that have been attained by any other nation'.[107]

In more moderate moments, however, and especially after the disappointments of the First World War and its immediate aftermath, the nationalist progressives admitted that Britain did not offer a model that they could realistically expect to emulate in its entirety. For all the talk of convergence and of the inevitable evolution of industrial societies, the nationalist progressives were aware that obstacles of a very different kind stood in the way of reform of social policy in the United States from those in Britain. Most importantly, the nationalist progressives recognized that the relative weakness of the central bureaucracy, even after 1918, entailed that the role of national governing institutions would have to be played down in the American context. Fresh from working in Washington during the war, Felix Frankfurter in particular warned nationalists not to try to emulate the British interest in developing a 'centralized administration' to deal with social policy concerns. 'I do not speak from any regard for traditional States' rights nor as the exponent of any theory of political science', the progressive jurist insisted, 'but as one with some knowledge of the Federal machinery and its power further to absorb and discharge effectively nationwide duties.' This is not to say that federal and State governments refused to accept *any* role in helping to alleviate poverty and distress. It was, rather, that bureaucrats working within those institutions understood that role solely in terms of the coordination of the activities of other voluntary and charitable agencies rather than in terms of the direct provision of support or protection.

Just as the United States did not have the bureaucratic apparatus to build a British-style welfare state, nor did it seem to possess the political will to set about constructing one.[108] Not only were there institutional barriers in the

---

[105] Editors, 'Health Insurance', 200.   [106] Ibid.
[107] Editors, 'Health Insurance', 201.
[108] See L. Scheweber, 'Progressive Reformers, Unemployment and the Transformation of Social Inquiry in Britain and the United States, 1880–1920', in D. Rueschmeyer and T. Skocpol (eds), *States, Social Knowledge and the Origins of Modern Social Policies* (Princeton: Princeton University Press, 1996), 163–200.

United States, the like of which the British had never known, but there was also a far greater perceived public unwillingness to countenance such large-scale federal activity. 'In this country', Croly argued, 'we have not yet been able to throw off that crass individualism which, carried to its logical consequences, forces each unfortunate to shift for himself while relieving the community of a distasteful and frequently expensive responsibility.'[109] While all the nationalist progressives agreed with Croly that it was impossible to 'trust the welfare of the mass' to 'automatic economic processes', they also agreed that until there was serious political reform it was no good trying to trust it to the American federal government either.[110] As Stephen Skowronek has argued, the pursuit of these movements' ideals 'did not entail making the established state more efficient; it entailed building a qualitatively different kind of state'.[111] The failure to maintain the Progressive Party and the collapse of efforts to build an American Labor Party to challenge such views confirmed Croly's pessimistic judgement still further. Without partisan support, the aspiration to build large-scale alternative political institutions was always going to be impossible. In this context, the greatest value of detailed investigation into British welfare practice, Ordway Tead argued, was that it revealed those elements which were ideologically essential and those which could more straightforwardly be discarded in the face of political difficulties. 'England's experiments need not be repeated in every particular', Tead thus argued, but 'they can and should be used as the basis for wiser measures designed specifically to meet American conditions and needs.'[112] However desirable the British model seemed in the ideal, alternative solutions would have to be sought in practice.

On the other side of the Atlantic, the British socialist pluralists' attitude to their own country's revolution in the nationwide state provision of social welfare was similarly ambiguous. Cole, Laski, and Tawney's distrust of the state bureaucracies obviously made it difficult for them or their immediate colleagues unreservedly to welcome the arrival of centrally directed labour exchanges, old- age pensions or national insurance. Even the latter scheme's acceptance of a role for non-state groups—the so-called 'approved societies'—did not prevent Cole from dismissing the programme as appealing only to the most 'Prussian of Prussians'.[113] All the pluralist theorists also continuously harboured considerable doubts about the deleterious psychological effects of state intervention. Harold Laski's first, brief, discussion on the issue welcomed

---

[109] Editors, 'The Doleless Unemployed', *New Republic*, 26 October 1921, 232.

[110] Croly, *Progressive Democracy*, 14.

[111] S. Skorownek, *Building a New American State: The Expansion of National Administrative Capacities 1877–1920* (Cambridge: Cambridge University Press, 1982), 4.

[112] O. Tead, 'Report of Investigation into the Operation of the British Health Insurance Act', Labor-Management Documentation Center, Cornell University, Ithaca, American Association for Labor Legislation (AALL) Papers, 50001/ 4/13/ii.

[113] Cole, *Labour in the Commonwealth*, 137.

the emergence of large-scale 'insurance against ill-health and unemployment', but also pointedly reminded his audience that such facilities used to be provided by the rather more invigorating process of 'private endeavour'.[114] Laski continued with a similar worry that Liberal welfare schemes left 'the ordinary citizen of to-day . . . so much the subject of administration that we cannot afford to stifle the least opportunity of his active exertions'.[115]

Despite these concerns, Cole, Laski, and colleagues were also aware that there were *some* advantages to the new British system of welfare provision. None of them endorsed the American Federation of Labor leader Samuel Gompers's dedication to pursuing advancement only through trade union activity. Though collective bargaining, of course, had enabled some unions to achieve an improvement in material conditions, the pluralists noted, even in the early post-war years many workers were campaigning from a position of relative weakness. It was simply 'a mistake', Tawney insisted, to think that a better distribution 'must always develop spontaneously'.[116] Some form of 'public intervention' was clearly required. Acceptance of a role for the state in this area was made easier by the fact that, although they shared many of the theoretical assumptions of their conservative anti-statist contemporaries, none of the socialist pluralists concurred with the dominant anti-statist account as to the *cause* of poverty. None of the theorists, that is, was willing to accept that 'where there is individual industry and perseverance, economic difficulties are overcome without any outside help at all'.[117] Poverty, the socialist pluralists accepted, was generally the result of the economic system, not of individual fecklessness. Some form of intervention was, therefore, required to rectify the situation and help to construct a new social order.

Stateless solutions: trade boards and industrial maintenance

The American nationalist progressives' concerns as to the limits of political possibility and the British socialist pluralists' ideological aspirations, therefore, led them both to attempt to design a welfare system that offered a compromise between reliance on state and on non-state bodies. As they sought to construct them, they were attracted to several shared ideas.

During the First World War, relatively full-employment enabled workers to forget about the worries of unemployment; but inflation threatened the purchasing power of their weekly wage. The central aspect of both movements post-war programme consisted, therefore, in securing a realistically

---

[114] See Laski, *Foundations*, 109.   [115] Laski, *Foundations*, 126.
[116] R. H. Tawney, 'Poverty as an Industrial Problem' (1913), reprinted in J. Winter (ed.), *The American Labour Movement and Other Essays* (New York: St Martin's Press, 1979), 123.
[117] E. T. Ogilvy, 'The Better Way', in J. Strachey (ed.), *The Manufacture of Paupers: A Protest and a Policy* (London: John Murray, 1906), 117.

enforceable minimum wage.[118] Both wished to avoid the general British
Labour Party recommendation of a state-determined and a state-inspected
minimum wage for all trades. Both pluralists and nationalist progressives were
impressed, however, by the work of the Trade Boards scheme that had first
been introduced by the Liberal government and expanded by the wartime
coalition. Under this programme, minimum wages were established industry-
by-industry at levels set by a board consisting of representatives of employers,
employees, and appointed members with no direct connection to the industry concerned.

For both movements, the Trade Boards were perceived not only to offer a
way of identifying and ensuring the suitable details of material provision for
workers but also as a mechanism for ensuring other, more fundamental, ideological goals. The *New Republic* celebrated the Boards because their 'real
achievements' were 'deeper and more far reaching' than 'the immediate
increase in wages'.[119] Most importantly of all, Tawney, Cole, and Laski
insisted, the Boards allowed workers a degree of self-government.[120] 'The
educational effect of this', Lippmann agreed from the United States, 'will
undoubtedly prove very great.' Trade Boards, he continued, offered 'a kind of
legislature for industry' in which workers 'will receive constant practice in
formulating their needs, exerting pressure, making intelligent their
demands.'[121] At the same time as ensuring a higher level of material reward,
then, the programme's deliberative mechanisms provided the 'actual experience of control' which was essential for workers to start taking 'the path to
industrial autonomy'.[122] 'No necessary or more valuable school of democracy
can be created,' Lippmann enthused, 'than these trade legislatures in which
people have a chance to learn how to govern the conditions of their work.'[123]

The Trade Board scheme was also celebrated as a means to improve productive performance and as a mechanism for improving communal ties. The
process of having wages set at least partially democratically was held to assist
in the provision of a new incentive for workers. 'It seems a not uncommon
experience', Tawney recalled, 'that an increase in output has followed the
establishment of minimum rates.'[124] Both groups of theorists were also, of
course, anxious that workers develop loyalties beyond those of their individual industry. As such, the 'presence of appointed members' from outside the
specific industry on each Trade Board was welcomed in both Britain and

---

[118] See S. B. Rowntree, *Poverty: A Study of Town Life* (London: Macmillan, 1901); Cole, 'First
Charge', 408; Editors, 'Meaning of Reconstruction', 183.

[119] J. Goldmark, 'Minimum Wage in Practice', *New Republic*, 25 December 1915, 204–5.

[120] See R. H. Tawney, 'The Unemployment Crisis in England', *New Republic*, 23 February 1921,
367–8; Laski, *Grammar*, 458; G. D. H. Cole, *Self-Government in Industry* (London: G. Bell, 1917), 168.

[121] W. Lippmann, 'The Campaign Against Sweating', *New Republic*, Special Supplement, 27 March
1915, 7–8.   [122] Cole, *Self-Government*, 170.

[123] Lippmann, 'Campaign Against Sweating', 8.

[124] R. H. Tawney, *Studies in the Minimum Wage*, ii (London: G. Bell, 1918), 121.

America as 'some guarantee that considerations of a larger kind ... will be taken into account'.[125] Ordway Tead was particularly excited by the prospect of combining a traditional progressive interest in scientific management and expertise with one in industrial democracy and self-government. The Trade Boards would enable all 'the interested parties' to come together 'with the financial and technical facts fully before them' and reach agreement through informed discussion.[126] In so far as they provided a mechanism which both assisted experimentation and aided the performance of functions, bringing together the ideals and aspirations of both movements, it is not surprising that Cole was able to describe the Trade Boards as 'perhaps the most important achievement of this century in the sphere of industrial reform'.[127]

Trade Boards, of course, helped only those who were able to find employment, and as the economy took a dramatic downturn in both countries in the early 1920s they became increasingly irrelevant. The groups' interest in minimum wages should not be taken to indicate any unwillingness on their part to consider the claims of the new masses of unemployed that quickly emerged in the trade depression. Initially, though, the unemployment crisis did not distract either groups from their search for a compromise solution between state and non-state activity. Leading the way in examining the cause of the increasing number of people not able to find permanent work, G. D. H. Cole devised a scheme that came to be known as 'industrial maintenance'. On this programme, unemployment insurance would be conducted on an industry-by-industry basis. The British national insurance programme would be abolished and both the state and the worker would be relieved from having to pay contributions. In its place a system would be constructed which would impose on *employers* the obligation of paying contributions to an insurance fund for their workers. The scheme itself was to be established by central government, which would legislate to ensure that payments were made by employers; but the day-to-day operation of the claim-and-payment system would be placed in the hands of the workers themselves. The government was thus required initially to 'use all its power and influence to promote the carrying into effect by every possible industry of its own scheme of maintenance'; but once it was up and running the administrative work and the 'payment of benefits from the fund' were to be 'placed absolutely in the hands of the trade unions'.[128]

In the first few post-war years, the idea of divorcing the operation of insurance schemes from their revenue raising rapidly took hold in both pluralist

[125] R. H. Tawney, *Studies in the Minimum Wage*, i (London: G. Bell, 1918), 35.

[126] O. Tead and R. Valentine, 'Work and Pay: A Suggestion for Representative Government in Industry', *Quarterly Journal of Economics*, 31 (1917), 253.

[127] G. D. H. Cole, 'The Attack on the Trade Boards', *New Statesman*, 2 September 1922, 89.

[128] G. D. H. Cole, 'The Spread of Unemployment', *New Statesman*, 16 October 1920, 39; G. D. H. Cole, 'Reflections on the Wage System', *New Age*, 29 March 1917, 513–15.

and nationalist progressive circles. The Cambridge economist Joseph L. Cohen calculated that by 1923 43 British trade unions had passed resolutions in favour of 'industrial maintenance' and the idea was quickly being exported to the United States.[129] Explaining the proposals in the *New Republic*, Tawney argued that the method of contribution would lead itself to a fall in unemployment. If 'employers have to pay for unemployment', he cogently argued, 'they will take every measure in their power to reduce it'.[130] As many in the American labour movement had always been sceptical of asking workers to contribute to a state-run unemployment scheme—unemployment, after all, was not believed to be the fault of the worker himself—this programme seemed to offer an attractive alternative to nationalist progressives. The balance which 'industrial maintenance' struck, with the state compelling employers to contribute and unions conducting the programme, seemed just right.[131]

These practical advantages did not exhaust the idea's appeal. As the 'administration of unemployment insurance' would be entrusted entirely to 'the trade union movement', there were again perceived to be lessons in self-government; lessons which could of course be equally well received by both pluralists and nationalist progressives.[132] In advancing the scheme, Cole presented it as a 'clear step in the direction of industrial autonomy'.[133] The operation of the programme would provide another training ground for more adventurous programmes of democratization. 'Before Labour can control' on any significant scale, he continued, 'it must learn how to control; and this it will do only by actual experience of control' offered by the programme of industrial maintenance.[134] Connectedly, the pluralists also hoped that the practice of running the scheme would inculcate a sense of significance in the workforce that would enable it to be more aggressive in its industrial life and more creative in the personal sphere. Whereas 'state maintenance would inevitably give the worker a sense of dependence', he insisted, 'industrial maintenance would give him a sense of freedom'.[135]

The return of the state

Whatever its early popularity, however, it did not take too long for the idea of 'industrial maintenance' to be rejected in both Britain and the United

[129] See J. L. Cohen, *Insurance by Industry Examined* (London: P. S. King and Son, 1923), 53.

[130] R. H. Tawney, 'The Unemployment Crisis in England', *New Republic*, 23 February 1921, 368.

[131] See Editors, 'The Meaning of Reconstruction', 182 and Editors, 'Unemployment', *New Republic*, 31 August 1921, 6.

[132] Labour Party and TUC, *Social Insurance and Trade Union Membership* (London: Labour Party, 1924), 18.   [133] Cole, 'Reflections', 515.

[134] Cole, 'Reflections', 515.

[135] G. D. H. Cole, *Unemployment and Industrial Maintenance* (London: National Guilds League, 1921), 5–6.

States.[136] The power of trade unions declined rapidly in both countries in the early 1920s, and as it did so the practical feasibility of the idea diminished considerably. Employers in a position of relative industrial strength were certainly not going to be willing to pay unilateral contributions, let alone accept that the administration of the scheme should be wholly wrested from them. While 'the tendency has been more and more to place the burdens of unemployment on those who are directly responsible for the conduct of industry', the *New Republic* thus reported in 1921, the 'task of convincing business men and industrial managers that theirs is the responsibility for the unemployment and that, therefore, they should support those who are involuntarily unemployed, is one that cannot be performed for a few years'.[137] Similarly, if industries were to run their own insurance system then all workers within a particular industry would have to be members of the same programme, and if trade unions were to operate the scheme then they too would have to follow boundaries coterminous with those of the industry itself. Such a programme therefore relied upon an industrial unionism which, although close to many reformers' hearts, always remained far from realization.

More fundamentally, the scheme was not obviously as conducive to the pluralists' and progressives' key conceptual commitments as it may at first have appeared. It would, many began to worry, seriously restrict the very labour mobility to which the pluralists were so dedicated. Individuals covered by a particular industrial insurance programme may not be able easily to exit an industry and move to another as they would under a universal scheme. Similarly, the nationalist progressives soon became anxious that industrial maintenance would have tied the fate of individuals very much to the fate of their particular industry. Insurance schemes, Ordway Tead reminded his colleagues, function well when they spread risk, but the programme of industrial maintenance would have ensured that those in industries worst affected by unemployment would have to shoulder the burden themselves.[138] All the theorists faced up to all these problems fairly quickly. By 1924, the idea's originator G. D. H. Cole was still willing to accept an 'experiment' in 'industrial maintenance' but even he was no longer willing to describe himself as an 'advocate of "insurance by industry" as a general system'.[139]

As faith in the system of 'industrial maintenance' faded, so too did the strength of adherence to the Trade Board scheme. Whereas in the immediate post-war years it seemed reasonable to expect that Trade Boards would continue to expand into more and more industries, by the mid-1920s they too were on the back foot. In industries in decline the popular demand was for lower labour costs rather than for more intervention, and in those where

---

[136] For a detailed account, see Cohen, *Insurance*, 50–76.
[137] Editors, 'The Doleless Unemployed', 231.   [138] Tead, 'Report', 2.
[139] G. D. H. Cole, 'Mr Shaw's Unemployment Bill', *New Statesman*, 28 June 1924, 342.

unions remained strong traditional practices of collective bargaining appeared to union leaders to offer a more satisfactory approach to wage negotiation. Again, theoretical doubts attended this practical decline. The democratic deliberations that were associated with Trade Board negotiations, although valuable in themselves, could always go awry in setting minimum levels. The possibilities of workers being outmanoeuvred and outvoted by employers always remained, as did the prospect of workers being arbitrarily better rewarded in some industries or locales than others. Again, the early to mid-1920s were something of a turning point. By 1924, Cole was still willing to accept that the 'argument in favour of local autonomy in fixing wages sounds well enough' but he also became publicly wary of 'the petty tyrannies and the pressures of locality' which could lead to unsatisfactory wage settlements.[140]

The limitations of both of these programmes reopened the door to advocacy of a more conventional, centrally organized, government-sponsored scheme of material protection and provision in both countries. Throughout the early 1920s, the major thinkers came to accept the necessity of some 'publicly provided maintenance' for those without work and a level of state protection for those fortunate to remain in employment.[141] As unemployment deepened in the United States, nationalist progressives once again turned to the federal government for help. Emphasis had to be placed on 'the national aspect' of the unemployment question, Ordway Tead insisted, and 'the ear of the Federal Commission on Industrial Relations should be shouted at in order that the establishment of a national unemployment insurance and a National Labor Exchange be given serious thought'.[142] As the sense of crisis deepened, the *New Republic* insisted on the need for 'the organization nationally of a series of well articulated employment offices, the institution, preferably national, of unemployment insurance and the formulation of a long-time program of public works'.[143] Even the idea of centralized state planning for economic efficiency once again enjoyed a vogue. No 'measure would be more helpful', the *New Republic* continued, 'than the creation, under federal auspices, of a commission of experts charged with studying depressions and with proposing a plan of action'.[144] In Britain, the socialist pluralists' conversion to a state-based solution was not quite as thoroughgoing but showed nonetheless signs of a real change. On the minimum wage, for example, Cole began to argue for a 'statutory Minimum Wage Commission' with powers to 'fix legally binding minimum rates of pay'.[145] This is not to imply that the socialist pluralists' practical suggestions entirely surrendered to a

---

[140] G. D. H. Cole, 'Wages in the Countryside', *New Statesman*, 7 June 1924, 244; G. D. H. Cole, 'The National Minimum Wage', , 58–62.

[141] G.D.H. Cole, 'Labour's Unemployment Proposals', *New Statesman*, 29 February 1921, 494; G. D. H. Cole, 'The Reduction of Wages', *New Statesman*, 18 June 1921, 295.

[142] Tead, 'Cure and Prevention', 14 and 27.

[143] Editors, 'Unemployment', *New Republic*, 31 August 1921, 7.

[144] Editors, 'Unemployment', 8.   [145] Cole, 'Minimum Wage', 60.

state-centred collectivism. The pluralists were still sharply critical of the 'intensely bureaucratic tradition' of government departments like the Ministry of Labour, but they were increasingly willing to accept that it was at least plausible that 'these activities can be provided' by central authority without 'huge bureaucratic apparatus'. And in so far as that was the case, then 'let them be provided'.[146]

Conclusion

In 1924, Cole wrote in the *New Statesman* that state welfare provision was now preferred to non-state assistance and so 'Mr Lloyd George has triumphed over Mr Belloc'.[147] It was telling, however, that Cole insisted that Lloyd George and the New Liberals had defeated only the conservative anti-statist Belloc. He did not admit they had triumphed over Mr Laski, Mr Tawney, and Mr Cole too. Undeniable vanity aside, the primary reason why Cole did not think that the socialist pluralists had lost the argument as badly as their other state-sceptical colleagues had lay elsewhere. There remained a strong element of continuity in the socialist pluralists' thinking even as they began to accept an increased role for government intervention. Whereas attitudes to the instruments of distribution may have changed through the 1920s, Cole was certain, as were Laski and Tawney, that the underlying principles of distribution had not. Liberty as experimentation and community as sentiment were both eventually seen as compatible with some form of state activity. The central commitments required 'a spirit' among the population at large and 'not merely a body of rules by an outside authority'. Nonetheless, the pluralists were now willing to accept that 'in the revolution needed to make the development of that spirit a possibility, the state can, if it pleases, play a considerable part'.[148] The nationalist progressives displayed a similar degree of practical flexibility and conceptual commitment in their dealings with poverty and poverty alleviation. They argued in this policy arena, as in all others, that, if they were to begin to try to realize their ideals, they would have to be prepared both to innovate and to compromise. New institutions would have to be built and old ones redesigned but only at the pace that politics realistically allowed. 'We are not wedded to means: only to ends', the *New Republic* editors argued in 1918, and the description was more than simply self-serving.[149] All of the nationalist progressives were certain that the political realities which shaped the practical possibilities of reform would have

---

[146] G. D. H. Cole, 'Can We Dispense with the Ministry of Labour?', *New Statesman*, 18 February 1922, 551.
[147] G. D. H. Cole, 'The Future of Social Insurance', *New Statesman*, 12 March 1924, 7–8.
[148] Tawney, 'Economic Liberty', p. 114.   [149] Editors, 'Meaning of Reconstruction', 183.

somehow to be accommodated without sacrificing conceptual essentials. One 'method' of social welfare reform 'may avail at one time and place, another at another', the *New Republic* insisted. Nationalist progressives did not expect to be able to realize a millennial dream 'when there shall be neither rich nor poor, when the soil will yield its fruits by any other title than hard and continuous labor'. But they did continually argue that 'national purpose' should 'permeate the system of industry from which the average man must win employment and the necessities of life'.[150]

This pragmatic and flexible attitude did not imply that the movements took the problem of poverty and poverty alleviation lightly. It did mean, however, as Daniel Rodgers has so eloquently suggested of other groups, that 'poverty was but a thread in the social question's tangles'.[151] The ideological programmes that the nationalist progressives and the socialist pluralists outlined in the early post-war years committed both movements to strive for the construction of a whole new political and social order to enable them to realize their core ideals; ideals themselves which rested not in a dedication to material equality but to human freedom and community. Seen in this light, the poverty of large sections of the population was only one problem among many others which prevented citizens of Britain and the United States from living their lives in liberty and in community with one another. It was a problem that had to be resolved, therefore, but not at the expense of any more fundamental means of attaining their goals. As Laski argued, 'shorter hours and higher wages' were to be welcomed but only if they could be achieved without engendering 'that mood which avoids the most vital of our problems'.[152]

[150] Ibid.   [151] Rodgers, *Atlantic Crossings*, 210.
[152] H. Laski, 'British Reconstruction Proposals and the American Attitude', *Proceedings of the Academy of Political Science*, 8 (1919), 197.

Conclusion

This book commenced with a paradox. Between 1909 and 1925, the American nationalist progressives and British socialist pluralists outlined two sharply distinct political philosophies: one apparently state-centred, the other fiercely anti-statist. The nationalist progressives, it appeared, wished to construct an entirely new central state machine in the United States, one capable of overcoming the obstacles of localism and sectionalism and imposing a nationwide political agenda and social identity across the several States. The socialist pluralists, on the other hand, seemed fiercely to reject the state-centred programmes of their contemporaries. They celebrated diversity, social difference, and group autonomy, and argued for a radical decentralization of authority in all aspects of social, economic, and political life. And yet, despite these stark differences, the ideological evolution of these two groups also appeared intricately intertwined. Indeed, not only did the groups' leaders involve themselves in a continual dialogue, they also identified individual programmes of concrete reform that could be shared between them. Both movements formulated proposals for the expansion of democratic mechanisms into industry, for the large-scale extension of educational opportunities for working adults, and for protection of all citizens from the perils of poverty. They also drew upon both state and non-state mechanisms as they did so. Somehow, the stark initial disagreement had yielded political consensus.

The resolution of this paradox provided the central focus of the remainder of the book. Part I began the search by examining the course of both these movements' initial ideological evolution. It established that both groups started their work by responding to the fundamental arguments of the British and American idealists and to the suggestions of the Fabians, positivists, pragmatists, and social psychologists who had inherited idealism's claims. The first chapter argued that this examination presented both movements with a clear agenda. Any new ideology of reform would have to begin not with an analysis of the role of the state per *se* but with a careful reconsideration of the meaning of the two fundamental political concepts that dominated idealist speculation: liberty and community. The next two chapters, however, demonstrated that, having started from the same point, the nationalist progressives and socialist pluralists responded in two starkly contrasting ways. The nationalist progressives first endorsed and then radicalized the idealists' conceptual suggestions; the socialist pluralists sharply rejected them.

Yet, despite the disagreements, the terms of debate were nonetheless shared and, when the upheavals of the First World War brought these movements into direct contact with each other, they could engage in a discussion directly, convinced, at least, that they were arguing about the same things and using the same terms. Part II of the book traced this wartime debate that took the relationship between the two movements to a new level. Looking into Britain to ascertain how British reformers had responded to the challenges of enhanced state power during the conflict, the nationalist progressives came face to face with the pluralist challenge. Chapter 4 showed how, for a brief moment, they were tempted to accept the pluralist agenda in full. Yet, as the conflict subsided and an era of social and political reconstruction appeared to beckon, the nationalist progressives refused to alienate themselves from their fundamental commitments. Their dedication to national communal loyalty went too deep. They preferred instead simply to give that dedication a pluralistic sheen. Groups of citizens and associations of workers were thus to be allowed to run their own affairs as long as they did so in a manner conducive to the development of a richer national project. Chapter 5 then turned back to Britain. It argued that the socialist pluralists were startled by this rejection and spent the first years of the post-war age reconsidering their own position. Concerned that their decentralizing and individualist ideals could lead to social conflict and to the domination of the weak by the strong, the pluralists attempted to graft an additional ideal into their ideological programme. They designed a conception of community that celebrated ties of sentimental attachment between diverse individuals without threatening a prescriptive authoritarian agenda. Individuality and communal connection would thus be reconciled.

The international discussion between these progressives and pluralists failed to resolve the disputes at the level of fundamental commitments. One movement remained committed, above all, to national communal improvement, the other to individual experimentation and social diversity; they did not agree, and would not pretend to agree. Yet Part III demonstrated that this was far from the end of their discussion. Rather, it opened up new and far more fruitful connections. Both movements possessed enough political sensitivity to realize that philosophical disagreement did not preclude the possibility that an international exchange of ideas might still offer powerful political suggestions. They understood that, although they were striving for very different fundamental goals, they were also facing political challenges of sharply contrasting character, and they also understood that such a combination of differences might actually result in paradoxical similarities. As the nationalist progressives sought to achieve their communalistic goals in a society characterized by social diversity, political decentralization, and a conservative political elite, that is, so the socialist pluralists pursued their individualistic and decentralizing ideals in a nation characterized by a centralized set of political institutions, relative social homogeneity, and governments prepared, occasionally at least, to pursue radical policy options.

Both movements thus found themselves on similar territory; attempting to realize ideological goals in societies which seemed better suited to commitments of their polar opposites. The result, as Chapters 6 and 7 showed, was that both movements turned to workers' education as a means of reaching a wider public than their ideas initially allowed; also, both designed programmes of redistribution based on a combination of public and private sectors and compulsory and voluntary participation because this appeared the only means of reaching their ideals.

These similarities were not the simple result of accidents of circumstance, however. They were the conscious result of a continued dialogue. Throughout their exchange, both movements displayed an admirable and sensitive combination of ideological commitment and political flexibility. Neither of these movements was prepared to sacrifice fundamental beliefs, even in the face of severe political difficulties, nor was it stubbornly dedicated to achieving its goals in one particular way. Rather, they continually sought new mechanisms to achieve their ends; mechanisms suitable to their own circumstances but not narrowly determined by them. They were not, therefore, movements characterized by statism or anti-statism. They were movements committed to pursuing distinctive ideas of human liberty and community in distinctive settings, and prepared to draw on the advice of others in order to help them do so. Seen this way, the paradox with which the book began is not only resolved, it dissolves entirely. The loss of the paradox leaves us with the new task of evaluating the movements' legacy.

Epilogue

Years of Decline

From the immediate aftermath of the First World War into the early 1920s, the nationalist progressives suggested a series of ideas for far-reaching reform. None of these measures succeeded. Their efforts to construct an American Labor Party foundered in the face of a wide collection of obstacles, ranging from the obstruction of the courts through the lack of interest of major trade unions to the inability of diverse groups of progressive intellectuals to put aside their differences.[1] Attempts at constructing programmes of industrial democracy in the workplace fared little better. The 1920s did not usher in an era of industrial citizenship, as had been hoped; rather, it witnessed a reversal of fortunes. Most employers withdrew the consultative mechanisms that had introduced during the war to improve industrial relations and returned to the 'open shops', company unions, and traditional management practices of the late nineteenth century, with the full support of Democratic and Republican administrations in Washington.[2] Proposals for social insurance to protect workers against unemployment and ill-health, with or without the support of State and federal legislatures, also collapsed. By 1924, as the American economy boomed, the post-war slump seemed a distant memory and risky adventures in social policy appeared both unwelcome and untimely. Although the American Association for Labor Legislation continued to pressure for change, most trade unions remained suspicious and both the public and the governing authorities continued to be unconvinced, as apparently demonstrated by the election of Calvin Coolidge to the presidency in 1924.[3]

It might not have come as too great a surprise that these rather grandiose plans should fall away. The nationalist progressives had always been well aware that they would struggle to construct a new political order in a society and political system not conducive to their ideas. They understood, therefore, that they might have to begin from below, to build up support for change by

---

[1] See S. Shapiro, 'Hand and Brain: The Farmer Labor Party of 1920', *Labor History*, 26 (1985), 405–22.

[2] See J. A. McCartin, *Labor's Great War: The Struggle for Industrial Democracy and the Origins of Modern American Labor Relations, 1912–1921* (Chapel Hill: University of North Carolina Press, 1997), esp. 221–2, and H. J. Harris, 'Industrial Democracy and Liberal Capitalism, 1890–1925', in N. Lichtenstein and H. J. Harris (eds), *Industrial Democracy: The Ambiguous Promise* (Cambridge: Cambridge University Press, 1996), 43–67.

[3] See D. Levine, *Poverty and Society: The Growth of the American Welfare State in Comparative Perspective* (New Brunswick: Rutgers University Press, 1988), 168–79.

reshaping the expectations, aspirations, and values of American citizens themselves. The growth of adult education in the early post-war years had offered a prime means of achieving such a conversion. Yet severe problems arose here too. Unable to seek state support in the conservative climate of post-war America, the Workers Education Bureau (WEB) was forced to turn to the trade union movement in the search for funding. The American Federation of Labor (AFL), however, demanded an immediate quid pro quo in the form of an effective veto on any aspect of the curriculum of which it did not approve. When this was not forthcoming, the hierarchy of the AFL turned swiftly against the WEB. In the mid-1920s, AFL inspectors began to attack the 'strange multiplicity' of views expressed in the classes and schools the WEB supported. Some 'who are serving as teachers in this workers' education movement', they reported, are 'talking about the class struggle and using only a materialistic interpretation of the labor movement'. Such views, however, stood in direct opposition to the AFL's stated position. This discrepancy, the inspectors insisted, was 'disconcerting': 'is not there a fundamental need of a development of terminology so that there may be unity of thinking among those considering the educational problems of labor?'[4] The signs were ominous. The WEB leaders, Spencer Miller and James Maurer, and teachers, including John Dewey, made continual efforts to resolve the tensions but conflict and crisis could not be avoided. By the latter half of the decade the AFL explicitly insisted that for funding to continue the WEB's classes should 'be controlled by trade unionists themselves', arguing that such control 'involves no question of academic freedom at all'.[5] A series of bitter struggles followed, culminating in the AFL's withdrawal of support from institutions of which it disapproved, including the largest of the residential colleges for workers, Brookwood, in upstate New York.[6] To the theorists who had worked so hard to make working-class education the foundations of a broader political movement, these attacks were a simple confirmation of the 'historic policy of the A F of L to squelch and smother intellectuals'.[7] For the nationalist progressives more generally, the one final hope of practical political engagement appeared lost.

All of these disappointments dramatically rocked an ideological movement already struggling to reshape itself in the aftermath of the war. A further series of personal tragedies compounded the political problems. Randolph Bourne, Willard Straight, and Walter Weyl had all died in the immediate aftermath of the First World War; and, although a new generation had replaced them, they

---

[4] American Federation of Labor, 'Workers Education Bureau Conference: A Memorandum', WEB Records (1924)

[5] J. Dewey, 'Address', American Federation of Labor Action of Brookwood, Local No. 5, American Federation of Teachers, A. J. Muste Papers (1928).

[6] See R. Altenbaugh, *Education for Struggle: The American Labor Colleges of the 1920s and 1930s* (Philadelphia: Temple University Press, 1990), 182–94.

[7] D. Saposs, cited in L. Fink, *Progressive Intellectuals and the Dilemmas of Democratic Commitment* (Cambridge, MA: Harvard University Press, 1997), 49–50.

too began to fall away by the middle years of the 1920s. The most promising of the new generation of nationalist progressives, Arthur Gleason, passed away. Gleason's health had suffered severely after a ship taking him to England during the last years of the war was torpedoed, and although he remained one of the most hard-working of post-war progressive theorists, he finally succumbed to meningitis in 1924.[8] At the same time, the other leading light of the immediate post-war period, Ordway Tead, withdrew from mainstream politics. His once-ceaseless attempts to resuscitate nationalist progressive politics by establishing close personal connections with radicals in the American trade union movement now came to nothing. As union leader after union leader turned him away, Tead became convinced that opportunities for nationalist reform had 'diminished to a vanishing point'. After a brief attempt to convince the leaders of large corporations to reconsider their management techniques, Tead retired to a life in publishing and the occasional teaching of social work.[9] Reflecting on such losses to the editorial offices of the *New Republic*, Herbert Croly felt it 'depressing to see so many of one's friends drifting away intellectually and spiritually, it makes one feel lonely'.[10] Indeed, Croly became so distressed that he adopted a highly spiritual form of Christianity to console himself, but his religiosity served only to alienate his remaining progressive friends more completely still.[11] In 1929, he retired to Santa Barbara, California a broken man. He died a year later.[12]

This pattern of death and disillusionment left Walter Lippmann as the only leading nationalist progressive still active in national politics by the mid-1920s. Yet relations between Lippmann and his colleagues had long since fallen apart. By 1925, Lippmann had become desperately disillusioned with the entire nationalist progressive project. This disillusionment took most celebrated form in his fierce rejection of the reformist potential of democratic governance, outlined most spectacularly in *The Phantom Public*. In this work, Lippmann argued that the average American citizen in his relationship to politics is 'rather like a deaf spectator in the back row' of the cinema. He knows he 'ought to keep his mind on the mystery off there, but cannot quite manage to keep awake'.[13] Lippmann also dismissed the expectation that any

---

[8] See collection of obituaries, Social Welfare History Archive, University of Minnesota, The P. Kellogg Papers, 2/17.

[9] O. Tead, in L. Finkelstein (ed.), *Thirteen Americans: Their Spiritual Biographies* (New York: Institute for Religious and Social Studies, 1950), 22–3.

[10] H. Croly to F. Frankfurter, cited in E. Stettner, *Shaping Modern Liberalism: Herbert Croly and Progressive Thought* (Lawrence: Kansas University Press, 1993), 161

[11] See H. Laski to O. W. Holmes, letter dated 29 April 1928, M. de Wolfe Howe (ed.), *The Holmes-Laski Letters: The Correspondence of Mr Justice Holmes and Harold J. Laski, 1916–1935* (Cambridge, MA: Harvard University Press, 1953), 1050.

[12] See H. Croly to L. Hand, letter dated 9 October 1929, Harvard Law School Library, Harvard University, The L. Hand Papers, 102/24, and Editors, 'Herbert Croly', *New Republic*, 16 July 1930, supplement.

[13] W. Lippmann, *The Phantom Public: A Sequel to 'Public Opinion'* (New York: Macmillan, 1925), 13.

democratic initiative which aimed to involve citizens—and especially work-ing-class citizens—more actively in politics would help in any way. The citizen 'will not have a better public opinion because he is asked to express his opinion more often', he insisted, 'he will simply be more bewildered, more bored and more ready to follow along'.[14] Even the educational endeavours of the WEB and the New School for Social Research were rejected. Although education 'has furnished the thesis of the last chapter of every optimistic book on democracy written for one hundred and fifty years', Lippmann suggested, it success has been limited indeed.[15] The 'usual appeal to education as the remedy for the incompetence of democracy', he concluded, is 'barren'.[16] Even if teachers are well-intentioned, they can never meet the demands of the task facing them. As the problems of 'the modern world appear and change faster' than any set of teachers or students 'can grasp them', they 'are bound always to be in arrears'.[17]

These criticisms catapulted Lippmann and *The Phantom Public* out of the nationalist progressive fold and straight to the forefront of a conservative political canon; the book is justifiably regarded to this day as one of the most powerful modern rejections of the possibilities of democracy. Yet Lippmann had a still more dramatic argument in store. Indeed, to former colleagues within nationalist progressivism the attack on democracy was not the book's most disturbing conclusion. *The Phantom Public* not only turned against democracy, about which Lippmann had always been fairly sceptical; it also totally dismissed the possibility of constructing any programme of political reform on the basis of a desire to craft deeper communal loyalties amongst American citizens. The disappointments of the post-war period, Lippmann insisted, demonstrated that it was simply impossible to bring the competing sections of American society together. Sectional loyalties and moral imperfections were just too deeply ingrained in the fabric of the nation. All individuals and groups were capable of thinking about, on such a view, was their own immediate concerns. 'The farmer decides whether to plant wheat or corn, the mechanic whether to take the job offered at Pennsylvania or the Erie shops, whether to buy a Ford or a piano.' Whatever the reformer tires to achieve, Lippmann insisted, the average American will always 'make no attempt to consider society as a whole'.[18] This lack of interest, moreover, was not even necessarily peaceful; differences would lead to tension and tension to conflict. It was a mistake, however, to think that such a pattern was anything other than inevitable. Reformers should 'no longer expect to find a unity which absorbs diversity', Lippmann insisted. In such terms even the old nationalist progressive criticisms of pluralism itself had to be laid to rest. 'The pluralistic

---

[14] Lippmann, *Phantom Public*, 37.
[16] Lippmann, *Phantom Public*, 26.
[18] Lippmann, *Phantom Public*, 45

[15] Lippmann, *Phantom Public*, 22.
[17] Lippmann, *Phantom Public*, 27.

theory, as its leading advocate, Mr Laski, has pointed out, seems to carry with it a hint of anarchy', Lippmann argued, 'yet the suggestion is grossly exaggerated.' There 'is most anarchy' not in pluralism but 'where separateness of purpose is covered up and confused, where false unities are worshipped, and each special interest is forever proclaiming itself the voice of the people and attempting to impose its purpose upon everybody as the purpose of all mankind'.[19] Instead of 'looking for an identity of purpose' reformers should content themselves to 'look simply for an accommodation of purposes'.[20]

So drastic was this rejection, Lippmann worried that his conclusions would lead to him being 'put on trial for heresy by my old friends on *The New Republic*'.[21] His concern was understandable. With this assault on the possibility of communal attachment, Lippmann removed the entire foundations of the nationalist progressive ideological project. Without a commitment to national communality, there could be no nationalist progressive ideology. Yet on a personal level he had little cause to worry, for the events of the 1920s meant that very few of those friends remained.[22] By the middle of the decade, nationalist progressivism was over.

The Erosion of Socialist Pluralism

In Britain, the socialist pluralists suffered none of the personal traumas of the Americans. They flourished in the post-war world. G. D. H. Cole enjoyed increasing success in the 1920s, leaving a post as adult educator in the University of London in 1925 to become the first Reader in Economics in the University of Oxford.[23] Laski was similarly 'shot into prominence' on his return to permanent academic life in Britain.[24] His election to a professorship at the London School of Economics (LSE) guaranteed him a sizeable income, the ear of eager students from across the British Empire, and access to the very highest echelons of the Labour Party. Tawney maintained a somewhat lower profile but he too enjoyed success at the LSE. After unsuccessfully standing for Parliament in 1924, he crafted a career as a major economic historian in the early 1930s.[25]

Yet the mid-1920s proved to be a turning point in Britain, just as in the

---

[19] Lippmann, *Phantom Public*, 161.   [20] Lippmann, *Phantom Public*, 98.
[21] W. Lippmann, cited in R. Steel, *Walter Lippmann and the American Century* (London: Boldey Head, 1980), 212.
[22] See Steel, *Walter Lippmann*, 220–34.
[23] See M. Cole, *The Life of G. D. H. Cole* (London: Macmillan, 1971), 139.
[24] See I. Kramnick and B. Sheerman, *Harold Laski: A Life on the Left* (London: Hamish Hamilton, 1992), 153–84.
[25] See R. Terrill, *R. H. Tawney and His Times: Socialism as Fellowship* (Cambridge, MA: Harvard University Press, 1973), 56–85.

United States. In Britain, however, it was economic bust rather than industrial boom that caused the difficulties. Politics in Britain were dogged by the
continual spectre of economic decline throughout the decade. As exports
collapsed, unemployment soared, never dropping below one million
throughout the decade, and employers responded by cutting wages and
increasing working hours. Trade unions responded as best they could; but,
although strikes continued throughout the mid-1920s, they were almost all
directly concerned with falling living standards, lower wages, and longer
hours of work, and not with any struggle for industrial democracy or
'encroaching control'. Unions were no longer hoping to build a better industrial order, they merely wanted to hold on to the best aspects of the current
one. A final break from the optimism of the early post-war years came when
the British General Strike of 1926 failed completely, and the incumbent
Conservative government passed restrictive trade union legislation that
restructured the balance of industrial power for the remainder of the inter-
war years. The problems of these years made the pluralists' turn towards
mainstream Labour politics and away from an anti-statist policy of
'encroaching control' even more definite. In such an environment, the
National Guilds League collapsed, with many of its members drifting away
into the Communist Party.[26] Membership of the Workers' Educational
Association also declined as workers became increasingly concerned with the
immediate necessities of life.[27] The practical possibilities for pluralism began
to disappear.

These developments did not just cause immediate political problems;
they also led the pluralists to challenge the essentials of their fundamental
ideals. Throughout the 1920s, it became very difficult to believe the workers themselves were the building-blocks of a participatory democratic society. There was, or so it appeared, a need to revise the pluralist 'conception
of the democratic inclinations and capacities of ordinary people'.[28] In so
doing, the pluralists began to abandon their earlier positions. The most
dramatic turn around was from Cole. In the months before the Labour
Party took office in 1929, he penned his first major revisionist work, *The
Next Ten Years*. Ostensibly a programme for the new government, Cole
actually used this work to distance himself from a wide range of earlier
arguments. He even suggested that his previous commitments to a thoroughgoing industrial democracy had been ill-considered, the result of little
more than the frustration of not being able to improve the lot of the industrial worker. 'I despaired of making work interesting in itself', Cole
explained, so 'I sought to find a substitute . . . in the adventitious interest

[26] See Cole, *Life of G. D. H. Cole*, 158–60, and A. Wright, *G. D. H. Cole and Socialist Democracy*
(Oxford: Oxford University Press, 1979), 111.
[27] See B. Jennings, *Knowledge is Power: A Short History of the WEA* (Hull: University of Hull, 1979).
[28] Wright, *G. D. H. Cole*, 115.

of collectively controlling a naturally uninteresting job.'[29] Now, as unions moved away from their demands for a greater say in management and back to a concern with wages and hours, the plea itself could be abandoned. 'It will be useless', after all, 'to make any provision for workers' control which the worker will not have the desire to use.'[30]

Laski was not so willing to give up on the pluralist project. Although Cole had abandoned his earlier commitments by 1929, and Tawney had fallen largely silent, Laski penned two major works in the late 1920s—the renowned *Liberty in the Modern State* and the equally powerful *The Dangers of Obedience*— both of which contained a detailed conceptual case for the connection between individual liberty and a substantial programme of industrial democratization unaltered from the position advanced in *A Grammar of Politics*. Even the phrasing remained the same. In any non-democratic system, Laski continued to argue, the worker is so remote from the ambit of decision-making that 'he becomes, increasingly, the mere recipient of orders he has to obey' and thus is transformed from 'a free man' into a mere 'tool in human shape'.[31] A democratization of industrial decision-making would 'multiply the chance of creativeness' and hence free the individual from the psychological constraints imposed by industrial autocracy.[32] Laski also forcefully resisted the contemporary trend away from a faith in democracy on the grounds that it would remove potentially vital safeguards against abuse. 'Government by experts' of the sort Lippmann advocated, Laski insisted, 'would, however ardent their original zeal for the public welfare' eventually mean 'government in the interests of experts.'[33] As the Fabian W. A. Robson commented, what was remarkable about Laski in the late 1920s and the first year of the 1930s was his continuing ability to 'plead so insistently the cause of freedom'.[34]

Despite this early show of resilience, Laski did eventually reconsider his pluralistic commitments, and when his move away arrived it was all the more significant for the delay. The catalyst for the change this time was not the collapse of union power but the failure of the second Labour government in 1931. Laski was not only disappointed by the loss of any immediate hopes for reform, he was disgusted by Labour Prime Minister J. Ramsay MacDonald's secret negotiations with the Conservative leader Stanley Baldwin. Desperate to stay in power as economic crises rocked his administration, MacDonald had abandoned the Labour Party to lead a coalition 'National' government even at the cost of significant reductions to unemployment benefits. The electorate

---

[29] G. D. H. Cole, *The Next Ten Years in British Social and Economic Policy* (London: Macmillan, 1929), 161.   [30] Cole, *Next Ten Years*, 115.

[31] H. Laski, *The Dangers of Obedience and Other Essays* (London: George Allen and Unwin, 1930), 64–6.   [32] Laski, *Dangers*, 88.

[33] H. Laski, 'The Limitations of the Expert', *Fabian Tract* 235 (London: Fabian Society, 1931), 235.

[34] W. A. Robson, 'The Problem of Liberty', *Political Quarterly*, 2 (1931), 132.

dramatically endorsed those deals in the ensuing general election: the National government gained well-over 50 per cent of the popular vote, reducing Labour's representation from 288 parliamentary seats to just 50.[35] Laski simply could not understand the British electorate's decision to reward MacDonald's underhand dealings and the National government's willingness to abandon the poorest sections of society; and, as a result, his commitment to the democratic ideal shattered. Indeed, the doubts these events spawned went far beyond Cole's questioning of the effective competency of industrial democracy; they even cast democratic forums in national politics into disrepute. 'Universal suffrage', Laski bitterly complained, 'confers political power upon the masses of citizens the greater part of whom are enfolded in a purely private life and devoid of interest in, or knowledge of the political process.'[36] The decisions of these citizens 'when they chose their governors' were thus dismissed as 'influenced by considerations which escape all scientific analysis'. Such citizens 'rush in . . . oblivious of their true interests' which they will begin to realize only long after 'the decision has been made'.[37]

In this mood of utter disillusionment, Laski turned to a brand of crude Marxism that ill suited his earlier conceptual contentions. His new ideological allegiance enabled him to insist that the political system of democracy and the economic structure of capitalism had reached a point of contradiction. The economic crisis of the depression had caused such polarization between left and right that a period of non-democratic governance was almost inevitable. Faced with increasing unemployment, desperate poverty, weakened trade unions, and National government electoral domination, reformers would have to consider radical alternatives as they battled to wrest economic power away from the current establishment. Laski tried to reassure critics that, at heart, he continued to possess 'a profounder confidence' in 'the inexpugnable rightness of democracy', but at the same time he blamed the collapse of the Labour government on the 'cumbrous' inertia of 'democratic governance'.[38] The future would not be characterized by the same mistakes. As the Labour Party disintegrated, it was now necessary to emphasize party unity rather than dissension and debate. 'We cannot afford to risk failure by being too democratic', Laski informed stupefied colleagues in 1933. And if Labour was ever to return to office, it had to ensure that it made full use of its opportunities. 'We cannot put limits to the degrees of dictatorial power' which a future 'socialist government may have to assume', Laski instructed Party workers in 1933.[39] This was language previously unthinkable from the

---

[35] For an introduction, see N. Riddell, *Labour in Crisis: The Second Labour Government, 1929–1931* (Manchester: Manchester University Press, 1999).

[36] H. Laski, *Democracy in Crisis* (London: George Allen and Unwin, 1933), 67.

[37] Laski, *Democracy*, 68–9.

[38] H. Laski, 'Mr Baldwin Seeks to Mislead', *New Clarion*, 12 August 1933, 155.

[39] H. Laski, cited in H. Morrison, 'A Reply to Harold Laski', *New Clarion*, 30 September 1933, 275.

pluralists. Laski even said the new suggestions had received their 'supreme embodiment' in the life and work of Lenin.[40]

Beyond Decline

This narrative of failure and decay has often been employed to discredit the efforts of both movements. If they could not succeed in their own time, it is argued, there can be little reason to take their arguments seriously now. Their ideas are, at most, interesting roads not taken rather than realistic visions which could then have been adopted or which should be seriously considered today.[41] As David Runciman has argued of the pluralists, their suggestions 'did not disappear through culpable neglect, but because of the very real limitations of the ideas themselves'.[42] There are those who would disagree, of course. In recent years both movements have found active champions. Communitarians and self-styled republicans have turned to the position of Croly, Lippmann, and Weyl, arguing that their emphasis on the priority of communal attachments provides a viable alternative to the implicit egoism of modern liberalism.[43] 'Associationalists' have likewise endorsed the arguments of Cole, Laski, Tawney, contending that their decentralizing ambitions are perfectly suited to an era in which 'big government' is discredited. Yet those who take up these positions now tend to stand significantly outside of the political mainstream. Michael Sandel, who employs Herbert Croly in his 'political economy of citizenship', does so largely because he is critical of the whole basis of recent American political culture for founding its political ideals on an excessively liberal dedication to personal choice.[44] Similarly, Paul Hirst, who has championed Laski and Cole in Britain, outlines plans for the large-scale deconstruction of the British state and its replacement with a network of voluntary associations that remain as much of a utopian pipe dream as Cole's, and infinitely less morally desirable.[45] These are hardly ringing endorsements for a new world.

A pessimistic evaluation of these movements and their work is, nonetheless, misplaced. Whatever the particular failures of these movements, there

---

[40] H. Laski, 'We Must Know What We Want', *New Clarion*, 4 March 1933, 243.

[41] See R. J. Lustig, *Corporate Liberalism: The Origins of Modern American Political Theory, 1890–1920* (Berkeley: University of California Press, 1982), esp. 223–6.

[42] D. Runciman, *Pluralism and the Personality of the State* (Cambridge: Cambridge University Press, 1997), 263.

[43] For a powerful discussion of this theme, see the superb D. M. Rabban, *Free Speech in its Forgotten Years* (Cambridge: Cambridge University Press, 1997), esp. 383–5.

[44] See M. Sandel, *Democracy's Discontent: America in Search of a Public Philosophy* (Cambridge, MA: Belknap Press, 1996), 201–26.

[45] See M. Stears, 'Needs, Welfare, and the Limits of Associationalism', *Economy and Society*, 28 (1999), 570–89.

are important general lessons for political theory to be found in the history
of the debate between nationalist progressives and socialist pluralists. Those
lessons, moreover, do not exist *despite* the problems the movements faced;
rather, they flow directly from the political difficulties they encountered and
the ambitions of the goals that they set. These lessons begin with a recognition that both movements struggled continuously against ill-suited political
environments; they faced enormous, and often apparently unconquerable,
institutional and social obstacles to the fulfilment of their ideals. But they
carried on nonetheless. In so doing, they recognized the importance of a key
distinction between the defining conceptual principles and values that characterize the essence of an ideology on the one hand, and the practical recommendations and policy suggestions required to realize those ideals on the
other. Moreover, both movements also understood that while this first cate-
gory—the core aims and ideals—must be stable over time, the second cate-
gory must be contingent; practical policies are required, or rejected, only as
times, events, and structures change. The acceptance of this distinction
entailed that these ideological movements had to engage both in careful
conceptual argument and in a constant reassessment of their own political
situation; they had to study the terms of the desirable *and* of the possible.
Even when they were confident that they had identified the right ideals,
therefore, they continually had to identify practical means of realizing them.
That meant a constant search for new ways to subvert prevailing tendencies
or different means of overcoming stubborn problems. Sometimes they were
overly optimistic in the practical judgements they reached—as when the
progressives attempted to construct an American Labor Party—and at other
times they were overly pessimistic—as when Cole abandoned his commitment to industrial democracy in the aftermath of the General Strike. Their
efforts, however, at combining fundamental ideals and practical political
assessment were thoughtful and considered, informed not only by close
observation of their own political circumstances but by a openness to the
workings of other political systems and social environments as well.

The movements did not accept this dual—theoretical and political—challenge simply because there were no alternatives available. It would have been
relatively easy for either group to seek refuge in the imaginary world of its
own ideal theory. They could have argued that as it was difficult to *realize*
their ideas they would restrict themselves simply to identifying the ideal position in the hope that it would be realizable at some point in the future.
Alternatively, it would also have been easy for the movements to capitulate
right from the start. They could have abandoned their fundamental commitments, redesigned their concepts of liberty and community, and confined
their programme to the need to ameliorate immediate conditions within the
confines of the available circumstances. Both of these approaches are familiar
to political theory and practice in the late twentieth and early twenty-first

centuries. All too often today, political philosophers advance ever more ambitious programmes of reform, in full knowledge that their suggestions remain unattainable.[46] Active politicians, on both left and right, meanwhile gravitate towards an ever more anodyne 'middle ground', suggesting that social, institutional, political, and economic realities render more far-reaching reforms impossible.[47]

Yet the efforts of both of these movements demonstrated that there is an alternative to these two options. Neither movement took the practical difficulties they faced as a licence for idle utopia-building, nor did they accept that a genuinely progressive political theory should be narrowly determined by contemporary institutional, social, or attitudinal constraints. Indeed, if the nationalist progressives and socialist pluralists had believed, as many early twenty-first century theorists suggest, that it 'is no use setting out principles for reforming the basic structure if in fact we have no means to implement these reforms', then they would not even have begun their project.[48] Instead, both movements were committed to the view that a democratic progressive politics must work to build a consensus in support of its values, especially when it operates in societies where its ideals are minority opinions at best. Both movements, thus, remained dedicated to a reformist agenda that was constantly informed by the aspiration of moving forwards by challenging preconceptions and undermining the constraints that prevented the attainment of their ideals. They were also particularly well informed about the means that would have to be employed. The socialist pluralists and the nationalist progressives did not seek to persuade sceptical publics through soap-box rhetoric; they were far from idle propagandists. Rather, both understood that political expectation, attitudes, and aspirations are shaped and continually reshaped by the political and social institutions in which citizens live their lives. As such, they consistently sought to craft new institutions—in industry, in education, and in social welfare—which would shape the public attitudes that would allow their conceptual goals one day to be realized. Every institutional reform they suggested, from the most minor to the most grandiose, was informed by the desire to lay the foundations for a better social order. As Cole argued, these were movements that constantly asked 'will this proposed change . . . help society along the road to the ideal . . . or will it retard its progress?'[49]

---

[46] For discussions of this trend, see D. Miller, *The Principles of Social Justice* (Cambridge, MA: Harvard University Press, 1999) and M. Stears, 'Beyond the Logic of Liberalism: Learning from Illiberalism in Britain and the United States', *Journal of Political Ideologies*, 6 (2001), 215–30.

[47] For excellent discussions of this trend, see D. Coates, *Models of Capitalism: Growth and Stagnation in the Modern Era* (Cambridge: Polity Press, 2000), esp. 258–9 and C. Hay, *The Political Economy of New Labour: Labouring under False Pretenses?* (Manchester: Manchester University Press, 2000).   [48] Miller, *Principles of Social Justice*, 6.

[49] G. D. H. Cole, *Labour in the Commonwealth: A Book for a Younger Generation* (London: Headley Bros, 1918), 140.

This is, perhaps, the single most important aspect of the legacy of the nationalist progressives and the socialist pluralists. Their recognition of the need for institutional innovation, together with their insistence that each of these innovations be informed by their fundamental ideals, sets these movements apart from both their contemporaries and from many of their successors. The nationalist progressives and socialist pluralists involved themselves in an intelligent international exchange seeking to discover new means of reconstructing the political institutions of their societies in order to achieve a series of fundamental ideals. They realized that their goals were not immediately attainable and they sought out an eclectic set of suggestions for how to move closer to them, almost irrespective of the sources from which those suggestions came. To both the socialist pluralists and the nationalist progressives, the quest for ideological fulfilment and the search for far-reaching institutional and social change were, therefore, mutually supportive projects.

Conclusion

In the second half of 1934, 20 years after he first wrote for *The New Age* and five years after he had abandoned his pluralist ideals, G. D. H. Cole wistfully retold the story of his political development for one of the many left-leaning journals then aimed at middle England. A dynamic, democratic socialism, he admitted, needed 're-stating in terms appropriate to the world to-day'. 'Would that I could re-state it', he continued, 'but very likely that must be for younger people who have not so many memories and clogging loyalties in their way.'[50] The nostalgia in the sentiment was borne out by a more general return to the older ideological commitments. Cole, Laski, and Tawney all moved back to their earlier understandings during the latter half of the 1930s, through the election of the post-Second World War Labour government and beyond. This period of conceptual reconsideration coincided remarkably clearly with the end of the Labour Party's period of convalescence after the election of 1931 and its return to electoral health. As the political and economic crises of the late 1920s and early 1930s became simply a part of the Party's folk memory, the socialist pluralists of old lost the urge to pursue revolutionary and authoritarian strategies and returned to the politics of democratic persuasion and individual freedom. The future of British reform, Harold Laski thus argued, again lay in 'decentralisation, participation . . . local self-government . . . ecclesiastical self-government . . . the trade unions and the consumers' co-operative movement'.[51]

---

[50] G. D. H. Cole, 'Guild Socialism Twenty Years Ago and Now', *New English Weekly*, 13 September 1934, 6.
[51] H. Laski, *Will Planning Restrict Freedom?* (Cheam: The Architectural Press, 1945), 8–9.

By itself, of course, the return to these original conceptual formulas no more demonstrated their validity than the socialist pluralists' abandonment of them in the early 1930s had illustrated their invalidity. The socialist pluralists were certainly not joined in such a reconsideration by Walter Lippmann, who railed against the reformism of Roosevelt's New Deal throughout the 1930s, even when those measures reflected many of the nationalist progressive ideals of old.[52] More fundamentally, the theories and suggestions the socialist pluralists and nationalist progressives developed are, of course, still open to a large number of potential criticisms. It may appear that the life of creative experimentation for which the pluralists' strove, while fitting for some, may be paradoxically stifling for others. Not every citizen, after all, would flourish in a society that demanded continual scepticism, questioning, and self-improvement. Similarly, the nationalist progressives' insistence on national communal loyalty, while responding positively to the sectional conflicts of class tension, may be less suited to societies that exhibit divisions along other lines, including gender, race, and religious allegiance.

The central aim of this book has not been, however, to argue that early twenty-first century theorists should simply pick up progressive or pluralist political theorizing and attempt to employ it in modern debates and controversies. Rather, it has been to establish a new detailed account of an ideological debate that exercised a wide range of talented and committed political theorists in the first few decades of the twentieth century. The book has established that this debate was not a simplistic argument about the position of the central state. It was, instead, a sophisticated exchange of views by two movements struggling to pursue deeply held political convictions in polities that were not conducive to them and in societies which often refused to accept even the most attractive of their ideals. In this light, the debate's continuing appeal becomes clearer still. The aspirations of the nationalist progressives and the socialist pluralists remain a vigorous counterblast to many of the dominant tendencies in political thought today, tendencies which too often embrace either an overly utopian form of ideal philosophizing or an excessively narrow and pessimistic form of determinism. Seen in this way, the arguments between Laski, Cole, and Tawney in Britain and Croly, Lippmann, and Weyl in the United States produced two movements in ideology that continue to assert their relevance to this day.

[52] See Steel, *Walter Lippmann*, 321–6.

SELECT BIBIOGRAPHY

Primary Sources

Manuscripts and personal papers

Balliol College, Oxford
   A. L. Smith Papers
Bodleian Library, Oxford
   Oxford University Archive
   A. Zimmern Papers
British Library of Political Science, London
   R. H. Tawney Papers
   G. Wallas Papers
Harvard Law Library, Harvard University, Cambridge MA
   L. Hand Papers
   F. Frankfurter Papers (Microform)
Labor–Management Documentation Center, Cornell University, Ithaca.
   American Association for Labor Legislation Papers
   A. J. Muste Papers (Microform)
   O. Tead Papers
   Workers' Education Bureau Records
Nuffield College, Oxford
   R. Bedford Papers
   G. D. H. Cole Papers
   National Guild League Pamphlet Collection
Ruskin College, Oxford
   F. Casey Papers
Ruskin College Archive
Rutgers University Library, New Brunswick
   W. Weyl Papers
Social-Welfare History Archive, University of Minnesota
   P. Kellogg Papers
   Survey Associates Records
Workers' Educational Association, Temple House, London
   Workers' Educational Association Papers
Yale University Library, New Haven
   W. Lippmann Papers

Official publications

Interim Report of the Adult Education Committee of the Ministry of Reconstruction, 1919
Report of the Adult Education Committee of the Ministry of Reconstruction, 1919

Report of the Royal Commission on the Coal Industry, 1919
Report on the Establishment and Progress of Joint Industrial Control, 1918
Report of the President's Committee on Unemployment, 1921

Conference proceedings, minutes

American Political Science Association, Proceedings
American Federation of Labor, Reports of Conventions
Aristotelian Society, Proceedings
British Institute of Adult Education, Annual Conference Reports
National Council of Labour Colleges, Reports and Directories
Rainbow Circle, Minutes
Rand School of Social Science, American Labor Year Books
Trade Union Congress, Annual Conference Reports
Labour Party, Annual Conference Reports
Labour Party, Report on Social Insurance and Trade Union Membership
Workers' Educational Association, Annual Reports and Yearbooks

Newspapers, periodicals, yearbooks

Adelphi
American Economic Review
American Political Science Review
Annals of the American Academy of Political and Social Science
Blue Book
Contemporary Review
Dial
Economic Journal
Fabian News
Freeman
Good Government
Guild Socialist
Guildsman
Harvard Law Review
Highway
Intercollegiate Socialist
International Journal of Ethics
Journal of Adult Education
Journal of Philosophy
Labor Age
Manchester Guardian
Nation
Nation (New York)
New Clarion
New Age
New Republic

New Standards
New Statesman
New York Call
Philosophical Quarterly
Political Quarterly
Political Science Quarterly
The Public
Rand School News
Socialist Review
Survey
Yale Law Journal
The World Tomorrow

Signed articles and books (editorial articles and anonymous works are as cited in the text)

Alder, F., *An Ethical Philosophy of Life* (New York: D. Appleton and Co., 1918).

Arnold, M., 'Democracy', in S. Collini (ed.), *Matthew Arnold: Culture and Anarchy and Other Essays* (Cambridge: Cambridge University Press, 1994).

Bakewell, C. M., 'Royce as an Interpreter of American Ideals', *International Journal of Ethics*, 27 (1917), 306–16.

Balmforth, R., 'The Influence of Darwinian Theory on Ethics', *International Journal of Ethics*, 21 (1911), 448–65.

Barker, E., 'The Discredited State', *Political Quarterly*, 5 (1915), 101–21.

Beard, C., 'Introduction', in S. Zimmand (ed.), *Modern Social Movements* (New York: Bureau for Industrial Research, 1921) .

Bellamy, E., *Looking Backward* (Toronto: G. N. Morang, 1897).

Bosanquet, B., *Essays and Addresses* (London: Swan Sonnenshein and Co., 1889).

—— *The Philosophical Theory of the State* (London: Macmillan, 1899).

—— 'A Note on Mr Cole's Paper', *Proceedings of the Aristotelian Society*, 15 (1915), 160–3.

—— 'The Function of the State in Promoting the Unity of Mankind', *Proceedings of the Aristotelian Society*, 17 (1917), 28–57.

Bosanquet, H., *Rich and Poor* (London, 1896).

Boudin, L. B., 'Government by Judiciary', *Political Science Quarterly*, 26 (1911), 238–70.

Bourne, R., 'A Moral Equivalent for Universal Military Service', *New Republic*, 1 July 1916, 217–19.

—— 'The Guild Idyll', *New Republic*, 2 March 1918, 151–2.

—— 'American Uses for German Ideals', *New Republic*, 4 September 1925, 117–19.

Bradley, F. H., *Essays on Truth and Reality* (Oxford: Oxford University Press, 1914).

—— *Ethical Studies* (Oxford: Oxford University Press, 1927).

Brandeis, L. B., *The Curse of Bigness: the Miscellaneous Papers of Louis D. Brandeis* (Port Washington, NY: Kennikat Press, 1965).

Brooks, J. G., *Labor's Challenge to the Social Order: Democracy its Own Critic and Educator* (New York: Macmillan, 1920).

Brown, H. C., 'Human Nature and the State', *International Journal of Ethics*, 26 (1915), 177–92.

Brown, I., 'Aspects of the Guild Idea', *New Age*, 24 June 1915, 175.

—— 'Democracy and the Guilds', *New Age*, 18 February 1915, 436–7.

—— 'Trade Unionism without Tears', *New Age*, 11 November 1915, 44.

—— 'Freedom and Dr Figgis', *Guildsman*, December 1919, 7.

—— *English Political Theory* (London: Methuen, 1920).

—— 'Freedom and Dr Figgis (continued)', *Guildsman*, February 1920, 7.

Burns, C. D., 'Principles of Social Reconstruction', *International Journal of Ethics*, 27 (1917), 384–7.

—— *The Philosophy of Labour* (London: George Allen and Unwin, 1925).

Calhoun, W., 'Education and the State', *Rand School News and Book Review*, 4 December 1920, 2.

Carrel, F., *An Analysis of Human Motive* (London: Simpkin, 1905).

Chesterton, G. K., *The Man Who Was Thursday: A Nightmare* (Bristol: Arrowsmith, 1908).

Clendenning, J. (ed.), *The Letters of Josiah Royce* (Chicago: Chicago University Press, 1970).

Cohen, J. L., *Insurance by Industry Examined* (London: P. S. King and Son, 1923).

Cohen, M., 'Communal Ghosts and Other Perils in Social Philosophy', *Journal of Philosophy*, 16 (1919), 673–90.

—— 'On American Philosophy: the Idealistic Tradition and Josiah Royce', *New Republic*, 3 September 1919, 148–50.

Cole, G. D. H. (ed.), *Jean Jacques Rousseau: The Social Contract and the Discourses* (London: Everyman, 1913).

—— 'An Oxford Summer School', *The Blue Book*, 5 (1913), 14.

—— *The World of Labour: A Discussion of the Present and the Future of Trade Unionism* (London: G. Bell, 1913, 2nd edn 1917).

—— 'Freedom in the Guild', *New Age*, 5 November 1914, 7–8.

—— 'Guild Socialism', *Fabian News*, November 1914, 83.

—— *The British Labour Movement* (London: National Guilds League, 1915).

—— 'Conflicting Social Obligations', *Proceedings of the Aristotelian Society*, 15 (1915), 140–59.

—— 'Democracy and the Guilds', *New Age*, 4 February 1915, 370–1.

—— 'National Guilds and the Balance of Powers', *New Age*, 16 November 1916, 58–9.

—— 'National Guilds and the Division of Power', *New Age*, 14 December 1916, 153–4.

—— 'The State and its External Relations', *Proceedings of the Aristotelian Society*, 16 (1916), 310–23.

—— 'Reflections on the Wage System', *New Age*, 29 March 1917, 513–15.

—— *Self-Government in Industry* (London: G. Bell and Sons, 1917).

—— 'British Labor in Wartime', *New Republic*, 1 June 1918, 142–3.

—— *Labour in the Commonwealth: A Book for a Younger Generation* (London: Headley Bros, 1918).

—— *The Payment of Wages: A Study in Payment by Results in the Wage–System* (London: George Allen and Unwin, 1918, 2nd edn 1928).

—— 'The Coal Question in Great Britain', *New Republic*, 10 September 1919, 171–3.

—— 'A Mining Guild', *New Age*, 8 May 1919, 22–3.

—— 'National Guilds and the State', *Socialist Review*, 16 (1919), 22–31.

—— 'A Wasting Asset of Industry', *New Statesman*, 20 December 1919, 342.

—— 'The Basis of Wages', *New Statesman*, 17 April 1920, 35.

Cole, G. D. H., *Chaos and Order in Industry* (London: Methuen, 1920).

—— 'The Consumer Pays', *New Statesman*, 20 March 1920, 700.

—— 'Guild Socialism', in *American Labor Year Book 1919–1920* (New York: Rand School of Social Science, 1920) .

—— *Guild Socialism* (London: Fabian Society, 1920).

—— *Guild Socialism Restated* (London: Leonard Parsons, 1920).

—— 'Motives in Industry', *The Venturer*, 1 (1920), 201–8.

—— 'Profit Sharing', *New Statesman*, 8 May 1920, 123.

—— *Social Theory* (London: Methuen, 1920).

—— 'The Spread of Unemployment', *New Statesman*, 16 October 1920, 38–9.

—— 'Trade Unions and Democracy', *New Statesman*, 30 October 1920, 97–9.

—— 'What is the State?', *The Venturer*, 1 (1920), 527–30.

—— 'The Gun That Did Not Go Off', *New Statesman*, 23 April 1921, 67–8.

—— 'Labour's Unemployment Proposals', *New Statesman*, 29 February 1921, 494.

—— 'The Reduction of Wages', *New Statesman*, 18 June 1921, 295.

—— 'The Swing of the Pendulum', *New Statesman*, 16 July 1921, 406–7.

—— *Unemployment and Industrial Maintenance* (London: National Guilds League, 1921).

—— 'The Attack on the Trade Boards', *New Statesman*, 2 September 1922, 87–9.

—— 'The Building Guilds', *New Statesman*, 25 February 1922, 585.

—— 'Can We Dispense with the Ministry of Labour?', *New Statesman*, 18 February 1922, 551.

—— 'The Doubtful Value of Lectures', *New Statesman*, 7 October 1922, 9.

—— 'The First Charge upon Industry', *New Statesman*, 15 July 1922, 409.

—— 'The Government and the Unemployed', *New Statesman*, 11 November 1922, 166.

—— 'Labour in the First Session', *New Statesman*, 23 December 1922, 349–50.

—— 'The New Spirit in Industry', *New Statesman*, 1 January 1922, 389–90.

—— 'On Payment by Results', *New Statesman*, 3 June 1922, 233.

—— 'Slave Virtues and Other Virtues', *New Statesman*, 14 January 1922, 413–4.

—— 'The Unity of Trade Unionism', *New Statesman*, 22 April 1922, 59.

—— 'The Cost of Idleness', *New Statesman*, 13 January 1923, 421–2.

—— 'Education in the New Parliament', *New Statesman*, 8 December 1923, 264–5.

—— 'The Industrial Outlook', *New Statesman*, 18 August 1923, 538–9.

—— 'The Leach Gatherer', *Socialist Review*, 21 (1923), 265–70.

—— 'The One Thing Needed', *New Statesman*, 24 November 1923, 201–3.

—— 'The Question of the Hour', *New Statesman*, 13 October 1923, 5–6.

—— 'The Future of Social Insurance', *New Statesman*, 12 March 1924, 7–8.

—— 'The Labour Government and Workers' Control', *New Standards*, October 1924, 361.

—— 'Mr Shaw's Unemployment Bill', *New Statesman*, 28 June 1924, 342.

—— 'The Minimum Wage', *Socialist Review*, 22 (1924), 58–63.

—— 'Wages in the Countryside', *New Statesman*, 7 June 1924, 244.

—— 'Wages: The Relativity Myth', *New Statesman*, 26 March 1924, 57–8.

—— 'Actual Wages', *New Statesman*, 21 March 1925, 684.

—— 'The Case for Higher Wages', *New Statesman*, 14 February 1925, 525–6.

—— 'Cross–Roads in Adult Education', *New Statesman*, 29 August 1925, 542.

—— 'Unemployment', *New Statesman*, 14 March 1925, 650.

—— *The Next Ten Years in British Social and Economic Policy* (London: Macmillan, 1929).

—— *Incentives under Socialism* (Girard, Kansas: Haldeman-Julius, 1931).

—— 'Why I am a Socialist', *Adelphi*, December 1932, 183–90.

—— 'Guild Socialism Twenty Years Ago and Now', *New English Weekly*, 13 September 1934, 415–17.

—— (ed.), *J. J. Rousseau: The Social Contract* (London: Everyman, 1993).

—— and Freeman, A., 'Why the Workers Should Demand Education', *WEA Year Book* (London: Workers' Educational Association, 1918), 56.

—— and Mellor, W., *The Meaning of Industrial Freedom* (London: George Allen and Unwin, 1918).

Cooley, C. H., 'The Process of Social Change', *Political Science Quarterly*, 12 (1897), 63–74.

—— *Human Nature and the Social Order* (New York: C. Scribner's Sons, 1902).

—— *Social Organization* (New York: C. Schribner and Son, 1909).

Cramp, C. T., 'What Education Means', *Highway*, February 1927, 92.

Croly, H., *The Promise of American Life* (New York: Macmillan, 1909).

—— 'State Political Reorganization', *Proceedings of the American Political Science Association*, 8 (1911), 122–35.

—— *Progressive Democracy* (New York: Macmillan, 1914).

—— 'The Obligation of the Vote', *New Republic*, 9 October 1915, 5–10.

—— 'The Future of the State', *New Republic*, 15 September 1917, 179–83.

—— 'A School for Social Research', *New Republic*, 8 June 1918, 167–71.

—— 'Education for Grown–Ups', *New Republic*, 12 December 1923, 59–61.

Dewey, J., 'Vocational Education', *New Republic*, 11 March 1916, 159.

—— 'A New Social Science', *New Republic*, 6 April 1918, 292–4.

—— 'Creative Industry', *New Republic*, 2 November 1918, 20–2.

—— *Democracy and Education* (New York: Macmillan, 1922).

—— *Human Nature and Conduct* (New York: The Modern Library, 1922, 2nd edn 1930).

—— 'The Principle of Nationality', in J. A. Boyd (ed.), *Collected Works of John Dewey: Middle Works* (Carbondale: Southern Illinois Press, 1980) .

—— 'The Ethics of Democracy', in A. S. Sharpe (ed.), *John Dewey: The Early Works* (Carbondale: Southern Illinois University Press, 1988) .

—— and Tufts, J. H., *Ethics* (New York: Macmillan, 1908).

Douglas, H., 'Apprenticeships and Industrial Education', in *American Labor Year Book 1917–1918* (New York: Rand School of Social Science, 1918).

Duffus, R. L., 'The Twilight of Natural Rights', *New Republic*, 2 March 1918, 139–40.

Dunning, W. A., *A History of Political Theories* (New York: Macmillan, 1920).

Elliott, W. Y., *The Pragmatic Revolt in Politics: Syndicalism, Fascism and the Corporate State* (New York: Macmillan, 1928).

Field, G., *Guild Socialism: A Critical Examination* (London: W. Gardner, Darton and Co., 1920).

Figgis, J. N., *The Gospel and Human Needs* (London: Longmans, Green and Co., 1909).

—— *Churches in the Modern State* (London: Longmans, Green and Co., 1914).

Fitch, J. A., 'Labor and Politics', *Survey*, 8 June 1918, 287–9.

Follett, M., *The New State: Group Organization the Solution of Popular Government* (New York: Longmans, Green and Co., 1918).

Ford, H. J., 'The Promise of American Life', *American Political Science Review*, 4 (1910), 614–16.

Frankfurter, F., 'The Constitutional Opinions of Justice Holmes', *Harvard Law Review*, 29 (1916), 683–99.

Freeden, M. (ed.), *Minutes of the Rainbow Circle* (London: Royal Historical Society, 1989).

Gaitskill, H., 'At Oxford in the Twenties', in A. Briggs and J. Saville (eds), *Essays in Labour History* (London: Macmillan, 1967).

Gleason, A., 'The Discovery', *Survey*, 19 May 1917, 151–9.

—— *Inside the British Isles* (New York: Century Co., 1917).

—— 'The Shop Stewards and Their Significance', *Survey*, 4 January 1919, 417–22.

—— *What the Workers Want: A Study of British Labour* (London: George Allen and Unwin, 1920).

—— 'Workers' Education in Britain', *New Republic*, 20 April 1921, 237.

—— *Workers' Education: American and Foreign Experiments* (New York: Bureau of Industrial Research, 1921).

—— and Kellogg, P., *British Labor and the War: Reconstructors of a New World* (New York: Boni and Liveright, 1919).

—— and Miller, S. (eds), *Workers' Education* (New York: Workers Education Bureau, 1921).

Golden, C. S., 'The Workers Educate Themselves', *Labor Age*, 4 April 1922, 1.

Goldmark, J., 'Minimum Wage in Practice', *New Republic*, 25 December 1915, 204–5.

Green, T. H., *Lectures on the Principles of Political Obligation* (Cambridge: Cambridge University Press, 1986).

Haines, C. G., *The American Doctrine of Judicial Supremacy* (Berkeley: University of California Press, 1932).

Halsey, O. S., 'Health Insurance', *Intercollegiate Socialist* , 6 (1918), 23–6.

Hammond, J. L., 'The New Outlook in Industry', *New Republic*, 7 March 1923, 50–1.

Hand, L., 'Due Process of Law and the Eight Hour Day', *Harvard Law Review*, 21 (1908), 495–509.

Harris, W. T., *Psychologic Foundations of Education: An Attempt to Show the Genius of the Higher Faculties of Mind* (New York: Macmillan, 1898).

Hearnshaw, F. J. C., *Democracy and Labour* (London: Macmillan, 1924).

Henderson, A., 'The Industrial Unrest: A New Policy Required', *Contemporary Review*, 115 (1919), 361–8.

Hetherington, H. J. W., 'The Conception of a Unitary Social Order', *Proceedings of the Aristotelian Society*, 18 (1918), 286–316.

Hobhouse, L. T., *Democracy and Reaction* (London: T. F. Unwin, 1909).

—— 'The Right to a Living Wage', in W. Temple (ed.), *The Industrial Unrest and the Living Wage* (London: Collegium, 1913).

—— 'The New Democracy', *Manchester Guardian*, 19 April 1920.

—— 'A Ground Plan for Socialism', *Manchester Guardian*, 21 September 1920.

Hobson, J. A., *The Crisis of Liberalism: New Issues of Democracy* (London: E. S. King and Son, 1909).

—— 'The New Industrial Revolution', *Contemporary Review*, 118 (1920), 638–45.

—— *Incentives in the New Industrial Order* (London: Leonard Parsons, 1922).

—— 'The Cry for Productivity', *Nation (NY)*, 18 March 1925, 291.

—— *Veblen* (London: Chapman and Hall, 1936).

Hobson, S. G., 'Guilds and their Critics: Nation, State and Government', *New Age*, 13 June 1918, 101.

Hodgen, M. T., 'Workers Education in England and the United States', *New Statesman*, 7 April 1925, 330.

Hodges, F., *Nationalisation of the Mines* (London: Leonard Parsons, 1920).

Hsiao, K., *Political Pluralism: A Study in Contemporary Political Theory* (London: Kegan Paul, 1921).

Hughan, J., 'Cultural vs. Vocational Training', *Intercollegiate Socialist*, 7 (1918), 25.

—— 'Changing Conceptions of the State', *Socialist Review*, 7 (1920), 165–8.

—— 'Guildsmen and American Socialism', *Intercollegiate Socialist*, 7 (1918), 19–23.

James, W., 'On Some Hegelisms', in W. James (ed.), *The Will to Believe and Other Essays* (New York: Longmans, Green and Co., 1909).

—— *Some Problems in Philosophy* (London: Longmans, Green and Co., 1911).

Johnson, A., 'Revolutionary Reconstruction', *New Republic*, 15 December 1920, 80.

—— 'The New School for Social Research', in S. Hook and M. R. Konovitz (eds), *Freedom and Experience: Essays Presented to Horace M. Kallen* (Ithaca: Cornell University Press, 1947).

—— *Pioneer's Progress: An Autobiography* (New York: Viking Press, 1952).

Laski, H., 'The Case for Conscription', *New Republic*, 6 November 1915, 22–3.

—— 'The Apotheosis of the State', *New Republic*, 22 July 1916, 302–4.

—— 'The Basis of Vicarious Liability', *Yale Law Journal*, 26 (1916), 105–35.

—— 'Sovereignty and Centralization', *New Republic*, 16 December 1916, 176–8.

—— 'A Wrong Kind of Textbook', *New Republic*, 1 July 1916, 232.

—— 'Can the State Survive?', *New Republic*, 21 April 1917.

—— 'Nietzsche's Religion: Review of Figgis', *New Republic*, 28 July 1917, 364.

—— *Studies in the Problem of Sovereignty* (New Haven: Yale University Press, 1917).

—— 'A Labor Programme', *New Republic*, 9 March 1918, 179–80.

—— 'Industrial Self–Government', *New Republic*, 27 April 1918, 391–3.

—— 'Labor and the State', *New Republic*, 1 June 1918, 151–2.

—— 'The Aims of Labor', *New Republic*, 8 June 1918, 179–80.

—— 'The Responsible State', *New Republic*, 14 September 1918, 203–4.

—— 'Federal Power', *New Republic*, 23 November 1918, 108–9.

—— 'Church and State', *New Republic*, 30 November 1918, 141–2.

—— 'Freedom', *New Republic*, 21 December 1918, 228–9.

—— 'The New State', *New Republic*, 8 February 1919, 61.

—— 'Adult Education', *New Republic*, 20 March 1919, 283.

—— *Authority in the Modern State* (New Haven: Yale University Press, 1919).

—— 'British Reconstruction Proposals and the American Attitude', *Proceedings of the Academy of Political Science*, 8 (1919), 193–7.

—— 'The Meaning of National Guilds', *Political Science Quarterly*, 34 (1919), 668.

—— 'The Pluralistic State', *Journal of Philosophy* 16 (1919), 717–18.

—— 'Rousseau', *New Republic*, 16 July 1919, 364.

—— 'The Workers as Citizens', *New Republic*, 11 February 1920, 322.

—— 'The Temper of the Present Time', *New Republic*, 18 February 1920, 335–8.

—— *The Foundations of Sovereignty and Other Essays* (New Haven: Yale University Press, 1921).

—— 'Mr. Wallace as Social Analyst', *Nation*, 9 April 1921, 60–2.

—— 'Surveying the Wreck', *Nation*, 23 April 1921, 133–4.

—— 'More of the Adams', *Nation*, 6 August 1921, 687.

Laski, H., 'The Student's Note Book', *Highway*, September 1921, 198–9.

—— 'The Co-operative Movement', *New Republic*, 14 June 1922, 80–1.

—— *The State in the New Social Order* (London: Fabian Society, 1922).

—— 'Can Political Democracy Survive?', *Fabian News*, November 1923, 42–3.

—— 'Birthday Greetings', *Nation (N Y)*, 26 August 1925, 33.

—— 'Knowledge', in O. Stanley (ed.), *The Way Out: Essays on the Meaning and Purpose of Adult Education* (Oxford: Oxford University Press, 1925).

—— 'Lecture on Political Freedom', *Fabian News*, December 1925, 51.

—— *Socialism and Freedom* (London: Fabian Society, 1925).

—— *A Grammar of Politics* (London: George Allen and Unwin, 1925, 2nd edn 1930).

—— 'Research and Adult Education', *Journal of Adult Education*, 1 (1926), 11–26.

—— *The Dangers of Obedience and Other Essays* (London: George Allen and Unwin, 1930).

—— *Liberty in the Modern State* (London: George Allen and Unwin, 1930).

—— *The Limitations of the Expert* (London: Fabian Society, 1931).

—— *Democracy in Crisis* (London: George Allen and Unwin, 1933).

—— 'We Must Know What We Want', *New Clarion*, 4 March 1933, 243.

—— 'Mr Baldwin's Seeks to Mislead', *New Clarion*, 12 August 1933, 155.

—— *Will Planning Restrict Freedom?* (Cheam: Architectural Press, 1945).

Lawson, J., 'Editorial', *Highway*, February 1922, 76.

Lindsay, A. D., 'The State in Recent Political Theory', *Philosophical Quarterly*, 1 (1914), 128–45.

Lippmann, W., *A Preface to Politics* (New York: M. Kennerley, 1913).

—— *Drift and Mastery: An Attempt to Diagnose the Current Unrest* (New York: M. Kennerley, 1914).

—— 'Our Stupid Anti–Trust Laws', *New York Call*, 6 July 1914, 6.

—— 'The Campaign Against Sweating', *New Republic*, 27 March 1915, Special Supplement.

—— 'The Hope of Democracy', *New Republic*, 1 July 1916, 231.

—— 'A Clue', *New Republic*, 14 April 1917, 316–17.

—— 'Authority in the Modern State', *New Republic*, 31 May 1919, 148–9.

—— 'Unrest', *New Republic*, 12 November 1919, 315–22.

—— 'Can the Strike be Abandoned?', *New Republic*, 21 January 1920, 224–7.

—— *Public Opinion* (New York: Macmillan, 1922).

—— *The Phantom Public: A Sequel to Public Opinion* (New York: Macmillan, 1925).

Lovett, R., 'The Farmer–Labor Fiasco at Chicago', *New Republic*, 18 July 1923, 198–200.

McBain, H. L., 'The New State', *Political Science Quarterly*, 34 (1919), 167–70.

MacDonald, J. R., *Democracy and Character* (London: Independent Labour Party, 1905).

—— *Socialism and Society* (London: Independent Labour Party, 1907).

—— *Socialism and Government* (London: Independent Labour Party, 1909).

—— *Socialism After the War* (Manchester: National Labour Press, 1918).

—— *Socialism: Critical and Constructive* (London: Cassell and Co., 1921).

MacIver, R., 'The S... macy of the State', *New Republic*, 13 October 1917, 304.

—— *Commu... Sociological Study* (London: Macmillan, 1917).

Maeztu, R. de, 'Not Happiness', *New Age*, 8 July 1915, 225–6.

—— 'On Liberty and Organisation', *New Age*, 19 August 1915, 377–8.

Mansbridge, A., *University Tutorial Classes: A Study in the Development of Higher Education among Working Men and Women* (London: Longmans, Green and Co., 1913).

Matson, M., 'Correspondence', *Highway*, February 1919, 47.

Meeker, R., 'The Promise of American Life', *Political Science Quarterly*, 25 (1910), 688–99.

Merz, C., 'Enter: The Labor Party', *New Republic*, 10 December 1919, 53–5.

Mill, J. S., 'On Liberty', in M. Warnock (ed.), *Utilitarianism, On Liberty, and Essay on Bentham* (London: Fontana, 1979).

Miller, S. (ed.), *Workers Education in the United States* (New York: Workers Education Bureau, 1921).

Mitchell, B., *How to Start Workers' Classes* (New York: Workers Education Bureau, 1921).

—— *Abstract of British Historical Statistics* (Cambridge: Cambridge University Press, 1971).

Morrison, H., 'A Reply to Harold Laski', *New Clarion*, 30 September 1933, 275.

Mufson, I., 'What Did I Get Out of It?', *Labor Age*, April 1924, 7.

Muirhead, J. H., *The Platonic Tradition in Anglo–Saxon Philosophy: Studies in the History of Idealism in England and America* (London: George Allen and Unwin, 1931).

Ogilvey, E. T., 'The Better Way', in J. Strachey (ed.), *The Manufacture of Paupers: A Protest and a Policy* (London: John Murray, 1906) .

Olds, L., 'The Temper of British Labor', *Nation (NY)*, 19 April 1919, 601–3.

Osborne, C. H. C., 'Self–Government in Schools', *Guildsman*, October 1921, 4.

Overstreet, H. A., 'The New State', *Journal of Philosophy*, 16 (1919), 582–5.

Patten, S. N., *The Theory of Social Forces* (Philadelphia: American Academy of Political and Social Science, 1896).

—— *The New Basis of Civilization* (New York: Macmillan, 1907).

Pease, E., 'Self–Government in Industry', *Fabian News*, February 1918, 11–12.

Penty, A., 'Can Our Industrial System Survive?', *Guildsman*, May 1921, 9.

Philips, H., 'The Control of Industry', *Economic Journal*, 33 (1923), 384–7.

Poole, E., 'Exploration', in M. Weyl (ed.), *Walter Weyl: An Appreciation* (Philadelphia: Privately Published, 1922) .

Post, L., *The Deportations Delirium of Nineteen–Twenty: A Personal Narrative of an Historic Official Experience* (Chicago: C. H. Kerr and Co., 1923).

Pound, R., 'Common Law and Legislation', *Harvard Law Review*, 21 (1908), 383–407.

Powell, T. R., 'Separation of Powers: Administrative Exercise of Legislative and Judicial Power', *Political Science Quarterly*, 27 (1912), 215–38.

—— T. R., 'The Logic and Rhetoric of Constitutional Law', *Journal of Philosophy*, 15 (1918), 645–58.

—— 'The Functional Organization of Society', *Nation (NY)*, 13 October 1920, 413–14.

Putnam, E. J., 'The New School for Social Research', *New Republic*, 4 February 1920, 294.

Randall, A. E., 'Autocracy and the Guilds', *New Age*, 11 February 1915, 408–9.

Randall, H. K., 'Why Workers' Education', *New Republic*, 16 November 1921, 351.

Ratcliffe, S. K., 'Enrolling the English Nation', *New Republic* 1915, 205–7.

Ritchie, D. G., *The Principles of State Interference* (London: Swan Sonnenshein and Co., 1891).

—— *Darwinism and Politics* (London: Swan Sonnenschein and Co., 1901).

—— *Studies in Political and Social Ethics* (London: Swan Sonnenshein, 1902).

Robertson, D. H., 'Mr Cole's Social Theories', *Economic Journal*, 30 (1920), 536–41.

—— 'Social Theory', *Economic Journal*, 31 (1920), 229–31.

Robieson, M. W., 'On Certain First Principles', *New Age*, 25 July 1918, 197–8.

Robson, W. A., 'A Grammar of Politics', *Fabian News*, September 1925, 38.

—— 'The Problem of Liberty', *Political Quarterly*, 2 (1931), 132–3.

Rockow, L., *Contemporary Political Thought in England* (London: Leonard Parsons, 1925).

Rowntree, S. B., *Poverty: A Study of Town Life* (London: Macmillan, 1901).

Royce, J., *The World and the Individual* (New York: Macmillan, 1901).

—— *The Philosophy of Loyalty* (New York: Macmillan, 1908).

Russell, B., *Principles of Social Reconstruction* (London: George Allen and Unwin, 1916).

—— 'The State and its External Relations', *Proceedings of the Aristotelian Society*, 16 (1916), 301–10.

—— 'Why I am a Guildsman', *Guildsman*, September 1919, 3.

Schutze, M., 'As I Knew Him in Woodstock', in M. Weyl (ed.), *Walter Weyl: An Appreciation* (Philadelphia: Privately published, 1922) .

Shelton, H. S., 'The Hegelian Concept of the State', *International Journal of Ethics*, 24 (1913), 23–37.

Smith, E., 'The New School for Social Research: Preliminary Lectures', *New Republic*, 18 January 1918, 350.

Smith, T. V., *The American Philosophy of Equality* (Chicago: Chicago University Press, 1927).

Starr, M., 'More About Education with a Punch', *Labor Age*, October 1924, 10–11.

Stevenson, C., 'The Demand for Output', *Guildsman*, November 1919, 5–6.

Taussig, F. W., *Principles of Economics* (New York: Macmillan, 1911).

Tawney, R. H., *Studies in the Minimum Wage* (London: G. Bell, 1918).

—— 'The Case for the Consumer', *Guildsman*, December 1919, 3.

—— 'The Coal Industry and the Consumer', *Contemporary Review*, 116 (1919), 144–54.

—— *The Educational Needs of Democracy* (Leeds: Yorkshire WEA, 1919).

—— *The Nationalisation of the Coal Industry* (London: Labour Party, 1919).

—— 'Recent Thoughts on Government in Industry', in P. Alden (ed.), *Labour and Industry* (Manchester: Manchester University Press, 1920).

—— *The Acquisitive Society* (London: G. Bell, 1921).

—— 'The Unemployment Crisis in England', *New Republic*, 23 February 1921, 367–8.

—— 'Industry and the Expert', *Guildsman*, June 1921, 4–5.

—— 'The Minimum Wage in Britain', *New Republic*, 28 June 1922, 126.

—— 'The Future of the WEA', *Highway*, October 1928, 3.

—— *Equality* (London: George Allen and Unwin, 1938).

—— *The Webbs in Perspective* (London: George Allen and Unwin, 1953).

—— 'The Conditions of Economic Liberty', in R. Hinden (ed.), *The Radical Tradition: Twelve Essays on Politics, Education and Literature* (London: George Allen and Unwin, 1964).

—— *The Commonplace Book* (Cambridge: Cambridge University Press, 1972).

—— 'Poverty as an Industrial Problem', in J. Winter (ed.), *The American Labour Movement and Other Essays* (New York: St. Martin's Press, 1979).

Tead, O., 'Trade Unions and Efficiency', *American Journal of Sociology*, 22 (1916), 30–7.

—— 'A National Labor Policy', *New Republic*, 17 November 1917, 67–9.

—— 'The Development of the Guild Idea', *Intercollegiate Socialist*, 6 (1918), 16–19.

—— 'National Control of Railroads', *Intercollegiate Socialist*, 6 (1918), 4–6.

—— 'Productivity and Reconstruction', *The Public*, 16 March 1918, 332–4.

—— 'Guilds for America', *Intercollegiate Socialist*, 7 (1919), 31–3.

—— 'The Meaning of National Guilds', *The Dial*, 23 August 1919, 150–2.

—— 'National Organization by Industries: England', *New Republic*, 8 February 1919, 48–51.

—— 'The Bases of Social Theory', *The Freeman*, 7 June 1920, 406.

—— 'Self–Government in Industry', *The Freeman*, 9 February 1921, 525.

—— 'The World Tomorrow', *The World Tomorrow*, March 1921, 87–8.

—— 'Partners and Citizens in Industry', *New Republic*, 22 March 1922, 116–18.

—— and R. Valentine., 'Work and Pay', *Quarterly Journal of Economics*, 31 (1917), 241–58.

Thompson, J. A., 'Progress in Evolution', *New Statesman*, 3 July 1920, 360–1.

Toynbee, A., 'Are Radicals Socialists?', in A. Toynbee (ed.), *Lectures on the Industrial Revolution* (London: Beacon Press, 1908) .

Veblen, T., 'A Policy of Reconstruction', *New Republic*, 13 April 1918, 318–20.

Vernon, H., *Industrial Fatigue and Efficiency* (London: G. Routledge and Sons, 1921).

Vivian, H., 'National Guilds and the State', *Economic Journal*, 30 (1920), 233–7.

Wallas, G., *Human Nature and Politics* (London: Constable and Co., 1910).

—— 'The Acquisitive Society', *Nation*, 11 June 1921, 401.

Walling, W. E., 'Progressive Democracy', *American Economic Review*, 5 (1915), 380–1.

Watson, F. D., *The Charity Organization Movement in the United States: A Study in American Philanthropy* (New York: Macmillan, 1922).

Webb, S., *The Necessary Basis of Society* (London: Fabian Society, 1906).

—— 'The Difficulties of Individualism', in S. Webb (ed.), *Socialism and Individualism* (London: Fifield, 1909).

—— *Towards Social Democracy: A Study of Social Evolution During the Past Three–Quarters of a Century* (London: Fabian Society, 1909).

—— 'The Living Wage', *Fabian News*, January 1913, 15.

—— *The Works Manager To-Day: An Address Prepared for a Series of Private Gatherings with Works Managers* (London: Longmans, Green and Co., 1917).

—— 'The Inter-Allied Labor Conference', *New Republic*, 23 March 1918, 225–7.

—— 'Historic', in G. B. Shaw (ed.), *Fabian Essays in Socialism* (London: George Allen and Unwin, 1948).

—— and Webb, B., *English Poor Law Policy* (London: F. Cass, 1910, reprinted 1963).

—— *A Constitution for the Socialist Commonwealth of Great Britain* (London: Longmans, Green and Co., 1920).

—— *The Consumers Co-operative Movement* (London: Longmans, Green and Co., 1921).

—— *Industrial Democracy* (London: Longmans, Green and Co., 1901).

—— *The Principles of the Labour Party* (London: The Labour Party, 1918).

Wells, H. G., *The Future in America: A Search After Realities* (New York: Harpers and Bros, 1906).

—— *The New Machiavelli* (London: John Lane, 1911).

Weyl, M. (ed.), *Walter Weyl: An Appreciation* (Philadelphia: Privately published, 1922).

Weyl, W., *The New Democracy: An Essay on Certain Political and Economic Tendencies in the United States* (New York: Macmillan, 1912).

—— 'Equality', *New Republic*, 23 January 1915, 13–14.

—— *The End of the War* (New York: Macmillan, 1918).

—— *Tired Radicals and Other Papers* (New York: B. W. Huebsch, 1921).

White, W. A., *The Old Order Changeth: A View of American Democracy* (New York: Macmillan, 1910).

Wilde, N., 'Plural Sovereignty', *Journal of Philosophy*, 16 (1919), 658–65.

—— 'The Attack on the State', *International Journal of Ethics*, 30 (1920), 349–71.

—— 'The Problem of Liberty', *International Journal of Ethics*, 33 (1923), 291–306.

—— *The Ethical Basis of the State* (Princeton: Princeton University Press, 1924).

—— 'Foundations of Sovereignty', *International Journal of Ethics*, 32 (1924), 442–4.

Wolfe Howe, M. de (ed.), *The Holmes–Laski Letters: The Correspondence of Mr Justice Holmes and Harold J. Laski, 1916–1935* (Cambridge, MA: Harvard University Press, 1953).

Secondary Works

Allswang, J., *The Initiative and Referendum in California* (Stanford: Stanford University Press, 2000).

Altenbaugh, R. J., *Education for Struggle: The American Labor Colleges of the 1920s and 1930s* (Philadelphia: Temple University Press, 1990).

Archer, R., *Economic Democracy: The Politics of Feasible Socialism* (Oxford: Oxford University Press, 1996).

Beilharz, P., *Labour's Utopias: Bolshevism, Fabianism, Social Democracy* (London: Routledge, 1992).

Bensel, R. F., *The Political Economy of American Industrialization, 1877–1900* (Cambridge: Cambridge University Press, 2000).

Berkowitz, P., *Virtue and the Making of Modern Liberalism* (Princeton: Princeton University Press, 1999).

Boucher, D. (ed.), *British Idealists* (Cambridge: Cambridge University Press, 1997).

Brandeis, E., *History of Labor in the United States: Labor Legislation* (New York: Macmillan, 1966).

Brinkley, A., *Liberalism and its Discontents* (Cambridge, MA: Harvard University Press, 1998).

Brody, D., *Workers in Industrial America: Essays on the Twentieth-Century Struggle* (New York: Oxford University Press, 1993).

Burrow, J., *Whigs and Liberals: Continuity and Change in English Political Thought* (Oxford: Oxford University Press, 1988).

Clendenning, J., *The Life and Thought of Josiah Royce* (Nashville: Vanderbilt University Press, 1999).

Coates, D., *Models of Capitalism: Growth and Stagnation in the Modern Era* (Cambridge: Polity Press, 2000).

Cobden, S., *A. Mitchell Palmer, Politician* (New York: Columbia University Press, 1963).

Cole, M., *The Life of G. D. H. Cole* (London: St Martin's Press, 1971).

Collini, S., *Liberalism and Sociology: L. T. Hobhouse and Political Argument in England, 1870–1914* (Cambridge: Cambridge University Press, 1979).

Corfield, J., *Epoch in Workers' Education: A History of the Workers' Educational Trade Union Committee* (London: Workers' Educational Association, 1969).

Cronin, T. E., *Direct Democracy: The Politics of Initiative, Recall and Referendum* (Cambridge, MA: Harvard University Press, 1989).

Cywar, A., 'John Dewey in World War One', *American Quarterly*, 21 (1969), 578–94.

Dam, H. N., *The Intellectual Odyssey of Walter Lippmann: A Study in his Protean Thought, 1910–60* (New York: Gordon Press, 1973).

Davis, A. F., 'Welfare, Reform and World War One', *American Quarterly*, 19 (1967), 516–33.

Dawley, A., *Struggles for Justice: Social Responsibility and the Liberal State* (Cambridge, MA: Belknap Press, 1991).

Dexter, B., 'Herbert Croly and the Promise of American Life', *Political Science Quarterly*, 70 (1955), 197–218.

Dinan, J. J., *Keeping the People's Liberties: Legislators, Citizens, and Judges as Guardians of Rights* (Lawrence: Kansas University Press, 1998).

Diner, S. J., *A Very Different Age: Americans of the Progressive Era* (New York: Hill and Wang, 1998).

DiNunzio, M. R. (ed.), *An American Mind: Selected Writings of Theodore Roosevelt* (New York: Penguin, 1997).

Eisenach, E., *The Lost Promise of Progressivism* (Lawrence: Kansas University Press, 1994).

Eisenberg, A., *Reconstructing Political Pluralism* (Albany: State University of New York Press, 1995).

Fieldhouse, R., 'The Liberal Tradition in Adult Education', in R. Fieldhouse, R. Taylor and K. Rockhill (eds), *University Adult Education in England and the USA: A Reappraisal of the Liberal Tradition* (Beckenham: Croom Helm, 1985).

Fine, N., *Labor and Farmer Parties in the United States, 1828–1928* (New York: Russell and Russell, 1961).

Fink, L., *Progressive Intellectuals and the Dilemmas of Democratic Commitment* (Cambridge, MA: Harvard University Press, 1997).

Finkelstein, L. (ed.), *Thirteen Americans: Their Spiritual Biographies* (New York: Institute for Religious and Social Studies, 1950).

Forcey, C., *The Crossroads of Liberalism: Croly, Weyl, Lippmann, and the Progressive Era, 1900–1925* (New York: Oxford University Press, 1967).

Freeden, M., *The New Liberalism: An Ideology of Social Reform* (Oxford: Oxford University Press, 1978).

—— *Liberalism Divided: A Study in British Political Thought, 1914–39* (Oxford: Oxford University Press, 1986).

—— *Ideologies and Political Theory: A Conceptual Approach* (Oxford: Oxford University Press, 1996).

—— 'Practising Ideologies and Ideological Practices', *Political Studies*, 48 (2000), 302–22.

Fuss, P., *The Moral Philosophy of Josiah Royce* (Cambridge, MA: Harvard University Press, 1965).

Gerstle, G., 'Liberty, Coercion and the Making of Americans', *Journal of American History*, 84 (1997), 524–58.

—— 'Theodore Roosevelt and the Divided Character of American Nationalism', *Journal of American History*, 86 (1999), 1280–307.

Goldman, L., *Dons and Workers: Oxford and Adult Education since 1850* (Oxford: Oxford University Press, 1995).

Graham, P. (ed.), *Mary Parker Follett—Prophet of Management: A Celebration of her Writings from the 1920s* (Cambridge, MA: Harvard Business School Press, 1995).

Gray, J., *Mill on Liberty: A Defence* (London: Routledge, 1996).

Greenleaf, W. H., 'Laski and British Socialism', *History of Political Thought*, 2 (1981), 573–91.

Gutmann, A., *Liberal Equality* (Cambridge: Cambridge University Press, 1982).

—— and Thompson, D., *Democracy and Disagreement* (London: Belknap Press, 1996).

Harp, G. J., *Positivist Republic: Auguste Comte and the Reconstruction of American Liberalism, 1865–1920* (University Park, Pennsylvania: Pennsylvania State University Press, 1995).

Harris, H. J., 'Industrial Democracy and Liberal Capitalism, 1890–1925', in N. Lichtenstein and H. J. Harris (eds), *Industrial Democracy: The Ambiguous Promise* (Cambridge: Cambridge University Press, 1996).

Harris, J., 'Political Thought and the Welfare State, 1870–1940', *Past and Present*, 135 (1992), 116–41.

—— *Private Lives, Public Spirit: A Social History of Britain, 1870–1914* (Oxford: Oxford University Press, 1993).

Harrison, B., 'Oxford and the Labour Movement', *Twentieth Century British History*, 3 (1991), 226–71.

Hartz, L., *The Liberal Tradition in America: An Interpretation of American Political Thought Since the Revolution* (New York: Harcourt Brace, 1955).

Hawkins, M., *Social Darwinism in European and American Thought* (Cambridge: Cambridge University Press, 1997).

Hay, C., *The Political Economy of New Labour: Labouring Under False Pretences* (Manchester: Manchester University Press, 2000).

Haydu, J., *Making American Industry Safe for Democracy: Comparative Perspectives on the State and Employee Representation in the Era of World War One* (Chicago: University of Illinois Press, 1997).

Hirst, P., *Associative Democracy: New Forms of Social and Economic Governance* (Cambridge: Polity Press, 1994).

Hollinger, D. A., 'Science and Anarchy: Walter Lippman's *Drift and Mastery*', *American Quarterly*, 29 (1977), 463–75.

Holmes, S., *Passions and Constraint: On the Theory of Liberal Democracy* (Chicago: Chicago University Press, 1995).

Hoopes, J., *Community Denied: The Wrong Turn of Pragmatic Liberalism* (Ithaca: Cornell University Press, 1998).

Horn, M., *The Intercollegiate Socialist Society, 1905–1921: Origins of the Modern American Student Movement* (Boulder: Westview Press, 1979).

Horowitz, D., *Beyond the Left and Right: Insurgency and the Establishment* (Chicago: University of Illinois Press, 1997).

Hovenkamp, H., *Enterprise and American Law, 1836–1937* (Cambridge, MA: Harvard University Press, 1991).

Jennings, B., *Knowledge is Power: A Short History of the WEA* (Hull: University of Hull, 1979).

Jordan, J., *Machine-Age Ideology: Social Engineering and American Liberalism, 1911–1939* (Chapel Hill: University of North Carolina Press, 1994).

Karl, B. D., *The Uneasy State: The United States from 1915 to 1945* (Chicago: University of Chicago Press, 1983).

Katz, M., *In the Shadow of the Poorhouse: A Social History of Welfare in America* (New York: Basic Books, 1986).

Kennedy, D. M., *Over Here: The First World War and American Society* (New York: Oxford University Press, 1980).

King, D., *Making Americans: Immigration, Race and the Origins of the Diverse Democracy* (London: Harvard University Press, 2000).

Kloppenberg, J., *Uncertain Victory: Social Democracy and Progressivism in European and American Thought, 1870–20* (New York: Oxford University Press, 1986).

Konefsky, S. J., *The Legacy of Holmes and Brandeis: A Study of the Influence of Ideas* (New York: Macmillan, 1956).

Kramnick, I., and B. Sheerman, *Harold Laski: A Life on the Left* (London: Hamish Hamilton, 1993).

Laborde, C., *Pluralist Thought and the State in Britain and France, 1900–25* (Houndmills: Macmillan, 2000).

Lee, A., *Workers Education in the United States* (New York: Workers Education Bureau, 1921).

Levine, D., *Poverty and Society: The Growth of the American Welfare State in Comparative Perspective* (New Brunswick: Rutgers University Press, 1988).

Levy, D., *Herbert Croly of the New Republic: The Life and Thought of an American Progressive* (Princeton: Princeton University Press, 1985).

— 'Shaping Modern Liberalism: Herbert Croly and Progressive Thought: Review of E. Stettner', *American Historical Review*, 99 (1994), 1407–8.

Link, A., *Woodrow Wilson and the Progressive Era, 1910–17* (New York: Harper and Row, 1996).

Lloyd, B., *Left Out: Pragmatism, Exceptionalism and the Poverty of American Marxism, 1890–1922* (Baltimore: Johns Hopkins University Press, 1997).

Lustig, R. J., *Corporate Liberalism: The Origins of Modern American Political Theory* (Berkeley: University of California Press, 1982).

MacBriar, A. M., *Fabian Socialism and English Politics, 1884–1918* (Cambridge: Cambridge University Press, 1962).

McCartin, J. A., *Labor's Great War: The Struggle for Industrial Democracy and the Origins of Modern American Labor Relations* (Chapel Hill: University of North Carolina Press, 1997).

McCluskey, N. G., *Public Schools and Moral Education: The Influence of Horace Mann, William Torrey Harris, and John Dewey* (New York: Macmillan, 1958).

McKibbin, R., *The Ideologies of Class: Social Relations in Britain, 1880–1950* (Oxford: Oxford University Press, 1989).

—— *Classes and Cultures: England, 1918–1951* (Oxford: Oxford University Press, 1998).

Mann, A., 'British Social Thought and American Reformers of the Progressive Era', *Mississippi Valley Historical Review*, 42 (1956), 672–92.

Marks, G., *Unions in Politics: Britain, Germany, and the United States in the Nineteenth and Early Twentieth Centuries* (Princeton: Princeton University Press, 1989).

Martin, K., *Harold Laski: A Biographical Memoir* (London: Gollancz, 1953).

Martin, R. L., *Fabian Freeway: High Road to Socialism in the USA, 1884–1960* (Chicago: Heritage Foundation, 1966).

Martin, W., *The New Age under Orage: Chapters in English Cultural History* (Manchester: Manchester University Press, 1967).

Mason, A. T., *Brandeis: A Free Man's Life* (New York: Viking, 1946).

Mattson, K., *Creating a Democratic Public: The Struggle for Urban Participatory Democracy in the Progressive Era* (University Park, Pennsylvania: Pennsylvania State University Press, 1998).

May, H. F., *The End of American Innocence: A Study in the First Years of Our Time, 1912–1917* (New York: Columbia University Press, 1992).

Meadowcroft, J., *Conceptualizing the State: Innovation and Dispute in British Political Thought, 1880–1914* (Oxford: Oxford University Press, 1995).

Miller, D., *The Principles of Social Justice* (Cambridge, MA: Harvard University Press, 2000).

Mohl, R. A., 'The Abolition of Public Outdoor Relief', in W. I. Trattner (ed.), *Social Welfare or Social Control?: Some Historical Reflections on Regulating the Poor* (Knoxville: University of Tennessee, 1983).

Montgomery, D., *The Fall of the House of Labor: The Workplace, the State and American Labor Activism, 1865–1925* (Cambridge: Cambridge University Press, 1987).

—— 'Industrial Democracy or Democracy in Industry? The Theory and Practice of the Labour Movement, 1870–1925', in N. Lichtenstein and H. J. Harris (eds), *Industrial Democracy in America: The Ambiguous Promise* (Cambridge: Cambridge University Press, 1996).

Morgan, K. O., 'The Future at Work', in R. Thompson (ed.), *Contrast and Connection: Bicentennial Essays in Anglo–American History* (London: Bell, 1976).

Morrow, J., 'Liberalism and British Idealist Political Philosophy: A Reassessment', *History of Political Thought*, 5 (1984), 91–108.

Nicholas, K., *The Social Effects of Unemployment in Teeside* (Manchester: Manchester University Press, 1986).

Nicholls, D., *The Pluralist State: The Political Ideas of J. N. Figgis and his Contemporaries* (London: St Martin's Press, 1994).

Nicholson, P., *The Political Philosophy of the British Idealists: Selected Studies* (Cambridge: Cambridge University Press, 1990).

Nuechterlein, J. A., 'The Dream of Scientific Liberalism: The New Republic and American Progressive Thought, 1914–1920', *Review of Politics*, 42 (1980), 167–90.

Orloff, A. and Skocpol, T., 'Why No Equal Protection? Explanation the Politics of Public Social Spending in Britain, 1900–1911, and the United States, 1880–1920', *American Sociological Review*, 44 (1984), 726–50.

Otter, S. den, *British Idealism and Social Explanation: A Study in Late Victorian Thought* (Oxford: Oxford University Press, 1996).

Pelling, H., *A History of British Trade Unionism* (Basingstoke: Macmillan, 1992).

Pemberton, J. A. C., 'James and the Early Laski: The Ambiguous Legacy of Pragmatism', *History of Political Thought*, 19 (1998), 264–97.

Phillips, A. and Putnam, T., 'Education for Emancipation: The Movement for Independent Working Class Education, 1908–1928', *Capital and Class*, 10 (1980), 18–32.

Pierson, P., 'Increasing Returns, Path Dependence, and the Study of Politics', *American Political Science Review*, 94 (2000), 251–68.

Plant, R. and Vincent, A., *Philosophy, Politics and Citizenship* (Oxford: Basil Blackwell, 1984).

Pollins, H., *The History of Ruskin College* (Oxford: Ruskin College, 1984).

Price, D. E., 'Community and Control: Critical Democratic Theory in the Progressive Period', *American Political Science Review*, 68 (1974), 1663–78.

Rabban, D. M., *Free Speech in its Forgotten Years* (Cambridge: Cambridge University Press, 1997).

Renshaw, P., *The Wobblies: The Story of Syndicalism in the United States* (London: Eyre and Spottiswood, 1967).

—— 'The Depression Years, 1918–31', in B. Pimlott and C. Cook (eds), *Trade Unions and British Politics: The First 250 Years* (Harlow: Longmans, 1991).

Richter, M., *The Politics of Conscience: T. H. Green and his Age* (London: Wiedenfield and Nicholson, 1964).

Riddell, N., 'The Age of Cole? G. D. H. Cole and the British Labour Movement, 1929–1933', *Historical Journal*, 38 (1995), 933–58.

—— *Labour in Crisis: The Second Labour Government, 1929–31* (Manchester: Manchester University Press, 1999).

Rochester, S. I., *American Liberal Disillusionment in the Wake of World War I* (University Park, Pennsylvania: Pennsylvania, 1977).

Rockhill, K., 'Ideological Solidification of Liberalism in University Adult Education: Confrontation over Workers' Education in the USA', in K. Rockhill, R. Fieldhouse, and R. Taylor (eds), *University Adult Education in the USA* (London: Croom Helm, 1985).

Rodgers, D., *Atlantic Crossings: Social Politics in a Progressive Age* (London: Belknap Press, 1998).

Rowbotham, S., 'Travellers in a Strange Country: Responses of Working Class Students to the University Extension Movement, 1873–1910', *History Workshop Journal*, 12 (1981), 62–95.

Runciman, D., *Pluralism and the Personality of the State* (Cambridge: Cambridge University Press, 1997).

Rutkoff, M. and Scott, W. B., *New School: A History of the New School for Social Research* (New York: Free Press, 1986).

Ryan, A., *John Dewey and the High Tide of American Liberalism* (New York: W. W. Norton, 1995).

Sandel, M., *Democracy's Discontent: America in Search of a Public Philosophy* (Cambridge, MA: Belknap Press, 1996).

Schaffer, R., *America in the Great War: The Rise of the War Welfare State* (New York: Oxford University Press, 1991).

Scheweber, L., 'Progressive Reformers, Unemployment and the Transformation of Social Inquiry in Britain and the United States, 1880–1920', in D. Rueschmeyer and T. Skocpol (eds), *States, Social Knowledge and the Origins of Modern Social Policies* (Princeton: Princeton University Press, 1996).

Shafer, B. and Stears, M., 'From Social Welfare to Cultural Values: The Puzzle of Postwar Change in Britain and the United States', *Journal of Policy*, 10 (1999), 331–66.

Shafer, B. E. (ed.), *Is America Different?: A New Look at American Exceptionalism* (Oxford: Oxford University Press, 1989).

Shain, B. A., *The Myth of American Individualism: The Protestant Origins of American Political Thought* (Princeton: Princeton University Press, 1994).

Shapiro, S., 'Hand and Brain: The Farmer Labor Party of 1920', *Labor History*, 26 (1985), 405–22.

Simon, B., *The Search for Enlightenment: The Working Class and Adult Education in the Twentieth Century* (London: Lawrence and Wishart, 1990).

Skinner, Q. and Tully, J. (eds), *Meaning and Context: Quentin Skinner and His Critics* (Cambridge: Polity Press, 1988).

Sklar, M., *The Corporate Reconstruction of American Capitalism, 1880–1916* (Cambridge: Cambridge University Press, 1988).

Skocpol, T., *Protecting Soldiers and Mothers: The Political Origins of Social Policy in the United States* (Cambridge, MA: Belknap Press, 1992).

Skowronek, S., *Building a New American State: The Expansion of National Administrative Capacities, 1877–1920* (Cambridge: Cambridge University Press, 1982).

Smith, J. E., *America's Philosophical Vision* (Chicago: Chicago University Press, 1992).

Smith, R. M., *Civic Ideals: Conflicting Visions of Citizenship in U.S. History* (New Haven: Yale University Press, 1997).

Soffer, R., *Ethics and Society in England: The Revolution in the Social Sciences, 1870–1914* (Berkeley: University of California Press, 1978).

Stapleton, J., *Englishness and the Study of Politics: The Social and Political Thought of Ernest Barker* (Cambridge: Cambridge University Press, 1995).

—— (ed.), *Group Rights: Perspectives since 1900* (Bristol: Thoemmes Press, 1995).

Stears, M., 'Guild Socialism and Ideological Diversity on the British Left, 1914–26', *Journal of Political Ideologies*, 3 (1998), 289–305.

—— 'Needs, Welfare and the Limits of Associationalism', *Economy and Society*, 28 (1999), 570–89.

—— 'Beyond the Logic of Liberalism: Learning from Illiberalism in Britain and the United States', *Journal of Political Ideologies*, 6 (2001), 215–30.

Steel, R., *Walter Lippmann and the American Century* (London: Bodley Head, 1980).

Stettner, E., *Shaping Modern Liberalism: Herbert Croly and Progressive Thought* (Lawrence: Kansas University Press, 1994).

Stocks, M., *The Workers' Educational Association: The First Fifty Years* (London: George Allen and Unwin, 1953).

Stokes, M., 'American Progressives and the European Left', *Journal of American Studies*, 17 (1983), 5–28.

Taylor, F. W., 'On the Principles of Scientific Management', in E. Boris and N. Lichtenstein (eds), *Major Problems in the History of American Workers* (Lexington, MA: D. C. Heath, 1991).

Terrill, R., *R. H. Tawney and his Times: Socialism as Fellowship* (Cambridge, MA: Harvard University Press, 1973).

Thelen, D. P., *Robert M. La Follette and Insurgent Spirit* (Madison: Wisconsin University Press, 1976).

Thompson, D., *John Stuart Mill and Representative Government* (Princeton: Princeton University Press, 1976).

Thompson, J., *Reformers and War: American Progressive Publicists and the First World War* (Cambridge: Cambridge University Press, 1987).

Thompson, N., *Political Economy and the Labour Party: The Economics of Democratic Socialism* (London: University College London Press, 1996).

Ulam, A., *Philosophical Foundations of English Socialism* (Cambridge, MA: Harvard University Press, 1951).

Vincent, A., 'The Poor Law Reports of 1909 and the Social Theory of the Charity Organisation Society', *Victorian Studies*, 27 (1984), 343–63.

—— 'Classical Liberalism and its Crisis of Identity', *History of Political Thought*, 9 (1990), 143–62.

—— *Theories of the State* (London: Basil Blackwell, 1993).

Weinstein, J. M., *The Decline of Socialism in America, 1912–1925* (New Brunswick: Rutgers University Press, 1984).

White, G. E., *Justice Oliver Wendell Holmes: Law and the Inner Self* (New York: Oxford University Press, 1993).

Wiebe, R., *The Search for Order, 1877–1920* (New York: Hill and Wang, 1967).

Wright, A., *G. D. H. Cole and Socialist Democracy* (Oxford: Oxford University Press, 1979).

—— *R. H. Tawney* (Manchester: Manchester University Press, 1982).

Wrigley, C., 'Trade Unions and Politics in the First World War', in B. Pimlott and C. Cook (eds), *Trade Unions in British Politics: The First 250 Years* (Harlow: Longmans, 1991).

Zylstra, B., *From Pluralism to Collectivism: the Development of Harold Laski's Political Thought* (Assen: Van Gorcum, 1968).

INDEX